Corrections

Corrections

Alejandro del Carmen
University of Texas at Arlington

BluePrints

coursewise
p u b l i s h i n g
inc.

Bellevue • Boulder • Dubuque • Madison • St. Paul

Our mission at **Coursewise** is to help students make connections—linking theory to practice and the classroom to the outside world. Learners are motivated to synthesize ideas when course materials are placed in a context they recognize. By providing gateways to contemporary and enduring issues, **Coursewise** publications expand students' awareness of and context for the course subject.

For more information on **Coursewise,** visit us at our web site: http://www.coursewise.com

To order an examination copy, contact Houghton Mifflin Sixth Floor Media: 800-565-6247 (voice); 800-565-6236 (fax).

BluePrints is a series of core texts that provide the basic framework for college courses in brief, inexpensive paperbacks. Each title offers concise, current coverage of material for a specific course. **Courselinks**™ and Chapter Plug-Ins™ provide statistical updates, late-breaking news, and additional resources and content.

Coursewise Publishing Editorial Staff

Thomas Doran, ceo/publisher: Environmental Science/Geography/Journalism/Marketing/Speech
Edgar Laube, publisher: Political Science/Psychology/Sociology
Linda Meehan Avenarius, publisher: **Courselinks**™
Sue Pulvermacher-Alt, publisher: Education/Health/Gender Studies
Victoria Putman, publisher: Anthropology/Philosophy/Religion
Tom Romaniak, publisher: Business/Criminal Justice/Economics
Kathleen Schmitt, publishing assistant
Gail Hodge, executive producer

Coursewise Publishing Production Staff

Lori A. Blosch, permissions coordinator
Mary Monner, production coordinator
Victoria Putman, production manager

Interior design and cover design by Elise Lansdon
Cover photo: CORBIS

Printed in the United States of America by Coursewise Publishing, Inc., 7 North Pinckney Street, Suite 346, Madison, WI 53703

10 9 8 7 6 5 4 3 2 1

Alejandro del Carmen

Alejandro del Carmen was born in the small town of Jinotepe, 40 kilometers south of Managua, Nicaragua. His family fled to the United States in 1979, at the end of the most violent civil war that has ever taken place in Nicaragua. At the time of arrival, Dr. del Carmen spoke very little English but was quick to grasp the language and learn about the customs of his adoptive nation. After living in several U.S. cities, the del Carmen family moved to Miami, Florida, where they resided for many years. It was in Miami that Dr. del Carmen attended both high school and college. Upon completion of his bachelor's degree in criminal justice from Florida International University, he attended the Florida State University's School of Criminology and Criminal Justice, where he earned a master's and Ph.D. degrees.

Dr. del Carmen's childhood experiences in large part shaped his decision to become a criminologist. Having been exposed to the horrors of war and the dehumanizing experience of being an immigrant, he chose a profession that facilitates an environment conducive of ideological tolerance and academic freedom. He firmly believes that the hope of humanity rests on the shoulders of those commissioned to shape the minds of future leaders.

Currently, Dr. del Carmen lives with his wife and two children in Arlington, Texas. Aside from being an assistant professor, he serves as director of the Center for Criminal Justice Research and Training at the University of Texas at Arlington. As director, he has established a close working relationship with the local police department and other governmental agencies. In the near future, Dr. del Carmen plans to travel to Central America to conduct criminological research.

Preface

Preface

In the advent of a new century, social issues seem to affect our daily lives more than ever. Violence seeks to find a home in America's schools, playgrounds, and churches. The public perception is that none of these places is safe anymore. Images of young children covered with blood attempting to escape a mad gunman remind us of the violent times in which we live. We strive to determine the motive of offenders in an attempt to bring closure to "inexplicable" violent incidents. Why does someone engage in violence against children? Why are children killing other children?

Although the motive of an offender is an important issue, this book is concerned with the reaction we invoke when a suspect is arrested and convicted. Once we apprehend the individuals responsible for violence, what are we to do with them? Is incarceration an effective method of punishment? Can we deter offenders from committing crimes again? This book addresses these all-important questions. I hope that, after reading this text, you will have an understanding of the historical significance of punishment, the alleged utility of punishment, and the social consequences that are a result of current penal practices.

The word *corrections* suggests that something must be fixed. Indeed, many view the correctional system as the component of the criminal justice system charged with the mission of "correcting" those who have violated social rules. Others feel that corrections involves nothing more than a jail cell, where the offender is housed until the completion of a sentence. This text will show you that corrections is a world unto itself and that it involves professionals from the correctional field and other disciplines who come together daily to carry out the provisions that the law mandates. To view a correctional facility and its functions is almost like watching the body of the criminal justice system on an X-ray machine. Corrections is the process that brought the law to life!

As you read this text, you will notice that I often refer to the Internet as a valuable tool for learning. My aim in doing this is to encourage you to use this powerful innovative tool as you seek further insights into the correctional issues discussed in the book. One way to do this is to visit the wonderful world of integrated web resources at the **Courselinks**™ web site for *BluePrints: Corrections* (http://www.courselinks.com). Here you will find carefully selected readings, web links, quizzes, worksheets, and more, tailored to your course and approved as connected learning tools.

This text examines a number of issues affecting today's correctional system, such as probation, parole, female and male offenders, prisons, and jails. I have purposely left out a discussion on capital punishment because it is my feeling that, in learning about this particular issue, students will benefit most by accessing the **Courselinks** site for Corrections and by reading the latest developments on this fascinating topic.

Coursewise Publishing, the publisher of this book, adheres to a philosophy of providing students with quality books for a reduced price. My wish is that this book gives merit to that important mission.

I sincerely hope that you enjoy reading this book as much as I have found delight in writing it. Have a wonderful journey through the world of corrections!

Acknowledgments

This book would not have been possible without the love and support of numerous individuals. My wife, Denise, supported and encouraged me to write this book. Her love and understanding were my constant companions. I could not have done it without her! My son Gabriel used to compete, unsuccessfully at times, with the attention I constantly paid to this book. His presence inspires me to be a better individual. The same is true of my daughter Gemma, whose birth was the source of much anticipation.

As always, my parents, Alejandro and Maria Cristina, have been the rock on which I seek refuge. Their courage in coming to the United States and beginning a new life for the sake of their children's freedom will never cease to inspire me. I hope that the publication of this book is evidence that their many sacrifices did not go unanswered.

My sister Marcela must also be mentioned here. Her love and kindness have always inspired me to be better. Marcela's dedication and passion for excellence drove me to complete this book, even when I was consumed with work. The same can be said of my brother Mauricio, who constantly strives to improve. I am proud of him—especially of the person he has become.

This book could not have been a reality without the assistance of Sue Titus Reid. Thank you, Sue, for being a mentor and friend. The Coursewise team has worked diligently in the production of this book. My friend and editor, Tom Romaniak, always exercised patience and care in the handling of this book. His constant advice and insights made this rookie author see "the light" at the end of the tunnel, even on very "cloudy" days. Also, Vickie Putman, production manager, along with Mary Monner, production coordinator, and Lori Blosch, permissions coordinator, held to a rigorous production schedule while always keeping sight of our goal. A special thanks to Sue Dillon, the best copy editor in the field. I enjoyed her numerous comments and suggestions. I truly feel that the merits of this book are largely due to her contribution.

I would like to express my sincere gratitude to my colleagues at the University of Texas at Arlington: Robert L. Bing, O. Elmer Polk, David McKenna, Michael Moore, Jill Clark, Caryl Segal, Gail O'Brien, and Martha Findlay. Their support was invaluable. In addition, a special thanks to Cathy Moseley, Arda Al-Khaiyat, and Ann Kelley for constantly being willing to help.

While I take full responsibility for any oversights in the final book, I want to express my gratitude to the following individuals for their reviews of the manuscript:

Mathew Kanjirathinkal, Texas A&M University–Commerce

Ronald Burns, Texas Christian University

Dennis J. Stevens, University of Massachusetts at Boston

Finally, I would like to thank the individuals who have made a difference in my life—my grandparents, Carlos, Luisa, Alejandro, and Aida. They each taught me, in their own special way, the value of education and the importance of exploring and understanding my roots. Also, a special thanks to Richard and Katie Zablah; Tyrone Duhart; Rick Smith; Larry Boyd; T. Bowman; Dennis, Rhonda, and Ashley Lesner; Carlos and Dianne Morales; Les Smith; Jonathan Odo; Rick Veach; and Emmanuel Onyeozili. I truly value their friendship and support. A special note of gratitude to Marcos Tolentino Barcenas, for teaching me to value life's every moment and to Fathers Michael Thomas, Jim Gigliotti, and Pedro Garcia for reminding me of the power and mercy of God. Finally, thank you to my students, who make it all worthwhile—especially Michael Linzmayer, Carolyn Rickett, Jamie Smith, Chris Jaquez, Jay Gustafson, and the many others who have challenged me to become a better professor and a more compassionate human being.

Alejandro del Carmen

Dedication

To

my wife, Denise,
children Gabriel and Gemma

and to

my parents, Alejandro and Maria Cristina

Brief Contents

Contents

Chapter 4

**The Modern Prison: Classification and Correctional
Programs   51**

Section 2

The Corrections Process   71

Chapter 5

The Pretrial Process (Bail and Jail)   73

Chapter 6

Sentencing   91

Chapter 7

Release from Prison   107

Section   3

The Correctional Client   129

Chapter   8

The Male Inmate   131

Chapter   9

The Female Inmate   155

Chapter   10

The Juvenile Offender   173

Section 5

Special Issues 275

Chapter 14

Corrections: Y2K and Beyond 277

At **Coursewise,** we're publishing connected learning tools. That means that the book you are holding is only a part of this publication. You'll also want to harness the integrated resources that **Coursewise** has developed at the fun and highly useful **Courselinks**™ web site for *BluePrints: Corrections.* Visit http://www.coursewise.com.

Philosophy and Overview of Corrections

Overview of the Correctional System

On March 11, 1999, CNN reported that "a judge dismissed murder charges Thursday against a man who spent nearly 17 years on death row before Northwestern University student journalists helped gather evidence to clear him. 'I'm personally and profoundly grateful that we were spared the unthinkable, unthinkable conclusion to this case,' Cook County Circuit Judge Thomas R. Fitzgerald said in clearing Anthony Porter, who had been just two days away from being executed in September."[1]

Key Terms

corrections
"Three Strikes and You're Out"

As we enter a new century, it is not hard to find stories such as this one, in which some aspect of the correctional field is discussed. In fact, if you were to go out to the streets of a major city and ask people their opinion about a particular aspect of corrections, you would find that most people have indeed formulated an opinion of the correctional system. However, despite the many opinions shared by citizens, you will probably find that most of the input they provide is not based on concrete, "hard" evidence; rather it is formulated around feelings or past experiences that have shaped their outlook of the correctional system.

One of the popular thoughts that come to mind for most people when they discuss the system of corrections is of inmates wearing striped clothing and holding metal cups awaiting their daily serving of cold rice. When you learn about the history of corrections you will realize that this popular image once existed. However, it is important to clarify, before going any further, that corrections involves much more than that. In fact, corrections encompasses a world unto itself. It is a world whose main concern is the correctional client while being inclusive of all of the personnel and equipment that support the existence of the incarcerated individual. The personnel are complex and often vary in their goals, duties, and performance. These personnel are often made up of doctors, counselors, guards, cooks, pharmacists, nurses, chaplains, and administrators, to name a few. They all have the same mission of custody and rehabilitation despite the fact that, at times, they seem to neglect or prefer one over the other. In addition to the personnel, the correctional system relies now more than ever on the use of technology and equipment to accomplish its mission. This includes computer systems, surveillance cameras, infrared equipment, and electronic gates. All of this makes up the complex world of corrections. Clearly, this is a much more serious and elaborate system than the image shared by most people. Having said that, it is important to note that corrections is only one of the three components of the criminal justice system (the other two being police and courts). As such, this chapter presents a brief overview of the criminal justice system with special emphasis on two of its components—police and courts—as they will relate, in later chapters, to the operation of the correctional system. In addition, this chapter provides a brief look at today's correctional trends. This should support your understanding of the complex yet exciting world of corrections.

Criminal Justice: An Overview

The criminal justice system in the United States is a multimillion dollar business. According to the U.S. Department of Justice, federal, state, and local governments spent $94 billion for civil and criminal justice in fiscal 1992. This constitutes a 59 percent increase over 1987 expenditures. For every resident, the three levels of government together spent $368. The largest percentage increase of those funds, 248 percent, was from corrections, while the judicial branch and police agencies increased their budgets by 170 percent and 117 percent respectively. These figures suggest that of the three components of the criminal justice system, corrections is growing the fastest while still being the least understood by the public. It is a component, however, that is extremely affected by the actions of the police, prosecutors, defense attorneys, and judges.

The System Aspect of Criminal Justice: Effect on Corrections

It is important to realize that the process of proceeding through the various stages shown in figure 1.1 is only one aspect of the system, for the criminal justice system in the United States is both a system and a process. The system aspect is important but is often overlooked. We can analyze what happens prior to arrest and at the various stages from arrest through trial, but in reality what happens at one stage may have a tremendous impact on what happens at another stage or in another component. When one part of the system changes, the effects may be felt in the rest of the system.

As figure 1.1 indicates, a person may be released from the system of criminal justice at any of the stages. Upon apprehension of a suspect, the police may decide not to arrest. After being arrested, even after booking, the accused may be released because the prosecutor decides not to proceed with the case. After the initial appearance before a magistrate or after the preliminary hearing, the charges may be dropped or the case dismissed. If the case must go before a grand jury, that body may refuse to return an indictment, thus ending the case before trial. Charges may also be dismissed at the stage of arraignment. At any time prior to trial, the charges may be reduced. This is usually done in exchange for an agreement by the defense to plead guilty to lesser charges, thus avoiding the time and expense of a trial. A large percentage of criminal cases are processed out of the system at one of these stages, a fact that has raised considerable criticism among those who argue that this occurs because of socioeconomic status or other nonlegal criteria.[2] You may notice in figure 1.2 that the correctional funnel becomes more narrow as the case processes through the system. This is significant because only a few of the many cases that are processed result in incarceration. In defense of processing some cases out of the system prior to trial, it is argued that such is done on the basis of the legal seriousness of the offense and that the system of criminal justice could not accommodate trial of the cases of all persons accused of crime. Further, it is held that it is in the interest of society as well as the accused not to try all cases.

Even if a case is tried and the evidence suggests beyond a reasonable doubt that the accused is guilty, the jury or judge (if the case is not tried before a jury) may decide not to convict. In those cases in which the defendant is found guilty, the sentencing judge may decide to suspend the sentence or impose only a fine, with the result that the defendant does not enter the formal stage of corrections.

It is also important to point out that referrals of juveniles to law enforcement officials are often handled informally. This may occur at the stage in which the complaint is first made to the police or after apprehension by the police. This informal handling of juveniles by the police will reduce the number of juveniles who ever enter the corrections phase of the criminal justice system.

During the following discussion of two components of the criminal justice system—the police and the courts—we note how actions within each component affect corrections. At this point, however, the interrelationship of the various elements of the criminal justice system may be dramatically illustrated by the system effect created by the *Gideon*[3] case, which established a right to counsel in felony cases. Since the Supreme Court applied the ruling of that case retroactively, 4,000 prisoners in Florida who had been convicted in felony cases in which they had not had counsel had to be retried. The county jails were temporarily overcrowded as a result, and since 2,000 of these inmates were not reconvicted, Florida, for the first time in years, had empty prison beds.

Another way in which one component of the criminal justice system affects corrections can be seen in the use of probation and parole. If the judges, who grant probation, begin imposing sentences instead of using probation in a significant number of cases, the prisons will be confronted with increasing populations. Likewise, if parole boards significantly decrease the number of cases in which they grant parole, thus increasing the amount of time inmates will spend in prison, the inmate population will increase. Prisons might also suffer staffing and other problems if the granting of probation and parole significantly increases, thereby decreasing the prison population.

Organization of State Criminal Justice Systems

One way to regulate the impact of one component of the criminal justice system on another is to have greater coordination of activities. The state system of criminal justice, has, however, suffered from a lack of central organization that would make such coordination possible. The fragmentation of the criminal justice system was noted by the President's Commission on Law Enforcement and Administration of Justice in 1967, the Advisory Commission on Intergovernmental Relations in 1971, the Committee for Economic Development in 1972, and the National Advisory Commission on Criminal Justice Standards and Goals in 1973. Some states did reorganize and establish planning networks, especially with federal funds dispensed after passage of the Omnibus Crime Control and Safe Streets Act of 1968.[4] But only eight states have grouped together at the state level more than one major component of their respective criminal justice systems.[5]

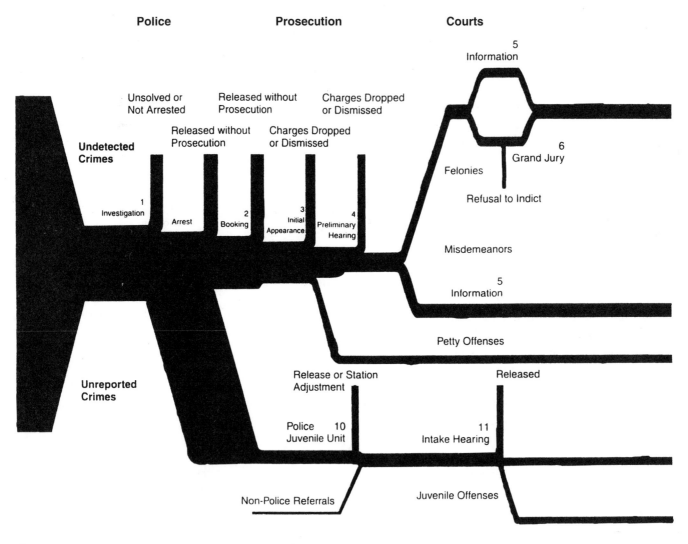

| Police | Prosecution | Courts |

Figure 1.1
A general view of the
criminal justice system.

Source: President's Commission on
Law Enforcement and Administration of
Justice, *The Challenge of Crime in a
Free Society* (Washington, D.C.: U.S.
Government Printing Office, 1967),
pp. 8–9.

1. May continue until trial.
2. Administrative record of arrest. First step at which temporary release on bail may be available.
3. Before magistrate, commissioner, or justice of the peace. Formal notice of charge. advice of rights. Bail set. Summary trials for petty offenses usually conducted here without further processing.
4. Preliminary testing of evidence against defendant. Charge may be reduced. No separate preliminary hearing for misdemeanors in some systems.
5. Charge filed by prosecutor on basis of information submitted by police or citizens. Alternative to grand jury indictment; often used in felonies, almost always in misdemeanors.
6. Review whether government evidence sufficient to justify trial. Some states have no grand jury system; others seldom use it.

Courts must be excluded from such executive reorganizations since to include the courts would violate the constitutionally required separation of powers of the judiciary and the executive branches of government. However, the courts may be included in some functions of the reorganization, such as the training of court personnel. The major components of the criminal justice superagency would include the state police organization, the state prosecution, and the state adult and juvenile corrections system. Coordination of these components would reduce the serious gaps and overlaps of the various state systems—systems that have grown in most cases because of political expediency rather than rational planning based on empirical evidence of what is effective.[6]

Corrections

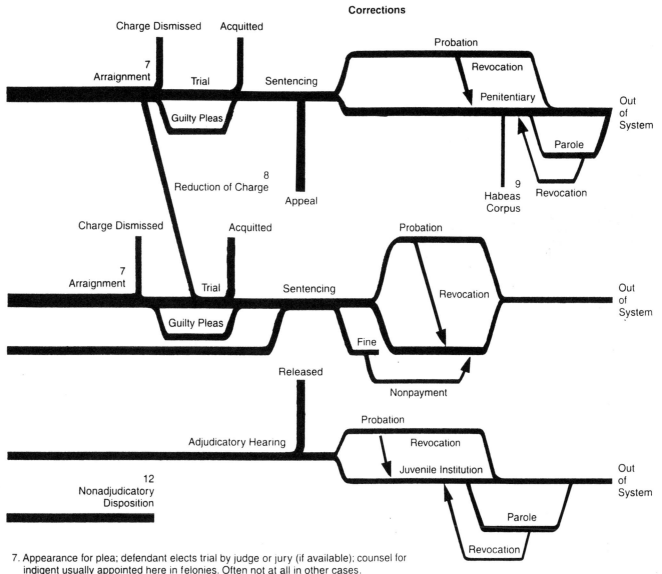

7. Appearance for plea; defendant elects trial by judge or jury (if available); counsel for indigent usually appointed here in felonies. Often not at all in other cases.
8. Charge may be reduced at any time prior to trial in return for plea of guilty or for other reasons.
9. Challenge on constitutional grounds to legality of detention. May be sought at any point in process.
10. Police often hold informal hearings, dismiss or adjust many cases without further processing.
11. Probation officer decides desirability of further court action.
12. Welfare agency, social services, counseling, medical care etc., for cases where adjudicatory handling not needed.

As mentioned previously, the components of the criminal justice system include the police, courts, and corrections. All of these components could be discussed at length.[7] Here, however, we look mainly at the ways in which each of the first two components directly affect corrections.

The Police

In this section we examine briefly the organization of police systems in the United States and then discuss the nature of policing. As stated earlier, our emphasis here, as with other components of the criminal justice system, is on the impact policing has on corrections.

Components of the Criminal Justice System

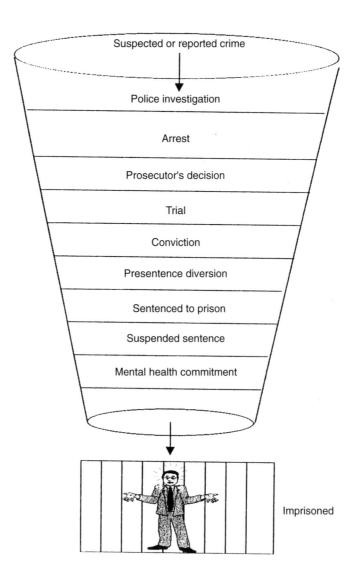

Figure 1.2
The correctional funnel.

The Contemporary Police System in the United States

The police system in the United States is a highly decentralized system. It exists on three levels: local, state, and federal, with the majority of law enforcement agencies located in counties, cities, and towns.[8]

At the state level, police are the main law enforcers. They patrol the highways, regulate traffic, and have the primary responsibility for the enforcement of some state laws. They provide some services, such as a system of criminal identification, police training programs, or a communications system for local law officials. The sheriff is the main law enforcement officer at the county level of government. That person is selected, usually for two to four years, to keep the peace, to preserve order and enforce court orders, to execute civil and criminal process, and to patrol the area. The main law enforcers in suburban townships and municipalities are police officers. At all of these levels, jurisdiction (the territory of authority) is limited to the state, county, or municipality in which the person is a sworn officer of the law, unless the officer is chasing a felon (referred to in legal terms as a "hot pursuit") across jurisdictional lines. At all of these levels, police officers have considerable control over the lives of people, a control that directly affects corrections, as the following discussion indicates.

The Nature of Policing

If you watch television programs such as Law and Order and/or Homicide, it is easy to understand why most people are led to believe that police officers are constantly engaged in shoot-outs and drug busts. However, the reality of police work is different. In general, police work is reactive rather than proactive. That is, the police spend most of their time responding to citizen calls rather than detecting crime. James Q. Wilson, in his pioneer work *Varieties of Police Behavior,* found that most police work involves some sort of "fixing up." Specifically, Wilson found that most calls to the police concerned such matters as accidents or illnesses, animals, personal assistance, drunk persons, escort vehicles, fire, power lines or trees down, lost or found persons, or property damage. The second-highest percentage of police calls, according to Wilson, involved "order maintenance." This included gang disturbances or family problems, problems with neighbors, or fights. Only a very small percentage involved law enforcement-related calls.[9]

Police Impact on the Correctional System

The police have considerable decision-making discretion in the performance of their jobs. It is that decision-making power that closely connects the police to corrections. They have immense authority in determining to what extent, if any, the apprehended person will be processed through the stages of the criminal justice system. They determine not only who is arrested, but in many cases, who will be detained in jail overnight. The evidence secured by the police will influence what charges, if any, will be brought and whether or not the apprehended person will eventually be tried. Police testimony at trial may be crucial on the issue of guilt or innocence. What the officer says about the conduct of the suspect upon arrest may influence the judge in sentencing. In all stages of the criminal justice system through sentencing, the police have potentially more influence over the accused than does any other component of the system.

Courts

The second major component of the criminal justice system is the courts. After a brief overview of the state and federal court system, we will examine the trial courts.

The Dual Court System

The United States has a dual court system consisting of state and federal courts. State crimes are prosecuted in state courts and federal crimes are prosecuted in federal courts. The crimes of the former are defined by state statutes and the latter by acts of Congress. Most criminal cases are tried in state courts—approximately 85 percent of the total of all cases tried.

State courts   The state court system differs from state to state. Basically, lower trial courts exist to try the less serious offenses. Higher trial courts have general jurisdiction and can try felonies and serious misdemeanors. All states have appeal courts. Some states have an intermediate appeal court; others have only one court of appeals, which is often called the state supreme court.

Federal courts   The federal court system consists of three basic levels, excluding special courts such as the United States Court of Military Appeals. The United States district courts are the trial courts. Cases may be appealed from those courts to the appellate courts. There are eleven courts at this level, and they are called circuit courts. Finally, the highest court is, of course, the Supreme Court, which serves as an appeal court although it has jurisdiction to serve as a trial court in a few cases.

It is important to realize that the lower federal courts and the state courts constitute separate systems. A state court is not bound by the decisions of a lower federal court in its district, but it must follow the decisions of the United States Supreme Court. Also, cases may not be appealed from a state court to a lower federal court.

Trial and Appellate Courts

The distinction between trial and appellate courts should be made. Trial courts hear the factual evidence of a case and decide the issues of fact. These decisions may be made by a jury or by a judge if a case is tried without a jury. Appellate courts do not try the facts, such as the guilt or innocence of a defendant but, in essence, review the lower court trial. The appellant (the party appealing the lower court decision) alleges "errors" in the trial court proceeding (for example, hearsay evidence admitted, illegal confession admitted, minority groups excluded from the jury) and asks for a new trial. The appellee (the winning party in the lower court decision and the party against whom the appeal is being brought) argues that errors either did not exist or, if they did, did not constitute "reversible errors"—that is, they did not prejudice the appellant—and therefore a new trial should not be granted.

When a trial court has ruled against the defendant, he or she has a right of appeal, both in the state and the federal court systems, although the defendant does not (except in a few specified types of cases) have the right to appeal to the highest court. For example, the United States Supreme Court hears only a small percentage of the cases for which an appeal is requested.

On appeal, the case is heard by a judge or judges, not by a jury, and the issues are confined to matters of law, not fact. The court looks at the trial court record and hears oral arguments from attorneys for both sides. It then determines whether any errors of law were committed in the lower court trial.

The appellate court may affirm or reverse the decision of the lower court. When a lower court decision is reversed, the case is usually sent back for another trial—that is, the case is "reversed and remanded."

Prosecutors may also appeal on points of law, but the defendant may not be retried because of the constitutional provision against double jeopardy. However, the prosecutor, if he or she wins on appeal, has a decision that may be of benefit in future trials.

Lower courts   The President's Crime Commission reported that the lower courts are the most important courts because they handle 90 percent of the criminal cases. Yet in some of these courts, defendants are not told their constitutional rights. Judges may have little time to get facts that they should consider in determining whether to grant bail, so they decide that important question on the basis of the charge and previous record. The trial may be brief and may not have the formalities of procedure required of a criminal trial in courts of general jurisdiction. Rules of evidence are often ignored. The defendant is usually sentenced immediately, and no presentence reports and no probation services exist in many jurisdictions. Judges are often perturbed at having to preside over petty offenses such as vagrancy, drunkenness or disorderly conduct, and prostitution. Often "defendants are treated with contempt, berated, laughed at, embarrassed. . . ."[10]

Some improvements have been made since the 1967 Crime Commission report, but lower courts are still plagued with many problems, one of which is a backlog resulting in serious delay in the trial of cases. The injustices created by an overworked court that must decide cases quickly and with little individualized attention are obvious, as is the lack of preparation time available to overworked prosecutors and defense attorneys. Crowded court dockets have created pressures that encourage plea bargaining and mass handling of some cases, which might lead to unreasonable pressures on defendants to plead guilty. The impact of such practices on corrections is extensive. During the long period in which defendants are awaiting trial, they may be detained in correctional facilities, usually jails, often in inhumane conditions. Continued court delays will place strains on the jail facilities in many jurisdictions, especially in the large metropolitan areas. Defendants who have court-appointed attorneys may not see them during this long wait because those attorneys are so busy with cases being tried. Such defendants are left with many questions and no answers, resulting in increased bitterness toward the criminal justice system. Such attitudes are not conducive to treatment programs and may result in less likelihood of success upon release from incarceration than would have been the case if the individual had been released on bail while awaiting trial.

Long delays are also often characteristic of the appeal process. An inmate who is successful in his or her appeal to a higher court to reverse the conviction at the trial court may have to spend more time imprisoned than would have been the case had the appeal been heard promptly.

Actions of trial courts affect corrections in another way. If the trial judge who imposes a sentence on the defendant does not have adequate information on which to base that decision, the defendant may receive a longer sentence than is necessary or a shorter sentence than is reasonable. Even with comprehensive information acquired before sentencing, such decisions are difficult; without such information they are generally impossible. Trial judges who have the power to sentence a defendant to a particular institution may err in that decision. Again, with extensive presentencing information, such problems might be avoided, resulting in greater opportunity within the correctional institutions for working with the incarcerated.

Corrections

The final component of the criminal justice system is **corrections,** which we may define broadly as covering all of the official ways in which society reacts to persons who have been accused of committing criminal acts as well as persons who are handled by the juvenile court. Although you will learn, in detail, about the history of the correctional system, it is important for now to become familiar with some of the major events that made a significant impact on the American correctional system. In addition, you will have an opportunity to get acquainted with the current correctional trends.

The Nature of Corrections

In October 1870, the National Prison Association met in Cincinnati, Ohio, and repudiated the concepts that characterized corrections at that time: the silent, lockstep system and rigid discipline with hard labor. The conference called for a new approach to corrections advocating an emphasis on changing or rehabilitating, rather than merely warehousing and punishing the offender. The twentieth century saw the development and expansion of concepts such as parole to allow the early release of the offender from prison, attempts to implement a system of classifying inmates according to abilities and needs, and the development of numerous types of treatment programs aimed at implementing the philosophy of rehabilitation. The 1960s, 1970s, and 1980s, however, were characterized by increasing crime rates and rising acts of violence within correctional institutions. These events led many to conclude that corrections had not met its goal of reducing crime and that a new approach should be taken. Some have argued that the problem is that not only corrections, but all of the components of the system of criminal justice, are characterized by discrimination against the poor and minorities who constitute the bulk of the incarcerated population. In fact, at the Million Man March in October 1995, Reverend Jesse Jackson argued that crack cocaine users (most likely to be of poor socioeconomic status) were more likely to receive longer prison sentences than those imposed on powder cocaine users (most likely to belong to the middle/upper class). Others have argued that, in general, treatment of offenders has not worked and we should return to a philosophy of punishment. Despite these disagreements, all agree that the future of corrections is a topic of great debate; the present can only be described as a state of transition. But one thing is clear: the field of corrections is attracting more attention today than it has in recent periods of our history.

Correctional Trends

In 1995, there were 125 federal and 1,375 state correctional facilities. At the federal level, there were 25,379 correctional employees, while the states employed 321,941.[11] The number of individuals under correctional supervision has increased in the past twenty years. There were 5.5 million people on probation, in jail or prison, or on parole in the United States at year-end 1996—in other words, 2.8 percent of all U.S. adult residents. On June 30, 1997, there were an estimated 436 prison inmates per 100,000 U.S. residents, an increase from the 292 inmates per 100,000 U.S. residents in 1990.[12]

The more recent jail trends suggest that by midyear 1997, an estimated 567,079 inmates were held in the nation's local jails, up from 518,492 at midyear 1996. Also, in 1997, jails reported adding 19,713 beds during the previous twelve months, achieving a total bed capacity of 581,733. It is estimated that since 1990 the number of jail inmates per 100,000 U.S. residents has risen from 163 to 212. There are some jurisdictions that hold the greatest percentage of jail inmates in the United States. These include Los Angeles County and New York City, which accounted for 7 percent of the national total.[13] Most experts are verbalizing their concern over this population growth in jails and prisons across the nation. It has been speculated that this trend will continue to grow to unprecedented proportions as incarceration continues to grow in popularity among Americans.

The Most Active States in Correctional Practices

Although most states' correctional systems have experienced growth in the past few years, most of the correctional activity takes place in four states—New York, Florida, Texas, and California. These states oversee approximately 36 percent of all offenders under correctional supervision.[14]

New York   Historically, the correctional system of New York has been regarded by many as the innovator of correctional policy. As you will learn in later chapters, New York gave birth to the reformatory. Although this state still plays an important role on the national correctional platform, it is no longer regarded as being an innovator of correctional policy. Some of the characteristics of the New York correctional system are as follows:

- Adult corrections operates under the supervision of the Department of Corrections.

- Juvenile corrections is supervised by the New York Division of Youth Services.

- The New York Correctional System is decentralized while enjoying strong state coordination efforts.

- Parole is administered by the New York Division of Parole while probation is considered a county function.

One of the greatest predicaments affecting the New York correctional system is its present condition of inmate overcrowding. This is primarily caused by the overwhelming amount of inmates entering New York's correctional system coupled with a lack of adequate correctional funding. In fact, soon after Governor Pataki took office, he proposed the loosening of laws for minor repeat offenders with the hope of lessening the pressure on the New York correctional system. Despite his efforts, many wonder how the state will continue to address the increasing number of inmates entering the correctional system as it continues to be the subject of an ill-funded correctional budget.

Florida   The state of Florida is the newest member of the "small" group of states that oversee most of the correctional activity in the United States. Experts regard Florida as the state that represents what the nation will be, in terms of correctional activity, by the year 2010.[15] Some of the characteristics of Florida's correctional system are:

- All correctional services are administered under the executive branch.

- The Florida Department of Health and Rehabilitative Services oversees juvenile corrections.

- All community-based and institutional services are administered regionally.

- Regional directors enjoy complete autonomy over their operations.

Florida, unlike New York, enjoys a well-appropriated correctional budget. However, despite this, Florida legislators argue that a good portion of these funds should be applied to divert offenders from entering prison. This has prompted the state to start the Community Control Project, a close supervision program that targets offenders bound for prison. This is the largest program of its kind in the United States and has diverted literally thousands of offenders from entering prison. Today, Florida's prison admissions have dropped significantly despite the fact that the prison population continues to grow. This phenomenon has taken place largely as a result of longer prison sentences issued in this state.

Texas   The leading state in incarceration rates is Texas. In fact, more Americans are under correctional supervision in Texas than in any other state. Ironically, this is the case despite the fact that Texas ranks as the fifth state to experience the highest crime rate in the nation.[16] When accounting for violent crime rate only, Texas ranks as number fourteen. These figures are interesting in light of the fact that this state is regarded as the most punitive in terms of its correctional practices. Some of the specific features of the Texas correctional system are:

- All adult correctional activity takes place under the supervision of the Texas Department of Criminal Justice (this is supervised by a board made up of nine individuals who are appointed by the governor).

- The Texas correctional system is made up of three divisions—institutions, parole supervision, and probation.

- The Texas Parole Board reports directly to the Board of Criminal Justice.

In recent years, the state of Texas, due to the state's aggressive correctional policy, has been the subject of several legal suits. As a result, Texas has established a strict prison population cap. This policy has had ramifications on the state's correctional system by forcing many jurisdictions to be cautious in their practices of incarcerating offenders. Despite this, the state of Texas as a whole continues to aggressively punish offenders by either submitting them to some form of correctional supervision or by executing them. In fact, in 1997, of the seventy-four persons executed in the United States, Texas was responsible for executing thirty-seven of them. Virginia followed, with nine executions.[17] Clearly, most U.S. executions took place in Texas.

California   Although this state is the last one in our discussion, it is by no means of little importance. In fact, the state of California has the largest prison population in the United States and ranks second-highest in terms of its rate of growth in the number of prisoners. This has taken place, for the most part, as a result of California's tough sentencing policies. Some of the characteristics of the California system are:

- The Adult Authority supervises the operation of the California adult correctional system.

- The correctional system is part of the executive branch of government.

- The Youth Authority supervises juvenile correctional institutions.

Some of the recent legislation enacted in California (i.e., **"Three Strikes and You're Out"**) will have a significant impact on the future of its correctional system. This legislation, which provides longer prison terms for third-time felons, will increase the number of permanent correctional clients. This phenomenon, coupled with a struggling correctional budget, will lead California's correctional system to a serious situation in the near future. Experts argue that in the years to come, California will have to resort to state funds not mandated by law in order to continue financing its correctional system.

As may be obvious, these four states have many characteristics in common. For instance, you may have noticed that most of them have struggling correctional budgets that barely pay for the construction of new correctional facilities. Despite this, most of the four states mentioned have a firm commitment to continue their imprisonment trend. Thus, it is not difficult to believe that they will continue to be among the states that oversee the most correctional activity in the United States in the years to come. Unfortunately, other states are following closely and almost seem to compete with these states for first place. As we enter a new century, more and more Americans are being imprisoned. This predicament is such that CNN reported recently that the United States is very close to being the nation that incarcerates the most citizens—a distinction that is presently held by Russia.[18]

Complexities in Correctional Management

As if the complexities previously mentioned were not enough, the management staffs of correctional facilities face numerous challenges almost on an everyday basis. For one, correctional management staff is constantly under pressure by the public to be more punitive. They receive this pressure by the news media as they immediately respond to stories in which an inmate is freed early due to his or her good behavior. The public reacts almost instantaneously by criticizing correctional managers and their staff for being "too lenient" on offenders. Second, correctional managers often feel isolated from the rest of society. They believe that most citizens do not understand the full scope of their jobs. This, coupled with the stress of their jobs, makes their role as correctional managers extremely hard to fulfill. Finally, correctional managers must face, on regular basis, legislators and other public figures who often regard the programs offered in prisons as not being aggressive enough to accomplish the mission of rehabilitating or punishing offenders. At times, the success or failure of these programs becomes the indicator of further funding. Although most states allocate a substantial amount of their budgets to corrections, state legislators and the public have unrealistic expectations that make the job of correctional managers almost impossible to bear.

WiseGuide Wrap-Up This chapter has given us a very brief overview of the three components of the criminal justice system, an overview that provides a basis for an in-depth discussion of the correctional system.

This chapter emphasized activities of the police and the courts that have a direct and indirect impact on the correctional system. This impact is particularly extensive at the beginning of the correctional system as laws are enforced by law enforcement agents. In addition, the court system has a substantial influence on the system of corrections as it makes a determination of whether or not to commit the offender to some form of correctional supervision. Thus, the actions taken by both law enforcement agencies and the courts constantly influence the welfare of the correctional system.

After examining both the police and the courts, you learned about some of the current correctional trends. Aside from recent statistics that demonstrate the activity of the correctional systems throughout the nation, we had an opportunity to examine the most notorious and active of these systems, expecially those of New York, Florida, Texas, and California. Learning about these systems will prove especially fruitful as we move to the next chapter on the theories of punishment.

Notes

1. CNN, March 11, 1999.
2. CNN, March 11, 1999.
3. *Gideon v. Wainwright,* 372 U.S. 335 (1963).
4. Those states are Maryland, Kentucky, Montana, Virginia, New Mexico, Pennsylvania, North Carolina, and New Jersey. See National Institute of Law Enforcement, *Criminal Justice Organization,* p. 94.
5. *Criminal Justice Organization,* p. 94.
6. For additional information on reorganization of state criminal justice agencies, see *Criminal Justice Organization.*
7. See Sue Titus Reid. *Criminal Justice,* 5th ed. (Coursewise Publishing, Inc., 1999).
8. The President's Commission on Law Enforcement and Administration of Justice, *Task Force Report: The Police* (Washington, DC: U.S. Government Printing Office, 1967), pp. 7–8.
9. Wilson, James Q. *Varieties of Police Behavior: The Management of Law and Order in Eight Communities.* (Cambridge, MA: Harvard University Press, 1968), p. 18.
10. The President's Commission, *Courts,* pp. 30, 31.
11. Bureau of Justice Statistics, U.S. Department of Justice *Sourcebook of Justice Statistics, 1996.* (1997), pp. 82–85.
12. Bureau of Justice Statistics, U.S. Department of Justice. (http://www.ojp.usdoj.gov/bjs/prisons.htm), 1998.
13. Bureau of Justice Statistics, U.S. Department of Justice.
14. Clear, Todd, and Cole, George. *American Corrections,* 4th ed. (Belmont, CA: Wadsworth Publishing Company, 1997).
15. Clear and Cole, *American Corrections.*
16. The Criminal Justice Policy Council of the State of Texas, *Testing the Case for More Incarceration in Texas: The Record So Far.* (Austin, TX: CJPC, Oct. 1995).
17. Bureau of Justice Statistics. U.S. Department of Justice. *Capital Punishment Strategies—Survey Findings.* (http://www.ojp.usdoj.gov/bjs/prisons.htm) Dec., 1998.
18. CNN, March 1, 1999.

The Social Response to Crime

Societies react to criminal behavior in various ways, only one of which is incarceration. Prior to the emergence of incarceration as a form of punishment, as opposed to the sole purpose of holding persons awaiting trial, numerous forms of psychological and physical punishments were administered. Fines, restitution, hard labor, and other forms of punishment were common. Various theories and justifications were used to support specific and general forms of punishment. We begin this chapter with a brief look at the main theories of punishment, thus setting the stage for a more detailed analysis of punishment and for the later chapters on sentencing and incarceration. Throughout the discussion of the history of punishment are hints of reasons or justifications for the implementation of penal sanctions. These reasons are so important that we devote a section of this chapter to considering the philosophies of incapacitation, reparation, maintenance of social solidarity, deterrence, reformation, rehabilitation, reintegration, retribution, and the "Justice Model." We also examine deterrence and crimes, placing specific emphasis on individual and general deterrence.

Key Terms

classical school of criminology
criminal law
criminologists
cultural consistency
determinism
deterrence
FBI Crime Index offenses
felicific calculus
free will
general deterrence
hedonism
incapacitation
incarceration
indeterminate sentence
individual deterrence
juries
"just deserts"
"Justice Model"
neoclassical school
positive school
positivists
recidivists
reformation
reintegration
restitution
retribution
revenge
scientific method
social contract
social-structural theory
utilitarianism

Theories
of Punishment

In their classic criminology book, Edward Sutherland and Donald Cressey discussed the major cultural, psychoanalytic, and sociological explanations for variations in punishment.[1] Such theories of punishment variation provide a framework for our discussion of punishment throughout the course of history. Although there are numerous theories of punishment, the following discussion includes the most significant of these. It is clear, then, that methods and theories of punishment vary from place to place and from one time period to another. What is the explanation for such variation? We examine the main approaches from a cultural and sociological perspective.

Cultural Consistency

The theory of **cultural consistency** suggests that methods and severity of punishment will be consistent with other developments within the culture at a given time. When physical suffering was regarded as the natural lot of people, severe forms of corporal punishment were utilized. When greater emphasis was placed on the dignity of the individual and the equality of citizens, uniformity in sentencing was in vogue. When the price system developed, with fair prices set for various commodities, the system of letting the punishment fit the crime was practiced.[2] Individualization in the treatment of criminals occurs when individualization becomes important in medical treatment. When punishment was emphasized in the home and other social institutions, it was easier for the state to gain support for severe punishment. Finally, penalties are increased in severity as the values that are threatened become more important. Over time, different values gain and lose importance.

Cultural consistency theory also suggests that as the freedom and liberty of the individual became more important characteristics of a culture, imprisonment came to be considered a severe form of punishment because it deprived a person of that freedom.

Social Structure

Punishment has been related in theory to characteristics of the social structure. For example, it has been argued that when labor is needed, punishment will be light since the prisoners are needed for the labor supply. When labor is in great supply, prisoners will be punished severely or killed. Thus, the social structure holds that the economic need of a capitalistic society has often been the best predictor of the different methods of punishment implemented throughout history. This social structure perspective has been modified since it was first developed.

A particular version of the **social-structural theory,** discussed by Sutherland and Cressey, is based on the relationship between the middle class and punishment. The explanation is that when the lower-middle class, which is composed of persons who most frequently repress their natural desires, is in control of punishment, severe and frequent punishment is inflicted. The literature suggests that if the lower-middle class is absent in a society, severe punishment is nonexistent. Sutherland and Cressey note, however, that one of the main problems with this approach is the absence of a precise definition of lower-middle class.[3]

Another version of the social-structural theory of punishment was proposed by Emile Durkheim. His most important proposition was that punishment varies with the complexity of the division of labor in a society. In societies characterized by mechanical solidarity—in which the society is cohesive and deviation is a serious threat—people provide most of their own needs. The division of labor is slight, and punishment is punitive in order to repress deviant behavior. In societies characterized by a more complex division of labor, known by what

Durkheim called organic solidarity, the emphasis is on **restitution;** therefore punishments are not as severe.[4] Restitution can be defined as the compensation to victims for the physical, financial, and emotional loss suffered as a result of a criminal incident. This compensation can be monetary or in the form of service to the community.

Recently, Durkheim's approach has been questioned. After stating the differences between his findings and Durkheim's theoretical conclusions, Steven Spitzer concluded that Durkheim's model was a valuable one for studying punishment. "In linking the nature of control to the organization of society Durkheim makes explicit what too many investigators ignore—the fact that punishment is deeply rooted in the structure of society. Whether we determine that Durkheim's explanation must be specified or completely disregarded, one thing is clear; the investigation of punishment must be sensitive to the present political and economic dimensions of social life."[5]

Finally, the degree of frequency of punishment has been associated with the degree of social disorganization within a society. When a society is basically homogeneous, few people deviate and therefore nonpunitive reactions are sufficient. As heterogeneity increases, often accompanied by increasing social disorganization, it becomes necessary to invoke more severe punishments. Sutherland and Cressey cite examples of increasing punitiveness during periods of revolution when there is an accompanying increase in social disorganization. They conclude that none of these perspectives explains the *process* by which the culture, psychic conditions, or social structure create the change in punishment.[6] All of these can be criticized for the lack of empirical evidence to support the particular point of view. Despite these criticisms, the cultural and sociological theories of punishment have some validity in helping us understand the history of punishment.

Historical Background of Punishment and Criminal Law

The formal development of criminology as a distinct discipline is very recent, but we can trace historically the ideas of people who might be called early **"criminologists."** Most of these people were lawyers, doctors, psychiatrists, or sociologists; basically all were reformers of the **criminal law** and contributed important ideas to the philosophy of punishment.

Hermann Mannheim's compilation of essays on these early "criminologists" has been an excellent source for the historical background of the philosophies of punishment that have been most influential in the development of criminology, and that source will be used in the following discussions.[7] Mannheim begins with the birth of Cesare Beccaria in 1738 and continues his discussions of these "pioneers" through the death of Gustave Aschaffendburg in 1944. He discusses their ideas about the causes of criminal behavior, as well as their philosophies of punishment (we will concentrate on the latter).[8] Not all of the pioneers can be discussed here, but the works of these men are extremely important as most of our philosophies of punishment today can be traced to one or more of the early pioneers in the field.

We begin by examining the background against which the **classical** and **neoclassical** theorists were writing. The efforts of these men were aimed at reform of the criminal law. The classical writers were rebelling against a very arbitrary and corrupt system of law in which judges held an absolute and almost tyrannical power over those who came before them. Laws were often vague and judges took it upon themselves to interpret "the spirit of the law" if the vagueness did not suit their purposes. Such widespread personal interpretation of the law led to a lack of consistency and impartiality, which usually meant that the lower-class defendant received the blunt end of justice. Accusations were often secret and trials were a farce. The law was applied unequally to citizens and corruption was rampant. Confessions were obtained by the use of hideous torture, and the death penalty was used for even trivial offenses. Due process and equality before the law were unknown. Once people were incarcerated, they were not classified—the old and the young, the hardened criminals and the first offenders, all were thrown into prison together. Specifically, let us look at the punitive methods used in two European countries—France and England.

The French Response to Crime

During the Middle Ages in France, decisions regarding sentencing of the accused were made in secret; judges could make decisions without any restrictions. The sentences were usually very severe, with the defendant having no right of defense at the trial. Punishments were decided by secret tribunals and defendants were punished "according to the authority of the secret bench."[9] Methods of torture differed from country to country, and from province to province within France. In some, the defendant would be tied to a chair that was moved closer and closer to a burning furnace. Another method was to shod the defendant in high boots made of spongy leather, tie the defendant to a table, and pour boiling water into the boots. The water would eat away the flesh and sometimes dissolve the bones. Stripping a man half naked, tying his hands behind him with a ring between them, placing a weight of 180 pounds on his feet, and then raising him with sudden jerks by means of a rope on the ring was another method. For more serious crimes, the weight was 250 pounds. This process completely dislocated the individual's arms and legs.

The body of the defendant might be stretched, with a doctor and surgeon standing by to check his pulse. When they determined that he could no longer bear the pain, they would release him, attempt to revive him, and as soon as he was somewhat revived, begin the method of torture again. Another form of punishment was execution by fire. If the accused died before the execution, the dead body would be burned. If it was discovered that a person was guilty of a crime after the person died and was buried, the body would be disinterred and the remains burned.

Possibly the most horrible torture was quartering. The offender was first put through preliminary torture, such as the burning of his or her limbs. Then the executioner would attach a rope to each of the four limbs and fasten each rope to a bar to which a strong horse was harnessed. First, the horses would be made to give short jerks, but as the offender cried out in agony, the horses would be suddenly urged on rapidly in different directions. If the limbs still were not dismembered, the executioner would finish the job with a hatchet, put all of the limbs in front of the torso (which might still show some signs of life, for this method took a long time), and burn them.[10]

Philosophers were unsuccessful in changing the barbarous punishments of the Middle Ages in France, and most of those laws remained until the eve of the French Revolution.

The British Response to Crime

The judicial system in England, prior to and during the time the classicists were writing about penal reform, was also severe and corrupt. According to a member of Parliament, a justice of the peace was "an animal who, for half-a-dozen chickens, would dispense with a dozen laws."[11] Graft and corruption were common among magistrates, watchmen, and constables, and lawyers did not always have good reputations. Dr. Johnson, referring to a man who had just left the room, said he "did not care to speak ill of any man behind his back, but he believed the gentleman was an attorney."[12] The popular belief was that laws were weak and punishments were severe. Criminal laws relied on **deterrence,** not on surveillance or detection. Capital punishment was provided for over 200 offenses.

By the eighteenth century, it was said that Englishmen were tough; they could take everything but death. One soldier was lashed 100 times for asking for a leave from the army in order to marry a prostitute. He returned the next day with the same request, and it was granted. One man said he received 26,000 lashes in the fourteen years he served in the English army and 4,000 more afterwards, but that he was well and healthy even after the punishments.[13]

In 1790, Parliament repealed a law providing that a woman convicted of murdering her husband or of treason was to be burned alive. The "humaneness" of the people was demonstrated by the custom of strangling her before she was burned. Men hanged at the gallows for treason were cut down while still alive and their bowels removed and burned in front of them, they would then be beheaded and quartered. Gallows existed in all districts in London and, on many, the victims were left for the birds to eat—presumably to serve as a deterrent to all who passed by. Some victims would hang as long as thirty minutes before they died, but they were given brandy to ease the pain. At times the executioner would pull on their legs to hasten death. Hanging and other punishments were public, and people lined the streets to see the victim on the way to the place of punishment. Food and drink were sold by peddlers and people sang ballads.

The English Code of the eighteenth century, often called the "bloody code," was one of the most severe in history. It barred torture and punishment by the wheel along with cutting noses and ears, but it permitted other severe forms of punishment and provided for capital punishment for such offenses as cutting down trees on an avenue or in a park, setting fire to a cornfield, taking part in a riot, shooting a rabbit, demolishing a turnpike gate, and escaping from jail. When the sentence was to be flogging at the end of a cart drawn through town, spectators would often pay the executioner to whip more vigorously.

It was against that background of severe punishment and harsh laws that Beccaria initiated what has been termed the **classical school of criminology.**

Classical School

The only two members of the classical school recognized in most criminology texts are Cesare Beccaria and Jeremy Bentham. In this section, we discuss their respective philosophies and examine the influences they had on penal and legal development since the mid-eighteenth century. We also discuss the influence of other thinkers of their day, especially Voltaire, Montesquieu, and Rousseau.

Cesare Beccaria

The leader of the classical school of thought was Beccaria, who was born in Milan, Italy, on March 15, 1738. Although his family was of aristocratic background, its political function had gradually ceased to be of any importance. After studying for eight years at the Jesuit College at Parma, Beccaria attended the University of Pavia, receiving his degree in 1758. He began as a mathematician and later became interested in economics and politics. In 1764, when he was only twenty-six years of age, his influential essay, *Des delitti e delles pene,* was published in Italy. In 1767, the essay was published in England under the title *On Crimes and Punishments.* There has been much debate in recent years over who wrote the essay, but most criminology texts still regard Beccaria as the only author.

The treatise drew attention from the Paris intelligentsia. Beccaria's work was widely accepted as an important cry for change and reform and was eventually translated into twenty-two languages. Beccaria's major contribution was the concept that the *punishment should fit the crime,* a philosophy that became the theme of the classical school of thought. He died in 1794, having produced only the one major work, which was, however, a great impetus to the penal reform movement and served as a basis for the alteration of penal practices.[14]

Beccaria's words were accepted and put into practice to varying degrees by the enlightened monarchs. In Austria, Maria Teresa called for a reform of the penal code in 1768, and her son Joseph II abolished the death penalty in 1787. In 1772, King Gustavus III of Sweden abolished torture and reduced the infliction of the death penalty. The treatment of criminals improved greatly in the United States after 1776, especially in Pennsylvania under the guidance of the Quakers. Reform came under Frederick the Great of Prussia; around the same time reform was introduced in England. Perhaps the most dramatic reforms came after the French Revolution of 1789, when the French Penal Code of 1791 was established.

Beccaria's work is extremely important today. "It is not an exaggeration to regard Beccaria's work as being of primary importance in paving the way for penal reform for approximately the last two centuries."[15] His short essay contains almost all of the modern penal reforms. But the greatest contribution of his work was "the foundation it laid for subsequent changes in criminal legislation."[16]

Social Contract Doctrine

At the time that Beccaria was writing, many philosophers and intellectuals were beginning to speak of the **social contract.** This concept held that an individual was bound to society only by his or her consent and, therefore, society was responsible to him or her as well. Such thinkers as Montesquieu, Voltaire, and Rousseau were making strong statements about the rights of people and the nature of society in general. Beccaria believed in the concept of the social contract and felt that each individual surrendered only enough liberty to the state to make society viable. Laws therefore should merely be the necessary conditions of the social contract, and punishments should exist only to defend the total sacrificed liberties against the usurpation of those liberties by other individuals. The basic principle that should guide legislation—and indeed form its backbone—is that the greatest happiness should be shared by the greatest number of people.[17]

Philosophy of Free Will

Another philosophy that strongly influenced Beccaria was that of **free will.** It was argued that human behavior is purposive and is based on **hedonism,** the pleasure-pain principle: People choose those actions that give pleasure and avoid those that give pain. Therefore punishment should be assigned to each crime in a degree that would result in more pain than pleasure for those who committed the forbidden act. This hedonistic view of human conduct prescribed that laws must be clearly written and not open to interpretation by judges. Only the legislature could specify punishment. The law must apply equally to all citizens, thus no defenses to criminal acts were permitted. The issue in court was whether a person committed the act; if so, a particular penalty prescribed by law for that act would be imposed. The state makes the laws but should not be granted the power to decide who violates the law; that must be done by a third party—a judge or a group of the defendant's peers. Judges were to be mere instruments of the law, allowed only to determine innocence or guilt and then prescribe the set punishment. The law became rigid and structured and, indeed, impartial. The philosophy was to "let the punishment fit the crime."

Punishment as a Deterrent

Beccaria did not believe in severe punishment. The only reason to punish was to assure the continuance of society and to deter people from committing crimes. Deterrence would come, not from severe punishment, but from punishment that was appropriate, prompt, and inevitable. As for the death penalty, Beccaria believed that it did not deter and was an act of brutality and violence. He also believed "that capital punishment wasted human material, which was the principal asset of the state. . . . He further observed that capital punishment shocked general moral sentiment. . . . The reality of the shock . . . was illustrated by the popular detestation of executioners; and its result must be to weaken popular morality which the law ought instead to strengthen."[18]

Influence on Contemporary Criminal Law

The impact of Beccaria's arguments on modern American criminal law can be seen in this statement from Roscoe Pound: "Our substantive criminal law is based upon a theory of punishing the vicious will. It postulates a free moral agent, confronted with a choice between doing right and doing wrong, and choosing freely to do wrong."[19]

The major weaknesses in Beccaria's ideas on crimes and punishments were the rigidity of his concepts and the lack of provision for justifiable criminal acts. These faults were acknowledged by the classical school.

Jeremy Bentham

Jeremy Bentham (1748–1832), a contemporary of Beccaria, was a *utilitarian hedonist.* One critic, considering the "nature and importance of his work, its originality, its enormous extent, its many-sided character, its universal influence, its far-reaching practical results, and its potential virtues" concluded that he was tempted to "proclaim Bentham the greatest legal philosopher and reformer the world has ever seen."[20] Among Bentham's famous concepts is one advocating that the greatest good must go to the greatest number. One of his most important theories is that of *felicific calculus*—it assumed that people are rational creatures who will consciously choose pleasure and avoid pain. Therefore a punishment must be assigned to each crime so that the pain would outweigh any pleasure derived from the commission of the crime. Thus, the philosophy of "let the punishment fit the crime" was derived.

Principle of Utilitarianism

Bentham was an armchair thinker who considered crime in the abstract. In fact, he totally failed "to consider criminals as human beings, as live, complicated, variegated personalities." Like Beccaria, he stood against the status quo and fought fiercely for reform in the criminal law. He saw a new ethical principle of social control, a "method of checking human behavior according to a general ethical principle." He called the principle **utilitarianism:** "An act is not to be judged by an irrational system of absolutes but by a supposedly verifiable principle . . . [which is] 'the greatest happiness for the greatest number' or simply 'the greatest happiness.'" Unfortunately, Bentham did not explain the theoretical basis for his principle, nor did he tell how the principle could be measured objectively and empirically.[21]

Like Beccaria, Bentham also believed in the doctrine of free will, although he hinted at the theory of learned behavior as the explanation for criminal behavior. "He deserves considerable credit . . . for his adherence to a theory of social (that is, pleasure pursuit) causation of crime rather than a concept of biological, climatic or other non-social causation."[22]

Bentham stated that the objectives of punishment were (1) to prevent all offenses, (2) to prevent the worst offenses, (3) to keep down mischief, and (4) to act as the least expense. He condoned severe punishment because of its reforming effect, but he acknowledged that severity of punishment must be accepted by the people before it would be effective. The criminal law should not be used as vengeance against the criminal, but only to prevent crime. His ideas on capital punishment were similar to Beccaria's. Capital punishment was carried out with extraordinary brutality, and should not be regarded as satisfactory punishment since it created "more pain than is necessary for the purpose."[23]

Other Influences

Voltaire contributed indirectly and directly to the success of Beccaria's reform measures. Voltaire's indirect contribution was his work in laying the foundation for the Enlightenment. "By fighting religious intolerance and fanaticism, he contributed, more than any other, to the building of a more reasonable and humane society in which there was no longer any place for a criminal law based on superstition and cruelty." Without Voltaire's work, criminal reform would have been greatly delayed; Beccaria's essay on crime and punishment probably would not have appeared. Voltaire contributed directly to the success of penal reform by publicizing Beccaria's work.[24]

Another philosopher who influenced the classical period of criminology, but who is infrequently mentioned in criminology texts, is the German jurist Paul von Feuerbach (1775–1833). He did not think that punishment should be retributive. The purpose of punishment was to protect the rights of others and the penalties, therefore, should be commensurate with the type of right violated. von Feuerbach argued that the definitions of crimes and the punishments provided by the state should be clearly stated in the law; he is regarded as a forerunner of the most important principles of civil and Anglo-American law.

Neoclassical School

The *neoclassical school* of criminology flourished during the nineteenth century. It had the same basis as that of the classical school—a belief in free will. The neoclassicists, however, found the penalties that resulted from the classical doctrine to be too severe and all-encompassing for the humanitarian spirit of the time. In particular, the French Code of 1791 was found to be unduly severe, and it was revised in 1810. The revisions provided for some judicial discretion, introducing minimum and maximum sentences, and it recognized the principle of extenuating circumstances, thus adhering to neoclassical penology. Further revisions in 1819 permitted more judicial discretion, but only under objective circumstances. There were still no exceptions in the law from subjective circumstances; that is, there was no consideration of the *intent* of the offender. The neoclassical criminologists, who were mainly British, began complaining about the need for individualized treatment of some offenders.

Perhaps the most shocking aspect of the harsh penal codes of the classical period is that they made no provision for separate treatment of children who committed crimes. One of the changes of the neoclassical period was that children under seven years of age were exempted from the law on the basis that they could not understand the difference between right and wrong. Mental disease was seen as a sufficient cause to impair responsibility; thus, defense by reason of insanity crept into law. Any situation or circumstance that made it impossible to exercise free will was seen as reason to exempt the person involved from conviction.

Although the neoclassical school was not a scientific school of criminology, it did begin to deal with the problem of causation, which the classical school most decidedly had not done. By making exceptions to the law, varied causation was implied, and the doctrine of free will could no longer stand alone as an explanation for criminal behavior. Even today, much modern law is based on the neoclassical philosophy of free will mitigated by certain exceptions.

The classical school, defining crime in legal terms, emphasized the concept of free will and advocated that punishment gauged to fit the crime would be a deterrent to crime. The **positivists** rejected the harsh legalism of the classical school and substituted the doctrine of determinism for that of free will. They focused on the constitutional, not the legal, aspect of crime. They paved the way for a philosophy of individualized, scientific treatment of criminals, based on the findings of the physical and social sciences. As Stephen Schafer said, "their emergence [in the late eighteenth century] symbolized clearly that the era of faith was over and the scientific age had begun."[25]

Cesare Lombroso, Rafaelle Garofalo, and Enrico Ferri were the three major figures in the **positive,** or *Italian,* **school.** Their approaches differed, but they all agreed that the emphasis in the study of crime should be on the scientific treatment of the criminal, not on the penalties to be imposed once the individual was convicted.

Cesare Lombroso

Cesare Lombroso (1835–1909) believed that the only justification for punishment is self-defense. Reforming the guilty rarely occurs. Lombroso believed that society has no right to impose any penalty on a criminal that is more harsh than the degree of wrong done by that person to society. He therefore excluded retribution and **revenge** as justifications for punishment. Unlike Beccaria, Lombroso believed that since different criminals have different needs, it is foolish to impose the same punishment on all who commit the same offense. He looked to Ferri, who argued that when a criminal can be rehabilitated in ten years, it is foolish to keep him or her in prison for twenty years when another person who needs to stay longer is released in five years. Lombroso thus became an early advocate of the **indeterminate sentence.**

Lombroso was not in favor of short prison terms, which only expose criminals to other criminals and allow no time for rehabilitation. He suggested that in such cases, alternatives such as "confinement at home, judicial admonition, fines, forced labor without imprisonment, local exile, corporal punishment, conditional sentence" might be imposed. He favored conditional sentencing or the probation system while advocating the death penalty only as a last resort.[26]

Rafaelle Garofalo

Baron Rafaelle Garofalo (1852–1934) was born in Naples, Italy, the son of a noble family of Spanish origin. He studied law, was interested in criminal law reform, served as a professor of criminal law and procedure during part of his career, and was also a member of the magistracy. At the request of the minister of justice, Garofalo wrote a reform of the Italian criminal procedure to be used in the criminal courts, but for political reasons, it was not adopted.

In 1885, Garofalo's major criminological work, a book entitled *Criminology,* appeared in Italian. In his work, Garofalo rejected most of the philosophies of the classical school: the legal definition of crime; the belief that punishment should fit the crime and that in doing so, it would deter criminal behavior; and the acceptance of the death penalty.

Positive School

Cesare Lombroso
CORBIS/Bettman

With regard to punishment, Garofalo believed that an offender's time in prison did not result in his or her moral **reformation.** Most prisons were too lenient; therefore, the offender did not suffer when incarcerated. Even if he or she suffered, that suffering was quickly forgotten. This did not mean that it was impossible to *"transform the activity of the offender."*[27] Garofalo had no doubts that "the manifestation of even the innate criminal propensities can often be repressed by 'a favorable concurrence' of external circumstances. The devising of appropriate measures of repression thus becomes the practical problem of central concern."[28] Garofalo warned, however, that one cannot expect too much in the attempt to change social conditions.

Enrico Ferri

Enrico Ferri (1856–1929) was the son of a poor shopkeeper. He was a problem student in his early life, became truant, and was almost expelled from school. Later, under the influence of Robert Ardigo, Ferri "found himself" and became interested in the scientific orientation. When he went to study with Lombroso for a year, Ferri had already become a positivist, and had published some of his main ideas. "While Ferri owed much of his system of ideas to the stimulation of Lombroso, he also became the catalyst who synthesized the latter's concepts with those of the sociologist and had no little influence on Lombroso's thinking."[29] Three years after he graduated, Ferri returned to his alma mater at Bologna as a professor of criminal law. There, in 1880, before he reached the age of twenty-five, he delivered a two-hour lecture on the new horizons in criminal law and procedure. This lecture became the basis for his best-known book, *Criminal Sociology.*

Ferri believed that crime was primarily produced by the type of society from which the criminal came. He postulated his *law of criminal saturation,* which states that "in a given social environment with definite individual and physical conditions, a fixed number of [crimes], no more and no less, can be committed."[30] Crime, then, can only be corrected by making changes in society. He called these changes "penal substitutes" or "equivalents" of punishment. Among them he lists changes in the tax structure (lower tax on necessities and increases on items such as alcohol), sanitary police regulations for dwellings in the city and the country, freedom of emigration, public improvements to supply work for the indigent, improved street lighting, substitution of metal for paper money to reduce counterfeiting, and cheap "workingmen's" houses. In addition to these economic reforms, he suggested electoral reforms, changes in marriage and divorce laws, an intelligent regulation of prostitution, and provisions for marriage of the clergy, which he believed would "avoid many infanticides, abortions, adulteries, and criminal assaults."[31]

Ferri strongly criticized legislators for their "blind worship of punishment," embodied in the philosophy of the classical school. This, he believed, resulted in an increase in punishment in an attempt to prevent crime. Thus, the criminal is not reformed and the crime-producing elements of society are not corrected.

Emphasis on the Scientific Method

Ferri advocated the use of the **scientific method,** not only in the study of causation of criminal behavior, but also in the system of criminal justice. Decisions concerning the punishment and treatment of criminals should not be made by **juries** and untrained judges, but by scientists. He advocated that the jury be abol-

T A B L E **2.1** **Comparison of Classical and Positive Schools**

Classical School	Positive School
1. Accepted legal definition of crime	1. Rejected legal definition; Garofalo substituted "natural crime"
2. Let the punishment fit the crime	2. Let the punishment fit the criminal
3. Doctrine of free will	3. Doctrine of determinism
4. Support of the death penalty for some offenses	4. Abolition of the death penalty
5. Anecdotal method—no empirical research	5. Empirical research—use of inductive method
6. Mandatory sentence	6. Indeterminate sentence

ished because jurors are not scientists and that decisions on sentencing should be made by judges trained in the social and psychological sciences. Ferri worked actively for penal reform.

Contributions of the Positive School of Thought

As indicated in our discussions of the three individuals in the positive school, the contributions of this school toward the reform of the criminal law have been extensive. These individuals wrote in reaction to the classical school, emphasizing the importance of empirical research in their work. They believed that punishment should fit the criminal, not the crime, as advocated by the classical school. The positivists substituted the doctrine of **determinism,** some arguing that it was physical, others that it was psychic, social, or economic; thus, introducing into the study of crime the concept of the environment. They spoke out against the death penalty as an effective deterrent to crime, and they advocated substituting the indeterminate sentence for the *definite sentence,* thereby giving further evidence of their rejection of the classical theory that the punishment should be tailored to fit the crime. Their main contribution, however, is that they began the empirical study of the etiology of crime.

Methodological problems in the research of the positivists limited their explanations of criminal behavior,[32] but their attitudes on punishment and sentencing, summarized in table 2.1, had a tremendous impact on developments in criminal law as well as in corrections.

Ferri, in comparing the positive and classical schools, said, "We speak two different languages."[33] Table 2.1 gives a brief comparison of the main points on which these schools of thought differed.

In a frequently quoted book published in 1968, Herbert L. Packer took the position that there are basically only two purposes to be served by punishment. In the first, the punishment is merited by the individual who committed the crime—the theory of **"just deserts."** Because of his or her transgression, the evildoer deserves to suffer. The second purpose of punishment is to deter crime. Each of these purposes can, however, be subdivided, an approach that is used in this discussion of justifications for punishment. Under the first purpose, we analyze retribution and revenge. Under the second purpose, we analyze what Packer calls utilitarian prevention, which involves general and specific deterrence; and behavioral prevention, which involves rehabilitation, reintegration, and reformation.[34]

Comparison
of the Classical
and Positive Schools

**Justifications
for Punishment**

Case Study 2.1

Commonwealth v. Ritter

The second theory which has been urged as a basis for the imposition of penalties is that of retribution. This may be regarded as the doctrine of legal revenge, or punishment merely for the sake of punishment. It is to pay back the wrong-doer for his wrong-doing, to make him suffer by way of retaliation even if no benefit results thereby to himself or to others. This theory of punishment looks to the past and not the future, and rests solely upon the foundation of vindictive justice. It is this idea of punishment that generally prevails, even though those who entertain it may not be fully aware of their so doing. Historically, it may be said that the origin of all legal punishments had its root in the natural impulse of revenge. At first this instinct was gratified by retaliatory measures on the part of the individual who suffered by the crime committed, or, in the case of murder, by his relatives. Later, the state took away the right of retaliation from individuals, and its own assumption of the function of revenge really constituted the beginning of criminal law. The entire course, however, of the refinement and humanizing of society has been in the direction of dispelling from penology any such theory. Indeed, even in classical times moralists and philosophers rejected the idea entirely . . .

The "Just Deserts" Approach: A Philosophy of Retribution

Historically, one of the most common justifications for punishment has been that the wrongdoer deserves to be punished. This position is explained in the excerpt from *Commonwealth v. Ritter*,[35] a 1930 case, in Case Study 2.1.

Revenge

It is important to distinguish the concepts of **retribution** and revenge, for many who advocate today that retribution is a valid justification for punishment are not looking at retribution as it has been used historically. It is the philosophy of "just deserts" that is embraced under retribution today. That is, the offender is punished based on what he or she deserves. Historically, however, retribution often meant revenge, which was generally manifested in the doctrine of *Lex Talionis*—"an eye for an eye and a tooth for a tooth," a doctrine that can be traced back to the Bible and the Code of Hammurabi. Under this doctrine, a person who violates the laws of society should be treated in the same way that he or she treated the victim. In its extreme form, this position would advocate capital punishment for those who murder. In the 1990s, this position gained popularity as the citizenry frequently elected political figures who advertised themselves as having little or no sympathy for those who violated society's rules. This, in turn, has resulted in higher incarceration rates, longer prison sentences, and a growing number of death-row inmates. Thus, it can be argued that today's society does not regard punishment as a means to obtain a rehabilitative goal but rather as a mechanism to seek revenge.

Retribution

After years of disfavor, retribution has gained its position as a justification for punishment in the United States. As will be seen later in the discussion of rehabilitation as a justification for punishment, retribution has probably replaced rehabilitation as the major reason for punishment. The acceptance of this justification for punishment can be seen in the capital punishment decisions of the United States Supreme Court, although not all of the justices accept the justification. In a 1972 opinion,[36] Justice Marshall argued that retribution for its own sake was improper, but Justice Steward took the position that retribution might prevent private revenge. He argued that retribution is instinctual with humans and it is the purpose of the criminal justice system to divert that drive into the proper channels.[37] Even stronger support for the philosophy of retribution can be found in the dissenting opinion of Chief Justice Burger, who concluded, "It would be reading a great deal into the Eighth Amendment to hold that the punishments authorized by legislatures cannot constitutionally reflect a retributive purpose."[38]

In 1976, the Supreme Court recognized retribution as an appropriate reason for capital punishment. It is no longer the dominant objective, said the Court, "but neither is it a forbidden objective nor one inconsistent with our respect for the dignity of men. . . . Indeed, the decision that capital punishment may be the appropriate sanction in extreme cases is an expression of the community's belief that certain crimes are themselves so grievous an affront to humanity that the only adequate response may be the penalty of death."[39] Referring to Justice Stewart's opinion in *Furman,* the Court noted that the instinct for retribution is a part of human nature, and if the courts do not handle these situations, private individuals might take the law into their own hands. With regard to retribution, the Court concluded, "In part, capital punishment is an expression of society's moral outrage at particularly offensive conduct. This function may be unappealing to many, but it is essential in an ordered society that asks its citizens to rely on legal processes rather than self-help to vindicate wrongs."[40]

In a classical article on the death penalty, Jack P. Gibbs argued that in the past, the Supreme Court justices have given more support to the doctrine of retribution as a justification for capital punishment because they have realized that the evidence on deterrence is not strong and that the public has become disillusioned with the doctrine of rehabilitation. Retribution is the only doctrine supporting punishment in general and the death penalty in particular, in which there need be no question of effectiveness. Effectiveness is not an issue. The argument under retribution is that an individual is incarcerated because that is what he or she deserves. Retribution is not *utilitarian.* Since its goal is "'doing justice' rather than the prevention of crimes, it makes no instrumental claims," and that is its principal merit. Its central defect, however, is that it "leaves so many questions about legal punishment unanswered that it cannot serve as a basis for a penal policy."[41]

In the first place, advocates do not give a clear, concise definition of retribution. They say one should be punished because that is what one "deserves," but that precludes answers to some important questions. First, what is the appropriate punishment for a given type of crime? If we use the doctrine "let the punishment fit the crime," then capital punishment is applicable only to murder, but it has not been so limited. Second, if one argues, as proponents of the retribution theory do, that punishment should be commensurate with the seriousness of the crime, how does one measure the latter? Can we assure that, for example, ten years in prison is twice as severe as five years? Even so, how do we compare imprisonment to death? Does the answer lie in what people perceive to be the severity of the crime—that is, public opinion? If so, how is that determined? Finally, in past decisions on capital punishment, the Supreme Court has said that aggravating or mitigating circumstances must be considered, but the doctrine of retribution does not answer the question of how much and what kind of discretion. Gibbs concluded: "[T]he fundamental shortcoming of the retributive doctrine is not that it seeks to justify a legal punishment as an end in itself; rather, the doctrine offers no solutions to the specific problems that haunt the criminal justice system . . . the retributive doctrine is attractive precisely because it is little more than an empty formula."[42]

The Justice Model of Punishment: A Recent Approach

Retribution as a justification for punishment is seen not only in past cases on the issue of capital punishment, but in addition constitutes the framework for what is known today as the **"Justice Model"** of punishment and sentencing. The focus of this discussion will be the philosophy of punishment on which the Justice Model is based.

Andrew von Hirsch represented the position of the report of the Committee for the Study of Incarceration in the book *Doing Justice: The Choice of Punishments.*[43] Indicating their basic mistrust of the power of the state, the committee members rejected rehabilitation and the indeterminate sentence and turned to deterrence and "just deserts" as reasons for punishment. In its rejection of rehabilitation as a reason for punishment, the committee, however, advocated shorter sentences and sparing use of incarceration.

The rehabilitation model has also been rejected by Ernest van den Haag,[44] who emphasized "just deserts"—deserved punishment—as well as the utilitarian aspect of punishment and the concept of justice.

> Justice is done by distributing punishments to offenders according to what is deserved by their offenses as specified by law. Legal justice involves neither less nor more than honoring the obligation to enforce the laws, which the government undertook in the very act of making them. Benefits, such as the rehabilitation of offenders, the protection of society from them while they are incapacitated, or, even more, the deterrence of others, are welcome, of course. But they are not necessary—and never sufficient—for punishment, and they are altogether irrelevant to making punishment just.[45]

The person most often cited as being responsible for the popularity of the Justice Model is David Fogel, who expressed his views in detail in his book *". . . We Are the Living Proof . . .": The Justice Model for Corrections.*[46] Fogel formulates twelve propositions on which he believes the Justice Model can be operationalized.[47] Essentially, he argues that punishment is necessary for the implementation of criminal law, a law based on the theory that people act as a result of their own free will and must be held responsible for their actions. Prisoners should be considered and treated as "responsible, volitional and aspiring human beings." "All of the processes of the agencies of the criminal justice system should be carried out in a milieu of justice." This precludes a correctional system that "becomes mired in the dismal swamp of preaching, exhorting, and treatment," a situation that, according to Fogel, results in a correctional system that is dysfunctional as an agency of justice. Discretion cannot be eliminated, but under the Justice Model, it will be controlled, narrowed, and subject to review.[48] In short, the emphasis is shifted from the processor (the public, the administration, and others) to the "consumer" of the criminal justice system, a shift from what Fogel calls the "imperial" or "official perspective" to the "consumer perspective" or "justice perspective." Justice for the offender must not stop with the process of sentencing, but must continue throughout the correctional process. "The justice perspective demands accountability from all processors, even the 'pure of heart.' *Properly understood, the justice perspective is not so much concerned with administration of justice as it is with the justice of administration.*"[49]

Under Fogel's Justice Model, a person sentenced to serve time in a correctional facility should retain all of the rights "accorded free citizens consistent with mass living and the execution of a sentence restricting the freedom of movement."[50] The inmate should be allowed to choose whether he or she wishes to participate in rehabilitation programs. The purpose of the prison becomes solely to confine for a specified period of time, not to rehabilitate the criminal. The offender receives only the sentence he or she deserves, and that sentence is implemented according to fair principles. "The entire case for a justice model rests upon the need to continue to engage the person in the quest for justice as he moves on the continuum from defendant to convict to free citizen."[51]

The influence of the classical school, which we discussed earlier in this chapter, can be seen in this recent return to a theory of "just deserts," or retribution. Bentham and Beccaria argued that the punishment "should fit the crime." The "just" and "humane" approach is to punish the criminal for what he or she has done, not to follow the treatment rehabilitation or so-called "humanitarian" approach. According to C. S. Lewis, that doctrine of humanitarianism, "merciful though it appears, really means that each one of us, from the moment he breaks the law, is deprived of the rights of a human being . . . when we cease to consider what the criminal deserves and consider only what will cure him or deter others, we have tacitly removed him from the sphere of justice altogether; instead of a person, a subject of rights, we now have a mere object, a patient, a 'case.'"[52]

What are the problems with this "justice" view of retribution as a justification for punishment? The model emphasizes due process, but it has been argued that although due process is important and meaningful during the stages of the criminal justice system prior to incarceration, the model faces some problems after incarceration. "It's one thing to furnish safeguards against administrative abuse and to promote expanded offender rights, but yet another to introduce those rights and remedies into correctional programming."[53]

Critique of the Justice Model

The retribution/Justice Model leaves many questions unanswered. In our previous discussion of retribution, we discussed some of those questions that were raised by Jack P. Gibbs. Essentially, the model is empty. It does not answer the important question: How *much* punishment is "deserved"? Further, it has been argued that the new approach is characterized by "an absence of rationale, of cement or framework. Most of the recommendations are 'reactions' to past abuses, not prescriptions for future successes."[54] Finally, for those members of our society who already see themselves as victims of the social structure of power held by the middle and upper classes, will the retribution/Justice Model appear "just"?

Prevention of Crime

In addition to the "just deserts" approach to punishment, Packer indicated that the second basic purpose of punishment is the prevention of crime. He divided this purpose into two categories: utilitarian prevention, in which he included **individual** and **general deterrence,** and behavioral prevention, which includes the goals of rehabilitation, reformation, and **reintegration.** We will examine each of these purposes.

Individual Deterrence

Individual deterrence refers to preventing the individual who is being punished from committing additional crimes. In the past, deterrence often took the form of **incapacitation**—usually corporal punishment, which would make it impossible for the individual to repeat the crime for which he or she had been apprehended. Thus, the hands of the thief would be cut off; the eye of the spy would be gouged; the rapist would be castrated. Less severe forms of punishment aimed at individual deterrence included such acts as branding the offender on the forehead with a letter representing the crime committed, such as a *T* for thief. The presumption was that public knowledge of the crime made it impossible for the offender to commit that crime again.

Today, it is assumed that individual or specific deterrence (as it is often regarded) can be accomplished by the **incarceration** of the particular offender. It is true that most people can be restrained from criminal acts if they are incarcerated and closely guarded. Clearly they are prevented from committing criminal acts if a sentence of capital punishment is imposed and carried out. In some cases, incarceration is sufficient to prevent individuals from committing additional crimes after their release, although even in those cases, one must look at such factors as the type of incarceration, treatment during incarceration, and the length of stay.[55]

There are some very important questions that remain unanswered with regard to individual or specific deterrence. How many convicted persons would be **recidivists**—repeat offenders—if they were not incarcerated or punished in other ways? How many people, especially those who are imprisoned, become *more* criminalistic because of the punishment they receive? Are most punishment efforts concentrated on those least likely to be deterred by such punishment—for example, the alcoholic, the drug addict, and the sex offender? Some studies indicate that, in fact, punishment is usually not effective in deterring these offenders.[56] In this area of drug abuse, efforts have not been concentrated on the sellers (who might be deterred by strict law enforcement), but on the users (who are not likely to be deterred). White-collar criminals, middle-class wives who shoplift, and traffic violators are probably more likely to be individually deterred after some reaction from law enforcement officials than those on whom most of criminal law efforts are concentrated.[57]

General Deterrence

The belief that punishment of one individual deters others from committing the same offense may be traced through the writings of Beccaria, Bentham, and Feuerbach and back to Greek philosophy. The brief excerpt from *Regina v. Jones*[58] in Case Study 2.2 shows this reliance on general deterrence, even at the risk of imposing a sentence that might be detrimental to the person convicted. The respondent had pleaded guilty to three charges of indecent assault on girls ages six, seven, and eight. He was fined $150 for each charge. The maximum penalty in that jurisdiction was five years in prison plus whipping. On appeal, the court changed the sentence to a prison term.

This reliance on general deterrence to justify punishment led Justice Holmes to remark: "If I were having a philosophical talk with a man I was going to have [executed] I should say, 'I don't doubt that your act was inevitable for you but to make it more avoidable by others we propose to sacrifice you to the common good. You may regard yourself as a soldier dying for your country. . . . But the law must keep its promises.'"[59] As an eighteenth century judge told the accused: "You are to be hanged not because you have stolen a sheep *but in order that others may not steal sheep.*'"[60]

Deterrence of Types of Crimes and Types of People

The debate over deterrence should be narrowed to examine types of crime and types of people. This is often overlooked in the debate concerning punishment as a deterrent. Perhaps punishment (or the threat of punishment) is effective in deterring a woman from shoplifting but not necessarily from poisoning her husband. Perhaps certain types of people are deterred by laws, while others are not.[61]

Case Study 2.2

Regina v. Jones

For the respondent it is urged that a prison sentence is not appropriate in the circumstances in this case. The reasons urged by counsel for the respondent against imposing a term of imprisonment are that the respondent is suffering from a form of sex perversion which Dr. McLarty, one of the psychiatrists, describes as sexual repression, that there is not much likelihood of a recurrence of the offense by the respondent, and that a prison term will be definitely detrimental to the respondent's condition. These are all considerations relating to the rehabilitation of the respondent and, in my opinion, entirely overlook the element of deterrence to others in the imposition of sentence for a criminal offense. It may be that this particular respondent, after continuation of psychiatric treat-ment, will not repeat the offense and there is a possibility of him being cured of his condition by such psychiatric treatment, but these are matters of grave uncertainty. I think I would agree that, so far as the condition of this particular respondent is concerned, a prison term may be detrimental to his recovery, but in my opinion the offense is too serious for punishment by a fine or by suspending sentence and placing the respondent upon probation. It is said that the prison term will not have any deterrent effect upon other persons who are truly sex perverts. That may be so, but I do not think it justifies disregarding the deterrent effect upon those persons whom sentence will deter and who might be disposed to commit an assault of this character. . . .

It is often the case that discussions of the theory of deterrence commit the fallacy of absolutism: Since all behavior is not deterred by penalties, punishment does not deter. But "to justify punishment it is not necessary to prove that it *always* prevents crime, but its deterrent quality. It is enough to indicate that there would be more crime if all punishment were abolished."[62]

Ernest van den Haag has argued that punishment deters all but "persons who have little to lose." He quoted Herbert L. Packer as saying "Deterrence does not threaten those whose lot in life is already miserable beyond the point of hope."[63] van den Haag argues that the stigmatizing effect of punishment is a deterrent to many, but it is influenced by their social status—the higher the socioeconomic status, the greater the effect. He also contends that although the stigmatizing effect of legal punishment today is at a low ebb, most people can be deterred by the threat of punishment.[64]

It has been argued that it is not the threat of punishment per se that is a significant deterrent, but rather the severity and certainty of that punishment. With regard to certainty, one argument is that the *actual* certainty of punishment influences people's perceptions about certainty—if they believe certainty of punishment is high, they will be afraid to violate the law. This proposition has not, however, been examined explicitly,[65] although the conclusions of several studies question its validity.[66]

A study conducted by Jack Gibbs and Charles Tittle is particularly relevant to this topic. Gibbs studied rates of homicide while Tittle analyzed crime rates for all **FBI Crime Index offenses,** considering both certainty and severity of punishment. They both found certainty and severity of punishment to be inversely related to homicide—as the degree of certainty and severity of punishment increased, the homicide rates decreased. Gibbs found the relationship to be stronger for severity and Tittle found it to be more significant between certainty and punishment.[67] A later study found "*no consistent* support for the hypothesis that severe punishment deters crime."[68]

Severity and Certainty of Punishment

Deterrence: The Need for Theory

Analysis of the issue of deterrence, both general and specific, is complicated by the fact that it is difficult, if not impossible, to identify those persons who have been deterred by the threat of punishment. Other variables that might be associated with deterrence are also difficult to measure, but Robert F. Meier, in analyzing the issue of deterrence, argued that the basic need is for more theoretical development. He concluded that the "inability to formulate valid deterrence models is likely to continue to plague the development of this field until there is sufficient theoretical progress to permit specifying pertinent variables in addition to strictly legal factors, and to stipulate the manner in which their presumed relationship with behavior can be best tested."[69]

Behavioral Prevention

A second way in which the "prevention of crime" can be analyzed is in Packer's conceptualization of behavioral prevention, which is often referred to by such terms as rehabilitation, reformation, and reintegration.

In the past century, the hallmark of "progressive" corrections in this country has been the belief that the purpose of punishment is to reform or rehabilitate the offender. This position has been strongly endorsed by social scientists and even acknowledged by the courts.[70] Rehabilitation has been described by one authority as the "rehabilitative ideal,"[71] characterized by the juvenile court, probation, parole, and individualized sentencing and treatment. The ideal is based on the premise that human behavior is the result of antecedent causes that may be known by objective analysis and that permit scientific control of human behavior. The assumption is, therefore, that the offender should be *treated,* not punished.

Recently, however, the doctrine of rehabilitation has lost popularity. Some argue that it should no longer be the guiding purpose of punishment because it does not work or because it is ethically objectionable. In short, the doctrine has experienced a quick decline in popularity. As David L. Bazelon, Chief Judge of the United States Court of Appeals in Washington, D.C., has concluded, "The guiding faith of corrections—rehabilitation—has been declared a false God."[72]

Judge Bazelon has argued that the problem with rehabilitation as a justification for punishment is that it "should never have been sold on the promise that it would reduce crime. Recidivism rates cannot be the only measure of what is valuable in corrections. Simple decency must count too. It is amoral, if not immoral, to make cost-benefit equations a lodestar in corrections."[73] Others have argued that treatment programs, though they may not have been effective in coerced situations, should be available in prisons for those inmates who want to be rehabilitated. It is noteworthy to mention that those who strongly support the doctrine of rehabilitation have not given up easily. Many have emphasized the importance of the *reintegration* of the offender into the community, resulting in a strong emphasis on community-based programs.

The argument that the doctrine of rehabilitation is unjust to the offender was raised in the early 1950s by the British theologian C. S. Lewis, who argued that the rehabilitative ideal removes the concept of "just deserts"—that is, people get what they deserve. Society is no longer interested in a "just" cure but only in a cure; not in a "just" deterrent but only in a deterrent.[74] It is this type of attack on the rehabilitation model of corrections that has formed the basis for the return to an emphasis on retribution, as noted earlier in our discussion of the "Justice Model," which appears to be the pervasive model of punishment today.

WiseGuide Wrap-Up This chapter provided instruction on the main theories of punishment, the historical background of punishment and criminal law, justifications for punishment, and the prevention of crime. We learned that the cultural consistency and social structure theories provide particular insights into the mechanisms that have provoked the implementation of different types of punishments throughout history. Some of these punishments were implemented in France and England, where torture and death became known concepts among the citizenry. Fortunately, individuals such as Cesare Beccaria and Jeremy Bentham contributed toward the reform of these punitive methods. Out of these reforms, the *classical school of criminology* was born. Although this school of thought was quite popular at the time, it faded away and was followed by the works of Cesare Lombroso, Rafaelle Garofalo, and Enrico Ferri. The writings of these three individuals gave rise to the positive school of criminology. This school of thought, unlike the classical school, promoted the concepts of predeterminism and rehabilitation. It is important to note that both the classical and positive schools govern some of the present-day policies that aim at both the punishment and rehabilitation of offenders.

In the latter part of this chapter, justifications for punishments, such as retribution and deterrence, were discussed. Both of these assume that offenders are rational and enjoy the benefit of exercising free will. Many consider these to be erroneous assumptions, holding that some offenders are "born bad,"[75] while others have a "limited" free will[76] that is constrained by their own realities.

Notes

1. Sutherland, Edwin H., and Cressey, Donald R. *Criminology,* 10th ed. (Philadelphia: J.B. Lippincott and Company, 1978), pp. 347–358.
2. Sutherland and Cressey, *Criminology,* 9th ed. (Philadelphia: J.B. Lippincott and Company, 1974), p. 337.
3. Sutherland and Cressey, *Criminology,* 10th ed., p. 355.
4. See Emile Durkheim. *The Division of Labor in Society,* paper ed. (New York: Free Press, 1964), p. 113.
5. Spitzer, Steven. "Punishment and Social Organization: A Study of Durkheim's Theory of Penal Evolution," *Law and Society Review* 9 (Summer, 1975), 634.
6. Sutherland and Cressey, *Criminology,* 10th ed., p. 358.
7. Mannheim, Hermann, ed. *Pioneers in Criminology,* paper ed. (Montclair, NJ: Patterson Smith, 1973).
8. For a discussion of the contributions of these "pioneers" to an understanding of the causes of criminal behavior, see Sue Titus Reid, *Crime and Criminology,* 8th ed. (New York: McGraw-Hill, 1997).
9. Lacroix, Paul. *France in the Middle Ages.* (New York: Frederick Ungar Publishing Co., 1963), p. 394. The examples of punishments in France are based on this source.
10. Lacroix, *France in the Eighteenth Century,* p. 291.
11. Durant, Will and Ariel, *The Story of Civilization,* vol. 7, *The Age of Reason Begins.* (New York: Simon and Schuster, 1961), p. 54. The examples of punishments in England are from that source.
12. Durant, *Civilization,* vol. 9, *The Age of Voltaire.* (New York: Simon and Schuster, 1965), p. 71. This book is the source of the remaining examples of punishment in England.
13. Durant, *Civilization,* vol. 9, *The Age of Voltaire.*
14. Beccaria, Cesare. *On Crimes and Punishments,* trans. Henry Paolucci. (Indianapolis, IN: Bobbs-Merrill, 1963), pp. ix–xxxiii.
15. Monochese, Eliott. "Cesare Beccaria," in Mannheim, *Pioneers,* p. 49.
16. Schaefer, Stephen, *Theories in Criminology.* (New York: Random House, 1969), p. 106.
17. Beccaria, *Crimes and Punishments,* pp. 11–13.
18. Heath, James. *Eighteenth Century Penal Theory.* (London: Oxford University Press, 1963), p. 60.
19. Roscoe Pound, quoted in Frank Tannenbaum, *Crime and the Community.* (New York: Ginn and Company, 1938), p. 4.
20. Phillipson, Coleman. *Three Criminal Law Reformers: Beccaria, Bentham and Romilly.* (New York: E.P. Dutton and Co., 1923), p. 234.
21. Geis, Gilbert. "Jeremy Bentham," in Mannheim, *Pioneers,* p. 54.
22. Geis, in *Pioneers,* p. 57.
23. Geis, in *Pioneers,* p. 59.
24. Maestro, M.T. *Voltaire and Beccaria as Reformers of the Criminal Law.* (New York: Columbia University Press, 1942), pp. 152–157.
25. Schafer, *Theories in Criminology,* p. 123.
26. Mannheim, *Pioneers,* pp. 386–388, 391.
27. Garofalo, Rafaelle. *Criminology,* trans. Robert W. Milllar (Boston: Little, Brown and Company, 1914), p. 32.
28. Allen, Francis. "Rafaelle Garofalo," in Mannheim, *Pioneers,* p. 327; for an excellent discussion on Garofalo, see this essay.
29. Sellin, Thorsten. "Enrico Ferri," in Mannheim, *Pioneers,* pp. 370–371.
30. Ferri, Enrico. *Criminal Sociology,* trans. Joseph Killey and John Lisle (Boston: Little, Brown and Company, 1917), p. 209.
31. Ferri, *Criminal Sociology,* pp. 242–277.

32. For a discussion, see Reid, *Crime and Criminology*.
33. Ferri, Enrico. *The Positive School of Criminology*. (Chicago: Charles H. Kerr and Co., 1913), p. 35.
34. Packer, Herbert L. *The Limits of the Criminal Sanction*. (Stanford, CA: Stanford University Press, 1968).
35. Court of Oyer and Terminer, Philadelphia, 13 D. & C. 285 (1930).
36. *Furman v. Georgia*, 408 U.S. 238 (1972).
37. 408 U.S. 238, 308.
38. 408 U.S 238, 395.
39. *Gregg v. Georgia*, 428 U.S. 153, 184–185.
40. 428 U.S. 153, 183.
41. Gibbs, Jack P. "The Death Penalty, Retribution and Penal Policy," *The Journal of Criminal Law and Criminology* 69 (Fall, 1978), 294.
42. Gibbs, "The Death Penalty," p. 299.
43. von Hirsch, Andrew. *Doing Justice: The Choice of Punishments*. (New York: Hill & Wang, 1976).
44. van den Haag, Ernest. *Punishing Criminals: Concerning a Very Old and Painful Question*. (New York: Basic Books, 1975).
45. van den Haag, *Punishing Criminals*, p. 25.
46. Fogel, David. *". . . We Are the Living Proof . . ." The Justice Model for Corrections*. (Cincinnati, OH: W.H. Anderson, 1975).
47. Fogel, *Living Proof*, pp. 183–184.
48. Fogel, *Living Proof*, p. 184.
49. Fogel, *Living Proof*, p. 192, emphasis as in the original.
50. Fogel, *Living Proof*, p. 202, emphasis deleted.
51. Fogel, *Living Proof*, p. 206.
52. Lewis, C. S. "The Humanitarian Theory of Punishment," *Res Judicatae* 6 (June, 1953), 224–225.
53. Carlson, Rich J. *The Dilemma of Corrections*. (Lexington, MA: D.C. Heath & Co., 1976), p. 135.
54. Carlson, *Dilemma of Corrections*, p. 126.
55. See, for example, the recent study of Anthony R. Harris, Imprisonment and the Expected Value of Criminal Choice: A Specification and Test of Aspects of the Labeling Perspective," *American Sociological Review* 40 (February, 1975), 71–87.
56. See David J. Pittman and C. Wayne Gordon. *Revolving Door*. (New York: Free Press, 1968).
57. Chambliss, William J. *Crime and the Legal Process*. (New York: McGraw-Hill, 1969).
58. 115 Can. Crim. Cas. 273 (1956).
59. Quoted in John Kaplan. *Criminal Justice: Introductory Cases and Materials*. (Mineola, NY: The Foundation Press, 1973), p. 16.
60. Quoted in Sanford H. Kadish and Monrad G. Paulsen. *Criminal Law and Its Processes*. (Boston: Little, Brown and Company, 1969), p. 85.
61. Andenaes, Johannes. "Determinism and Criminal Law," *Journal of Criminal Law, Criminology, and Police Science* 47 (November–December, 1956), 406–413.
62. Cohen, Morris. "Moral Aspects of the Criminal Law," *Yale Law Journal* 49 (April, 1940), 1015–1016.
63. van den Haag, *Punishing Criminals*, p. 64.
64. van den Haag, *Punishing Criminals*, pp. 64-65.
65. See the discussion of Gibbs, *Crime, Punishment, and Deterrence*, and Johannes Andenaes, "General Prevention Revisited: Research and Policy Implications," *Journal of Criminal Law, Criminology, and Police Science* 66 (September, 1975), 338–365.
66. See Assembly Committee (1968) *Deterrent Effects of Criminal Sanctions*, Progress Report of the Assembly Committee on Criminal Procedure, California Legislature; N. Walker, *Sentencing in a Rational Society* (Harmondsworth, England: Penguin Press, 1969), cited in Jerry Parker and Harold G. Gransmick, "Linking Actual and Perceived Certainty of Punishment," *Criminology* 17 (November, 1979), 366–379.
67. Gibbs, "Crime, Punishment and Deterrence," *Southwest Social Science Quarterly*, 515–530; and Charles R. Tittle, "Crime Rates and Legal Sanctions," *Social Problems* 16 (Spring, 1969), 409–423.
68. Chiricos, Theodore G., and Waldo, Gordon P. "Punishment and Crime: An Examination of Some Empirical Evidence," *Social Problems* 18 (Fall, 1970), 200.
69. Meier, Robert F. "Correlates of Deterrence: Problems of Theory and Method," *Journal of Criminal Justice* 7 (Spring, 1979), 18–19.
70. See *Williams v. New York*, 337 U.S. 241, 248 (1949).
71. Allen, Francis. "Criminal Justice, Legal Values and the Rehabilitative Ideal," *Journal of Criminal Law, Criminology, and Police Science* 50 (September–October, 1959), 226–232.
72. Bazelon, David L. "Street Crime and Correctional Potholes," *Federal Probation* 41 (March, 1977), pp. 3–9.
73. Bazelon, "Street Crime," 10.
74. Lewis, "The Humanitarian Theory of Punishment," 225. See also Nicholas Kittrie, *The Right To Be Different* (New York: Penguin, 1973). For a discussion of the right to treatment, see Ronald Goldfarb and Linda Singer, "Redressing Prisoners' Grievances," *George Washington Law Review* 39, (December, 1970), 175.
75. Raine, Adrianne. *The Psychopathology of Crime*. (New York: Academic Press, 1993).
76. Golden, Renny. *Disposable Children: America's Welfare System*. (Belmont, CA: Wadsworth, 1997).

The Development of Imprisonment As a Form of Punishment

In chapter 2 we examined the various theoretical justifications of punishment that have been used in reaction to those who violate the laws and mores of society. Although many of the punishments were cruel and unusual, it must be kept in mind that in the past the world was less populated, police protection was nonexistent, and capital punishment and torture were quick methods of incapacitating the offender. "Under the more unstable conditions of the past it would have been difficult to carry out long, continued forms of punishment such as imprisonment."[1] Prison, therefore, is a recent development, although society has for a long time confined criminals. Until recently that confinement was only temporary—while awaiting execution, transportation, or whipping—and was not perceived or used as a form of punishment in itself.

This chapter traces the historical development of prisons, focusing attention on the influence of the prison reformer John Howard. In discussing the emergence of prisons in the United States, we contrast the two basic types of systems—the Pennsylvania and the Auburn—and observe the influence each had on today's modern prison systems. Reformation of those incarcerated, a later concern, led to the development of the Elmira Reformatory, which placed emphasis on rehabilitation through education, parole, and indeterminate sentences. Architecture assumed an important role in all of these systems, and even today it is strongly argued that architecture is related to treatment. Thus, we will carefully examine prison architecture and the custodial emphasis in the evolution of prisons.

Key Terms

Auburn System
Cherry Hill
early release
Elmira Reformatory
halfway houses
indeterminate sanctions
"panopticon"
parole
penitentiary
Pennsylvania System
prerelease centers
prison overcrowding
Progressives
solitary confinement
wardens

Outline

We also look at the development of the prison system in the United States throughout the twentieth century. Specifically, emphasis is placed on the Progressives and their role throughout the evolution of American corrections. An analysis is made on various historical periods, including the transition period and the modern era. Finally, when discussing the latter, attention is placed on various dimensions of prison overcrowding, including its effects on the present correctional system.

Historical Development

The transition from corporal punishment to incarceration as punishment took place in the eighteenth century. This transition became evident in 1704 when Pope Clement XI erected the papal prison of San Michele in Rome, and Hippolyte Vilain XIII established a prison in Ghent, Belgium in 1773. Once established as a preferred form of punishment, incarceration became the subject of several reforms. In fact, in the mid-1700s, John Howard, one of the greatest prison reformers of all time, visited prisons throughout Europe and brought to the attention of the world the sordid conditions under which prisoners were being kept. His classic work *State of Prisons,* published in 1777, was extremely influential in the reform of prisons in Europe and the United States. In fact, Howard is often credited with the beginning of the penitentiary—a facility built with the intent of isolating offenders from society and from each other so that they can reflect, repent, and undergo reformation. The word "penitentiary" is suggestive of the penance that offenders were encouraged to undergo. It is important to note that all of these characteristics made the penitentiary different from prisons and jails.

In 1776, England was faced with prison overcrowding due to a rising crime rate, the elimination of the need for galley slaves, and decreasing opportunities for "transportation" of criminals to other countries. In responding to the need for new arrangements for the handling of convicts, England legalized the use of "hulks," which were abandoned ships converted to hold prisoners. By 1828, at least 4,000 convicts were confined in prison hulks. "The ships were unsanitary, ill-ventilated and full of vermin." Contagious diseases would often kill a great number of prisoners. Punishments were brutal and particularly severe. There was little work for prisoners and such idleness was demoralizing. Moral degeneration inevitably set in because of the "promiscuous association of prisoners of all ages and degrees of criminality."[2] This system of penal confinement in England lasted until the mid-nineteenth century.

Among the reasons for the substitution of imprisonment for corporal and capital punishment was the spirit of humanitarianism that arose during the Enlightenment. The influence of the classical criminologists and philosophers can also be seen. The emphasis on "rationalism" served as the ideological basis that provoked and demanded change. This approach was important in the history of prisons because of its influence on social and political philosophy. The philosophers believed that social progress and the "greatest happiness for the greatest number" would occur only through revolutionary social reform. Such social reform could be brought about only by applying "reason."[3]

It was logical that those ideas would flourish in America because many French people lived in the United States during the French Revolution, and many influential Americans lived in France. Since the Constitutional Convention was greatly influenced by French political philosophers, it is not unreasonable to assume that its members were also aware of the French social philosophy. The fact that those who were probably most influenced were concentrated in Philadelphia, and that this city was the birthplace of early penal reform, lends further support to the belief that French philosophy influenced American criminal justice reform.

Emergence of the Penitentiary System in the United States

Several explanations have been given for the rise of the **penitentiary** system in the United States; some of those reasons are examined in the following discussion. David J. Rothman, in his classic book *The Discovery of the Asylum*,[4] discusses the development of the penitentiary and other institutions in the United States. Prior to the Jacksonian period, he notes, Americans handled orphans by placing them in private homes, expected families to care for their insane members, used corporal or capital punishment to punish those who violated the laws or mores of the society, and placed the poor with relatives or friends. Why did Americans develop orphanages, asylums, penitentiaries, and almshouses to care for these classes of deviants during the Jacksonian period?

Rothman maintains that, contrary to the beliefs of some historians, the development of such institutions was not inevitable. He looks upon the development of all of these types of institutions as an effort to "promote the stability of the society at a moment when traditional ideas and practices appeared outmoded, constricted, and ineffective." Circumstances were changing rapidly and the people sought a way to maintain stability and retain community cohesion. Students of such social problems, legislators, and philanthropists believed that the nation faced unprecedented dangers. They believed that such institutions could eliminate long-standing problems while restoring social balance.[5]

Rothman begins his analysis with the colonial period, taking the position that the social structure of that period must be understood before one can understand the changes that took place in the nineteenth century. During the colonial period, it was thought that crime, poverty, mental illness, homeless children, and other social problems were not indicative of a defective social organization and that they could not be eliminated through social action. So there seemed to be no reason for the development of institutions to handle such persons. After the Revolution, considerable endorsement was given to the position that the roots of crime and poverty are in the social structure—the faulty organization of the community. The belief in social action to solve such problems was also prevalent. In the case of criminals and delinquents, it was thought that institutionalization would serve the dual purposes of rehabilitating the inmates as well as setting an example for others;[6] it would serve the purposes of both individual and general deterrence.

According to Rothman, the penitentiary was not developed as a place of last resort, but rather as a place of temporary confinement in which the criminal could be changed while society could retain its stability. Prisons would also serve the society as demonstrations of proper social organization. The early penologists believed strongly that the penitentiary was a model not only for reforming the criminal but also for society in general; the architecture of the penitentiary would serve as a model for other social institutions.[7]

Walnut Street Jail

The Walnut Street Jail was typical of the earliest institutions developed for the purpose of incarceration as punishment in this country. In 1787, Quakers were among the elite in the city of Philadelphia who formed the Reformist Society for Alleviating the Miseries of Public Prisoners. Under the leadership of individuals such as Dr. Benjamin Rush and Benjamin Franklin, the society aggressively moved to replace corporal and capital punishments with incarceration. Moreover, Rush proposed a new system for the treatment of criminals, which included classification, individualized treatment, and prison labor to make them self-supporting. In

1790, under Rush's leadership, the society influenced the enactment of a law that established the principle of solitary confinement. The Walnut Street Jail was to be remodeled so that this philosophy could be implemented. Individual cells would be provided for serious offenders, and other prisoners would be separated by gender and by whether they had been sentenced or were only being detained awaiting trial. In this manner, offenders could be isolated from society's bad influences and from one another to allow time for reflection, repentance, and reformation. This law was the beginning of the modern prison system in the United States, for it established the philosophy that was the basis for the Pennsylvania System and later, the Auburn System.

The prisoners at Walnut Street Jail worked eight to ten hours a day and received religious instruction. They worked in their cells and were paid for their work. Guards were not allowed to use weapons, and corporal punishment was forbidden. Prisoners were allowed to talk only in the "nightrooms" before retiring. But by 1800, problems with the system were obvious. Crowded facilities made work within individual cells impossible, and there was not enough productive work for the large number of prisoners. Vices flourished, and the pardon power was abused. The Walnut Street Jail ultimately failed because of lack of finances, politics, lack of personnel, and crowding, but not before it gained recognition throughout the world. It has been called the "birthplace of the prison system, in its present meaning, not only in the United States but throughout the world."[8]

Problems Faced by the Early Prisons

The Walnut Street Jail and other early prisons faced serious problems. Despite tight security and thick walls, escapes occurred. To combat this problem, some **wardens**—chief administrators of correctional institutions—required inmates to wear uniforms. In some prisons, the color of the uniform indicated whether the convict was a first-, second-, or third-time offender. Wardens faced the problem of what to do with inmates who broke rules. In some cases, administrators reacted with a return to corporal punishment, especially whippings, while others used solitary confinement. The prisons faced the problem of the expense of keeping the inmates, especially those with long sentences. Work programs such as gardening were devised to alleviate this problem, while allowing the inmates opportunities for exercise. Generally, however, those programs did not work either. The inmates were not reliable or efficient and administrators were not skilled in managing the labor situation. The result was that most prisons operated at a loss. "By 1820, the viability of the entire prison system was in doubt, and its most dedicated supporters conceded a near total failure. Institutionalization had not only failed to pay its own way, but also encouraged and educated the criminal to a life of crime."[9]

Development of the Pennsylvania and Auburn Systems

In response to such problems, two distinct types of prison systems were developed—the **Pennsylvania System** and the **Auburn System.** The Pennsylvania System was based on solitary confinement whereby inmates were isolated at all times, while the Auburn System was based on the congregate system that placed inmates in workshops during the day, but forbade communication among them. These two systems were the subject of intense debate during the 1800s, and the intensity of these debates on the merits of the two systems was not diminished by the fact that most prisons in the United States were modeled after the Auburn System. The two systems were actually very similar, but the arguments over the merits of the systems involved an "extraordinary amount of intellectual and emotional energy." When a state adopted one or the other of the two systems, it

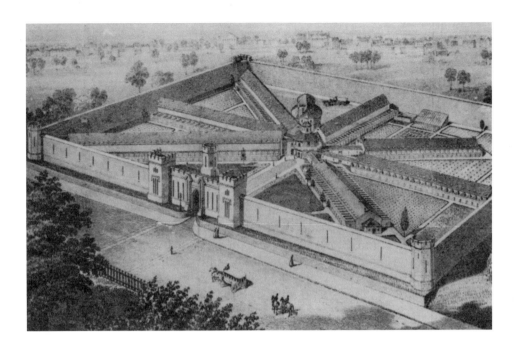

Cherry Hill Eastern Penitentiary
American Correctional Association.

entered the debate "with the zeal of a recent covert."[10] Tourists flocked to see the prisons, and foreign nations sent delegates to examine the two systems. In 1831, France, for example, sent Alexis de Tocqueville and Gustave Auguste de Beaumont, who wrote that "nothing distracts in Philadelphia, the mind of the convicts from their mediations; and as they are always isolated, the presence of a person who comes to converse with them is the greatest benefit."[11] By the 1830s, the Pennsylvania and Auburn systems were famous around the world.

Development of the Pennsylvania System

With the failure of the Walnut Street Jail, solitary confinement at hard labor did not appear to work. Consideration was given to a return to corporal punishment. But in 1817, the Philadelphia Society for the Alleviation of the Miseries of Prisons began a reform movement that eventually led to a law providing for the establishment of solitary cells without labor. The first such prison was opened in Pittsburgh in 1826 and was later known as the Western Penitentiary. Based on the experiences with this prison, however, the law was changed to permit work in solitary confinement prior to the establishment of the Eastern Penitentiary in Philadelphia. The design of this building eventually became the basic architectural model for the Pennsylvania System.

Cherry Hill Eastern Penitentiary, or Cherry Hill as it was called because it was located in a cherry orchard, opened in 1829. It was the first large-scale attempt at implementing the philosophy of **solitary confinement** at *all* times with work provided in the cells. The law that authorized the construction of this prison clearly specified that the principle of solitary confinement must be incorporated, although the commissioners could make some alterations and improvements in the plan used for the Western Penitentiary. John Haviland, the architect who designed the Eastern Penitentiary, was faced with the problem of creating a design that would permit solitary confinement but would not, at the same time, injure the health or permit the escape of the occupant. His solution was to build seven wings, each connected to a central hub by covered passageways. Each prisoner would have a single inside cell with an outside exercise yard. Prisoners were blindfolded when

The Auburn System
American Correctional Association.

taken to the prison and were not permitted to see other inmates. They were not even assembled for religious worship. The chaplain spoke from the rotunda—a circular hall—and prisoners listened to him while remaining in their individual cells.

Before Cherry Hill was completed, it became the focus of discussion among prison reformers around the world. It served as the architectural model for most of the new prisons in Europe and South America and, later, in Asia. The architectural design was not popular in the United States, although even today it "dominates the penitentiary system of continental Europe."[12] In Scandinavia, for instance, the "traditional structure is straight out of Pennsylvania, and . . . one of the finest surviving examples of Pennsylvania prison design is the Vestrefaengsel in Copenhagen, where, until not so long ago, chapel seats were still boxed off in vertical coffin-shaped compartments so that privacy of the prisoner would be maintained and his contamination prevented."[13]

Development of the Auburn System

The Auburn System became the architectural model for prisons in the United States. In 1796, New York passed a law that provided for the construction of two prisons. Newgate, a prison built in New York City, was first occupied in 1797 and soon became overcrowded. To make room for new inmates, the number of prisoners released had to equal the number admitted. The second prison opened at Auburn in the winter of 1817. At first, it followed the same type of system as that of Newgate—workshop groups during the day and several prisoners to a cell at night. Discipline was a problem in this setting, and this method eventually failed, thus allowing the development of a new system—the Auburn System.

The Auburn System, or *congregate system,* espoused congregate work during the day with an enforced rule of silence, but it also demanded that the prisoners be housed in isolation at night. The architecture created a fortress-like appearance with a series of tiers set in a hollow frame, a much more economical system than that used at Cherry Hill.

The *silent system* was strictly enforced at Auburn. Inmates were not allowed to talk or exchange glances at any time. They had to stand with their arms folded and their eyes facing the floor so they could not communicate with their hands. They had to walk in lockstep with a downward gaze, and ate face-to-back.

To further isolate the inmates, there was strict regulation of letters and visits with outsiders, and few or no newspapers were provided. Prisoners were brought together for religious services, but they sat in booth-like pews that prevented them from seeing anybody except the speaker. The underlying philosophy of the silent system was the notion that convicts were incorrigible and that industrial efficiency was the main purpose of correctional facilities.

Discipline was also enforced at Auburn. The warden, Captain Elam Lynds, believed that the spirit of a person must be broken before reformation could truly occur. He was largely responsible for the Auburn philosophy of punishment. It is said that he changed the disciplinary rules without legislative authority, instituted the silent system, fed the inmates in their cells, and required lockstep marching. A committee from the legislature visited the prison, approved of the way it was being run, and persuaded the legislature to legalize the new system.

A system of classification that placed dangerous criminals in solitary confinement was instituted in 1821. This led to mental illness, the death of some inmates, and the pleading of others to be let out to work. As a result, the practice of solitary confinement was abolished in 1822.

Comparison of the Pennsylvania and Auburn Systems

Architecture is extremely important in distinguishing the Auburn and Pennsylvania systems. The latter emphasized solitary confinement while the former was based on the congregate system. Both systems placed emphasis on the importance of a disciplined routine while isolating the individual from bad influences. Both systems reflected the belief that since the inmate was not inherently bad, but rather the product of a defective social organization, he or she could be reformed under the proper circumstances. "Just as the criminal's environment had led him into crime, the institutional environment would lead him out of it."[14] The discussions of crime centered around the advantages and disadvantages of these two systems, but no one seriously questioned the premise on which both rested—that incarceration was the best way to handle criminals.

The differences in architecture of the two systems resulted in differences in cost. Even though the design of the Auburn System was more economical to build, it has been argued that the Pennsylvania System was more economical to administer. Furthermore, the Auburn System was more conducive to productive labor of inmates and less likely to cause mental illness among the inmates.[15] Finally, it must be noted that the Pennsylvania System sought to produce honest individuals, while the Auburn System aimed at producing obedient citizens.

Prison Architecture

The close relationship between architecture and behavior was visualized by the early proponents of penal and criminal law. Tarde, one of the most influential prison reformists of the eighteenth century, examined the prison system and decided that prisoners should have individual cells to keep them away from each other. Tarde developed a law of imitation that was based on the notion that individuals committed crimes through their association with others who engaged in crime. Based on this premise, Tarde thought inmates should have a "stream of kindly disposed visitors whose good influence would be brought to bear" on them.[16] In 1797, Bentham proposed a prison plan called the **"panopticon,"** or "inspection house." He emphasized the importance of prison architecture: "Morals reformed, health preserved, industry invigorated, instruction diffused, public burdens lightened, economy seated, as it were upon a rock, the Gordian knot of the poor laws not cut, but untied, all by a simple idea in architecture."[17]

The panopticon was the first circular prison plan, and although Bentham got a permit to build such a structure, "fortunately for penology, this monstrosity was never built."[18] The structure was to be built of cast iron and glass. Although Bentham's project was never completed, some prisons and jails that resembled his circular plan were built in Europe and America. Pittsburgh's Western State Penitentiary, which opened in 1826, was modeled after Bentham's prison design. It was rebuilt in 1833 because it was "wholly unsuited for anything but a fortress."[19] The plan was also followed in the first four cell houses built at Stateville Prison in Illinois, between 1925 and 1935. The plan was then abandoned because of the impracticality of the design. A noted prison architect evaluated the design, saying that it was "the most awful receptacle of gloom ever devised and put together with good stone and brick and mortar."[20]

Those early ideas no doubt influenced John Haviland, who designed the Eastern Penitentiary's central rotunda and seven wings in 1820. He gave admirable attention to proper lighting, adequate plumbing, ventilation, and space for exercise and warmth. His plan, as we have seen, was the basic architectural design for the Pennsylvania System. It became quite popular in Europe, but lost out to the Auburn System in the United States. Nevertheless, his contributions to prison architecture in America cannot be overlooked. "Compared with the penitentiaries of their day, Haviland's prisons were overwhelmingly superior, both technically and stylistically. . . . Haviland's great service to penology would seem to be in establishing high standards of construction, standards which were to have an influence on almost all of the prison construction of the nineteenth century."[21] Furthermore, Haviland's prisons were built in accordance with a treatment philosophy.

The architect of the Auburn prison system, John Cray, also embodied a treatment philosophy in his architecture. Both Cray and Haviland's designs emphasized strict discipline and noncommunication in an institution that was "fearsome and forbidding."[22] Prison architecture was the key to treatment philosophy. To a great extent, the philosophy of those early prisons has dominated the prison system in the United States for over 100 years. Although many would disagree with the philosophy of noncommunication, which was the basis of these early prisons, prison architecture should be considered in terms of the effect the structure might have on the person being confined.

Emergence of the Reformatory System

Elmira

On October 12, 1870, penologist Enoch C. Wines led a meeting in Cincinnati, Ohio that resulted in the organization of the National Prison Association, later called the American Correctional Association. The group drew up thirty-seven principles calling for, among other things, indeterminate sentences, classification of prisoners, cultivation of the inmate's self-respect, and advancement of the philosophy of reformation, not punishment. What emerged from this meeting was the **Elmira Reformatory,** which was established in 1876. This institution became the model for reformatories designed for young offenders. The architecture was similar to that of the Auburn System, with the exception that greater emphasis was placed on educational and trade training. Indeterminate sentences with maximum terms, opportunity for parole, and classification of inmates according to conduct and achievement were the greatest contributions of this new institution.

It was predicted that Elmira would dominate the prison system of the United States. The great contribution of the Elmira reformatory system was its emphasis on rehabilitation through education and the use of indeterminate sentence and parole. The system eventually declined mainly because of the lack of trained personnel to conduct the education system and to carry on the classification system adequately.

A great increase in the prison population in the late 1800s resulted in overcrowding. The overcrowding in prisons was largely due to the perceived threat of the numerous immigrants arriving in America. As will be explained later, most of these immigrants were viewed as potential criminals whose only way out of poverty was through a life of crime. The fear of crime and immigrants influenced correctional policy to the extent that new prisons had to be created to house the numerous individuals being incarcerated. In addition, during the late 1800s and early 1900s, the United States was the subject of numerous political and social changes that also influenced correctional practices. New prisons were built, including Attica in New York in 1931 and Stateville in Illinois in 1925. Most of these followed the Auburn architectural plan and were characterized by increasing cost per inmate, Sunday services, a chaplain on duty most of the time, and insufficient educational and vocational training. Vocational training was based on the needs of the institution, not on the interests or needs of the inmates. Moreover, insufficient funds were available for adequate prison personnel. As a result, a new era was born in American corrections.

The Progressives

The period from the 1890s to the 1930s came to be known as the Progressive Era. Immense industrialization, technological advances, and urban growth characterized this period. With these new developments, however, came a new array of social concerns. "The assimilation of immigrants and minorities into the industrial urban centers was particularly difficult to achieve, creating a deep anxiety about social order among many Americans. Some of them responded by advocating exclusionary policies, such as immigration restriction. But others sought answers in a paternalistic vision of the state and in the articulation of a broad reform plan."[23]

The **Progressives,** as this group of people became known, espoused social reforms, including individualized treatment of criminals to achieve their rehabilitation. They believed that treating criminals as individuals, each with a different set of needs and problems, would achieve rehabilitation and prepare them for mainstream society. The Progressives worked toward changing the criminal justice system as it existed. They believed that the reasons for crime were biological, psychological, economical, or sociological, and they relied on scientific methods for solutions. "Under this banner, the field of penology became as much territory for social workers, psychologists, and psychiatrists as lawyers."[24]

By the early 1900s, the Progressives had been successful in achieving acceptance of four components of their program: indeterminate sentences, probation, parole, and juvenile courts.[25] These components made a permanent impact on the correctional system in America. Clearly, the contributions made by the Progressives are unprecedented in the history of corrections.

At the state level, old facilities were stretched to house the increasing number of inmates. In fact, "ten new prisons of the Auburn type style and one modeled after Jeremy Bentham's Panopticon"[26] were built during the period of 1900–1935. Due to the large number of inmates entering correctional facilities, little or no attempt was made to classify or segregate the different types of inmates. Furthermore, no effort was made to prevent communication among those incarcerated. The conditions were so strict that only on Sundays were inmates allowed to get out of their cells for an hour. This was considered a luxury during an otherwise unbearable period lasting from Saturday night to Monday morning.

The role of prisons began to change as they adopted the reformatory philosophy. Thus, most reformatories became more like prisons.[27] In fact, the only characteristic that distinguished prisons from reformatories in some states was the age of the inmates. Despite this, some reformatories continued to support vocational and educational programs while holding military drills.

For the most part, most American prisons during the period of 1900–1935 held programs that were custodial, industrial, and punitive in nature. It was clear that the era of prisons that adhered to the notion of classification and moral instruction of offenders had ended. The end of this era is often attributed to the fast-growing number of inmates at that time. Also, the death of the reformatory program that was in place before the 1900s was made possible by the change in political attitudes about the roles of prisons. Interestingly, custody, hard labor, and punishment, which were the goals of prisons at the time, had come into existence 100 years earlier. Toward the end of this period, many prisons had eliminated hard labor, thus adhering to custodial and punitive goals. The federal government also participated in the prison changes. In 1929, the U.S. Congress passed the Hawes-Cooper Act. This "diverted prison products of their interstate character on arrival at destination, thus making them subject to state laws."[28] Once again, six years later, the U.S. Congress passed the Ashurst-Sumners Act, which prohibited transportation companies from accepting products made in prison for purposes of transporting them into any state. This act also provided for the labeling of all packages that contained prison-made products. "With the passage of these laws, the Industrial Prison was eliminated. In 1935, for the great majority of prisoners, the penitentiary system had returned once more to its original status: punishment and custody."[29]

Transition Period (1935–1960)

The penitentiary system, returning to its original purpose of custody and punishment, coupled with the Great Depression and the increasing criminality characteristic of this period, provoked a punitive attitude toward crime.[30] However, this was not the case among many scholars who were beginning to develop an interest in developing reforms in the treatment of prisoners. Their efforts met with resistance and hostility in the words and actions of J. Edgar Hoover, Director of the FBI, as he led the battle against some of these activist professors. The opening of the Alcatraz prison in 1934, under the auspices of the U.S. government, was a way to show the public that the government was indeed taking serious action to stop the increasing criminality of those years.

Alcatraz, a twelve-acre island in San Francisco Bay, was used by the U.S. Army for more than eighty years as barracks. In 1909, it was transformed into a prison with the intent of holding military prisoners. In 1934, Alcatraz was transformed into a maximum security prison with minimum privileges, and came to be known as "The Rock." Alcatraz was considered to be "escape-proof."

Prison life at Alcatraz can be explained simply by saying that an inmate had four rights—clothing, shelter, food, and medical care. Everything outside these categories was considered a privilege, and had to be earned. Working, recreational activities, visits and letters from family, and library access were privileges that an inmate could earn. After an average of five years in Alcatraz, a prisoner was eligible to be transferred back to another federal prison to serve the remainder of his sentence, provided he was no longer considered a threat and was considered capable of following rules. Alcatraz remained a prison for twenty-nine years, closing in 1963 because operating costs were too high. It was almost three times more costly to run Alcatraz than other federal prisons, primarily because of its physical isolation. In 1972, Alcatraz became a national park by an act of Congress.

Between 1915 and 1930, prison administrators began discussing the need for diagnosis and classification. Some of the early efforts include those of Bernard Glueck at Sing Sing, Edgar Doll and W. G. Ellis in New Jersey, and A. W. Stearns in Massachusetts.[31] In 1930, the Bureau of Prisons Act placed federal prisons under the authority of the Federal Bureau of Prisons. In 1934, the act was reorganized under the leadership of Sanford Bates. The Bureau emerged as the leader in corrections nationwide and, thus, introduced ideas of diagnosis and classification. The hope of diagnosis was an eventual "cure of the patient." Various forms of treatment emerged to aid this process. The emergence of the treatment approach was strongly influenced by several disciplines, including, but not limited to, social work, psychology, and psychiatry. Classification has enjoyed a longer history than has diagnosis, and it is not a specific treatment, a process of labeling, or specific training. Rather, it is a process of analyzing an individual and then making a decision about the most effective manner in which to apply the resources of the institution to the inmate. All diagnostic techniques available were to be employed in analyzing the problems of the individual, and treatment programs were to be tailored to meet his or her needs. All of these happenings did much for corrections, and the Federal Bureau of Prisons provided a pattern in correctional programs that other states followed.

Despite all of these changes, prison conditions and treatment of inmates still remained very much a matter of discussion. Conditions were not optimal—time spent idly, overcrowding, monotony, and repression led to riots in several prisons, including Alcatraz in 1946. These and other notable problems gave way to a time marking changes in the field of corrections—a time known as the Modern Era.

The Modern Era

France was one of the leaders in changing its penal system in 1945. In May of that year, "the Commission for the Reform of French Penitentiaries explicitly endorsed the humane treatment and betterment of prisoners through general and professional instruction. Medical, psychological, and social services were available in every penitentiary, and prison personnel were required to receive specialized, technical training."[32]

In the United States, a great advocation for human rights issues started to come about. The field of corrections did not escape criticism, and came under pressure to change the changing ideological climate of the time. The conditions that led to the climate during this era in the United States were diverse, yet cannot be ignored—the Vietnam War, the civil rights movement, reinterpretations of criminal law, demonstrations in the streets, and the assassination of President Kennedy.[33] Prisons did not go untouched by these pressures, and riots focusing on poor medical care, poor quality of food, and excessive brutality on the part of the guards occurred in prisons throughout the country. Inmates demanded the same basic rights that were advocated outside prison walls. These riots had an impact on corrections, and some of the changes that were implemented came about as a result of the unrest.

In 1953, the American Prison Association identified the reasons for the riots as official indifference, lack of financial support, enforced idleness, lack of professional leadership and professional programs, overcrowding of institutions, substandard personnel, political motivation and domination of management, and unwise sentencing and parole practices.[34] As a result of the climate of this time, the federal government funded many corrections administrators at both local and state levels to create and carry out new policies. The major thrust of these changes was increased rehabilitation in order to treat the psychological disturbances that were considered to be at the root of the individuals' criminality. Treatment-oriented corrections were set in place to ameliorate the existing conditions in prisons.

In 1954, the American Prison Association changed its name to the American Correctional Association. Its members were instructed to "redesignate their prisons as 'correctional institutions' and to label the punishment blocks in them as 'adjustment centers.'"[35] Programs focused on more favorable conditions for inmates and provided libraries, vocational programs, counseling opportunities, and exercise-educational facilities. This period of change, which began circa the 1960s, became known as the "Modern Era."

The 1970s saw a movement opposing the idea of prisoner rehabilitation because of abuses and therapies that were considered intrusive. To this day, no consensus exists on the best way to initiate prison reform.

Prison Overcrowding

Although **prison overcrowding** has been in existence for over 100 years, its popularity as a social phenomenon has recently taken front stage as one of America's most frequently discussed topics. This is mostly due to the war on drugs campaign originally established by the Reagan administration, which gave rise to longer sentences. In addition, President Clinton's "get tough on crime tactics" have given continuance to the Reagan crime policy. The news media have also contributed to this effort by convincing the public that society should continue to build more prisons to effectively fight crime. Thus, the combination of longer sentences and a powerful media campaign has given rise to public awareness of the increasing problem of prison overcrowding. This is most evident in states such as Florida and Texas, where the public expresses steady support for the increase of correctional budgets aimed at constructing new and more expensive prison facilities.

In 1994, the nation's prisons had to find room for 83,294 more prisoners. The Bureau of Justice Statistics reported this 9 percent increase as the second-largest annual increase in U.S. history. This increase places the prison population over the 1 million mark. This means that in the last decade, the prison population in the United States doubled on a per capita basis.[36] This increase has brought with it an inevitable overcrowding of prisons, coupled with the construction of new prisons to accommodate new inmates. The building of private prisons and those run by private organizations has also become a trend.

This so-called "privatization of prisons" has alarmed many. "The delegation by government, to private business, of the power to imprison and, necessarily, the power to use force to maintain order, prevent escape, and the like raises troublesome legal and ethical questions." Furthermore, many are concerned with the idea of an industry with a vested interest "in maintaining, or even increasing, the number of people incarcerated."[37]

This increasing number of inmates limits the ability of correctional officers to do their job and causes escalating tensions among prisoners. Population ceilings have been established by the U.S. Supreme Court as a way to avoid crowding. Among the proposed solutions to the problem of overcrowding has been the use of **indeterminate sanctions.** These, which include boot camps, community service, and home confinement, among others, have been suggested as a way to reduce the total number of inmates within prison walls. **Early release, parole, halfway houses,** and **prerelease centers** have also been suggested as solutions to the problem of overcrowding.[38] These will be discussed in more detail in later chapters.

WiseGuide Wrap-Up Since the development of the Walnut Street Jail in the late 1700s, the U.S. prison system has undergone many changes. These changes have evolved within the context of an ever-changing society, and they have been accompanied by turmoil and constant disagreement on the best way to handle the most current issues. However, many questions remain a matter of disagreement. Some still frequently debated questions include how and which inmates are to be imprisoned; how inmates should be treated when being detained and released; what is the best type of architectural format that prisons should follow to ensure safety and an appropriate environment for inmates; how overcrowding can best dealt with; and what reforms are needed within the system. Nevertheless, these problems continue in existence to the present day, and whether any progress has been made is still a subject of great debate among scholars.

Notes

1. Parmelee, Maurice. *Criminology*. (New York: Macmillan, 1918), p. 367.
2. Barnes, Harry Elmer. *The Story of Punishment*. (Boston: Stratford, 1930), pp. 117, 122.
3. Barnes, p. 121.
4. Rothman, David J. *The Discovery of the Asylum: Social Order and Disorder in the New Republic*. (Boston: Little, Brown and Company, 1971).
5. Rothman, *Discovery of the Asylum*, pp. xiii–xviii.
6. Rothman, *Discovery of the Asylum*, p. xix.
7. Rothman, *Discovery of the Asylum*, p. xix.
8. Menninger, Karl. *The Crime of Punishment*. (New York: Viking, 1968), p. 222.
9. Rothman, *Discovery of the Asylum*, pp. 92–93.
10. Rothman, pp. 81–82.
11. See Gustave de Auguste Beaumont and Alexis de Tocqueville, *On The Penitentiary System in the United States and its Application in France*. (Carbondale, IL: Southern Illinois University Press, [1833] 1964), p. 146.
12. Barnes, *Story of Punishment*, p. 144.
13. Conrad, John P. *Crime and Its Correction*. (Berkeley, CA: University of California Press, 1965), p. 128.
14. Rothman, *The Discovery of the Asylum*, p. 83.
15. Barnes, *Story of Punishment*, pp. 142–143.
16. Mannheim, Hermann, ed. *Pioneers in Criminology*. (Montclair, NJ: Patterson Smith, 1960), p. 300.
17. Cited in Negley K. Teeters, "State Prisons in the United States: 1870–1970," *Federal Probation* 33 (December, 1969), 18.
18. Barnes, Harry Elmer, and Teeters, Negley K. *New Horizons in Criminology*, 3rd ed. (Englewood Cliffs, NJ: Prentice-Hall, 1959), p. 484.
19. Harry Elmer Barnes. Quoted in Mannheim, *Pioneers in Criminology*, p. 65.
20. Alfred Hopkins, quoted in Mannheim, p. 65.
21. Norman B. Johnson. "John Haviland," in Mannheim, *Pioneers in Criminology*, p. 122.
22. Gill, Howard B. "Correctional Philosophy and Architecture," *Journal of Criminal Law, Criminology, and Police Science* 53 (March, 1962), 312–322.
23. Rotman, Edgardo. *The Failure of Reform, The Oxford History of the Prison*. (New York: Oxford Press, 1995), pp. 176–177.
24. Rotman, *Failure of Reform*, p. 187.
25. Clear, Todd, and Cole, George, *American Corrections*, 4th ed. (Belmont, CA: Wadsworth Publishing Co., 1997), p. 65.
26. Killinger, George G., Wood, Jerry M., and Cromwell, Paul. *Penology: The Evolution of Corrections in America*, (St. Paul, MN: West Publishing, 1979).
27. Killinger, Wood, and Cromwell, *Penology*, 53.
28. Killinger, Wood, and Cromwell, *Penology*, 53.
29. State Prisons in America 1787–1937, in George C. Killinger and Paul F. Cromwell, eds., *Penology* (St. Paul, MN: West Publishing, 1973), p. 53.
30. "State Prisons in America 1787–1937," eds., p. 53.
31. Allen, Harry, and Simonsen, Clifford. *Corrections in America*, 5th ed. (Upper Saddle River, NJ: Prentice-Hall, 1998), p. 46.
32. O'Brien, Patricia. *The Prison on the Continent, The Oxford History of the Prison*. (New York: Oxford Press, 1995), p. 218.
33. Allen, Harry, and Simonsen, Clifford. *Corrections in America*, 5th ed. (Upper Saddle River, NJ: Prentice-Hall, 1998), p. 47.
34. Rotman, *The Failure of Reform*, p. 189.
35. Rotman, *Failure of Reform*, p. 190.
36. United States Department of Justice, Bureau of Justice Statistics. August 9, 1995.
37. Morris, Norval. *The Contemporary Prison, The Oxford History of the Prison*. (New York: Oxford Press, 1995), p. 255.
38. Allen and Simonsen. *Corrections in America*, p. 231.

The Modern Prison: Classification and Correctional Programs

Early advocates of imprisonment in this country believed that incarceration was not only an appropriate form of punishment, but that it would also have a reforming effect on offenders. The Pennsylvania System was based on the assumption that if offenders had time to think and reflect, and to read and to study the Bible, they would repent and be reformed. In the Auburn System, whipping was assumed to have a reforming effect. Wardens believed that the inmate's spirit had to be broken before reformation could take place. Later, reformers argued that hard work would have a reformative effect on inmates. Others emphasized vocational training as a prerequisite for changing the offender.

In the twentieth century, reformation of offenders has been viewed through a medical model. The principles of diagnosis and treatment have been utilized, with the hope of an eventual "cure" of the "patient." Various forms of treatment programs have been developed to aid in this process. More recently, however, the philosophies of reform and rehabilitation have been seriously questioned. It has been argued that treatment has not worked and that we should return to a philosophy of retribution—of "just deserts." Most people feel that prison should be a place of punishment and not a source of rehabilitation. Furthermore, they feel that inmates should not enjoy any free services for which citizens in the community have to pay. According to the **principle of least eligibility,** inmates should be the "least eligible" of all citizens to receive any social benefits beyond those required by the law. If this principle was to be taken to the extreme, it would prohibit inmates from receiving a free college education while in prison. In

Key Terms

behavior modification
classification clinic
contract system
diagnostic or reception center
Federal Bureau of Prisons
group psychotherapy
individual psychotherapy
integrated classification system
lease system
maximum security prisons
medium security prisons
minimum security prisons
piece-price system
principle of least eligibility
public or state account system
reality therapy
reception program
social therapies
state-use system
"super-max" prisons
transactional analysis

reality, this principle has created many problems for correctional administrators. They face constant criticisms from the general public for the free services provided to inmates while in prison. Most people feel that it is not fair for law-abiding citizens who have "obeyed the rules" to struggle in making payments for services that law-breakers receive free of charge.

The principle of least eligibility has also influenced the performance and existence of prison programs. Most people feel that inmates should enjoy the opportunity of being rehabilitated, but no one wants to incur the monetary cost associated with the funding of such programs. Thus, the end result is that most prison programs suffer from inadequate funding, poor staffing, and poor success rates. It is also important to mention that some of these public criticisms of prison programs have been provoked by inmates who claim that it is their constitutional right to have a sex change operation or receive plastic surgery. In their claims, inmates have argued that a denial of their request would constitute a violation of their constitutional rights. Needless to say, this has angered many people who feel that the cost of such "luxuries" should not be funded from taxpayers' funds.

In this chapter, we look at the programs designed to aid in the reformation and rehabilitation of inmates and the techniques that have been used toward this end. We begin with a discussion on the organization of corrections. This is followed by an examination of the classification process of correctional institutions and inmates, which is considered to be very important in the placement of inmates in treatment programs. We also discuss treatment, educational, and vocational programs while paying particular attention to the various effects of incarceration.

Organization of Corrections

There are various systems of corrections in the United States. One system is administered at the federal level while the others are managed in each of the fifty states. Since all of these systems vary in terms of operations, management, and programs offered, it is safe to make the statement that there are fifty-one correctional systems in the United States.

The Federal Bureau of Prisons

The **Federal Bureau of Prisons** was created in 1929 by the House Special Committee on Federal Penal and Reformatory Institutions. After a great deal of deliberation, this committee offered various recommendations, including the establishment of a centralized administration of federal prisons at the bureau level, increased expenditure for federal probation officers, the establishment of a full-time parole board, and the provision of facilities by the District of Columbia for its inmates. This legislation was signed into law by President Hoover on May 14, 1930, creating what is now known as the Federal Bureau of Prisons within the U.S. Department of Justice.

Today, the Federal Bureau of Prisons oversees ninety-two correctional institutions throughout the United States. As of December 1997, the total number of inmates it supervises is 113,191 (101,845 in Bureau of Prison facilities and 11, 346 in contract facilities). Contract facilities are run by the private sector under contract with the federal government. Overall, the federal inmate population is mostly made up of males (93 percent) and whites (56.3 percent). However, it is important to note that African Americans are the second largest group (40.5 percent) in federal prisons.[1]

Statistics also show that at the federal level, the average age of an inmate serving time is thirty-seven, while the most common sentence imposed is five to ten years (30.4 percent). Interestingly, most inmates at a federal correctional facility are serving time for a drug-related offense (59.5 percent). Although this num-

Spotlight 4.1

Highlights of States' Correctional Systems in 1995

- In 1995, states operated 1,375 facilities.
- More state facilities of all security levels were in operation in 1995 than were present five years earlier.
- Facilities operating under state authority in 1990 grew 14 percent from 1,207 to 1,375.
- State prison authorities operated more than four-fifths of the nation's correctional facilities.
- More than nine of every ten inmates were held in facilities operated by state authorities.
- The South accounted for nearly 50 percent of state correctional facilities and more than 40 percent of state prisoners at midyear 1995.
- State facilities housed nearly 150,000–200,000 inmates in the Northeast, Midwest, and West regions; the South housed more than 400,000 prisoners.
- The South had the largest number of prisoners per 100,000 state residents (437), and the Northeast had the lowest number (293).

- 49 percent of inmates were African American non-Hispanic; 35 percent were white non-Hispanic; 14 percent were Hispanic; 1 percent was Native American; and 1 percent was Asian or Pacific Islander.
- In both 1990 and 1995, about equal proportions of state prisoners were kept in each of the maximum (under 40 percent of all inmates), medium (almost 50 percent), or minimum (10 percent) security facilities. (These levels of security will be discussed later in this chapter.)
- The number of inmate deaths rose from 2.4 per 1,000 state inmates in 1990 to 3.4 in 1995.
- 378 correctional facilities (27 percent) were under court order or consent decree for specific conditions—to limit population—or for the totality of conditions at midyear 1995.
- At midyear 1995, the overall number of inmates per correctional facility employee was lowest in state confinement institutions (2.9 to 1).

Source: Census of State and Federal Correctional Facilities, 1995. (August, 1997). U.S. Department of Justice. Bureau of Justice Statistics.

ber has changed in the past few years, it is close to the all-time high recorded in 1994, when 61.4 percent of sentenced inmates were serving time at a federal facility for a drug-related offense.[2]

As stated previously, each of the fifty states operates its correctional system in a specific way. Thus, it is very hard to describe all of the state prison systems because most of them are unique in one way or another. The states of California, Texas, Florida, and New York are known for their correctional systems. Despite the fact that we cannot look at each of these systems, we can still examine some generalities that are common to most of the states' correctional systems. These are highlighted in Spotlight 4.1.

The State Prison Systems

It has been reported that as early as the 1800s, inmates were being classified. In fact, at the Elmira Reformatory, Zebulon Brockway began the process of classifying inmates according to their security level and program needs. Consequently, this trend continued through the years. A century ago, the American Prison Association articulated the concept of individualized treatment in its Declaration of Principles. Ironically, that concept became popular long before anyone realized

Classification

that in order for treatment programs to succeed, there must be an understanding of the particular offender. It was not until the 1920s that a few prison administrators began talking about the need for diagnosis, which resulted in the establishment of some diagnostic centers for prisons. This was also the result of the rehabilitation ideal, which was based on the notion that inmates could be rehabilitated through appropriate treatment.

Classification was regarded as the diagnostic method necessary to assess the treatment needs of offenders. One of the most influential figures in the continuing use of classification was psychiatrist Karl Menninger. In the 1950s, Menninger advocated the use of the classification method for the effective treatment of offenders. His rehabilitative principles were based on the notion that prison life could be compared to an individual's childhood. Menninger asserted that both of these rely heavily on a state of dependency in which the necessities of food, shelter, clothing, and supervision have to be met by a supervising authority.[3] Thus, he concluded, there is a good possibility that offenders subconsciously seek a more "secure" environment (i.e., prison) when they commit a crime.

Despite Menniger's attempts, classification has really meant segregation—by race, age, and sex. No serious attempt has been made in the classification process to assess the problems of a particular offender within the context of a treatment program. As a result of the emphasis given to confinement in the 1980s, classification is understood today by many to mean only segregation. Despite this, most criminologists regard classification as a process with a deeper meaning. Classification can be defined as "a method by which diagnosis, treatment planning and the execution of the treatment programs are coordinated in the individual case."[4] Classification begins when the inmate first arrives at the diagnostic center. A custody assessment and a treatment program are then determined for him or her. For the most part, the process requires the reevaluation of an inmate's program during the course of treatment.

Despite the fact that classification is supposed to be a process by which the individual is assessed according to his or her custody requirement and a decision is made about the most effective way to apply the resources of the institution to the individual's case, it is often a process in which inmates are labeled as "predators" of a specific offense. Unfortunately, this label stays with them throughout their tenure in prison and sometimes even after they fulfill their sentence. All available diagnostic techniques should be used in analyzing the individual's problems, and a treatment program should be tailored to each individual's needs. The plan should then be executed and revised when necessary. Finally, the program should be coordinated with the activities of the individual on parole or unconditional release. This is the way that classification programs should ideally work. In reality, however, this is not always the case. It is worth noting that classification does not only take place among inmates—correctional facilities are also classified according to their security level. Before examining the inmate classification process, it is important to look at the various levels of security attributed to American correctional facilities.

Prison Classification

Once the inmates have been exposed to the classification process, a determination of the inmate's security level is made. Factors such as the seriousness of the offense, the possibility of escape, and the potential for violent behavior are taken into consideration when determining the appropriate security level. Most states do not enjoy the benefit of having a specific institution for each level of security, thus facilities are often divided into sections for different categories. It is important to mention that because there are no universal standards for designing a prison, an institution that holds high-risk offenders in one state may be regarded as a low-security facility in another. Despite this, we can make general statements about the different security levels attributed to correctional facilities in the United States.

U.S. prisons are classified according to their level of security. Any correctional site can be categorized as being a maximum, medium, or minimum facility. Recently, as many as thirty-eight states have built prisons that are considered to have higher security mechanisms than those of a maximum facility—these are often referred to as "maxi-max" or **"super-max" prisons.** The concept began in 1983 at a federal prison in Marion, Illinois when, after inmates killed two correctional officers, a prison-wide twenty-three hour "lockdown" was implemented—allowing inmates to leave their cells for only one hour during the day for solitary exercise. As the concept grew, the number of maxi-max prisons increased. All of these facilities have been built with the aim of housing the most violent and aggressive individuals in the correctional system. Some of the most notorious maxi-max institutions include California's Pelican Bay institution and the super-max prison built in Florence, Colorado. Despite their rapid growth, experts argue that the solitary confinement of maxi-max prisons is harmful to inmates, who have been found to suffer from symptoms ranging from "memory loss to severe anxiety to hallucinations to delusions and, under the severest cases of sensory deprivation, people go crazy."[5] It can only be speculated that the debate over the effect of these prisons on inmates will continue as more of these facilities are built. Another factor giving rise to the recent attention these facilities are receiving is the fact that more and more inmates (some of them involved in well-known cases) are being sent to maxi-max facilities. On January 9, 1998, the man behind the World Trade Center bombing, Ramzi Yousef, received one of the harshest sentences in history. Judge Kevin T. Duffy sentenced Yousef to 240 years plus life in solitary confinement. Judge Duffy recommended that Yousef be allowed to see only his lawyers and not be allowed to make telephone calls, even to his family. Despite the fact that some welcomed the sentence, other argued that it violated Yousef's constitutional protection against cruel and unusual punishment. Thus, as stated previously, the debate regarding the constitutionality and effectiveness of the maxi-max prisons continues.

Maximum Security Prisons

In 1995, **maximum security prisons** comprised 25 percent of state and federal facilities in the United States. Larger states usually have one or more maximum security prisons. In 1995, over half of these institutions housed 1,000 inmates or more.[6] These facilities are usually surrounded by high walls that contain guard towers, leaving the impression that their aim is to punish the most serious offenders the system can house. In addition, they are often located in rural areas away from society.[7] Inside the maximum security prison, inmates live in small cells that contain their own sanitary facility. When one walks through the corridors of these facilities, there is no question that their purpose is custody and discipline. To add insult to injury, some of these facilities are very old. In fact, it is estimated that in 1995, 10 percent of inmates housed in maximum security prisons lived in facilities that were over 100 years old.[8]

In maximum security prisons, head counts are conducted frequently despite the fact that inmates are allowed out of their cells only if they are accompanied by a guard. This has had a severe effect on inmates who have been incarcerated in these types of facilities for an extended period of time. Critics hold that such treatment constitutes cruel and unusual punishment.

Medium Security Prisons

Although the architecture of these prisons usually resembles that of maximum security institutions, in reality their method of operation is somewhat different. The **medium security prisons** were born in an attempt to seek alternatives to the maximum security institution. Most of the construction in corrections in the past half century has been for medium security institutions. The most recent architecture of the medium security facilities is based on the "campus design," which includes residence areas with single rooms and dormitories for inmates. In most of these medium security prisons, inmates are allowed to have more freedom than that offered in maximum security institutions. In fact, inmates in medium security facilities have privileges and contact with the outside world via visitors, television, radios, and mail. For the most part, these facilities aim at rehabilitating offenders through the implementation of various programs (some of which will be discussed later in this chapter). In 1995, medium security facilities comprised 38 percent of the total number of state and federal facilities. In 1995, medium security facilities were of every size: 31 percent small, 29 percent medium, and 40 percent large capacity.[9] In 1995, at the state level, approximately 43 percent of inmates were classified as being medium security, in contrast with 32 percent at the federal level.[10]

Minimum Security Prisons

The architecture of **minimum security prisons** is substantially different from that of maximum and medium security prisons. Because these prisons do not house the most serious offenders in the correctional system, they do not need guard towers or high walls. Most of the inmates who reside in these institutions are allowed to live in private rooms or in dormitories, allowing them to have a substantial level of personal freedom. In fact, some of the minimum security prisons of today allow inmates to choose and wear their own clothing, and inmates are privileged to have their own television sets. In 1995, inmates in minimum security facilities were the least likely (85 percent) to be in male-only institutions. In that same year, approximately 2 percent of the inmates in minimum security prisons resided in buildings that were at least 100 years old. In 1995, most inmates at the federal level (57 percent) resided in minimum security prisons—this constitutes an increase of inmates (35 percent) since 1990.[11] Despite this growth, most of these prisons still offer rehabilitative programs to inmates. In fact, it is a common sight to find inmates working outside these campus-like facilities wearing regular working clothes. Although this may give the impression to the general public that these inmates are not receiving sufficient punishment for their wrongdoing, it should be remembered that they are still deprived of their freedom. Every aspect of their lives is controlled by the correctional staff.

Types of Inmate Classification Systems

After having examined the different security classifications of correctional institutions in the United States, it is important for us to discuss the various types of inmate classification systems that have been used, or in some cases, are still in use. The first type, the **classification clinic,** was a failure because it was autonomous within the institution that incarcerated the individual under study. Elaborate diagnosis could take place and then be ignored by the administrative officials of the institution, for they were in no way bound by the recommendations of the classification clinic. This represented a clash of opinions between those seeking treatment and correctional personnel whose priority was custody.

The **integrated classification system,** one of the most popular methods in the not-so-distant past, involved both the professional and the administrative personnel of the institution. A classification committee was formed that was usually chaired by the warden or superintendent of the institution. The decisions of the committee were binding on the administration, and any changes in the inmate's treatment program had to be approved by the committee. An important advantage of this system was that it permitted professional and administrative personnel to work together and to gain insight into the problems that each group faced.[12]

A third type, which is the most widely used system today, is the **diagnostic,** or **reception center.** The convicted individual can be sentenced to a particular institution and then classified, while others can be sentenced to the diagnostic center. In the reception center, inmates are usually diagnosed for approximately three to six weeks. The inmate is studied carefully and examined by psychologists, psychiatrists, physicians, social workers, and other personnel. Then a treatment program is planned, including a decision concerning which of the institutions in the jurisdiction would be most appropriate for the rehabilitation of the particular individual. This system reflects the alleged goal of the existing classification system—to classify inmates based on their security and rehabilitative needs.

Some states have a reception center at each institution while others have a reception center that receives all inmates before they are diagnosed and sent to a specific prison to serve their prescribed sentence. A number of criminologists have regarded the reception center as a place where the individual inmate begins to accept his or her reality of being an inmate. After contemplating the possibility of loss of freedom in a court of law, the convicted offender now begins to accept his or her reality of incarceration for the next few months or perhaps the next few years. In reception centers, inmates are often stripped of their street clothing and are given a uniform, a code of conduct book, and in most cases, a full medical examination. In some cases, this occurs as soon as the inmate arrives from the local jail.

In some jurisdictions, inmates are classified based on only their past criminal history, age, severity of the criminal act, and institutional conduct, if any. Thus, the priority in these cases is to assign the individual to a proper security level (minimum, medium, or maximum). This has been the norm of late, as the existence and function of rehabilitative programs continue to be challenged by the general population who is constantly demanding a more punitive approach toward the handling of inmates.

However, at jurisdictions in which rehabilitation is considered a realistic goal, inmates in reception centers are often given a series of psychological and medical examinations to determine their program needs as well as their custodial level. Those inmates who are in most need of assistance usually receive it. However, it is important to mention that before considering the program needs of the inmate, the institution's needs are almost always met. To add insult to injury, the enrollment in some programs is sometimes very high and, as a result, the availability of these programs is limited. This is becoming more of a trend as rehabilitative programs suffer from budgetary cuts and public scrutiny.

Most reception facilities have committees that often make the classification decision. These committees are often made up of the deputy warden and the heads of each department, including, among others, those who oversee custody, industry, education, and treatment. In most cases, an inmate appears before the committee, which makes a recommendation regarding the inmate's program as well as his or her custody status. At the time of consideration, the committee is often presented with enough information to make a decision regarding the inmate. This information often includes presentence reports, police records, and the results of the various examinations conducted in the reception center. It is worth noting that in some jurisdictions, the committee often consists of a few staff members who are appointed to make these decisions. This occurs because top-level prison administrators are often unavailable due to their hectic schedules and long hours.

An Ideal Inmate Classification System

As noted previously, most of the current classification systems are far from ideal. To assess the weaknesses and strengths of the existing classification systems, it is important to examine the traits associated with an "ideal" inmate classification system. The first element of a classification program should be a **reception program.** New inmates should be segregated for purposes of medical tests and for orientation. Traditionally, inmates were initiated into the correctional system by other inmates. Under modern reception programs, orientation is, theoretically, conducted by professional staff. The inmate should be taken on a tour of the institution where he or she will be confined. The rules and regulations of the institution should be carefully explained. Personnel should be trained to work with the individual on personal problems, such as the loss of family and friends, as well as with the hostilities the individual may have developed toward the police or other elements of the legal process.

Activities are an important element in the orientation process. Most people committed to a correctional facility have already spent time in jail, a time usually characterized by idleness. "Further idleness during the admission period tends to increase the tensions and ill feelings it is so necessary to break down."[13]

It is important to build a case summary of the diagnostic studies. This summary should contain a legal history of the case, a history of previous criminal record (if any), a social history, physical conditions, vocational abilities and interests, educational and religious background, recreational interests, reports of psychologists and psychiatrists, and the initial reaction of the individual to any treatment programs. The behavior of the individual at the reception center (if one exists) should also be noted in the case summary. This initial adjustment phase should be only the beginning of a complete record on the inmate. The final case history should include not only the case summary, but all correspondence about the inmate, a photograph, fingerprints, reports of probation officers, progress reports, and legal documents. Staff members should be trained to use these documents effectively and the documents should be kept confidential from other inmates. It is worth noting that current prison overcrowding coupled with a growing punitive attitude among the citizenry prevent us from having an ideal classification system.

Classification Committee

The classification committee is the key element in classification. Therefore, it is important to have well-trained staff members on the board. If the recommendations of the committee are to be binding throughout the institution, the warden or superintendent should chair the committee. Other committee members should be staff persons who will help evaluate and work with the inmate. The composition of the committee would thus vary from inmate to inmate, to include the appropriate work supervisor and counselor, a staff member from the prison school if the inmate has expressed an interest in education, the psychiatrist, psychologist, and physician who tested and examined the inmate, and so on.

The inmate should be allowed to participate in the initial classification meeting, and he or she should be made to feel comfortable and at ease during the interview. The committee may have to decide on (1) whether to transfer the inmate to another institution, (2) how much custody will be required, (3) work assignments, (4) academic program, (5) religious classes and counseling, on the chaplain's recommendation, and (6) recreational programs. In special cases, the committee may recommend psychiatric counseling, or participation in Alcoholics Anonymous (AA), Check Forgers Anonymous, or other such organizations.[14]

In addition to facilitating the treatment of inmates, classification in its ideal state makes other positive contributions to corrections. It aims at facilitating the ordinary administration of a prison. While breaking down many of the problems created by overspecialization, classification aims at facilitating discipline, increasing productive industrial output, and improving the morale of inmates. If utilized properly, it results in success that the inmate can see.

Contributions of the Inmate Classification System

> Classification has demonstrated that [inmates] appreciate real effort to help them and the opportunities for self-improvement provided. Classification results in the development of materials which will aid the parole board in making a decision. It provides data for criminological research. Finally, it provides the information needed for long-range planning for building correctional facilities.[15]

Just as we have examined the classification process as it pertains to institutions and inmates, it is equally important to take a look at the various correctional programs offered to inmates in today's prison system. As we discuss these programs, it is important to keep in mind that they sometimes aim at achieving goals that have been regarded by some correctional administrators and staff personnel as being "unrealistic" in nature. Also, it is equally important to remember that most, if not all, of these correctional programs suffer from budgetary constraints and public criticisms for being "too soft" on inmates. Some of these public sentiments are often based on well-publicized cases in which a particular prison program failed in its attempt to treat, train, or educate an inmate who committed a serious offense after being released from prison.

Correctional Programs

Treatment Programs

Don Gibbons, in his classical treatise on the treatment of delinquents and criminals, emphasized the need to distinguish between treatment and humanitarianism. The rise of the spirit of humanitarianism has often been confused with the belief that people, in general, and inmates, in particular, should be treated humanely. The result has been that any efforts implemented to make prisons more humane have been interpreted by some as an attempt to treat or rehabilitate inmates. In fact, many argue that there is no convincing evidence suggesting that attempts to make prisons more humane places in which to serve time have resulted in the rehabilitation of inmates.

What is the difference? According to Gibbons, "Humanitarian reform designates those changes that have been introduced into corrections in recent decades which serve to lessen the harshness or severity of punishment."[16] In essence, the humanitarian movement in prisons is based on the early philosophy that deprivation of liberty is the punishment. It would be excessive punishment, and therefore inhumane, to force the person deprived of his or her liberty to live in filth or among rats, in damp, cold, dark cells, to eat poorly prepared food constituting an unbalanced diet, and to suffer corporal punishment. Likewise, in the past, changes have been made in privileges for inmates, such as increases in the number of visits they may have with their families and friends. Gibbons points out that such visits may decrease tension in prisons and may have positive effects on the inmates. They might also, however, have negative effects. The point is that the visits are not "treatment" and should not be considered therapeutic in character. Increased visits, classification, and educational and vocational training might be referred to as *adjuncts* to treatment. Religious activities, recreational participation, and prerelease planning are other adjuncts. These programs are not aimed at particular therapy problems of inmates and therefore do not constitute treatment per se.[17]

Types of Treatment

What, then, is treatment? The term "treatment" is often used very broadly with regard to what takes place in prisons or in alternatives to incarceration. Since there is no consensus on its meaning, we refer to the definition given by the American Heritage Dictionary (1985) on treatment—"the application of remedies with the object of effecting a cure."[18] Treatment is broadly considered to include all of those "programs" or approaches that are aimed at the reformation or rehabilitation of the inmate. Volumes have been devoted to discussion of treatment, and it is impossible to discuss any or all of the issues in detail. Our discussion, therefore, is confined to a brief overview of the kinds of treatment that have been used in prison facilities in the United States.

Throughout this discussion of treatment types, the reader should keep in mind that some inmates do not have adequate access, if they have access at all, to treatment. In part, this is due to the fact that some inmates are regarded as being "too dangerous" to be given an opportunity to participate in a treatment program in the company of other inmates. Another reason for the lack of inmate accessibility to treatment programs is the overcrowding prison conditions that make these programs scarce and extremely competitive.

Finally, it is important to keep in mind that not all offenders should be treated alike. Offenders are not a homogeneous group; different variables influence each offender to turn to crime. Thus, no one treatment technique is effective with all inmates.[19]

In his classical work, Don Gibbons constructed a "typology" of treatment forms that contained two categories representing the two basic orientations toward causation of crime—psychological and social therapies.[20] Psychological therapies include individual "depth" psychotherapy, group psychotherapy, and client-centered therapy. Included among social therapies are group therapy and milieu management. Both types are examined in the following sections.

Psychological Therapies

Individual "Depth" Psychotherapy

It has been asserted that the treatment of criminals implies changing their personalities, beliefs, or motivations so that they have internal controls to prevent criminal behavior. Some believe that a psychiatrist's most effective therapeutic tool is psychotherapy. In general, the aim of psychotherapy is to bring about a process of growth in patients so that they can manage their own affairs. When therapists work individually with patients, they try to help individuals understand the early life experiences that are thought to be important in causing personal problems. Through this psychoanalytic technique of in-depth therapy, therapists bring out these experiences and assist their patients in dealing with them. Gibbons has referred to the basic elements of psychotherapy proposed by Richard Jenkins:

1. A sense of emotional security which the patient develops from interaction with the therapist.

2. Respect for the integrity and self-determination of the individual or respect for the patient's identity.

3. The release of pent-up emotional tension.

4. Reduction or stimulation of the patient's sense of responsibility for his actions.

5. Attenuation or stimulation of the guilt-anxiety of the person.

6. Reduction of feelings of inferiority or inadequacy of patients.[21]

Despite the aims of this type of therapy, it is important to note that in a controlled environment such as prison, **individual psychotherapy** seldom works. One of the most obvious impairments is that the therapist is not working for the patient, as is common in clinics outside the correctional system, but rather he or she is working for the government with the aim to develop a crime-free mentality in the offender. Thus, this problem, among others, has challenged the existence of programs addressing the emotional state of inmates. In fact, in most prisons, counselors and other correctional staff members attempt to address directly some of the most common problems of inmates (i.e., adjustment into the correctional facility, concerns with existing dependants outside the facility) instead of practicing in-depth psychotherapy techniques.

Group Psychotherapy and Human Potential Therapies

Gibbons distinguishes between **"group psychotherapy,"** which is essentially aimed at an individual within a group setting, and "group therapy," which is therapy aimed at changing an entire group. S. R. Slavson argued that group therapy is valuable because the group members give support to one another, and that reduces their individual fears and defenses. But Jenkins contended that some problems may be so painful that an individual may not want to discuss them in a group.[22]

Since Gibbons formulated his treatment typology, the term "human potential" therapies has become widely used in society and, in the past few decades, has been introduced into prison. Since their introduction, these types of therapies have retained their popularity because they address inmates' emotions and thoughts in a group setting, thus allowing inmates to develop a support mechanisms with their peers. Here we look at several kinds of human potential therapies. All are a form of group psychotherapy, but they are at times "led" by persons who are not trained as extensively as are clinical psychologists or psychiatrists.

Reality Therapy

Unlike "depth" psychotherapy, **reality therapy** does not involve delving into the past. Rather, it operates on the principle that the past is significant in an individual's behavior only to the extent that he or she so permits. The focus is therefore on the present. Reality therapy has been developed by those who question the value of conventional psychiatric treatment.

The use of reality therapy in the treatment of offenders was started by Dr. William Glaser, otherwise known as the "Father of Reality Therapy," in the early 1960s. The therapist begins with the assumption that the basic problem of inmates is irresponsibility. Then the therapist tries to teach offenders to become responsible for themselves, achieving their own needs without harming others.

Reality therapy is based on the assumption that all people have two basic psychological needs: the need to give and receive love and the need to feel that they are important to others as well to themselves. It is further believed that behavior has some meaning to the actor, but that people who are not meeting their own needs "refuse to acknowledge the reality of the world in which they live. This becomes more apparent with each successive failure to gain relatedness and respect. Reality therapy mobilizes its effort toward helping people accept reality and aims to help them meet their needs within its confines."[23] People meet their needs through involvement with others; so the therapist must become involved with patients and not reject them because of their deviant behavior. As therapists become involved with patients, they help these patients adapt to reality by being both a model and a mirror of reality. In so doing, they take a more active role in the relationship with patients than has been the traditional. In reality therapy, in contrast to traditional therapy, patients are encouraged to face the moral aspect of their behavior. They must decide whether behavior is right or wrong. No attempt is made to delve into the unconscious; reality therapy forces the individual to examine the conscious self and behavior.

Rachin notes that patients who have not responded well to conventional treatment methods often do not respond to reality therapy. In addition, it is less costly than traditional methods since it does not require as much time. He concludes: "The principles of reality therapy are common sense interwoven with a firm belief in the dignity of man and his ability to improve his lot. Its value is twofold: it is a means by which people can help one another, and it is a treatment technique, applicable regardless of symptomatology."[24] After having explored the methodology used in reality therapy, it is easy to understand why it is a popular therapy in corrections. Not only does this type of therapy adhere to the concept that society's rules are real and cannot be escaped, but it is feasible that this type of therapy can also be implemented over a short period of time in any type of correctional setting. The latter makes reality therapy very attractive to correctional administrators concerned with the rehabilitation of inmates.

Transactional Analysis

Transactional analysis, or TA, was originated by Dr. Eric Berne, author of *Games People Play*.[25] Some correctional institutions use transactional analysis in treatment programs. William Nagel briefly referred to TA, stating that it is based on the belief that each person has three persons within: a parent, an adult, and a child. By the use of games, psychodrama, and script analysis, individuals are helped to understand how these three persons control his or her behavior. The goal is to understand and "develop spontaneity and a capacity for intimacy."[26] Some institutions have space problems that prevent them from offering TA programs; they must have room for the small groups to meet and offices for the back-up counseling sessions. According to Nagel, transactional analysis has been used as a treatment method at the federal penitentiary at Marion, Illinois, and at the O.H. Close School near Stockton, California. This type of therapy has been considered to be appropriate for most correctional facilities since it is simple, short term, and straightforward.

Social Therapies

Gibbons regards **social therapies** as environmental therapies, and divides them into three categories—environmental change, group therapy, and milieu management. Environmental change takes place outside correctional facilities and in the community and thus is not discussed here. Group therapy and milieu management can be utilized within correctional institutions.

Group Therapy

Group therapy is designed to change the behavior of an entire group through a process of socialization. Thus, group therapy is believed to be highly effective in prison settings that aim at improving inmate socialization skills. In showing that the principle of differential association could be utilized in treatment, Donald R. Cressey stated that if criminals or delinquents are to be changed, they must become assimilated into groups that emphasize law-abiding behavior and alienated from those that emphasize law-violating behavior. The "more relevant the common purpose of the group to the reformation of criminals, the greater will be its influence on the criminal members' attitudes and values" and the "more cohesive the group, the greater the members' readiness to influence others and the more relevant the problem of conformity to group norms." In addition, all of the members of the group must be able to achieve status within the group for activities that are conducive to reform. The more effective reformation groups will be those in which criminals join with noncriminals for the purpose of changing other criminals. Finally, when the entire group is the focus of change, the process of reformation can be enhanced by convincing the group that change is needed. The group will then exert the pressure for change on its members.[27]

Group therapy can be used within institutions by utilizing groups that are already formed or by forming new groups. Group therapy has been distinguished from group counseling by some who argue that the former is more intensive. Gibbons believes that the distinction is unfortunate. He has argued that if the purpose is to "create real groups with new attitudinal and normative patterns," it is group therapy.[28]

Milieu Management

Milieu management has the same goals as does group therapy, but is more extensive in that it includes the entire environment of the group in the treatment program. It is therefore usually conducted within institutions. One example is the Synanon method for treating drug addicts. Synanon houses have been established with the total environment structured toward treatment and rehabilitation of the addict. Great success has been claimed for such programs. It should be noted, however, that the patients in many of these programs participate voluntarily, which clearly distinguishes these situations from those of the correctional facility. One of the crucial criticisms of the milieu approach is that the participants may learn to live within the structured milieu but are not able to live within society without the protection of the group. That criticism could, of course, be made of any program that does not attempt to integrate the person into society.

In addition to the categories of treatment discussed by Gibbons, we now look at behavior modification, which has been used extensively by corrections.

Behavior Modification

Traditional psychotherapy is based on the theory that deviant behavior is symptomatic of some deep, underlying personality problem that must be uncovered and treated. **Behavior modification,** on the other hand, is based on learning theory and is concerned with observable behavior. According to the argument, it is not the unconscious that is important, but rather the behavior that can be observed and manipulated. It is assumed that neurotic symptoms and some types of deviant behavior are acquired through an unfortunate quirk of learning and are in some way rewarding to the patient. The significant aspect of this approach is the belief that deviant behaviors are learned in the same way that all other behavior is learned. The undesirable behavior can be eliminated, modified, or replaced by taking away the reward value. Or, the behavior can be replaced by rewarding a more appropriate behavior that is incompatible with the deviant behavior.

Following the theories of B. F. Skinner and his associates, the basic premise of behavior modification is that behavior is controlled by its consequences. "Behavior modification, then, is the systematic application of proven principles of conditioning and learning in the remediation of human problems."[29] In dealing directly with behaviors that are undesirable, behavioral therapy attempts to produce a change in the person's long-established patterns of response to himself or herself and to others.[30]

Let us look at a classical illustration of how behavior modification works. Blaine, a fourteen-year-old boy whose IQ was in the low eighties, had adjustment problems both at school and at home. He was antagonistic toward his peers and incorrigible at school. At home, he messed up the house and set fires. School officials tried various punishments with little success. His father tried spankings and lectures with little result, but experienced some success with denying television privileges. Under the behavior modification program devised for Blaine, a daily chart was kept. For each day he did not play with matches, he received a star on his chart, praise from his father, and an opportunity to watch television in the evening. If he got a star each day for a week, he received twenty-five cents. If he played with matches one day, he lost the star and the television privileges for that day and the quarter for the week. In the six months that the chart was used for Blaine, he missed only one opportunity for reinforcement. Furthermore, he and his brothers began doing their chores at home regularly; for this action they received praise and reinforcement. Blaine's behavior at school improved greatly. "Follow-up showed no changes—the school was full of praise for his behavior and playing with matches" did not recur.[31] This type of treatment is also available in most correctional facilities. In fact, statistics suggest that in 1995, psychological, life skills, and psychiatric counseling was available in 69 percent of correctional facilities, while in the same year, 67 percent of these institutions offered community adjustment counseling.[32]

Physiological Behavior Control

Considerable attention has been given recently to the "mind-controlling" behavior techniques, such as the use of drugs, psychosurgery, chemotherapy, and electrode implantation. Such popular attempts to control behavior are included under the umbrella of "behavior modification." It has been argued that even though these procedures are used to control behavior, "they should not be confused with behavior-modification procedures for they are not applications of the principles of conditioning and learning. Techniques such as these involve instead physiological alterations that fall within the domain of the physician, the surgeon, the psychiatrist—certainly not the behavior modifier."[33] Nor does the controversy end with the definition of the treatment program. There is disagreement on the issue of what constitutes consent to these treatment methods and whether or not the methods have actually been administered without consent.

Today, most correctional facilities enjoy the benefit of having drug rehabilitation programs. This is not surprising considering the fact that most offenders housed in today's prisons have been convicted for drug-related offenses. In fact, the Clark Foundation report "Americans Behind Bars" concluded that "much of the growth in prison population has resulted from a doubling of the number of arrests for drug law violations and a tripling of the rate of incarceration for arrested drug offenders."[34] Some of the psychological therapies explained earlier are being used as part of the inmate's drug treatment program. Some studies on the effectiveness of long-term residential treatment programs have indicated that without aftercare and follow-up support, offenders are more likely to relapse into drug use and crime. Specifically, these studies, which evaluated the Federal Bureau of Prisons's drug treatment programs in public health service hospitals in Lexington, Kentucky, and Fort Worth, Texas, revealed a 96 percent relapse rate among treatment participants. Thus, it has been recommended that the implementation of additional months of drug and job treatment programs would reduce the reoccurrence of drug use among those released.[35] Other studies have suggested that intensive case management delivered for six months to drug-involved arrestees released after booking has significantly reduced drug use and lowered criminal recidivism.[36] Other types of programs are offered in today's institutions to support those who suffer from various problems, including the HIV virus and mental disorders. Each state offers a different type of program, thus making a discussion of each a very difficult task.

Education Programs

Despite today's punitive attitude, society supports educational programs offered in correctional facilities. It has been long held that individuals who are educated will turn away from a life of crime. This belief has been substantiated by various research studies that suggest that education may be a key to preventing criminal behavior.

According to statistics released in 1995, 80 percent of the correctional facilities in the United States provide secondary educational programs, while 75 percent of them provide basic adult education. In that same year, vocational training was offered in 54 percent of the correctional institutions while college-level course work was available in 33 percent of these same institutions. In addition, about 23 percent of inmates were enrolled in some type of education in 1995, including 22 percent of state inmates and 29 percent of federal inmates.[37]

Historical Overview

Prison education programs of any significance are recent in development. "The first school system for all prisoners was established in Maryland in the 1830s followed by a New York law of 1847 appointing instructors in its prisons."[38] High rates of illiteracy among the early prisoners gave impetus to prison education programs. The ministers who went to prison for religious training and to attempt to convert the inmates were really the first teachers. The ministers had to teach the inmates how to read before they could read the Bible. The Quakers, who initiated many early prison reforms, were the first laypeople to advocate education of criminals. But they ran into opposition from individuals who thought that educated criminals would be more dangerous to society than uneducated ones upon their release.

Prison education in the United States began formally with the development of the reformatory system, which started at Elmira in 1876 under the leadership of Zebulen Brockway. His desire was to establish an educational system that would teach inmates self-discipline as well as academic subjects. The division of academic and moral education was headed by college professors. Specific courses were taught by professors, public school principals, and lawyers.[39] It is rather ironic that in 1876, prison courses were taught by highly qualified professionals, while in the "modern, progressive" prisons of recent decades, courses are often taught by people who do not have college degrees. Brockway's other contributions were the industrial program at the Detroit House of Corrections in 1861, the "first grading system based on the degree of reformation (reformation attitude), [and] one of the first trade schools and manual arts programs for those prisoners incapable of benefitting from the more academic courses."[40]

Current Programs

As stated previously, it is impossible to discuss all of the education programs offered in prisons because they vary from state to state. However, we will briefly review the existing literature regarding the evaluation of some of these programs.

It is important to note that education programs not only serve the interest of the inmate, but also that of the correctional administrator. These programs provide incentives to inmates in surroundings that are otherwise devoid of constructive activities. In addition, these programs provide exposure to positive civilian role models while engaging inmates for many hours in quiet, productive activity. Some have even claimed that education programs make up a key component of what has been referred to as "dynamic security" within correctional facilities.

The review of studies regarding education programs offered in prisons suggests that participation in prison education programs is related significantly to lower recidivism rates. Also, some studies have also suggested that pre-college programs have a significant relationship with post-release employment, meaning that offenders who participated in pre-college education programs were more likely to continue their education after release. Some of the findings have suggested that participation in college programs in prison is associated with lower recidivism rates, higher rates of post-release employment, and higher rates of participation in education programs after release.[41] Overall, positive benefits for those who attend education programs in prisons were seen. Although there are some studies that suggest the contrary, most experts argue that the benefits of these programs outweigh any negative effects.

Vocational Training

Vocational training programs attempt to teach offenders job skills that they can hopefully employ once released. This is one of the oldest approaches toward the rehabilitation of offenders. At times, these programs are designed to keep the prison running or to at least provide some type of an income. At the federal level, industries operated by the Federal Bureau of Prisons (UNICOR) produce furniture, electronic equipment, graphics, etc. In fact, in some states such as Florida, the desks, tables, and stationery often found in colleges are produced by inmates. It is often the case that vocational training suffers from the principle of least eligibility in that it offers training only for less desirable jobs. If programs were to offer training for better jobs, the public would, in all likelihood, resent it, arguing that inmates do not deserve quality training. By virtue of this, inmates often learn trades that are not marketable outside the prison facility. This leads the released offender to resort to the "old illegitimate ways" in order to survive. Historically, the vocational training programs offered in prisons have been impacted by the economic needs of society. In the following discussion, we will have the opportunity to examine the previous and existing developments in prison labor, keeping in mind that these developments have had an effect on the vocational programs currently offered in correctional institutions.

Prison Labor and Industry

It has been said that "the most difficult prison to administer is the one in which prisoners languish in idleness. Absence of work leads to moral and physical degradation and corrupts institutional order."[42] This view leads to the attitude that "no single phase of life within prison walls is more important to the public or to the inmate than efficient industrial operations and the intelligent utilization of the labor of prisoners."[43] This attitude toward prison labor reflects a belief that work is an important element in the program of rehabilitation that society likes to think takes place in prisons. It probably also reflects the popular belief that prisoners should work and help support themselves. Yet, prison labor in the past has resulted in restrictive legislation, as we shall see.

Historical Overview

Work was an important element of the early U.S. prisons. Even in the solitary confinement cells of the Pennsylvania System, prisoners were expected to work at crafts. That system, of course, became outmoded with the Industrial Revolution.

The early prison labor systems, beginning at Auburn, New York in 1823, were profitable, although in the process they exploited prisoners, who were often treated like slaves.[44] In prison industry, "hard labor" was often considered to be the major component in the daily routine, discipline, reformation, and profit in institutions across the country. The first programs of prison labor in the United States operated within a free and open market, but were later curtailed by legislation. Several forms of prison labor were characteristic: the lease system, the contract system, the piece-price system, and the public, or state, account system.

Under the **lease system,** the entire prison labor force was placed in the hands of a lessee for an agreed-upon fee. "The system developed in the South where prisoners where sent to lumber camps, in effect as slave laborers, and the state received a fixed rate per man per month."[45] The state thus "worked" the prisoners and realized revenue from them, but had no responsibility for their custody. In the 1920s, public indignation finally killed this system. The **contract system** then developed whereby the state maintained the prisoners, but sold their labor to a contractor who provided the necessary machinery and supervised the inmates. This system also exploited the inmates and provided revenue for the state and for the contractor. It was abolished, in essence, by federal legislation.

Under the **piece-price system,** the contractor paid a fixed price for each finished piece of work done by inmates. The state was in charge of maintaining the prisoner and supervising his or her work. Federal legislation also eliminated this system.

The **public,** or **state account, system** brought the entire labor system within the control of the state. The state maintained the inmates, supervised their work, and marketed their products.

All of these systems were affected by legislation that resulted from complaints of private industry that they could not compete with the cheap prison labor. Although some states passed laws regulating prison industry, the biggest blow came in 1929 with the passage of the Hawes-Cooper Act, which was to become effective five years later. This act prohibited prison goods from being shipped into states that had laws prohibiting their sale. The power to regulate the sale of such goods is now essentially with the states. In 1925, the passage of the Ashurst-Sumners Act made it a federal offense to transport prison goods into states that prohibited their sale and also required the labeling of prison-made goods shipped in interstate commerce. The United States Supreme Court upheld the constitutionality of these laws.

As more states passed laws prohibiting the sale of prison-made products within their borders (by 1940 all fifty states had done so), the prison labor system was forced to change. The **state-use system** developed, which permits the sale of prison-made goods only to state institutions. Consequently, most prison labor is geared to the production of soap, clothing, office furniture, license plates, road signs, and other products used by state agencies and institutions.

Recent Developments

In 1979, Congress authorized the Prison Industry Enhancement (PIE) program through the Justice System Improvement Act. This program brings the private sector into the prison industry by exempting certified correctional agencies from any type of legislative restriction imposed on the transportation and sale of prison-made goods in interstate commerce. This exemption is made provided that inmates are paid minimum wage and that certain other criteria are met. In addition, the PIE program authorizes deductions of up to 80 percent of gross wages for taxes, room and board, family support, and victim compensation. This program was revised in 1984 under the Justice Assistance Act and amended again in the Crime Control Act of 1990.[46] It is important to note that while this program does not repeal the Ashurst-Sumners Act, it does deny its application to specific certified prison industries. Despite this, however, the program's popularity has grown in recent years, thus prompting Congress to gradually expand the number of allowable certifications from seven to fifty.

As can be expected, the PIE program offers various advantages to states that implement it in addition to the benefits it provides inmates. Specifically, the PIE program offers a strong financial incentive to the state by generating goods and services that produce income, and offenders can make a contribution to society while defraying their own cost of incarceration. Statistics show that between December 1979 and September 1994, $2,914,236 had been contributed to victim's programs; $8,251,225 had been collected for room and board; $2,875,088 had been paid for family support; and $5,189,950 had been collected in taxes.[47] Despite this, PIE remains a small program, employing only 1,663 inmates nationwide.[48]

Some states such as California have implemented programs that allow inmates to help in the fight for a better environment. For example, the California Prison Industry Authority established a waste recycling plant inside the premises of Folsom State Prison to enable parole violators to engage in community service while generating revenues for the state. Some of these revenues were aimed at offsetting prison costs and alleviating the city's waste problem. Inmates were asked to sort out garbage that was moving through a conveyor. Preliminary evaluations indicate that this program is a success.[49] Other states have implemented similar programs in an attempt to defray incarceration costs while allowing inmates to spend their time in a fruitful activity.

WiseGuide Wrap-Up This chapter considered the important issue of treatment of offenders within institutions. We began with a discussion of the federal and state correctional systems. We then looked at the classification process of institutions and inmates. We examined the various characteristics associated with maximum, medium, and minimum security prisons while looking at the psychological impact of the inmate classification process. We then moved on to the various programs offered in most correctional settings in the United States. We looked at the establishment and operation of the various treatment, educational, and vocational programs offered by many correctional systems in the United States.

When discussing the treatment programs, we emphasized the typology offered by Don C. Gibbons, which is based on two areas—psychological and social therapies. We then considered the various dimensions of behavior modification, and discussed education programs in terms of their growing popularity in today's correctional settings. We looked at the historical development of these programs, while paying attention to the most recent studies in this area that have shown a very strong, positive correlation between attendance at correctional educational programs and low recidivism.

Finally, we examined some of the vocational programs offered in today's prisons. Again, we presented the historical background of these programs to show their evolution and continuing popularity. As explained earlier, these programs are popular among the citizenry and correctional administrators because they reduce some of the costs associated with imprisonment while reducing incidents of violence and recidivism rates among inmates. However, at times, inmates refuse to accept the positive effects of prison programs, resulting in violence and at times death.

Notes

1. Federal Bureau of Prisons. *Quick Facts.* (Dec. 27, 1997). Automated Information Systems.
2. *Quick Facts.*
3. Menninger, Karl. *The Crime of Punishment.* (New York: Viking Press, 1968), p. 176.
4. Loveland, Frank. "Classification in the Prison System," in Paul W. Tappan, ed. *Contemporary Correction.* (New York: McGraw-Hill, 1951), p. 91.
5. CNN, January 9, 1998. *Trend Toward Solitary Confinement Worries Experts.* Statement made by Dr. Henry Weinstein.
6. Census of State and Federal Correctional Facilities, 1995. (August, 1995). U.S. Department of Justice Statistics.
7. Prison Research Education Action Project. "Prisons Cannot Protect Society," in Bonnie Szumski, *America's Prisons: Opposing Viewpoints,* 4th ed. (St. Paul, MN: Greenhaven Press, 1985), p. 46. See also *America's Prisons,* Charles P. Cozic, (St. Paul, MN: Greenhaven Press, 1997).
8. Census of State and Federal Correctional Facilities, 1995. (August, 1977). U.S. Department of Justice. Bureau of Justice Statistics.
9. Census of State and Federal Correctional Facilities, 1995.
10. Census of State and Federal Correctional Facilities, 1995.
11. Census of State and Federal Correctional Facilities, 1995.
12. Loveland, Frank. "Classification in the Prison System," in Paul W. Tappan, ed., *Contemporary Correction.* (New York: McGraw-Hill

1951), p. 91. For a discussion of team work in the classification of inmates, see John Hepburn and Celesta A. Albonetti, "Team Classification in State Correctional Institutions: Its Association with Inmate and Staff Attitudes," *Criminal Justice and Behavior* 5 (March, 1978), 63–73.
13. Loveland, Frank. "Classification in the Prison System," p. 95.
14. American Correctional Association. *Manual of Correctional Standards.* (Washington, DC, 1996), pp. 285–287.
15. Loveland, "Classification in the Prison System," pp. 100–103.
16. Gibbons, Don C. *Changing the Law Breaker: The Treatment of Delinquents and Criminals.* (Englewood Cliffs, NJ: Prentice-Hall, 1965), pp. 130–131.
17. Gibbons, *Changing the Law Breaker,* pp. 133–135.
18. *The American Heritage Dictionary,* 1985. 2nd ed. (Boston, MA: Houghton Mifflin Company).
19. Gibbons, *Changing the Law Breaker,* p. 142.
20. Gibbons, Don C. *Society, Crime, and Criminal Careers.* (Englewood Cliffs, NJ: Prentice-Hall, Inc., 1968), p. 493.
21. Quoted in Gibbons, *Changing the Law Breaker,* p. 145.
22. Slavson, S. R. "Group Psychotherapy," *Scientific American* 183 (December, 1950), 42.
23. Quoted in Richard L. Rachin, "Reality Therapy: Helping People Help Themselves," *Crime and Delinquency* 20 (January, 1974), 49.
24. Rachin, "Reality Therapy," p. 53.

25. Berne, Eric. *Games People Play.* (New York: Grove Press, 1962).

26. Nagel, William. *The New Red Barn: A Critical Look at the Modern American Prison.* (New York: Walker, 1973). p. 134. See also John Blackmore, " 'Human Potential' Therapies, Behind Bars," *Corrections Magazine* 4 (December, 1978) 29–38.

27. Cressey, Donald R. "Changing Criminals: The Application of the Theory of Differential Association," *American Journal of Socioloy* 61:9 (September, 1955), 116–120. See also Vold, George B., Bernard, Thomas J., and Snipes, Jeffrey B., *Theoretical Criminology,* 4th ed. (New York: Oxford University Press, 1998).

28. Gibbons, *Changing the Law Breaker,* p. 163.

29. Milan, Michael A., and McKee, John M. "Behavior Modification; Principles and Applications in Corrections," in Daniel Glaser, ed., *Handbook of Criminology.* (Skokie, IL: Rand McNally, 1974), p. 746.

30. For an excellent review of the literature on behavior modification, see V. Scott Johnson, "Behavior Modification in the Correctional Setting," *Criminal Justice and Behavior* 4 (December, 1977), 397–428.

31. Thorne, Gaylord L. et al. "Behavior Modification Techniques: New Tools for Probation Officers," *Federal Probation* 31 (June, 1967), 21.

32. Census of State and Federal Correctional Facilities, 1995.

33. Quoted in Milan and McKee, "Behavior Modification," p. 746.

34. Edna McConnell Clark Foundation. *Americans Behind Bars* (New York: Edna McConnell Clark Foundation, 1994), p. 8. For more discussion on drug offenders see Samuel Walker, *Sense and Nonsense About Crime and Drugs,* 4th ed. (Belmont, CA, Wadsworth Publishing Company, 1998).

35. Corrections-Based Continuum of Effective Drug Abuse Treatment. (June, 1996). National Institute of Justice.

36. Case Management With Drug-Involved Arrestees. (November, 1995). National Institute of Justice.

37. Census of State and Federal Correctional Facilities, 1995.

38. Tappan, Paul. *Crime, Justice, and Correction.* (New York: McGraw-Hill, 1960), p. 390.

39. Johnson, Elmer Hubert. *Crime, Correction, and Society.* (Homewood, IL: Dorsey, 1978), pp. 371–372.

40. Morris, Delyte W. "The University's Role in Prison Education," in Harvey S. Perlman and Thomas B. Allington, eds., *The Tasks of Penology.* (Lincoln, NE: The University of Nebraska Press, 1969), p. 199.

41. Adams, Kenneth et al. *A Large-Scale Multidimensional Test of the Effects of Prison Education Programs on Offenders' Behavior.* (December, 1994) Prison Journal, vol. 74, n. 4, p. 433 (17).

42. Johnson, *Crime, Corrections, and Society,* p. 559.

43. U.S. Bureau of Prisons, Handbook of Correctional Institutional Design and Construction, quoted in Tappan, *Crime, Justice and Corrections,* p. 681.

44. See Thorsten Sellin, *Slavery and the Penal System* (New York: Elsevier, 1976).

45. Handbook of Correctional Institutional Design and Construction, in Tappan, *Crime, Justice and Corrections,* p. 682.

46. Misrahi, James J. *Factories with Fences: An Analysis of the Prison Industry Enhancement Certification Program in Historical Perspective.* (Winter, 1996). American Criminal Law Review, 33, n. 2, 411–436.

47. Misrahi, *Factories with Fences,* p. 413.

48. Misrahi, *Factories with Fences,* p. 414.

49. Harrison, Larry, and Lovell, Douglas G. "Inmate Work Program Helps Solve City's Waste Problem." (April, 1996). *Corrections Today.* vol. 58, n. 2, p. 132 (3).

The Corrections Process

The Pretrial Process
(Bail and Jail)

 One of the most critical periods of the criminal proceedings—if not *the* most critical—is the time between arraignment and trial. It is a time "when consultation, thoroughgoing investigation and preparation . . . [are] vitally important."[1] During this period, the defendant either retains an attorney or is assigned counsel by the court. The defense counsel and the prosecutor negotiate and consider the possibility of plea bargaining. The defense may consider it important to a fair trial that the location of the trial be moved, and the judge must rule on the motion for a change of venue. Witnesses are interviewed and other attempts are made by both sides to secure evidence for the trial. The uncovering of additional evidence may change the nature of the case and can even result in the dropping or reduction of charges.

Because of the importance of this period before trial, we will consider carefully the ways in which accused persons are handled at this time. First, we look at the bail system, which permits some defendants to be free while awaiting trial. We begin with the history and purpose of bail and then look at the effects that denial of bail has on defendants. Criticisms of the bail bondsman system, in particular, as well as any money bail system lead us to a discussion of various attempts to reform the system. Finally, we look at evaluations of bail reform.

Bail and jails are interrelated to a much greater extent than simply the sound of the terms. Changes in the granting of bail directly affect the numbers of inmates detained in jails. Because of this interrelationship, and because jails are used to detain defendants awaiting trial as well as to incarcerate convicted persons, jails are discussed in this chapter rather than in the chapter on the prison system (these terms will be distinguished later in the chapter). Attention is given to the subject of pretrial

Key Terms

bail
direct supervision
interaction space
jails
Law Enforcement Assistance
 Administration (LEAA)
Manhattan Bail Project
personal space
podular design

detention, centering around United States Supreme Court decisions that considered some of the rights of pretrial detainees. In our discussion of jails, we look at the historical background of the use of jails as well as the organization and administration of local and county jails. We examine some of the conditions of "modern" jails, looking closely at court decisions, especially those in which the courts ordered that jail conditions be changed.

The Bail System

History

The American **bail** system originated from feudal practices in twelfth-century England. It was instituted, at the time, to assure the presence of defendants at trials. These defendants were often supervised by the *reeve* (an officer of the court) who was appointed to represent the crown in a specific *shire* (county). The *shire reeve* (origin of the word "sheriff") preferred to have someone else take care of defendants while they awaited trial and would often relinquish them to other people, usually friends or relatives. These people would serve as *sureties* (guarantees). When the bail system first began, the surety would be tried if the defendant did not appear for trial after he or she had been placed on bail. The party furnishing bail would be reminded that he or she had the powers of a jailer and was expected to produce the accused for trial. This policy of private sureties was also followed in America as English settlers brought these traditions to the American colonies. This practice was later replaced by a system of posting bond to guarantee a defendant's presence at trial.

Purpose of Bail

The purpose of bail is to *assure the presence of the defendant at trial.* In the United States, it has generally been held by courts that this is the only legal reason for bail. The courts have not only established the legal reasons for bail, but have also regulated the monetary boundaries of the bail system. In fact, the U.S. Supreme Court ruled that "bail set at a figure higher than that reasonably calculated to [secure assurance that the defendant will stand trial] is 'excessive' under the Eighth Amendment."[2] But many judges use bail for this purpose, especially in connection with people who are considered dangerous or who have been involved in riots and demonstrations. A classic example of this is illustrated in a CNN story[3] of a gunman who took dozens of people hostage at a day-care center in Texas. The man, James Monroe Lipscomb, Jr., ended up surrendering to police after thirty hours of negotiation. Apparently, Lipscomb was having marital problems and entered the Rigsbee Child Development Center to see his wife, who fled after her husband entered the day-care center. As a result of this, Lipscomb proceeded to take over the entire day-care facility. After surrendering, police charged him with various crimes, including one count of aggravated kidnaping. The Texas courts felt that Lipscomb posed a threat to society and set bail at $1 million. This case illustrates the practice followed by judges to set bail at high amounts in order to assure that the defendant will not pose a threat to society before the trial begins. However, it is important to recognize that sometimes even bail does not serve the claimed purpose of protecting society. Wealthy dangerous offenders who have adequate financial resources may be set free, while persons who are not dangerous to themselves or to society may languish in jail.

Bail Bondsman/woman

The professional bondsman/woman* emerged due to the profitable nature of the bail system. In return for a fee, the bondsman posts the bond for the accused. Theoretically, if the accused does not appear, the bondsman is required to forfeit

*For simplicity, the term "bondsman" will be used throughout this discussion to refer to both males and females.

the money to the state. In practice, the forfeitures of bonds are vacated by courts in many cases, on the theory that the bondsman has been diligent in his or her attempts to produce the accused for trial. The bondsman often has a lucrative job with little risk. Some bondsmen have, however, been "straw" men in that they have not had the necessary money to produce in cases of forfeiture. Because the bond system has been abused by some bondsmen, laws have been passed to minimize the abuse. Some laws require the bondsmen to prove their ability to pay in case of forfeiture, and other laws place statutory limits on the fees that can be charged.

Generally, the bondsman charges the accused 10 percent for posting bond. He or she may require the accused to sign over a home mortgage or, in some other way provide collateral security. If a professional bondsman is not used, the accused may post bail by paying the court a specified percentage of the amount of bail or by placing securities with the court. In the case of monetary payment, the money paid by the defendant is seldom returned even if he or she appears for trial. Bail, therefore, does cost money. If bail is high, it can be costly for the defendant even if he or she can raise the money through family and friends or can hire a professional bondsman. In 1988, a survey of 88,120 pretrial detainees presented evidence suggesting that of the 87 percent whose bail had been set, 94 percent were incarcerated only because they could not afford bail or the fees of a bondsman.[4]

In the past, the professional bondsman system has been severely criticized.[5] Some of these criticisms are still pertinent to the bondsman system today. The bondsman may require a larger premium from an offender whom he does not know—a "poor business risk"—and thereby have considerable control over a defendant. Professional criminals, on the other hand, may be considered by a bondsman to be better "risks" and may not be required to post as much money. As one judge said:

> The effect of such a system is that the professional bondsmen hold the keys to the jail in their pockets. They determine for whom they will act as surety—who in their judgment is a good risk. The bad risks, in the bondsmen's judgement, and the ones who are unable to pay the bondsmen's fees, remain in jail. The court and the commissioner are relegated to the relatively unimportant chore of fixing the amount of bail.[6]

Alternatives to Bail

The bail system has been the focus of a great deal of criticism in recent years. Most of these criticisms are based on the notion that a large number of defendants are indigent and cannot afford bail while others who can afford it are not inclined to appear in court.[7] Due to these criticisms, alternative forms of pretrial release have been created. These forms of pretrial release are financially and non-financially based. They range from requiring the defendant to post the entire amount of bail, to the release of defendants on their own promise that they will appear at trial. This method is often referred to as *release on recognizance* (ROR or OR). Spotlight 5.1 illustrates the various methods of pretrial release.

Some of these methods of pretrial release have been created as a result of the various reforms made to the bail system. As mentioned earlier, these reforms have been made, in part, due to the heavy criticisms attributed to the bail system. We will examine some of these reforms in the hopes of understanding the mechanisms that led to their existence.

Spotlight 5.1

Methods of Pretrial Release

Financial Bond

- **Fully secured bail.** The alleged offender posts the entire amount of bail.

- **Privately secured bail.** A bondsman/woman signs a promissory note to the court for the bail amount and charges a defendant a fee for the service. This fee is usually 10 percent of the bail amount. If the defendant does not appear in court, the bondsman/woman must pay the court the full amount. In most cases, the bondsman/woman requires the defendant to post collateral in addition to the fee required.

- **Deposit bail.** The court allows the accused to deposit a percentage (10 percent in most cases) of the full bail with the court. The complete amount of the bail is required if the defendant fails to appear. The percentage of bail is returned after disposition of the case, but the court frequently retains 1 percent for administrative costs.

- **Unsecured bail.** The accused does not pay any money to the court but is liable for the full amount of bail should he or she fail to appear.

Alternative Release Options

- **Release on recognizance (ROR).** The court releases the accused based on the promise that he or she will appear in court as required.

- **Conditional release.** The court releases the accused subject to specific conditions as set by the courts. These conditions may include attendance at drug treatment therapy, or staying away from the complaining witness.

- **Third-party custody.** The defendant is released into the custody of an agency or individual that promises to assure his or her appearance in court. No monetary transactions are involved in this type of release.

- **Citation release.** Arrested individuals are released pending their first appearance in court on a written order issued by law enforcement personnel.

Source: Bureau of Justice Statistics, *Report to the Nation on Crime and Justice: The Data,* 2nd ed. (Washington, D.C. U.S. Department of Justice, 1988), p. 76.

Manhattan Bail Project

In the 1960s, industrialist Louis Schweitzer became concerned with poor youths who could not make bail and were imprisoned while awaiting trial. As a result of this concern, Mr. Schweitzer established the Vera Foundation, which along with other organizations such as the New York University School of Law and the Institute of Judicial Administration, conducted an experiment on bail. This experiment, the **Manhattan Bail Project,** was based on the notion that "more persons can successfully be released . . . if verified information concerning their character and roots in the community is available to the court at the time of bail determination."[8] The publicity received by this experiment led to bail reform initiatives throughout the country.

The project, which began in 1961, allowed New York University law students to interview defendants in order to gain information that would be relevant to pretrial release. Some of this information included: (a) present or recent residence at the same address for six months or more; (b) current or recent employment for a period of time of six months or more; (c) relatives in the New York City area with whom the defendant was in contact; (d) no previous crime conviction; and (e) residence in the New York City area for ten years or more.

Once the interview took place, the staff would then decide whether or not to recommend release for the defendant. If the staff decided to recommend release, the recommendation would be sent to the arraignment court, where the accused would be assigned randomly to control or experimental groups. For the control group, the recommendation would not be committed to the court. For the experimental group, copies of the recommendation were issued to various courtroom actors such as the judge, prosecutor, and assigned counsel. However, the decision whether or not to grant release was left up to the judge. Of those individuals recommended for release by the staff, 60 percent were released by the judge, compared to only 14 percent of those not recommended by the staff. Thus, due to the existence of the project, four times as many persons were released pending trial. In regard to those who were released and did not appear for trial, the staff reported that numerous factors (i.e., illness, ignorance of legal processes, family emergencies, and confusion about when and in what court to appear) were responsible for nearly all of the nonappearances. This was usually corrected by a telephone call to their work, to relatives not living with them, or to their home.

Other cities have adopted bail reform plans that involve, among other methods, release of defendants on their own recognizance pending trial. It has been established that most of the defendants that were released on ROR have appeared for trial, and according to the Advisory Commission, this method of release has become a significant alternative to money bail bonds. Despite this, the commission criticizes the plans, noting that in cases involving ROR and other money bail alternatives, the "criteria for these options for the most part have been applied either too conservatively (releasing mostly persons who could have posted bond anyway) or too carelessly (with substantial increases in the default rate)." The commission concluded by asserting that, despite the fact that the system of using means other than money bail for releasing defendants prior to trial is a sound one, there have been some administrative problems.[9]

In 1966, the federal government passed the Bail Reform Act. It did not preclude the use of bail as a condition of release in federal courts. It lessened its importance by requiring that before the judge makes a decision, he or she must consider alternatives for releasing the accused. The act required a specific procedure for analysis. Judges were to consider alternatives to bail and base decisions on specific types of information. The act established a preference for release without security. It provided that the defendant "shall . . . be ordered released pending trial on his personal recognizance or . . . upon the execution of an unsecured appearance bond in an amount specified by the judicial officer, unless the officer determines, in exercise of his discretion that such a release will not reasonably assure the appearance of the person as required."

The debate over whether to release defendants on bail continued, as evidenced in the following reactions to bail. In his annual state of the judiciary address to the American Bar Association in 1979, Chief Justice Warren E. Burger of the U.S. Supreme Court called for a "fresh examination" of the conditions of bail release for those charged with serious crimes. Burger referred to what he called the "startling increase" in the number of crimes committed by persons on bail while awaiting trial.[10] On the other hand, the former Director of the Federal Bureau of Prisons, Norman A. Carlson, citing crowded jail conditions and inadequate facilities, said "our first concern should be to keep as many detainees as possible out of jail."[11] These reactions, followed by the public's growing reluctance to grant bail, created the conditions necessary for yet another bail reform act.

As mentioned previously, the Bail Reform Act of 1966 established that the judicial officer was to impose the minimal conditions of release needed to assure only that the defendant will appear in court. Also, while an individual could have been held

The Bail Reform Act of 1966

The Federal Bail Reform Act of 1984

for failure to post bail, detention without bail was allowed only in cases involving capital offenses.

The Bail Reform Act of 1984 changed these provisions. Specifically, the act provided that, in reaching decisions on bail and release, the court should give consideration not only to ensuring the defendant's appearance in court but also to protecting the safety of individuals and the community.

The provisions of the act, as they relate to pretrial detention, make specific reference to particular categories of offenses and offenders. The act authorizes pretrial detention for defendants who are charged with crimes of violence, offenses with possible life sentences or death penalties, major drug offenses, and felonies in which the accused has a specific criminal record. In addition, the act creates a rebuttable presumption that no condition of release will assure the appearance of the defendant and the safety of the community under the following circumstances: The accused committed a drug felony with a ten-year maximum sentence; the defendant used a firearm during the commission of a violent or drug trafficking offense; or the defendant was convicted of specified serious crimes within the preceding five years while the individual was on pretrial release.[12]

The Federal Bail Reform Act of 1984 does not require that prosecutors request pretrial detention for all defendants in these groups. It also contains provisions for temporary detention (up to ten working days) of illegal aliens or persons under pre- or post-trial release, probation, or parole at the time of the current offense. This provision was included for the purpose of allowing time for other agencies (i.e., law enforcement or immigration officials) to take the appropriate course of action.[13]

Pretrial Detainees

Pretrial detainees, unlike prisoners, have not been convicted of any crime for which they are being detained. Although they are considered to be innocent, they are misfortunate in that they were either denied bail or did not have the funds to attain bail. Furthermore, to add insult to injury, they are held under the worst conditions of incarceration. As will be explained later, jails are the least desirable correctional facilities due to the nature of their clientele and poor funding sources. Thus, pretrial detainees are exposed to serious and nonserious offenders in a vulnerable and inadequate environment.

The law prescribes that pretrial detainees remain in jail until their trial date. Needless to say, the consequences of this are numerous and have an impact on the outcome of the case. Research suggests that individuals held in jail until the time of trial are at a disadvantage in the preparation of their defense. In addition to the predicaments mentioned earlier, pretrial detainees are often in need of an attorney, which most of them cannot afford. Thus, they have to rely upon court-appointed counsel, who, as statistics suggest, are often overwhelmed with cases and cannot spend the necessary time preparing for a good defense. In fact, this is one of the reasons why detainees usually have only one or two quick conversations with their attorneys before appearing in court. At the time of their appearance, detainees are often escorted in shackles while wearing jail-issued clothing. This image may make an impact on the judge and jury, as they could begin to think that the individual in question "looks" like a criminal, thus he or she "must be a criminal."

Pretrial Detainees' Rights

Because pretrial detainees are considered to be innocent until proven guilty, several courts argued in the 1970s that these individuals should not suffer any more restrictions than those necessary to assure their attendance at trial. Furthermore, the courts also reasoned that the rights of pretrial detainees should exceed those of already sentenced inmates. However, as is always the case in the field of corrections, this reasoning did not last long. In fact, in 1979, the U.S. Supreme Court overruled the decisions made by the lower courts, and limited the rights of all pretrial detainees. A clear example of this is illustrated in the discussion of *Bell v. Wolfish* in Case Study 5.1.

What is the meaning of this important case? It should be noted that the Court limited its holding to those issues involving double bunking, the "publisher-only" rule, receipt of packages, visual inspection of bodily cavities after contact visits, and inspection of rooms while inmates are not present. It must also be emphasized that the Court was looking at these conditions as they relate to pretrial detainees, not to convicted persons serving time in jails. Finally, the court distinguished this case from those in which inmates are locked in their cells for long periods of time and in which facilities are not as modern and as sanitary as were the facilities at MCC.

The case reaffirmed the Court's position that persons not convicted of a crime may not be subjected to punishment. The disagreement between the dissenters and the majority, however, was over what constitutes punishment. The majority makes it clear that jail officials should have wide discretion in determining what measures are necessary for "security" within their facilities, and that within reason, such restrictions are not to be considered punishment.

More recently, in *U.S. v. Salerno*, the courts also questioned the constitutionality of the Bail Reform Act of 1984 as it pertains to the preventive detention of "dangerous" offenders. This case involved the detention of several individuals who were charged with various acts associated with organized crime. At the time of the pretrial detention hearing, the government presented evidence suggesting that Salerno and another individual in this case were prominent figures in the La Cosa Nostra crime family. Thus, the government held, the only method used to protect the community from these "high-risk" offenders was to detain them before trial.[17] The constitutional question posed by this case was whether or not the Bail Reform Act of 1984 violated the Fifth Amendment's due process clause.

In *Salerno*, the Court held that the Bail Reform Act was constitutional due to the fact that when the government's interest in protecting the community outweighs individual liberty, pretrial detention can be "a potential solution to a pressing societal problem." In the Court's opinion, the Bail Reform Act applied only to a specific list of serious offenses, placed heavy burdens on the government to prove that the individual arrested posed serious threats to others, and did not prevent the accused from enjoying a speedy trial. In its final resolution, the Court also dismissed Salerno's argument that the act had violated the Excessive Bail Clause of the Eighth Amendment.[18] For the time being, the Bail Reform Act of 1984 and its impact on pretrial detainees remains unchanged.

Bail and Pretrial Detention: A Conclusion

Our discussion thus far indicates that pretrial detention clearly places the detainee at a disadvantage in comparison to his or her counterpart who is released pending trial. Beginning with the Manhattan Bail Project in the early 1960s in New York City, and continuing through the Bail Reform Act of 1984, we also examined the evidence that suggests that the present system of bail is being modified according to the needs of the criminal justice system. Thus, it can only be expected that scholars and practitioners alike will continue to pay close attention to the system of bail and pretrial detention as the inmate population continues to grow to unprecedented proportions.

Case Study 5.1

Bell v. Wolfish

Bell v. Wolfish involved inmates at the Metropolitan Correctional Center (MCC), a federally operated facility for short-term custody in New York City. The facility was designed primarily to detain those awaiting trial. It was constructed in 1975 to replace a covered waterfront garage that had served as the federal jail in the city since 1828. The case is particularly interesting because of the type of facility involved. The MCC is not the dungeon-type structure with unsanitary facilities that characterizes many of our jails. It is a modern facility that, according to the Court of Appeals, "represented the architectural embodiment of the best and most progressive penological planning." The facility was overcrowded, however, shortly after it opened. Rooms designed for one inmate were used for two, and some inmates had to sleep on cots in the common areas.

Less than four months after the MCC opened, several inmates filed a petition that resulted in this appeal to the Supreme Court. Numerous charges were filed, including inadequate phone service, strip searches, searching of inmates' rooms in their absence, interference with and monitoring of mail, inadequate classification system, inadequate and arbitrary disciplinary and grievance procedures, restrictions on religious freedom, excessive confinement, overcrowded conditions, inadequate facilities for education and recreation and employment opportunities, insufficient staff, and excessive restrictions on the purchase and receipt of books and personal items. The lower court enjoined many of these practices, noting that the pretrial detainees are "presumed to be innocent and held only to ensure their presence at trial." Consequently, a compelling necessity must be shown if they are deprived of any rights beyond those necessary for confinement alone. Most of the rulings of the District Court were affirmed by the Court of Appeals. Not all of the issues were on appeal to the Supreme Court; the four basic issues considered by the latter are discussed briefly here.

"Double Bunking."   The first major issue on appeal to the Supreme Court was the use of *double bunking*—housing two inmates in a room designed for one. The lower courts held that a compelling necessity must be shown before this practice would be acceptable. The Supreme Court rejected that test and discussed the issue of whether double bunking constituted "punishment." The Supreme Court

noted that although punishment is permitted in the case of convicted persons (although cruel and unusual punishment is unconstitutional), punishment is not permissible for those not yet convicted. The latter may be detained for trial, but not punished. The Court held, however, that double bunking does not constitute punishment. Unless it can be shown that by engaging in a particular practice the jail officials intend to punish pretrial detainees, a practice will not be considered "punishment" if the restriction is reasonably related to a legitimate government purpose. The government has a legitimate purpose not only in assuring the presence of the accused at trial, but also in managing the jail and keeping the facilities secure. "Restraints that are reasonably related to the institution's interest in maintaining jail security do not, without more, constitute unconstitutional punishment, even if they are discomforting and are restrictions that the detainee would not have experienced had he been released while awaiting trial."

The "Publisher-Only" Rule.   Under the *publisher-only* rule, inmates could receive hardback books only from publishers. The assumption was that publishers could be trusted not to include drugs, weapons, and other contraband items with the shipment. Such books would presumably therefore not have to be inspected. The Bureau of Prisons amended that rule prior to this hearing to allow inmates to receive books and magazines from bookstores as well as from publishers and book clubs. The bureau had also already announced plans to allow receipt of paperbacks, magazines, and other soft-covered materials from any source. The bureau argued that hardback books were the "more dangerous source of risk to institutional security." The Court agreed that prohibiting inmates from receiving hardback books from sources other than publishers, bookstores, and book clubs did not violate First Amendment rights.

Receipt of Packages.   The Court also agreed with officials of the institution that receipt of packages from outside the institution (except one package per inmate at Christmas) was a security problem and, therefore, the regulation prohibiting such was upheld. It was argued that the probability that such packages will contain contraband is high, thus requiring extensive searches—a time-consuming and expensive process.

Case Study 5.1 (continued)

Searches. The Court agreed with officials that it was reasonable, in light of security needs, to search inmates' rooms when they were absent. Although the Court deems unapproved searches of homes as a violation of their "sanctity," the same does not apply to searches of a cell. In fact, correctional officers often disrupt any degree of privacy an inmate may find in a cell by conducting cell searches. These, for the sake of security, are viewed by correctional personnel and the courts as necessary and imminent. The most controversial issue, however, was body searches, which involved visual inspection of body cavities after each contact visit of inmates. Although the Court had difficulty with this practice, it held that such was reasonable in light of security problems.

Mr. Justice Powell concurred with part of the majority opinion but dissented on the holding on body cavity searches, which he called a "serious intrusion on one's privacy." Powell advocates some "level of cause, such as a reasonable suspicion, should be required to justify the anal and genital searches described in this case."[14]

Mr. Justice Marshall, in his dissent, argued that the Court's emphasis on the issue of punishment was misplaced. The issue, said Marshall, is what effect the acts have on the pretrial detainees who are presumptively innocent. "By its terms, the Due Process Clause focuses on the nature of deprivations, not on the persons inflicting them. If this concern is to be vindicated, it is the effect of conditions and confinement, not the intent behind them, that must be the focal point of constitutional analysis." He suggested requiring "that a restriction is substantially necessary to jail administration. Where the imposition is of particular gravity, that is, where it implicates interests of fundamental importance or inflicts significant harms, the Government should demonstrate that the restriction serves a compelling necessity of jail administration."[15] With regard to the visual inspection of body cavities, Marshall said:

> In my view, the body cavity searches of MCC inmates represent one of the most grave offenses against personal dignity and common decency. After every contact visit with someone from outside the facility, including defense attorneys, an inmate must remove all of his or her clothing, bend over, spread the buttocks, and display the anal cavity for inspection by a correctional officer. Women

inmates must assume a suitable posture for vaginal inspection while men must raise their genitals. And, as the Court neglects to note, because of time pressures, this humiliating spectacle is frequently conducted in the presence of other inmates.

The District Court found that the stripping was "unpleasant, embarrassing, and humiliating." A psychiatrist testified that the practice placed inmates in the most degrading position possible, a conclusion amply corroborated by the testimony of the inmates themselves. There was evidence, moreover, that these searches engendered among detainees fears of sexual assault, were the occasion for actual threats of physical abuse by guards, and caused some inmates to forego personal visits.

Not surprisingly, the government asserts a security justification for such inspections. These searches are necessary, it argues, to prevent inmates from smuggling contraband into the facility. In crediting this justification, despite the contrary findings of the two courts below, the Court overlooks the critical facts. As respondents point out, inmates are required to wear one-piece jumpsuits with zippers in the front. To insert an object into the vaginal or anal cavity, an inmate would have to remove the jumpsuit, at least from the upper torso. Since contact visits occur in a glass-enclosed room and are continuously monitored by corrections officers, such a feat would seem extraordinarily difficult. There was medical testimony, moreover, that inserting an object into the rectum is painful and "would require time and opportunity which is not available in the visiting areas," and that visual inspection would probably not detect an object once inserted. Additionally, before entering the visiting room, visitors and their packages are searched thoroughly by a metal detector, fluoroscope, and by hand. Correction officers may require that visitors leave packages or handbags with guards until the visit is over. Only by blinding itself to the facts presented on this record can the Court accept the Government's security rationale.

Without question, these searches are an imposition of sufficient gravity to invoke the compelling necessity standard. It is equally indisputable that they cannot meet that standard. Indeed, the procedure is so unnecessarily degrading that it "shocks the conscience."[16]

Some of the inmate population is housed in jail facilities. Thus, we now turn our attention to the study of jails and their role in the criminal justice system.

Jails

Jails are one of the most important facilities in the system of justice in the United States because they affect the most people. However, even their definition is inconsistent. Hans W. Mattick, in discussing the problem of defining jails, pointed out that the Latin root of the term "jail" is *cavea*, which means cavity, cage, or coop. Generally, the term *jail* is used to refer to "locally-operated correctional facilities that confine persons before or after adjudication."[19] Inmates that are sentenced to jails usually have a sentence of a year or less, however jails also house persons in a wide variety of other categories—including offenders who are not released on bail and must remain in prison until the end of their trial. The number of individuals who are housed in jails across America varies from year to year. At midyear 1997, an estimated 567,079 inmates were held in the nation's jails, up from 518,492 at midyear 1996.[20] The consistency in these high numbers suggests that jails are "a major intake center not only for the entire criminal justice system, but also a place of first or last resort for a host of disguised health, welfare, and social problem cases."[21] A federal court affirmed that "the chilling impact of these numbers dictates the necessity to come to grips with the constitutionality of conditions in the jails in America."[22] As will be noted in the following discussion, the institution of jails has not resisted the change mandated by the different historical eras.

History of Jails

It is ironic that despite the fact that jails are the oldest American penal institutions, less is known about them than about any other institution. Although the existence of jails has been tolerated for centuries, little or no attention is given to this penal institution. It was not until 1970 that some type of data became available, when the first national jail census was conducted by the **Law Enforcement Assistance Administration (LEAA)**.

Historically, jails can be traced back to the twelfth century when they made their debut "in the form of murky dungeons, abysmal pits, unscaleable precipices, strong poles or trees, and suspended cages in which hapless prisoners were kept."[23] At the time, the purpose of jails was mostly to detain individuals awaiting trial, transportation, the death penalty, or corporal punishment. These old jails were not escape-proof, and individuals in charge received additional fees for shackling prisoners. Inmates were not classified according to their special needs, physical conditions were awful, food was inadequate, and there were no treatment rehabilitation programs. In fact, the great prison reformer, John Howard, asserted in 1773 after touring European institutions, that more prisoners died of jail fever than were executed.[24] This statement was regarded as "alarming" considering the fact that executions were very common at the time.

In the 1600s, the Pennsylvania Quakers argued for a more humane form of treatment to those who violated the law. At the time, criminals were exposed to the harsh effects of corporal punishments. Due to the humanitarian contributions left by the Quakers, the Walnut Street Jail was founded in 1790 in Philadelphia. Other jails were built soon after, marking a period of a "more" humanitarian handling of criminal offenders. However, it could be argued that despite these attempts, jails still depicted the worst conditions possible to those unfortunate enough to be incarcerated. In fact, these horrible conditions were best depicted in

1923 by Joseph Fishman, the only federal prison inspector, investigator, and consultant in the United States. In his book, *Crucible of Crime,* Fishman described the jails in the United States at the time. He based these descriptions and evaluations of jails on his visits to 1,500 of these facilities. In his book, he stated that some convicts would ask for a year in prison instead of six months in jail due to the horrible conditions of the jails at the time.[25] Note that prisons, unlike jails, were better facilities since they enjoyed better staff that provided adequate support to inmates.

Fishman's conclusion might be summarized by his definition of jail as:

> An unbelievably filthy institution in which are confined men and women, serving sentences for misdemeanors and crimes, and men and women not under sentence who are simply awaiting trial. With few exceptions, having no segregation of the unconvicted from the convicted, the well from the diseased, the youngest and most impressionable from the most degraded and hardened. Usually swarming with bedbugs, roaches, lice, and other vermin; has an odor of disinfectant and filth which is appalling; supports in complete idleness thousands of able-bodied men and women, and generally affords ample time and opportunity to assure inmates a complete course in every kind of viciousness and crime. A melting pot in which the worst elements of the raw material in the criminal world are brought forth blended and turned out in absolute perfection."[26]

Today, jails have changed their physical appearance dramatically, although they still suffer from inadequate funding and inadequate resources. In large cities like Miami, jails often blend with suburban neighborhoods in their design, which makes them appear as if they are large corporate offices. Despite this, residents of these suburban neighborhoods often plead for legislators to advocate the moving of these facilities to other locations in an attempt to "save" the integrity of the community. Although most modern jails do not require inmates to wear uniforms, more and more facilities are beginning to change this policy by requiring inmates to wear the classic jail uniform of black and white stripes. This is becoming more evident as the public demands the implementation of more sanctions to jail inmates.

Jail Populations

In general, it can be said that jail populations are characterized by a high rate of turnover and that the population is more heterogeneous than the populations of other types of facilities for incarceration. Jails are occupied by persons awaiting trial, witnesses being held for trial, and convicted persons serving short sentences—men and women, adults and juveniles included. Most of the convicted inmates are serving sentences for the commission of misdemeanors rather than felonies. Misdemeanors are the less serious types of offenses, such as disorderly conduct, prostitution, and public drunkenness. Sentences for such violations are generally short, usually less than one year. The more serious offenders, who are called felons, have been convicted of felonies—the more serious kinds of offenses, such as murder, armed robbery, and rape. Such persons generally receive sentences for longer than a year and are confined in prisons or similar institutions, not in jails. Today's emphasis on crime control has prompted inmates to receive longer sentences, thus overcrowding both jail and prison facilities.

The popularity of imprisonment as a preferred form of punishment is evident in the growth of jail inmates. The Bureau of Justice Statistics (BJS) conducted the first national jail census in 1970. Since then, the BJS has conducted a jail census in 1972, 1978, 1983, 1988, and 1993. It has been reported that since

T A B L E **5.1** Jail Population, 1980–1995

Year	Jail Population	Year	Jail Population
1980	182,288	1988	341,893
1981	195,085	1989	393,303
1982	207,853	1990	403,019
1983	221,815	1991	424,129
1984	233,018	1992	441,781
1985	254,986	1993	455,500
1986	272,736	1994	479,800
1987	294,092	1995	499,300

Source: Bureau of Justice Statistics Correctional Surveys (The National Probation Data Survey, National Prisoner Statistics, Survey of Jails, and The National Parole Data Survey).

1990, the number of jail inmates per 100,000 U.S. residents has risen from 163 to 212. Since 1990, there has been a yearly increase of 9.4 percent in the jail population—this constitutes nearly twice the average annual increase of 4.9 percent since 1990. In 1997, jails responded to the increasing number of inmates by adding 19,713 beds during the previous twelve months, bringing the total rated capacity to 581,733. Furthermore, from 1992 through 1994, jails increased the number of part-time and full-time employees by 9.9 percent. In 1997, the twenty-five largest jail jurisdictions held 27 percent of all jail inmates in the United States. The largest jurisdictions, Los Angeles County and New York City, accounted for 7 percent of the national total of jail inmates.[27] The growth of the jail population (since 1980) is further illustrated in table 5.1.

Administration of Jails

Typical American jails are very small and were built between 1880 and 1920. Most of these facilities have been exposed to very little or no renovation. They are located in small towns that are, in many cases, the county seat of a predominately rural county. These small, rural jails make up the majority of jails but house only a minority of the jail population. Some of these jails are seldom used and are rarely crowded. This is not the case in urban settings, where jails are often crowded and are subject to numerous lawsuits.

The typical jail is locally financed and administered, which inevitably involves the administration of the jail in local politics. Throughout history, American jails have been under the direction and supervision of the sheriff, who is usually an elected official. For the most part, these administrators have shown little interest in jail inspections or improvements. However, that trend has changed since the 1980s when the American Correctional Association sponsored the Commission on Accreditation for Corrections. This commission not only developed standards for jails, but it also certifies those that meet such standards. This has led to a movement in which states have assumed partial control of their jails, thus establishing minimum standards. Despite this, today's jails suffer from limited budgets that are often under a fee system—the costs of food, housing, and services are averaged and a specific amount is allocated to the sheriff's department. This practice results in poor jails that often experience inadequate food, lack of inmate support, and poor services.

Staffing of Jails

Today's jails face serious staffing problems. For the most part, staff members receive low pay and usually have very little or no training for working with the incarcerated. As mentioned earlier, most jails have low budgets because they are considered the lowest priority of local governments that often have less money to spend than do state or federal governments. Jails are sometimes administered by law enforcement officials who adhere to a law-abiding administrative approach while ignoring any rehabilitative goal. Since the 1970s, jails have been largely understaffed. A 1970 jail survey revealed an average of 1.6 full-time staff per jail working during any given shift, and that person would (on the average) have to supervise about forty inmates. This phenomenon has continued in the 1990s despite the increases in funding for some local jails. The absence of adequate jail supervision has had numerous effects on the inmate population, including an increase in the rate of jail violence.

Due to budgetary constraints, jails have few professional staff members, including medical personnel. The irony of jails is that most of their population is often in need of medical, psychiatric, and social care. Inmates are often drug addicts; they may suffer from venereal diseases, and some are HIV positive. This presents even greater problems for jail administrators who are constantly avoiding legal challenges introduced by inmates. Under the Civil Rights Act of 1971 (codified as 42 U.S. Code 1983), employees in jails may be held legally liable for their actions. This provision includes wardens, who are also liable for the actions of their employees. Many critics of this legislation have argued that inmates have an open door to sue the jails and their administrators. Statistics have proven these critics right—inmates often sue on every conceivable aspect of incarceration, including among others, the "poor" quality of food.

The present wave of inmate lawsuits is in many ways inherited by previous judicial action that emphasized the need for change in jail facilities. In the not-so-distant past, an initiative was taken by the federal courts in their rulings that certain deprivations of medical care constitute cruel and unusual punishment. Such rulings led the Law Enforcement Assistance Administration (LEAA), which ceased to exist in 1982, to appropriate $902,000 to the National Sheriff's Association, the American Correctional Association, and local and state medical societies of the American Medical Association for a project to develop standards to improve health care in jails and prisons.[28]

In addition to the predicaments mentioned previously, another problem facing jails today is the conflict that exists between professional and nonprofessional jail staff. Robert G. Culbertson pointed out that the primarily custodian-oriented jail personnel view with suspicion the court decisions regarding the rights of jail inmates as well as the attempts on the part of state departments of corrections to place correctional personnel in jails. This problem, combined with inadequate numbers of personnel, creates predicaments, one of which is "role overload." "The role occupant finds it impossible for him to complete all the tasks requested by various people. He is placed in a position whereby he must deny some of the requests, creating conflict, or be taxed beyond the limits of his abilities." When that occurs, one might expect that the personnel, to avoid the problems of role overload, will seek ways in which to reduce the conflict. One of those ways might be to ignore the requests that come from treatment personnel. "The consequence again, is the escalation of conflict between rehabilitation and custody personnel."[29]

The New Generation Jail

Despite the fact that some jail cells are old, an unprecedented wave of jail constructions has taken place in the past few years. It is estimated that the construction of jails can cost as much as $100,000 per cell. However, those who follow these statistics closely argue that it is more expensive to run the facilities than to build them.

Most of the new jails under construction follow a different philosophy of design and management than that of the old jails. The new jails are designed in a way to improve the staff's ability to manage the inmate population. The new generation jails, as they are often called, are built upon three architectural concepts: **podular design, interaction space,** and **personal space.**

Podular units are self-contained living areas that house approximately twelve to twenty-four inmates. These units are composed of single-occupancy rooms for inmates and a common multipurpose dayroom to interact recreationally. Podular units are also characterized by living areas with comfortable furniture, porcelain lavatories, tile and carpet floor coverings, and windows. The pods are equipped with radios, telephones, outdoor exercise areas, and televisions. All daily activities (i.e., meal service, recreation, visitations, mail distribution, and clothing exchange) occur within the pod.[30]

The design of the new generation jail is based on the philosophy that an environment will be provided in which normative, civilized behavior of inmates housed in podular units is expected. In addition, each living area is designed for the purpose of enhancing the observation and communication (i.e., interaction) between inmates and staff members. This management philosophy, which is referred to as **direct supervision,** is one of the most crucial components of the new generation jail philosophy. It makes reference to a method of correctional supervision in which one or several jail officers are stationed inside the living area and, thus, are in direct contact (i.e., interaction) with those housed in the pod.

This new management philosophy is slowly becoming accepted by jail practitioners in the United States. This is the case, in part, due to the reported success of the effectiveness of the operation and design of these new jails as they aim at reducing negative inmate behavior. Today, longitudinal studies are being conducted to follow what happens when a traditional jail makes the transition to a podular, direct supervision facility.[31]

Trends and Profiles of Jail Inmates

As stated previously, the number of jail inmates has grown to unprecedented proportions in recent years. Since 1985, the nation's jail population has nearly doubled on a per capita basis. This has also been the case among juveniles. On June 30, 1997, an estimated 9,105 persons under age eighteen were housed in adult jails in the United States.[32]

At midyear 1997, male inmates made up 89 percent of the local jail inmate population. This constitutes nearly 3 percentage points less than the number at midyear 1985. However, female inmates increased in numbers. In 1995, female inmates made up 10.2 percent of the local jail inmate population. This constitutes an increase from 8 percent in 1985. On average, the adult female population has grown 9.9 percent every year since 1985, while the adult male inmate population has grown by 6.4 percent yearly. On June 30, 1997, jails were reported to have held nearly one in every 191 adult men and one in every 1,732 women in the United States.[33]

Statistics also suggest that fewer than half of adult jail inmates were convicted. Specifically, on June 30, 1997, an estimated 42 percent of the adult jail inmates in the United States had been convicted on their current charge. An estimated 235,200 of the 558,000 adults held in local jails were serving a sentence in jail, awaiting sentencing, or serving time for a violation of their parole or probation condition. In terms of the race of jail inmates, statistics suggest that at midyear 1997, a majority of jail inmates were African American or Hispanic. White non-Hispanics made up 40.6 percent of the jail population; African American non-Hispanics, 42 percent; Hispanics, 15.7 percent; and those from other races (i.e., Asians, Pacific Islanders, American Indians, and Alaska Natives), 1.8 percent. In relation to the number of U.S. residents, African American non-Hispanics were over six times more likely than white non-Hispanics, over twice as likely as Hispanics, and almost eight times more likely than individuals from other races to have been held in a jail on June 30, 1997.[34] Despite the fact that these statistics are alarming to those concerned with the issue of minority over-representation in jails, one must take into account the fact that some Hispanics may consider themselves to be white and, thus, they may be classified as such. If this is true, the Hispanic inmate population in jails may be greater than that reported by the statistics.

In the literature, both historic and recent, statements indicate that, in general, jails warehouse inmates and provide few services. To add insult to injury, many of those inmates who participate in the few programs offered in jails do so for reasons that do not include self help. However, in some rare cases, inmates regard their participation in these jail services as positive. For instance, an inmate in the Orange Country Jail (Florida) stated:

Jail Services

> I didn't want to participate in any programs, but that was the only way I could get out of 33rd Street [the main facility] into one of the buildings that have open spaces, only two guys to a cell, and good visitation rights. So I wouldn't have taken MRT [a substance abuse education program] if I didn't have to, but I'm glad I did. I learned about myself: I used to blame drugs as the source of my problems, but I learned it's my own attitudes and behavior that's responsible. Once you learn that, other things fall into place. Drug classes I had taken before never did this for me. In the life skills classes, I learned how to write a resume and present myself at a job interview, like sitting up straight. But you have to obey the rules in the program facilities if you want to stay. I've seen guys get busted back to 33rd Street because of shouting matches between inmates, for example. A few come back here again, but then they're careful to behave, because the other facility stinks. There's loud noise that keeps you from sleeping, it's cold, and there's no carpeting, so they like it here much better.

Some jail facilities offer services to treat the medical needs of inmates. They also offer substance abuse services, which are usually running to their maximum capacity. This is mostly due to the fact that substance abusers are being arrested now at greater proportions than before. However, these programs are scarce and often suffer from budgetary constraints. Advocates of these programs urge the funding of more jail services. They base their argument on the fact that many jail inmates have very poor reading skills, few job skills, and substance abuse problems. Thus, they have a hard time finding jobs after they are released from jails, leaving them with few options (one of which is a life of crime). Jail services supporters often quote studies that have found that inmates who improve their educational level during confinement are less likely to reoffend than those who don't. However, these supporters ignore the fact that these studies could be regarded as inconclusive because they do not include the possibility that motivated inmates—who would have done better after release even without the programs—are the ones who improve their basic academic skills. A study of federal inmates that attempted to adjust for this selection bias found that inmates who participated in educational programs were less likely to commit offenses again.[35] Similarly, a study of inmates in Wisconsin concluded that education programs in prison were cost-effective because they reduced recidivism or increased the

Spotlight 5.2

Services Provided by Florida's Orange County Jail

- Structured educational and vocational programs (from adult basic education to carpentry) designed to accommodate the inmate's short stay
- Job readiness and placement services
- Incentives to participate in programming —and to avoid misconduct

- Management of most inmates through direct supervision to contain costs, promote inmate responsibility, and allow for open areas that are often used as classrooms

Source: U.S. Department of Justice, Office of Justice Programs, The Orange County, Florida Jail Educational and Vocational Programs; December, 1997.

amount of time before released inmates returned to prison.[36] Although most prisons include the programs researched in these studies, few jails offer them. This is the case because most jails lack the necessary funding to build suitable classroom space, while at the same time, the population of jail inmates is usually locked up for a brief period of time.

One of the few jail divisions in the United States that overcame these predicaments is the Orange County, Florida, Corrections Division. This division provides intensive educational and vocational services to its 3,300-bed jail. This jail is the ninth largest in the United States.[37] When these services began to be implemented, dramatic changes were made in how the jail was run. Today, the entire jail revolves largely around its educational and vocational programs. Spotlight 5.2 illustrates the major services offered by the Orange County Jail.

Each of the services mentioned in Spotlight 5.2 forms a part of a comprehensive corrections strategy aimed at saving the county money while keeping inmates occupied and out of trouble. The hope is that this strategy will ultimately reduce recidivism. It is also important to note that all of the services provided by jail facilities are supposed to be administered to all inmates without regard to their ethnicity, socioeconomic status, religious affiliation, or any other prejudice that may exist. Unfortunately, this is not always the case. On March 12, 1998, the *Chicago Tribune*[38] reported that favoritism was shown to the famous actor Robert Downey, Jr. in a California jail. In its report, the *Chicago Tribune* argues that some of the favoritism given to Downey included a film furlough that allowed him to travel via a shuttle to a Hollywood studio as he put the finishing touches on a movie he was working on. In another instance, Downey was allowed to leave jail to visit his plastic surgeon due to an altercation with another inmate that left him with a facial wound. Other less notorious jail inmates are given preferences based on the color of their skin, among other factors. One of the biggest hurdles that may impede the implementation of programs such as those offered at the Orange County Jail is the overcrowding of inmates in the correctional system.

As was evident from the previous discussion of jail trends, jails in some areas of the country have not been exempted from the evils associated with inmate overcrowding. In fact, as demonstrated earlier, these jails are almost running at their full capacity. This problem is exacerbated by the overcrowding predicament of prisons that seems to get worse every day. Prisons are, at times, transferring inmates to jails so they can serve the remainder of their sentences.

Thus, jail administrators are faced with yet one more challenge—that of a "new," experienced inmate. It can only be speculated that the trend of prison and jail overcrowding will continue its current path of growth. States such as Missouri have had to hire private prisons in other states to handle some of their correctional clientele. This trend will continue to harm programs offered in jails, and at a time when offenders in need of the programs are being incarcerated and monetary allocation continues to decline.

WiseGuide Wrap-Up In this chapter, we examined the handling of the accused after arrest and before trial. It was argued that this may be one of the most crucial periods in the entire criminal justice process. A person detained in jail will probably be adversely affected by the experience. But if the person is released, society may be endangered. This time is also the period during which the accused, with his or her attorney, is preparing for trial.

We began our discussion with the system of bail, whose purpose is to secure the presentence of the accused at trial. We noted, however, that judges often use bail for preventive detention without statutory authority. We looked at various attempts to reform the bail system. We also considered pretrial detainees, especially their constitutional rights as determined by the U.S. Supreme Court. We then turned to a discussion of jails, beginning with a history of the use of jails as a form of social control. In the discussion of jails, we examined various characteristics of today's jail system, including the population increase in jails, the administration and staffing of jail inmates, the new generation of jails, the trends and profiles of jails, as well as the services provided by jails in the United States. Hopefully, this discussion has provided you with a comprehensive understanding of the functions performed by the systems of bail and jail in the United States.

Notes

1. *Powell v. Alabama,* 287 U.S. 45, 57 (1932).
2. *Stack v. Boyle,* 342 U.S. 1, 5 (1951).
3. CNN, December 19, 1997.
4. National Institute of Justice. *Report to the Nation on Crime and Justice.* (Washington, DC: U.S. Department of Justice, 1998), p. 76.
5. See Forrest Dill. "Discretion, Exchange and Social Control: Bail Bondsmen in Criminal Courts," *Law and Society Review* 9 (Summer, 1975), 639–674.
6. *Pannell v. U.S.,* 320 F. 2d 698, 699 (1963), (Judge Skelley Wright, concurring).
7. Clear, Todd, and Cole, George. *American Corrections.* (Belmont, CA: Wadsworth Publishing Co., 1997).
8. Ares, Charles E., Rankin, Anne, and Sturz, Herbert. "The Manhattan Bail Project," *New York University Law Review* 38 (January, 1963), 68. See this article, which is the basis for the comments in this section, for a more detailed discussion of the project.
9. National Advisory Commission on Criminal Justice Standards and Goals. *Corrections.* (Washington, DC: U.S. Government Printing Office, 1973), p. 103.
10. "Burger Seeks Study of Bail Releases in Major Crime," *The New York Times* (February 12, 1979), p. A14, col. 3.
11. *The New York Times* (May 5, 1977), p. A19, col. 1.
12. Bureau of Justice Statistics. *Pretrial Release and Detention: The Bail Reform Act of 1984.* (Washington, DC: U.S. Department of Justice, February, 1988), p. 2. The Bail Reform Act is codified in U.S. Code, Chapter 18, Sections 3141 et. Seq. (1994).
13. Bureau of Justice Statistics. *Pretrial Release and Detention: The Bail Reform Act of 1984.*
14. *Bell v. Wolfish,* 441 U.S. 520 (1979).
15. *Bell v. Wolfish.*
16. *Bell v. Wolfish.*
17. *U.S. v. Salerno,* 481. U.S. 739 (1987), remanded, 829 f. 2d. 345 (2d circ, 1987) cases and citations omitted.
18. *U.S. v. Salerno,* no. 86–87.
19. U.S. Department of Justice. Bureau of Justice Statistics, 1988. *Jail Statistics.*
20. U.S. Department of Justice. Bureau of Justice Statistics, 1988. *Jail Statistics.*
21. Mattick, Hans. "The Contemporary Jails in the United States: An Unknown and Neglected Area of Justice," in Daniel Glaser, ed., *Handbook of Criminology.* (Skokie, IL: Rand McNally, 1974), p. 781.

22. *Rhem v. Malcolm,* 371 F. Supp. 594 (1974). On appeal, the "findings of fact and conclusions of law that various conditions at the Tombs are unconstitutional" was affirmed, but the case was remanded for "further consideration . . . of the relief to be granted." 507 F. 2d 333, 342 (1974).

23. Flynn, Edith Elisabeth. "Jails and Criminal Justice," in Lloyd E. Ohlin, ed., *Prisoners in America.* (Englewood Cliffs, NJ: Prentice-Hall, 1973), chap. 2, p. 49.

24. Hall, Jerome. *Theft, Law and Society.* (Boston: Little, Brown and Company, 1935), p. 108. See also John Howard, *State of Prisons,* 2d. ed. (Warrington, England: Patterson Smith, 1792).

25. Fishman, Joseph F. *Crucible of Crime: The Shocking Story of the American Jail.* (New York: Cosmopolis Press, 1923), p. 82.

26. Fishman, *Crucible of Crime,* pp. 13–14.

27. U.S. Department of Justice. Bureau of Justice Statistics, 1998. *Jail Statistics.*

28. LEAA Newsletter 6 (June-July, 1977), p. 6.

29. Culbertson, Robert G. "Personnel Conflicts in Jail Management," *American Journal of Correction* 39 (March-April, 1977), 29.

30. Bayens, Gerald J., Williams, Jimmy J., and Smykla, John Ortiz. (1997). Jail Type Makes a Difference: Evaluating the Transition from a Traditional to a Podular, Direct Supervision Jail Across Ten Years. *American Jail Magazine.*

31. For more information, see Bayens, Williams, and Smykla. *Jail Type.*

32. Bureau of Justice Statistics (1997). U.S. Department of Justice. *Prison and Jail Inmates.* (January, 1998) by Darrell K. Gillard and Allen J. Beck.

33. Bureau of Justice Statistics. *Prison and Jail Inmates.*

34. Bureau of Justice Statistics. *Prison and Jail Inmates.*

35. Harer, M.D. "Recidivism Among Federal Prison Releases in 1987: A Preliminary Report" Unpublished paper. (Washington D.C., U.S. Department of Justice, Federal Bureau of Prisons, Office of Research Evaluation, March, 1994).

36. Piehl, A.M. "Learning While Doing Time," Unpublished paper. (Cambridge, MA: Harvard University, John F. Kennedy School of Government, April, 1994).

37. Finn, Peter. (1997). The Orange County, Florida, Jail Educational and Vocational Programs. U.S. Department of Justice. Office of Justice Programs. National Institute of Justice.

38. *The Chicago Tribune* (March 12, 1998), p. 2.

Sentencing

Sentencing is one of the most important stages in the criminal justice system. For the offender, it is the culmination of a series of traumatic events in his or her life as well as the determination of how the coming months or years will be spent, or in the case of capital punishment, whether the defendant will be allowed to live. For society, it is a time for decision making that necessitates not only action in a particular case, but recognition of society's philosophy of punishment and rehabilitation. Sentencing is also an extremely time-consuming activity.

Key Terms

determinate sentences
jail confinement
mandatory sentencing
prison confinement
probation
sentencing disparity

Sentencing, broadly defined, includes all of those decisions the court makes with regard to the official handling of a person who pleads guilty or is convicted of a crime. This may include probation, with or without specified restrictions on the behavior of the defendant, imposition of a fine, capital punishment, commitment under a special statute such as a sexual psychopath law, work assignments, restitution to the victim, corporal punishment, incarceration, or a combination of forms of punishment. Due to the frequency with which probation is used, it will be discussed in a later chapter. In this chapter, you are introduced to the concept and philosophy of sentencing, as well as the procedures and trends associated with sentencing. Sentencing strategies are examined for the purpose of providing a better understanding of this complex concept.

The Sentencing Decision

The sentencing decision is, for the most part, exercised by judges. This is the case unless the legislature of a particular jurisdiction has removed all judicial discretion. Also, in some serious cases, juries have sentencing power. However, it is important to mention that in some cases, the judge is not required to follow the sentencing recommendation given by the jury.

Recently, the United States Supreme Court examined the issue of jury input in two states—Alabama and Florida. When examining the system used by the state of Alabama, the U.S. Supreme Court declared that the Alabama system did not deny the defendant's Eighth Amendment rights.[1] Alabama's system is based on the principle that the trial judge is to consider the sentence issued by the jury, but the weight the judge places on the recommendation is not specified. After examining the system used in the state of Florida, the U.S. Supreme Court declared (in *Proffitt v. Florida*) that the existing capital punishment procedures were constitutional.[2]

In general, the U.S. Supreme Court has upheld the Arizona plan, which makes provisions establishing that after an individual is found guilty of first-degree murder, a different sentencing hearing needs to be conducted before the court to determine whether to impose life imprisonment or the death penalty. This statute refers to specific factors that must be considered for and against leniency when making that particular decision.[3]

In instances when the jury exercises sentencing power, the judge issues instructions to the jury regarding the law and its application to sentencing. As we will discuss in a subsequent chapter, several factors are taken into consideration when the sentencing decision is made. Although some of these factors may be designated by statute, some states have formalized and restricted their usage.

Sentence Disparity

In the past, it was the responsibility of judges to determine criminal sentences. They considered all of the facts of a specific criminal case, including, but not limited to, the circumstances of the offense and the life history of the offender, with the aim of choosing a sentence they regarded as fair. The only legal requirement for judges to meet was that the sentence was within a statutory range. It is important to note that this requirement was not too strict in that the ranges that existed were often extremely broad. In fact, statutes typically authorized sentences like "not more than five years," or in some instances, "any term of years or life."[4] The bottom line was that judges could impose any sentence as long as it was within the range specified by the statutes. In the mind of many, this gave judges too much discretionary power.

Once the sentence was imposed and the person was in prison, it was up to the parole board to determine the actual release date. Among the circumstances considered by the parole board were the individual's behavior in prison and the efforts made toward his or her rehabilitation. For the most part, parole boards released people when they thought they were ready. In most cases, this occurred after just half of the individual's sentence had been completed. If for some reason the released person did not behave as expected, parole could be revoked and incarceration became the only option.

In the 1970s, discretionary sentencing became strongly opposed as a result of the disparity in sentencing.[5] A large number of judges were found to sentence similar offenders differently, while a great deal of power was acquired by parole boards. In fact, the sentence disparity became so extreme that offenders were often serving different sentences in prison despite the fact that their offenses and backgrounds were similar. Thus, there was a strong accumulation of evidence that suggested that the system led to arbitrary decision making and sometimes discrimination against poor individuals, including members of minority groups.

Sentencing disparity is based on the concept that offenders with similar backgrounds and similar offenses may receive different sentences with no reasonable justification. In his book, *The Rich Get Richer and the Poor Get Prison,* Jeffery Reiman argued that it is a "simple fact that the criminal justice system reserves its harshest penalties for its lower-class clients and puts on kid gloves when confronted with a better class of crook."[6] In addition to Reiman's arguments, various studies have been conducted to measure whether sentence disparity does indeed exist. All of the studies concluded that not only does it exist, but it occurs more frequently than expected. We will explore some of these studies and the contributions they have made to the literature in regard to the sentencing disparity issue.

D'Alessio and Stolzenberg studied a random sample of 2,760 offenders who had been committed to the care of the Florida Department of Corrections in 1985. Despite the fact that they did not find any sentence disparity for poor offenders found guilty of property crimes, they found that poor offenders received longer sentences for violent crimes and narcotics possession.[7] Others have made similar findings. Chiricos and Bales found that unemployed defendants with similar records who were found guilty of similar offenses were more likely to be incarcerated while awaiting trial and for longer periods than were employed defendants. Furthermore, these authors also found that these unemployed defendants were more than twice as likely as their employed counterparts to be incarcerated upon a guilty finding.[8]

Other studies have explored the question of whether or not criminal justice officials' discretionary choices in the application of **mandatory sentencing** laws are made in a racially neutral manner. Results of these studies are particularly relevant. A study done by Meierhoefer, which involved cases of federal offenders, examined whether sentencing severity varied by the amount and type of drugs involved in the current crime, the use of weapons, and the defendant's offense record, role in the offense, history of drug use, age, gender, and race.[9] Meierhoefer found sentencing differences associated with the offender's race, even after taking into consideration differences associated with these other traits. Despite this, it is important to note that the magnitude of this difference was small.

In addition, the U.S. Sentencing Commission expanded this study and found that there were significant differences in the proportion of whites (54 percent), Hispanics (57 percent), and African Americans (68 percent) who received mandatory minimum sentences for the most serious offense they had been charged with.[10] Interestingly, a reanalysis of the data used by the U.S. Sentencing Commission in 1991 gave rise to a different conclusion.[11] In fact, the reanalysis showed that when legally relevant case-processing factors were considered, a defendant's race and ethnicity were not related to the sentence imposed.

In 1995, this same commission reached a different conclusion than the one made earlier. The U.S. Sentencing Commission reassessed the sentencing disparity between crack and powder cocaine offenses. These sentences were created in 1986 by the United States Congress when it enacted mandatory minimum sentences for cocaine and crack trafficking—the sale of 5 grams of crack or 500 grams of powder cocaine is punishable by a mandatory minimum sentence of five years in federal prison. Consequently, the sale of 50 grams of crack or 5,000 grams (5 kilos) of powder cocaine is subject to a mandatory minimum of ten years in federal prison. In addition, by 1988, Congress enacted a five-year mandatory minimum prison term for possession of more than 5 grams of crack. The same law mandated a maximum of one year in prison for first-time offenders who were convicted of possession of any other drug, including powder cocaine.[12] It was on these laws that the U.S. Sentencing Commission based its findings in 1995. In its 242-page report, the commission details the disparate impact that crack sentences have had on African Americans and makes recommendations for changes in the current sentencing strategy. Specifically, the report found that over 88 percent of those sentenced for crack offenses were African Americans, while only 4.1 percent of those sentenced for that same offense were white. This is the case, according to the commission, despite the fact most of those who use crack are white (52 percent) while 38 percent of users are African Americans.[13] The commission's recommendations involved (1) establishing methods within the guidelines' structure to deal with the crimes of possession and distribution of both crack and powder cocaine; (2) revisiting the 100-to-1 ratio (100 grams of crack or powder cocaine equals one year in prison); and (3) reassessing the penalty structure for simple possession. The recommendations were turned down by several officials, including President Clinton. In a statement, Clinton said that "we have to send a constant message to our children that drugs are illegal, drugs are dangerous, drugs may cost you your life—and the penalties for dealing drugs are severe." He also added that he was "not going to let anyone who peddles drugs get the idea that the cost of doing business is going down."[14]

In April 1997, the U.S. Sentencing Commission made recommendations suggesting reformation on the disparity between powder cocaine and crack cocaine mandatory sentences.[15] These recommendations, unlike those made in 1995, have not encountered much resistance from officials. This is mostly due to the fact that the recommendations made by the commission in 1997 are based on an effort to compromise with Congress and President Clinton, who were not in agreement with the commission's earlier advice that the 100-to-1 quantity ratio to trigger mandatory penalties for crack and powder cocaine be eliminated. The commission now acknowledges that crack selling should be more harshly punished than powder cocaine selling on a quantity basis. For the five-year mandatory sentence, the commission recommended that the 500-gram powder cocaine trigger be reduced to between 125–375 grams, and that the 5-gram cocaine trigger be raised to between 25–75 grams. Among those who support this latest recommendation is Judge Richard P. Conaboy, chairman of the commission, who states, "The ranges suggested provide Congress the flexibility to make an informed judgement about the appropriate penalties for these two forms of cocaine. . . . We feel strongly, though, that the current policy must be changed to ensure that severe penalties are targeted at the most serious traffickers. Adopting a ratio within the ranges we recommend will more accurately accomplish this purpose."[16]

Despite the lack of resistance by some officials, it is important to note that the recommendations made by the U.S. Sentencing Commission in 1997 have also found criticism among some individuals, including Eric W. Sterling, President of the Criminal Justice Policy Foundation. Sterling has been involved in analyzing drug sentencing in the United States since the early 1980s. He said that "there are at least six reasons why this proposal stinks. First, sentences should not be raised or lowered simply to include or exclude more offenders of a given race. Second, the quantity triggers were established irrationally. The low quantities have no relation to the high level of culpability that Congress wanted to punish in 1986 when it wrote this law. This tinkering does not bring rationality. Three, lowering powder cocaine quantity triggers means more low level cocaine mules, couriers, and look-outs will be subject to kingpin level sentences. Four, more blacks—who remain at the low rungs of the cocaine trafficking ladder—will get long mandatory sentences for powder cases. Five, Federal prosecutors will decline cases they now accept and accept cases they now decline, and the percentage and number of black low level crack defendants will remain largely unchanged. Six, this proposal is offered in the spirit of we have to do something. It will delay real reform."[17] Despite these criticisms, the good news for the commission is that Republicans in Congress, including Senate Judiciary Committee Chairman Orrin Hatch (R-UT), have agreed with the suggestion that there should be an increase in punishment for powder cocaine for low-level dealers. In addition, as stated previously, President Clinton has agreed with the recommendations set forth by the committee and has acknowledged his interest in giving the plan consideration.

It is important to mention that the administration's effort to end sentencing disparity has not stopped in a mere agreement to consider the commission's proposal. In July 1997, Attorney General Janet Reno and Drug Czar Barry McCaffrey recommended to the President that the 100-to-1 disparity between cocaine and crack possessions be reduced to 10-to-1 for federal sentencing purposes. It has been reported that after reviewing the plan, the President endorsed it and directed Reno and McCaffrey to seek congressional approval.[18] This took place in addition to the efforts described earlier, which were made by the U.S. Sentencing Commission for the purpose of modifying some of the disparity that presently exists in sentences. We must take into account that sentence disparity has been in existence for many years and will, in all likelihood, continue to take place. The main difference between the past and present sentence disparity practices is that, in earlier days, it was regarded as part of the judge's "wise" discretion, whereas now it is, for the most part, subject to public outrage. Most conflict criminologists regard sentence disparities as evidence that the criminal justice system is often the source of exploitation and unfair treatment toward the underclass—the most likely group to use the cheapest form of cocaine—crack.[19]

Sentencing Guidelines

In 1984, the U.S. Congress addressed sentence disparity concerns by forming the United States Sentencing Commission with the aim of promulgating the Federal Sentencing Guidelines. The new system curtailed parole and confined sentences imposed by judges into narrow ranges. A few years later, the U.S. Congress enacted the guidelines into law, and in 1989 the U.S. Supreme Court held that this effort was constitutional.[20]

In general, judges who use sentencing guidelines utilize worksheets to calculate a sentence. In many ways, this process has often been associated with the calculation of income taxes using the federal 1040 form. The worksheet used by judges when calculating a sentence is complex and intricate, but in theory it is supposed to guide all judges to the same conclusions. A sample of the worksheet used in the state of Minnesota can be seen in table 6.1. The numbers in italics within the grid represent the range within which judges may impose a sentence. The criminal history of the offender is calculated by adding a point for each prior felony conviction, half a point for each prior conviction including a gross misdemeanor, and one-quarter point for each prior conviction involving a misdemeanor.

T A B L E **6.1** Minnesota Sentencing Guidelines Grid (Presumptive Sentence Length in Months, Effective August 1, 1994)

The italicized numbers within the grid denote the range within which a judge may punish without the sentence being deemed a departure. The criminal history score is computed by adding one point for each prior felony conviction, one-half point for each prior gross misdemeanor conviction, and one-quarter point for each prior misdemeanor conviction.

Severity of Offense (Illustrative Offenses)	Criminal History Score 0	1	2	3	4	5	6 or more
Sale of simulated controlled substance	12	12	12	13	16	17	19 *18–20*
Theft-related crimes ($2,500 or less) Check forgery ($200–$2,500)	12	12	13	15	17	19	21 *20–22*
Theft crimes ($2,500 or less)	12	13	15	17	19 *18–20*	22 *21–23*	25 *24–26*
Nonresidential burglary Theft crimes (over $2,500)	12	15	18	21	25 *24–26*	32 *30–34*	41 *37–45*
Residential burglary Simple robbery	18	25	27	30 *29–31*	38 *36–40*	46 *43–49*	54 *50–58*
Criminal sexual conduct, second degree	21	26	30	34 *33–35*	44 *42–46*	54 *50–58*	65 *60–70*
Aggravated robbery	48 *44–52*	58 *54–62*	68 *64–72*	78 *74–82*	88 *84–92*	98 *94–102*	108 *104–112*
Criminal sexual conduct, first degree Assault, first degree	86 *81–91*	98 *93–103*	110 *105–115*	122 *117–127*	134 *129–139*	146 *141–151*	158 *153–163*
Murder, third degree Murder, second degree (felony murder)	150 *144–158*	165 *159–171*	180 *174–188*	195 *189–201*	210 *204–216*	225 *219–231*	240 *234–246*
Murder, second degree (with intent)	306 *299–313*	326 *319–333*	346 *339–353*	366 *359–373*	386 *379–393*	408 *399–413*	426 *419–433*

Less Serious ⟵ ⟶ More Serious (over Criminal History Score)

Less Serious ↑ More Serious ↓ (Severity of Offense axis)

Source: Minnesota Sentencing Guidelines Commission.

▭ At the discretion of the judge, up to a year in jail and/or nonjail sanctions can be imposed instead of prison sentences as conditions of probation for most of these offenses. If prison is imposed, the presumptive sentence is the number of months shown.

▭ Presumptive commitment to state prison for all offenses.

Note: First-degree murder is excluded from the guidelines by law and is punished by life imprisonment.

In the state of Florida, a similar worksheet is printed and distributed quarterly to clerks of the circuit courts, state attorneys, and probation and parole services field staff. Using an Innovations Incentive Grant of $35,000, Florida contracted an agency to develop a computer system to automate score sheet preparation and to allow for storage and retrieval of offender information. The resulting software, Sentencing Analysis Guidelines Entry System (SAGES), is currently operational in the Florida Department of Correction's mainframe computer. Thus, SAGES is not only available to the Department of Corrections but also to probation/parole field staff as well as half of the state attorneys offices in Florida.[21]

The guidelines assign an offense level to each specific crime—low offense levels for minor crimes and high offense levels to major criminal acts. This offense assignment takes place while the guidelines direct the calculation of the criminal history of each individual defendant. For instance, a person with a clean background starts with zero criminal history points, with a possibility of having points added for the first and each subsequent offense. Thus, the goal of the judge is to "look up on a grid the spot where the offense level intersects the criminal history."[22] The grid automatically assigns light sentences to individuals who have low criminal histories and who commit less serious crimes, while it assigns stiff sentences to those who have long criminal histories and commit severe crimes. The judge then imposes a sentence that is in accordance with the sentencing guidelines grid unless there is a strong reason to depart from this norm.

The concept of the guidelines has been welcomed because it attempts to reduce the high number of cases that have been victims of sentencing disparity. Thus, due to the popularity of these sentence guidelines, they are currently used in the federal system and in approximately one-third of the states. However, as expected, this popularity has met some resistance. In an analysis of the federal sentencing guidelines, researchers found that African Americans received longer sentences than whites, not because of differential treatment by judges, but because they made up the large majority of those convicted of trafficking crack cocaine.[23] In addition, critics argue that the attempt of sentencing guidelines to reduce discretion in sentencing is a failure because the discretionary power has shifted to prosecutors and others in the criminal justice system. However, despite these criticisms, it is important to mention that various jurisdictions use distinct guidelines and have different experiences with them. The overall experience has been that guidelines are representative of an improvement over unfettered federal discretion, but they must be well structured and subject to careful scrutiny to be successful.

Strategies in Sentencing

There are three major sentencing strategies in the United States—indeterminate, determinate, and mandatory sentences. The philosophies of punishment discussed in previous chapters are often represented in the various sentencing strategies. These strategies are often used in combination by some states. Spotlight 6.1 illustrates the major characteristics of each of the three sentencing strategies.

Mandatory Sentences: The "Three-Strikes Law" and "Truth in Sentencing"

"Three-Strikes Law"

Of all of the strategies mentioned earlier, mandatory sentences have gained the most popularity in recent years. Due to the growing conservative public attitude toward crime, many state officials have recently considered proposals to enhance sentencing for adults and juveniles who have been convicted of violent crimes. These sentences usually involve longer prison terms for violent offenders who possess a record of serious crimes. A prominent example of this is the creation of the new form of mandatory sentencing called the "Three-Strikes Law" (and in some jurisdictions, Two-Strikes Law), which by 1994, had been enacted in all fifty states. In general, the Three-Strikes Law is based on the notion that a repeated violent offender will be incarcerated up to life after he or she has been convicted three times for the same violent offense. The state of California was a pioneer in the implementation of this type of mandatory sentence. California Governor Pete Wilson argued that by implementing the Three-Strikes Law, crime would be substantially reduced.

It is not surprising to learn that the implementation of Three-Strikes Laws has resulted in longer prison terms for recidivists than did earlier mandatory minimum sentencing laws. For instance, the state of California's Three-Strikes Law requires that offenders who are convicted of a violent crime, and who have had two prior convictions, serve a minimum of twenty-five years.[25] This same law

Spotlight 6.1

Sentencing Strategies

- **Indeterminate sentence.** This strategy involves specifications of sentence ranges made by the legislature that allow correctional personnel to exercise discretion in determining sentences. This type of sentence usually involves a maximum and a minimum term for each offense, and is based on the rehabilitative ideal. The idea is that a correctional professional will have total discretion to release an offender once the individual has been rehabilitated successfully. Most penal codes with indeterminate sentences dictate a minimum and maximum amount of time to be served in prison (i.e., one–five years, three–ten years, twenty years to life).

- **Mandatory sentence.** This strategy is based on the notion that a sentence must be imposed upon conviction. Mandatory sentences, which often involve incarceration, are usually specified by legislatures (or at times by Congress). These sentences are designed to deny the judge of his or her discretionary powers regarding incarceration. If the sentence dictates a specific prison term, the judge does not have the ability to impose a

different term or an alternative to prison. Mandatory prison sentences are mostly given to violent and habitual offenders, drug offenders, and those who used a weapon in the commission of a crime. An example of this type of sentence is a Massachusetts gun law that mandates a one-year jail term to anyone convicted of possessing an unregistered firearm.[24]

- **Determinate sentence.** As society encourages a punitive approach toward offenders, more support is being given to **determinate sentences.** These sentences mandate fixed periods of incarceration minus any good time credits that offenders may earn. Thus, the release of an inmate is not based on his or her participation in a rehabilitation program offered in prison and is not subject to the discretion of a parole board. Today, as different states adopt intermediate sentencing laws, some have incorporated determinate sentences into penal codes that mandate a specific prison term for a particular crime, while others still allow judges to decide a particular prison sentence from an array of choices.

---

also doubles the prison terms for those offenders who are convicted of a second violent felony.[26] However, it is important to recognize that the Three-Strikes Law varies in breadth. For instance, some stipulate that both of an offender's prior convictions and the current offense should be violent felonies while others require that the offender's prior felonies be violent. Some Three-Strikes laws count only past adult violent felony convictions; others allow consideration of juvenile adjudications for violent crimes.

"Truth in Sentencing"

Another type of mandatory sentencing enhancement is "truth-in-sentencing." Provisions for this type of mandatory sentence are found in the Violent Crime Control and Law Enforcement Act of 1994. Truth-in-sentencing requires that all imprisoned offenders serve at least 85 percent of their sentences and aim at achieving two goals—deterrence and incapacitation. By passing mandatory sentencing laws, legislators are attempting to convey the message that some crimes are considered to be especially grave and that people who commit such crimes deserve, and may even expect, punitive sanctions. The creation of these laws has been attributed to the public outcry for more severe sanctions as a result of high-profile crimes. It can only be expected that such laws will continue to grow in popularity as the fear of crime continues to grow among Americans.

Spotlight 6.2

Tonry's Research Findings on the Impact of Mandatory Sentencing Laws

- Criminal justice officials and practitioners (i.e., police, lawyers, and judges) exercise their discretion in order to avoid the application of the laws they consider unduly harsh.

- Arrest rates for specific crimes decline soon after the implementation of mandatory sentencing laws.

- Dismissal and diversion rates increase at the early stages of case processing after the implementation of sentencing laws.

- For defendants whose cases are not dismissed, plea-bargain rates decline while trial rates increase.

- Sentencing delays increase for convicted defendants.

- The implementation of mandatory sentencing laws has very little impact on the probability that offenders will be imprisoned. This is the case when the effects of declining arrests, indictments, and convictions are taken into consideration.

- In general, sentences become longer and more severe.

Impact of Mandatory Sentencing Laws

Due to the growing popularity of mandatory sentences in recent years, scholars have devoted their attention to the evaluation of these sentences. Most of the evaluations have focused on two types of crimes—those committed with handguns and those related to drugs. It is important to note that drug offenses are most commonly subjected to mandatory minimum penalties in state and federal courts. In terms of crimes committed with handguns, an evaluation of a Massachusetts law that imposed mandatory jail terms for those convicted of possession of unlicensed handguns concluded that the law was not an effective deterrent of gun crime.[27]

Similarly, studies in Michigan[28] and Florida[29] found no evidence that mandatory sentences reduced the number of crimes committed with firearms. Interestingly, other evaluations of mandatory gun-use sentencing in six major cities (Detroit, Tampa, Miami, Jacksonville, Pittsburgh, and Philadelphia) concluded that these mandatory sentences deterred homicide but they did not have the same effect on any other violent crime.[30] Another study of New York's 1973 Rockefeller drug laws did not support the long-held claim that these laws were efficient in deterring drug-related crimes in New York City.[31] It is important to note that although these studies questioned the efficiency of mandatory sentencing laws, a few of them measured the incapacitation effects of these laws.

Studies have also been done in order to assert the impact of mandatory sentencing laws on the criminal justice system. Instead of summarizing each study independently, it is best to refer to the study conducted by Tonry (1987), which summarizes the findings of all of these studies.[32] In general, he found that officials make earlier and more selective arrests, charges, and diversion decisions while bargaining less. Spotlight 6.2 summarizes some of Tonry's findings. Spotlight 6.3 presents the research review that Tonry conducted on the most important studies of mandatory sentencing laws.

Impact of Sentencing on Corrections

In previous chapters, we discussed the purposes of punishment, a subject closely connected to sentencing. The adoption of a punishment philosophy of retribu-

Spotlight 6.3

Tonry's Research Review on the Impact of Mandatory Sentencing Laws

- Mandatory sentences do not achieve certainty and predictability since officials circumvent them if they believe that the results are unduly punitive.

- Mandatory sentencing laws are redundant in regard to proscribing probation for serious cases since such cases are generally disposed of by

sentencing the offender to imprisonment anyway.

- Mandatory sentences are arbitrary for minor cases.

- Mandatory sentences usually result in an unduly severe punishment for a marginal offender.

---

tion or rehabilitation, deterrence or reintegration, incapacitation or reparation, or a combination of these purposes, will affect the nature of sentencing. Such choices will in turn affect corrections. If capital punishment is used frequently, the number of inmates who are incarcerated for long periods of time, perhaps for life, will be reduced. If probation, a form of sentencing in which the offender is placed under supervision in the community and is not incarcerated, is used extensively, persons who would otherwise be incarcerated only for short periods of time will be freed. Any sudden, significant change in the use of probation could seriously affect correctional institutions and the programs they offer. A quick drop in the use of probation could increase the inmate population to even larger proportions. A sudden increase in the use of probation could result in employee layoffs in correctional institutions and reduction in the number of programs, medical care, and so on, of those institutions. Also, a change in the use of one type of sentence over another could change the length of the sentence for those in prison, thus either reducing or increasing the number of inmates incarcerated.

The impact of sentencing on corrections, however, goes beyond the numbers of people who will enter or remain in the correctional system. The goals of sentencing, which are controlled by the judicial branch, may actually be incompatible with those set by professionals in the correctional field. For instance, if sentencing is based on a philosophy of justice or social defense, the implementation of that philosophy will, in some cases, be in conflict with a correctional goal of changing or rehabilitating the offender. The recent strong movement toward viewing punishment (and therefore sentencing) in terms of "just deserts," or retribution, instead of in terms of rehabilitation, is not necessarily the philosophy taken by professionals in the field of corrections. To a large extent, they are still involved with the approach of attempting to change, assist, or resocialize the offender. Whether such goals have been accomplished continues to be a hot topic of debate. This conflict of interest and goals between those in the judicial branch who advocate a punitive sentence and those correctional professionals who support rehabilitation illustrates one of the internal contradictions of the criminal justice system. The struggle between these two components over the "just deserts," or retribution, approach, as compared to the rehabilitation approach, can be expected to continue unless those in corrections abandon the philosophy of rehabilitation. On the other hand, if one takes the position that the new approaches to sentencing have not abandoned the philosophy of rehabilitation, but that they represent only a shift from rehabilitation as a reason or justification for punishment, the conflict may not be so great. This approach might even enhance the goals of corrections if the result is to view corrections only in terms of voluntary programs for offenders. Only those offenders who wish to be "treated" need enter the treatment programs while they are confined, resulting in greater success rates for such programs.

After having examined some of the complexities associated with the sentencing system in the United States, it is time to discuss some of the sentencing trends in recent years—especially those implemented in 1994. Overall, between 1992 and 1994, the number of felony convictions decreased 2 percent in state courts and 5 percent in federal courts. In 1994, state and federal courts together imposed a prison sentence on 46 percent of all of the individuals convicted of a felony offense. Federal courts sentenced 62 percent of felons to prison, and state courts, 45 percent.[33] As stated previously, in 1994, federal courts convicted 39,624 persons of violent, property, drug, and other felonies while state courts convicted 872,218 individuals—bringing a combined U.S. total to 911,842 felons convicted.

In 1994, three types of sentences comprised most of the judgements that were imposed in federal and state courts for felony convictions. These included **prison confinement** (usually for a year or more), **jail confinement** (usually for under a year), and **probation** (this will be discussed in another chapter—for now, it is worth noting that it accounted for most of the sentences that state and federal courts imposed as punishment for a felony conviction). However, it is important to note that state and federal sentences are not entirely comparable, since there are differences between the type of offense processed in state and federal courts.

Interestingly, violent crimes made up 19 percent of felony convictions in state courts but only 7 percent of those in federal courts. Similarly, violent crimes made up 26 percent of state prison sentences but only 10 percent of federal prison sentences. In addition, drug-related offenses comprised 31 percent of all felony convictions in state courts while they made up 41 percent of those in federal courts. Consequently, drug crimes made up 30 percent of state prison sentences but 55 percent of federal prison sentences. When comparing these statistics, it is important to note that individual offense categories differ in state and federal courts. For instance, federal offenses labeled "robbery" are almost entirely bank robberies (approximately 95 percent), while state robbery offenses seldom include those of banks. Similarly, large-scale international drug crime makes up a relatively large fraction of federal drug trafficking cases, but involve few state cases. Federal weapons offenses may entail importation or manufacture of large numbers of weapons, while state weapons-related offenses usually involve a single firearm.[34] These statistics can be confusing. However, they all show that states' criminal justice systems oversee much more activity than does the federal government.

Lately, there has been a great deal of debate regarding the necessary amount of prison time each defendant should receive. In light of this, it is interesting to examine the direction that state and federal courts have taken regarding the length of sentences. Felons sent to state and federal prisons have an average imposed sentence length of approximately six years.[35] It is important to note that while these averages may differ slightly from those in 1990 and 1992, the direction of the changes since 1990 has not been toward either consistently longer or consistently shorter sentences. Unlike the lengths of jail sentences, which for the most part vary little from the seven-month overall national average, prison sentence

Sentencing Trends

Comparison of State and Federal Sentences for Felonies

Average Sentence Length

lengths vary widely from offense to offense. For instance, the average prison sentence for murder is approximately twenty-two years; for rape, thirteen years; for robbery, nine years; for motor vehicle theft, four years; and for drug possession, four years. Interestingly, the only category that exceeds the average prison sentence of six years is that of violent offenses.[36] For the complete listing of lengths of felony sentences imposed by state and federal courts, see table 6.2. When you review these statistics, please note that states, for the most part, impose longer sentences for serious violent offenses. This coincides with the fact that states oversee most of the criminal justice activity, as mentioned earlier.

Sentence Length versus Time Served

As we move toward a more punitive sentencing approach, it is important to examine the relationship between the sentences imposed by the courts and the time actually served by inmates.

The amount of prison time an offender is prescribed at sentencing is almost always longer than the actual amount of time the offender will serve. According to the Bureau of Justice Statistics,[37] there are two primary reasons that explain the main difference between the sentences imposed and the actual time served by inmates:

- Most states, but not the federal system, have a parole board that usually decides the time when a prisoner is released. In those particular states, the sentence imposed is the same as the amount of time the offender serves before being released only if the offender is never paroled. Since almost all offenders are eventually paroled, relatively few serve their entire sentence before release.

- In most states as well as the federal system, inmates can earn early release through time credits for good behavior or special achievements. Furthermore, automatic good-time credits are awarded in many states.

Due to the public outcry demanding that inmates serve longer periods of their sentence, any federal prisoner who is sentenced for a crime committed after November 1987 is subject to the law setting the 85 percent minimum. This federal law is based on the notion that all federal inmates have to serve at least 85 percent of their specified sentence. Obviously, the only exception to this involves those inmates sentenced to life in prison—these prisoners have to serve their sentences in full. By contrast, state inmates are subject to laws that vary from state to state. However, statistics suggest that in 1994, at the state level, rapists served 55 percent of their sentence while drug traffickers served 38 percent of their sentence. If one is to assume that state inmates sentenced in 1994 will serve the same percentage of their sentence as those released in 1994, state felons sentenced in 1994 will serve about two and one-half years (41 percent of a six-year sentence).[38]

In summary, the average federal prison sentence (six and one-half years) and the average state sentence (six years) do not differ substantially. However, newly sentenced federal inmates are expected to serve, on the average, three years longer than do newly sentenced state offenders (five and one-half years versus two and one-half years). One of the reasons for this difference is based on the fact that federal drug traffickers receive longer sentences than those received by state inmates. Also, federal drug traffickers make up over half of all federal prison sentences while serving a larger percentage of their sentence (85 percent) than state offenders who usually serve 41 percent of their sentence.

TABLE **6.2** Length of Felony Sentences Imposed by State
and Federal Courts, by Violent Offenses, 1994

Most Serious Violent Offense	Mean Maximum Sentence Length for Felons Sentenced to Incarceration			
	Total (in months)	Prison (in months)	Jail (in months)	Straight Probation (in months)
Murder/manslaughter [a]				
State and federal	260	267	7	58
State	262	269	7	59
Federal	148	153	8	41
Rape				
State and federal	132	157	7	60
State	133	158	7	60
Federal	69	79	9	48
Robbery				
State and federal	104	115	9	51
State	104	116	9	51
Federal	100	102	8	44
Aggravated Assault				
State and federal	54	79	6	42
State	54	79	6	42
Federal	49	59	6	39
Other Violent Crimes [b]				
State and federal	47	70	6	43
State	47	70	6	43
Federal	93	110	8	39

Source: U.S. Department of Justice, Department of Justice Statistics (July, 1997). *Felony Sentences in the United States, 1994.*

Note: For individuals who received a combination of sentences, the sentence designation was originated from the most severe penalty imposed—prison being the most severe, followed by jail, then probation. All of the mean sentence lengths excluded sentences to death or life in prison.

[a] Includes non-negligent manslaughter

[b] Includes offenses such as negligent manslaughter, sexual assault, and kidnaping

WiseGuide Wrap-Up The sentencing process presents a perplexing problem in the system of criminal justice. On the one hand, some people believe in the philosophy of individualized treatment. But those who hold that philosophy are faced with insufficient knowledge of treatment to implement it successfully. On the other hand, some believe in "justice," along with the realities of current sentencing disparities. There is no easy answer to the question of how to combine "justice" and "individualization." Some discretion must exist, or the system regresses to the mechanical and harsh philosophy of Beccaria, who argued successfully in the eighteenth century that the punishment should fit the crime. It was a philosophy that made sentencing easy. The legislature determined the sentence for each offense, and the court's only function was to determine whether the accused had committed the offense. That system was soon abolished in many countries because it was felt that such "justice" was cold and cruel. It did not take into account mitigating circumstances, which were emphasized by the neoclassical school. In the United States, a philosophy of individualized treatment developed in the twentieth century that was supported by legislatures and recognized by the courts. This philosophy reached its most extreme form in the indeterminate sentence. Recently, this philosophy has come under attack. At the time of this writing, the American Criminal Justice System is experiencing a "get-tough" policy with regard to sentencing. Some states have already returned legislatively to a mandatory sentencing process, and others have started procedures to abolish parole.

In this chapter, we examined several dimensions of the sentencing dilemma. We began with a brief look at the impact that sentencing has had on the system of justice. We also examined the various sentencing strategies developed as a result of the public outcry for a tougher approach toward criminals. We devoted considerable attention to mandatory sentences and the complexities surrounding these types of sentences. We then turned our attention to the characteristics associated with sentencing disparity. In the process of this discussion, we looked at several studies that had been done in recent years for the purpose of determining if there is, in fact, a sentencing disparity and, if so, how severe the problem is. After examining sentencing disparity, we examined the history and function of sentencing guidelines while paying particular attention to the role these have played in reducing the sentencing disparity. We then finalized this analysis of sentences by looking closely at some of the recent trends associated with the sentencing procedures of federal and state courts.

It therefore seems reasonable to conclude that the control, not the abolition, of discretion is one of the main issues associated with sentencing. The legal profession should recognize and accept the challenge of successful control of judicial and prosecutorial discretion, especially as discretion relates to sentencing decisions. Some of the problems of the criminal justice system, however, cannot be solved by the legal profession alone. Society must take responsibility for providing the necessary resources that will enable us to provide adequate legal services for all. We should realistically appraise the total social structure, realizing that the criminal justice system does not exist in isolation from the rest of society. Research must be fostered and supported. The tendency to abandon philosophies, such as treatment, before they have been given a real trial, should be reexamined. Criminology professor Sue Titus-Reid came to the following conclusion in an article that examined the attacks on the indeterminate sentence:

> It is easier to put the offender out of sight than to examine the social structure for cracks. It is easier to punish than to treat. It is easier to abolish the entire system of discretionary sentencing by attacking the abuses than to correct those abuses and provide the resources needed for adequate implementation of the philosophy of individualized sentencing. It is easier to attack the judges for "leniency" than to examine the need to decriminalize the criminal code or to provide sufficient and trained probation and parole officers or adequate community treatment facilities. It is also easier to lose than to win the war against crime.[39]

Notes

1. See *Harris v. Alabama,* 115 S. CT. 1031 (1995), Rehg. denied, 115 S. CT. 1725 (1995).
2. *Proffitt v. Florida,* 428 U.S. 242 (1976).
3. See *Walton v. Arizona,* 497 U.S. 639 (1990), Rehg. denied, 497 U.S. 639 (1990).
4. Coalition for Sentencing Reform. *History of the Guidelines.* (February, 1997).
5. *History of the Guidelines.*
6. Reiman, Jeffery. *The Rich Get Richer and the Poor Get Prison,* 5th ed. (Needham Heights, MA: Allyn & Bacon, 1998).
7. D'Alessio, Stewart J., and Stolzenberg, Lisa. "Socioeconomic Status and the Sentencing of the Traditional Offender," *Journal of Criminal Justice* 21 (1993), 71–74.
8. Chiricos, Theodore, and Bales, William. "Unemployment and Punishment: An Empirical Assessment," *Criminology* 29, No. 4 (1991), 701–24.
9. Meierhoefer, B.S. (1992). "General Effect of Mandatory Minimum Prison Terms." (Washington, DC: Federal Judicial Center, 1992); Meierhoefer, B.S. "Role of Offense and Offender Characteristics in Federal Sentencing," *Southern California Law Review* 66, 1 (November, 1992): 367–404; Meierhoefer, B.S. *General Effect of Mandatory Minimum Prison Terms: A Longitudinal Study of Federal Sentences Imposed.* (Washington, DC: Federal Judicial Center, 1992).
10. U.S. Sentencing Commission. *Federal Sentencing Guidelines: A Report on the Operation of the Guidelines System and Short-Term Impacts on Disparity in Sentencing, Use of Incarceration, and Prosecutorial Discretion and Plea Bargaining.* (Washington, DC: U.S. Sentencing Commission, 1991).
11. Langan, P. *Federal Prosecutor Application of Mandatory Sentencing Laws: Racially Disparate? Widely Evaded?* (Washington, DC: U.S. Department of Justice. Bureau of Justice Statistics, 1992).
12. News Brief. (March, 1995). "U.S. Sentencing Commission Releases Long Awaited Report on Crack/Powder Sentences."
13. News Brief. "U.S. Sentencing Commission."
14. News Brief. (December, 1995). "Clinton Signs Bill to Disapprove of Equalizing Crack Powder Cocaine Sentences."
15. U.S. Sentencing Commission. *Cocaine and Federal Sentencing.* (April, 1997); Mary Pat Flaherty and Joan Biskupic, "Hill Urged to Reduce Gap Between Sentences for Crack and Powder Cocaine," *Washington Post* (April 30, 1997), p. A12.
16. News Brief. (May-June, 1997). "Sentencing Commission Proposes Reduction in Disparity in Powder and Crack Cocaine Sentences."
17. News Brief, "Sentencing Commission."
18. News Brief. (August, 1997). "Reduction in Crack-Powder Cocaine Sentencing Disparity Proposed by Clinton Administration."
19. See Richard Quinney. *The Social Reality of Crime.* (Boston: Little, Brown, 1970), and M. Lynch and W.B. Groves. (1989). *A Primer in Radical Criminology.* (New York: Harrow and Heston).
20. *Mistretta v. U.S.,* 488 U.S., 361 (1989).
21. Sentencing Guidelines. "1994–1995 Annual Report." *The Guidebook to Corrections in Florida,* 1995.
22. Coalition for Sentencing Reform. *History of the Guidelines.*
23. McDonald, D. C., and K. E. Carlson. "Sentencing in the Courts: Does Race Matter? *The Transition to Sentencing Guidelines, 1986–90.* (Washington, DC: U.S. Department of Justice. Bureau of Justice Statistics, 1993).
24. Tonry, Michael. "Mandatory Penalties" in *Crime and Justice,* Vol. 16, Michael Tonry, ed. (Chicago: University of Chicago Press, 1990), p. 243.
25. U.S. Department of Justice. Office of Justice Programs. National Institute of Justice. *Mandatory Sentencing.* (January, 1997).
26. In mid-1996, the California Supreme Court ruled that the state's Three-Strikes Law constituted an undue intrusion on judges' sentencing discretion. State legislative leaders immediately announced plans to introduce legislation that would reinstate the law.
27. Tonry, *Crime and Justice,* p. 243.
28. Loftin, C., Heumann, M., and McDowall, D. "Mandatory Sentencing and Firearms Violence: Evaluating and Alternative to Gun Control." *Law and Society Review,* 17 (1983): 287–318.
29. Loftin, C., and McDowall, D. "The Deterrent Effects of the Florida Felony Firearm Law." *Journal of Criminal Law and Criminology* 75 (1984): 250–259.
30. McDowall, D., Loftin, C., and Wiersema, B. "A Comparative Study of the Preventive Effects of Mandatory Sentencing Laws for Gun Crimes." *Journal of Criminal Law and Criminology* 83, 2 (Summer, 1992): 378–394.
31. Joint Committee on New York Drug Law Evaluation, the Nation's Toughest Drug Law; Evaluating the New York Experience, a Project of the Association of the Bar of the City of New York; the City of New York and the Drug Sentencing Council, Inc., (Washington, DC: U.S. Government Printing Office, 1978).
32. Tonry, Michael. *Sentencing Reform Impacts.* (Washington DC: U.S. Department of Justice, National Institute of Justice, 1987).
33. U.S. Department of Justice. Office of Justice Programs. Bureau of Justice Statistics. *Felony Sentences in the U.S., 1994.* (July, 1997).
34. Dept. of Justice, *Felony Sentences.*
35. Ibid. Dept. of Justice, *Felony Sentences.*
36. Ibid. Dept. of Justice, *Felony Sentences.*
37. Ibid. Dept. of Justice, *Felony Sentences.*
38. Ibid. Dept. of Justice, *Felony Sentences.*
39. Titus-Reid, Sue. "A Rebuttal to the Attack on the Indeterminate Sentence." *Washington Law Review* 51 (July, 1976), 606.

Release from Prison

In the late 1970s, after spending thirty years in prison in Indiana, Ralph Lobaugh was released. The freedom for which he had fought for fourteen years, however, was too much for him. After two months, Lobaugh decided he could not cope with life outside the walls and went back to prison. According to Harold G. Roddy, director of the work-release program in Indiana, Lobaugh "just wanted to live in a cell again and be with his old friends."[1] His case is unusual, but the problems of readjusting to life outside prison walls were so severe that it was concluded, "The real punishment of prisoners begins when they return to society."[2] Although that statement may be extreme, it is clear that if inmates are not prepared for their return to life outside the walls, if they cannot find jobs, and if they face continued discrimination and harassment, their chances of returning to the institution on another charge are greatly increased.

This chapter explores the problems that inmates face upon release from prison, and considers the programs that have been designed to prepare inmates for that release. We begin with a discussion of furlough and work-release programs, which have been designed to provide the inmate with a gradual reentry into society. We then examine prerelease programs within the institutions—programs that do not actually place offenders in the community, but instead attempt to provide them with an opportunity to discuss some of the problems they will encounter. We then move to a discussion of some of the problems inmates most frequently encounter upon release: financial problems, lack of employment, and social concerns.

The last major section of this chapter is devoted to a discussion of parole, the most frequent form of release from prison. We look at parole historically, consider the purposes of parole, and discuss various ways in which parole may be organized. Considerable attention is given to the process of parole decision making and the conditions that may be imposed on the individual on

Key Terms

continuing custody theory
contract theory
due process theory

parole. Parole supervision, both in terms of the services offered to the client as well as the qualifications and functions of parole officers, is discussed. During our discussion of parole revocation, we describe several court cases that have placed limitations on the authority of the state to remove an individual from parole. Finally, we look at attempts to evaluate the success or failure of parole and consider the future of this method of release.

Preparation for Release

Furlough and Work-Release Programs

The regular use of work-release and furlough programs in the United States is very recent, stemming from the provision for these programs in the federal system by the Prisoner Rehabilitation Act of 1965. The first work-release law was the Huber Law, which was passed in Wisconsin in 1913. The next statute, that of North Carolina, was not passed until 1957. The first furlough program was introduced by legislation in Mississippi in 1918. A few states passed laws providing for work release or furloughs prior to 1965, but most of the programs in existence today were established by state laws after the 1965 federal law was passed.

It is necessary to distinguish work-release programs from furlough programs. A furlough allows an inmate to leave the institution once or occasionally for a specified purpose other than work or study. For example, the offender may be given a furlough to visit a sick relative, to attend a family funeral, to look for a job, or for other business reasons. The leave is only temporary, however, and is usually granted for only a short period of time.

In work-release programs, the inmate is released from incarceration to work or attend school. Inmates may participate in work-study, may take courses at an educational institution, or may work at a job in the community. The primary aim of such programs is to allow "selected prisoners to hold normal, productive, paying jobs and returning to the prison for all non-working hours."[3] Work release is also referred to by other names, including day parole, outmate program, day work, daylight parole, free labor, intermittent jailing, and work furlough.

State legislation varies in terms of who decides whether an inmate should be put on work release. State legislation also differs with regard to how the money earned by the inmate is to be used. Most legislation permits states to contract with other political subdivisions for housing of inmates because they cannot always find work near the institution. Some states provide halfway houses, a nonconfining residential facility designed for the purpose of readjusting offenders to the community after incarceration, while others use county jails.

Among the conditions for outside employment are that inmates cannot work in areas where there is a surplus of labor; they must be paid the same wage as others receive for the same job; if a union is involved, it must be consulted; and the releasee cannot work during a labor dispute.

Evaluation

The first and perhaps most important advantage of these programs is that they place the offender in contact with his or her family and the community. In the past, several studies have shown that "those inmates with strong family ties, and who have maintained those ties during incarceration, are more successful on release than those offenders without such ties."[4] Work-release programs enable offenders to engage in positive contact with the community, assuming, of course, that work placement is satisfactory. It also permits men and women (most of the programs have been for male inmates) to support, to some extent, themselves and their families. This can eliminate the self-concept of failure that may be the result of the loss of the supportive role that is so important in American society. The offender may also obtain more satisfying jobs than the prison could provide. Work-release and furlough programs provide a transition for the incarcerated inmate—from a closely supervised way of life in prison to a more independent life within society. These programs also give the community a transition period during which it accepts the offender back into society. Finally, the programs have permitted some states to close one or more correctional facilities, thus decreasing the cost to the taxpayer. However, it is important to mention that the popularity of these benefits has been obscured lately by the public's demand that inmates serve most, if not all, of their prison sentence.

A study of the work furlough program was conducted in San Mateo County, California. It involved 201 men with an accumulation of thirty-two years in jail sentences and twenty-seven years in prison terms. It reported that "not only is work furlough effective in overall terms, but the positive effects of the program are felt more strongly during the immediate post-release period when recidivism rates are the highest . . . the major finding . . . is that work furlough is most beneficial to those having the highest risk of failure after release."[5]

Others have questioned the findings that work release is effective, usually citing the problems with methodology in the samples. Gordon P. Waldo and Theodore G. Chiricos, in their classic review of the studies of work release, maintain that most of those who favor such programs "have ignored both theoretical premise and empirical evidence in asserting" the advantages of work release.[6] Based on their own study of the effects of work release, in which they used random assignments of subjects to both the control and experimental groups, Waldo and Chiricos concluded:

> At this initial point in our analysis, it would appear that participation in work release has no bearing on the rates of recidivism for all subjects in the present inquiry. In short, there is no evidence that participation in work release makes any difference in recidivism, regardless of the operational definition of recidivism or the control variables utilized.[7]

Another study, however, found that work release is effective with some male offenders who have been incarcerated in a minimum security facility. "The best predictors of success on work release were the level of institutional adjustment immediately before entering the program, whether the inmate had been convicted of auto theft, history of drug use, and age at first arrest." Conviction of auto theft, as well as early age at first arrest, were considered to be indicative of an impulsiveness that would not be conducive to success on work release.[8]

Work-release programs face two basic problems: (1) selecting inmates to enter the program; and (2) finding jobs in the community. Three investigators who studied work release in Virginia concluded that the literature has given no indication that the most appropriate people are being selected for such programs. They referred to a system devised after 120 variables were analyzed on a sample of 879 male work-release participants in the District of Columbia. Analysis indicated that seventeen of those variables were highly predictive of success in the program. The instrument was not used, however, "due to apparent administrative uncertainty and changing philosophies." The Virginia study found eight variables to be predictive of success. Like many studies, however, this one did not involve a comparison of a control group of persons not participating in work release.[9]

Problems with Work Release and Furloughs

The second basic problem of work-release programs is finding a job for the offender. Normally, the offender must have a job before work release will be granted. Most incarcerated persons do not have good work records. Many people are reluctant to hire offenders, making the job hunt even more difficult.[10]

Some additional problems with work release are related to the offender-participants in the programs. The releasees may have problems in adjusting to the community during the day and then to the institution at night. It might be easier to make the break with the institution completely and attempt to readjust to society without having to return to prison. Release during the day may eliminate or interrupt participation in some prison programs that are beneficial to the offender. Problems may arise over use of the money earned. Transportation is often a problem because many correctional institutions are not located in urban areas where inmates are most likely to find jobs.

Inmates on furloughs experience many challenges, much in the same way as those on work-release programs. One of these challenges is based on the notion that some offenders on furloughs may decide to escape once given the opportunity. In fact, it is hard to believe that an inmate will not at the very least, contemplate escaping, especially after being subjected to the rigors of prison and then given the opportunity to be temporarily free from any correctional supervision. Thus, the danger of furloughs lies in that the offender may violate the terms specified in the furlough program and escape. Despite the careful selection of inmates to participate in this program, some do escape, or attempt to escape, although most studies indicate that the rates are very low. However, when inmates do escape, the possibilities of recidivism are very high.[11] Another predicament is that once an inmate has been granted temporary freedom via a furlough, it is extremely difficult to readjust back to the rigors of prison life, creating a second prisonization process. Finally, furloughs represent a political risk to those who grant them. If an inmate decides to escape while on furlough, the public may interpret the policy as being "soft on crime"—a political deficiency in today's punitive society.

Prerelease Programs

Use of furloughs and work-release programs is limited by staff, resources, and the possibility that some offenders will commit crimes while participating in the programs. Consequently, not all offenders may participate. All offenders must, however, be released when they have served their court-imposed sentences. Prerelease programs have been developed to assist offenders in making the adjustments back to life in the community.

It has long been recognized that most offenders who eventually commit more crimes do so within a very short period of time after release. This suggests that immediate adjustment problems might be quite severe for offenders. It was not until the 1940s that prison officials began to develop programs *within* their institutions aimed at assisting inmates with these adjustment problems.[12]

In Iowa, a prerelease program began in 1962 for inmates scheduled to be released from the state penitentiary at Fort Madison. Most of the men had been in prison at least three years, and one had been incarcerated for eleven years. They were taught how to dress, how to tie a tie, what kind of clothes to wear for a job interview, and what to say to a prospective employer. They were also instructed in the rules and regulations of parole, the role of public welfare agencies, communication skills and social graces, community and family adjustment problems, law enforcement, and traffic safety. One inmate described these programs as "the decompression chamber before you get into the pressure cooker."

The Texas Department of Corrections began a prerelease program in 1963. Volunteers, businesspeople, and others talked to the inmates about subjects of interest in potential problem areas. In addition to the topics just mentioned, they discussed how to keep a job, problems of social security, legal problems, motor vehicle operation, income tax, credit, human relations, insurance, veterans benefits, personal and religious habits, and personal health. It was reported that fourteen months after the beginning of the program, the measured recidivism rate of those who participated in the program was 10 percent, compared to 33 percent for inmates released during the five years preceding the adoption of the program.[13]

A study at the United States Penitentiary in Lewisburg, Pennsylvania suggested that prerelease programs need to adopt part of the philosophy of Alcoholics Anonymous. That is, inmates need to recognize that they must want help, they do not want to be recommitted, and they accept the fact that release to the community will present problems. This prerelease program involved three types of programs: mandatory considerations (legal problems, rules of supervision, and so on); planning and resources (employment information, job responsibilities, financial planning, community resources, and so on); and emotional factors (race relations, attitude problems, and so on). Attendance was required at some, but not all, meetings. Special sessions were held on clothing, alcoholism, and other topics.

Inmates who participated in the program at Lewisburg were asked to complete a questionnaire ninety days prior to leaving the institution and again six months after their release. In the prerelease questionnaire, the main interest expressed by inmates was in finding a job, having money to meet their needs, and staying out of trouble. But in the group meetings of the prerelease program, they had additional concerns—being accepted by others, relationships with police, and so on. The post-release questionnaire revealed that the predominant problems were in the areas of employment, finances, and becoming adjusted to a free society. Two-thirds of the releasees thought the prerelease program had helped, but said that group sessions should have been longer because the individuals profited most by discussing problems with others who were also soon to be released. Respondents said that the most valuable things they received in prison were job training, academic improvement, and better understanding of interpersonal relationships.[14] Today, the effectiveness of prerelease programs remains unclear. A consensus, however, does exist in the belief that the absence of these programs would result in even more extreme overcrowded conditions for the prison system.

Halfway Houses: Traditional Prerelease Centers

Halfway houses are often used as transitions from prison to the community, and they have a long history. The earliest documentation of a proposal for a halfway house in this country was in 1817 in the Commonwealth of Massachusetts, but the first one actually established was the "Temporary Asylum for Discharged Female Prisoners" in 1864 in Boston. Not many followed, however, until 1950, when the disenchantment with rehabilitating persons within prisons began to gain momentum. In the 1950s, a movement to develop halfway houses began; it grew during the 1960s with the formation of the Halfway House Association.[15]

Traditionally, there have been two types of halfway houses: (1) places for released persons to receive assistance in adjusting to the community—a general purpose residence; and (2) places for specific problems of adjustment, such as drug treatment centers. The Shaw Residence in Washington, D.C., which was regarded as one of the general purpose types, has been known to provide assistance to people released from the Federal Bureau of Prisons. It operates like a real family home. Residents are given financial counseling assistance and help in adjusting to an independent life. For example, they are encouraged to spend weekends away from the residence.

Halfway Programs: Prerelease Guidance Centers

In the early 1960s, the Federal Bureau of Prisons opened six prerelease centers where prisoners could serve out the last few months of their sentences while becoming adjusted to the community. Some were located in YMCA facilities—in these centers, offenders ate in the cafeteria and used the recreational facilities. They usually traveled to the prerelease center by public transportation and without escort. Offenders were confined to the center for a few days of orientation, but then were fairly mobile. They were permitted to move out of the facility before the end of their term, returning only for conferences. These prerelease centers were staffed by people associated with the correctional institution who visited the offenders for counseling sessions, and by some permanent staff. The centers were tied in with some probation offices. The basic advantage of having this counseling available is that the professional staff handled problems as they took place. Even though some of the offenders got into trouble (for example, getting drunk), their actions did not invalidate the program. They would probably have these problems when released from prison anyway, and here they had access to counseling when the problem occurs.[16]

Recently, halfway houses have lost some of their attractiveness. States are now facing a great deal of criticism on the idea of rehabilitating offenders and, thus, the popularity and funding of halfway houses have suffered. This problem has been augmented to such proportions that some jurisdictions have transformed already-built halfway houses into museums or other public facilities—this has occurred because citizens see a halfway house in their community as a presence that will devalue their property. Despite this, halfway houses continue to offer offenders an opportunity for an "adequate" transition to life after prison. In addition to halfway houses, some prerelease programs, such as that described in Spotlight 7.1, continue to make a difference as they ease the transition from prison life to the outside world.

Problems Encountered upon Release

Inmates who have been incarcerated face many problems upon release. Currently, one of the most obvious problems is the labeling that occurs. This is most evident in states that make it a point of releasing photographs of offenders and placing them in local newspapers and on bulletin boards. Some states have gone as far as placing photos of inmates on the Internet so the whole world can be informed as to who was an offender and why he or she was incarcerated. This practice makes it very difficult for the recently released offender to attain a job or lead a crime-free lifestyle—the label of being a criminal can indeed hamper job marketability. We will look at three of the most frequently encountered areas of problems by inmates upon release: financial, employment, and personal (including family problems).

Financial Needs of Inmates upon Release

In the early 1960s, the results of the National Survey of Financial Assistance to Released Prisoners were published. The survey revealed that the most frequent kind of assistance that American prisons gave to released prisoners was civilian clothing. This is even more true today, as most institutions require that prisoners send their personal clothing home; thus, at the time of release it is necessary for the institution to replace prison clothing with something less conspicuous. Some

Spotlight 7.1

LASER Treatment: A Program That Changes Criminal Behavior

The Dauphin County Prison in Pennsylvania implemented the Life, Attitude, Skills, Educational Retraining (LASER) project in January, 1994.[17] This program aims at changing the criminal behavior of the individual by altering lifestyle patterns. Although it is cited here as an example of a prerelease program, it must be noted that this program aims not only at those who are incarcerated, but also to those on parole or on release. The program usually lasts thirteen weeks and teaches participants skills that will improve their quality of life, while decreasing in-house disciplinary infractions and reducing recidivism. A recent evaluation of the program revealed that recidivism rates for LASER participants were 62 percent for a control group, as opposed to 78 percent for the Dauphin County prison population.[18] It was also found that LASER graduates also committed fewer in-house disciplinary infractions while showing increased self-esteem and a higher educational level. It is claimed that the LASER program "whole" person approach teaches inmates the skills required to give them what they need most—freedom. Although the findings of this particular evaluation are encouraging, we must exercise a certain degree of caution before we can claim conclusively that this program is a success and, thus, should be replicated in other jurisdictions.

institutions save the personal clothing of inmates and give it back to them upon release. Others permit relatives to ship clothing to inmates. The survey, which included all state prison systems in America except the Arkansas system, revealed that all states except Hawaii issue the clothing free to a released inmate who otherwise would have none.

The next most frequent type of assistance is money for transportation from the prison to the individual's destination. These grants are minimal, however, and are usually given only for transportation to an approved destination. Some states give cash only to dischargees and not to parolees. Some states base the amount of cash given to the releasee on length of term or financial need; others give the same sum to all; however, the amount is small.[19] Out of those funds, releasees must pay for additional clothing, room and board, and, in many cases, debts incurred prior to incarceration. They may also have to support a family, and they usually don't have a job immediately upon release. Inmates are thus thrown into the outside world with few financial resources and usually with no moral support.

A change of clothing, a ticket home, and a few dollars will not get one very far in today's inflationary world. Add to that a person who is "marked," who is rejected by society as well as by his or her family in many cases, and the ex-offender, in the words of Norman C. Colter, is a "handicapped human being, one who needs all the things the rest of us need and a little bit more." Colter advocates giving the inmate a large subsidy upon release. He concludes:

> The choice is simple. We can continue the current practice of releasing a man with so little money that we virtually guarantee he will return to prison and thus add about $50,000 to our tax burden to pay for his arrest, trial, and several years of wasteful and destructive support. Or we can give him about $1,200 over a six-month period, an investment in the likelihood that this assistance will do much more to make him law-abiding than a $20,000 cell would.[20]

Employment

A second major problem faced by offenders upon release is employment. Although offenders who have served all of their time must be released whether or not they have already secured employment, those who have been granted parole generally will not be released without a job. The institution may or may not provide assistance in seeking employment to offenders. Again, as mentioned previously, their inability to attain a job is exacerbated by their lack of skills, their criminal label, and a lack of support from correctional agencies. This proves to be a negative cycle as the offender cannot be released until he or she obtains employment, while at the same time, he or she lacks the skills or the background to successfully attain a job. Unfortunately, this problem is most evident among drug offenders who, having been used to the high monetary rewards of selling drugs, refuse to be paid minimum wage in jobs they regard as "undesirable." They often argue that they could make as much money in a single drug transaction as they would be paid during an entire month at a "regular" job.

Legal Reactions

Many states have statutes that prohibit granting licenses to ex-offenders to become members of certain professions, such as law and medicine. The American Bar Association's Commission on Correctional Facilities and Services and its Criminal Law Section sponsored the National Clearinghouse on Offender Employment Restrictions, funded by contract with the United States Department of Labor's Manpower Administration. Through its newsletter and other publications, the clearinghouse has made available to interested persons "information on the laws, regulations, and administrative practices and procedures which prevent the ex-offender from obtaining employment," as well as information on manpower programs.[21]

Statutes that restrict the employment of ex-offenders are not, however, always upheld by the courts. In a case heard in the mid-1970s, the Seventh Circuit held as an unconstitutional violation of equal protection, a city ordinance that provided that a person who had been convicted of specified crimes could not obtain a public chauffeur's license, whereas retention of such license was discretionary in the cases of persons who committed such crimes after acquiring it.[22] Despite this, it is very difficult for former inmates to successfully find a job because most employers consider hiring an ex-con a liability. You can clearly see this trend when you apply for a job. Have you noticed that, in most cases, you are asked if you have been arrested and/or convicted of a crime in the past?

Social Problems of Ex-Offenders

Daniel Glaser, in his classic study of the federal correctional system in this country, devoted an entire chapter to "The Ex-Prisoner's Social World." Glaser found that the blood ties of inmates improve during incarceration but that relationships with friends and spouses are weakened. Over 90 percent of ex-offenders return to the communities in which they resided before the time of incarceration. That means that they return to an area where their offenses may be known, but where they can usually expect to receive the greatest assistance from others, mainly their families. This situation may be disadvantageous, however, in the case of ex-offenders who have experienced or are experiencing discord with relatives in the town to which they return. Of particular interest, however, was the finding that the "most unfavorable postrelease residential arrangement, in terms of postrelease failure rates, is that in which the exprisoner lives alone."[23]

Other studies have revealed some of the problems faced by inmates and their families. The spouses and children of inmates have been called the "hidden victims of crime."[24] Spouses usually face problems of acceptance, of understanding the legal process, economic problems, sexual adjustment, caring for children without the help of their spouse, and so on. One study of the families of African American inmates revealed that among poor African Americans, acceptance of incarceration was not a problem, but sexual-emotional and economic problems did exist.[25] In addition, maintaining the family, especially marital ties, is strongly related to success upon release.[26]

Ideally, counseling for families should take place while the spouse/parent is in prison and should continue after release.[27] The problems of inmates' children should also be considered. One study indicated that when a father is committed to jail, the performance of his children in school goes down, and although the differences are not great, girls seem to have more trouble adjusting to the incarceration than do boys.[28] In the words of a recently released inmate, "The first few days I was out were about the roughest days of this entire period . . . no money, no transportation, no job, and no place to live."[29]

Parole

Since we only briefly mentioned parole earlier, it is important that we examine this complex correctional program here. In the United States, most offenders reenter society on some form of a parole program after serving time in correctional facilities. The Attorney General's Survey of Release Procedures has defined parole as "the release of an offender from a penal or correctional institution after he has served a portion of his sentence, under the continued custody of the state and under conditions that permit his reincarceration in the event of misbehavior."[30]

Parole resembles probation in that both permit a convicted person to live in the community under supervision. Theoretically, the decision to parole someone is made after careful study of the person's background, behavior, and potential for success. Both parole and probation are based on the philosophy that the rehabilitation of some individuals might be hindered by imprisonment (or further imprisonment) and will be aided by supervised freedom. The processes differ in that parole is granted after a portion of the prison term is served, while probation is granted in lieu of incarceration. In other words, probation is a sentence while parole is not. In addition, probation is granted by a judge, while the decision to parole is usually made by a parole board appointed specifically for that purpose.

Parole should also be distinguished from other forms of release that occur when a person has served his or her full term, or when there is a statutory provision that a person may be released for "good behavior" after serving a specified portion of his or her term. In other words, good behavior entitles inmates, in some cases, to a reduction in the amount of their sentence that must be served. Their release is not, however, dependent upon the administrative decision of a parole board. Parole should also be distinguished from mandatory release, in which release is granted to an offender who has served all of his or her term. Such persons are released without supervision, in contrast to the continued supervision that the state (or the federal government in the case of a federal offender) exercises over one released on parole. The government is entitled to continue that supervision until the parole period expires.

Historical Overview

The origin of parole has been traced to the English system of transporting criminals to the American colonies. Criminals were pardoned by the English government after being sold to the highest bidder in America. The buyer then became the master of the individual, whose new status was that of indentured servant. The system is similar to parole in that the individual, in order to receive the change in status, agreed to certain conditions similar to the ones currently imposed by parole boards.[31]

Others have claimed that the concept of "conditioned liberty" was first introduced in France around 1830. It was an intermediary step of freedom—supervision between prison confinement and complete freedom in the community. This system does sound like the beginning of what is today known as parole. In the United States, parole for juveniles goes back to the last half of the nineteenth century to the house of refuge for children. In 1876, New York's Elmira Reformatory gave the first official recognition to a parole system.[32] The parole idea in the United States was closely linked to the introduction of indeterminate sentences. Parole began to be widely used upon states' adoption of indeterminate sentences. It is reported that by 1900, twenty states had parole systems, and by 1925, forty-eight states.[33] By 1910, each federal correctional facility had its own parole board. These were replaced in 1930 when Congress created the U.S. Board of Parole. Today, all states have some sort of mechanism in place to release offenders back to the community while under some form of supervision.

Data on Parole

By the end of 1995, there were more than 700,000 individuals on parole in the United States. This constitutes an increase of 1 percent from the previous year. The federal government oversaw 59,136 parolees by the end of 1995, while the states supervised 641,038 individuals on parole.[34] Clearly, most of the parole-related activity takes place at the state level. In terms of regions of the country that supervise the most parolees, these statistics revealed that the southern region of the United States experiences the most activity. The northeastern and western regions of the country follow closely. The states with the largest population of parolees in 1995 were Texas (103,089), California (91,807), and Pennsylvania (73,234).[35] This trend continues today.[36]

In looking at the characteristics of offenders placed on parole, statistics suggest that 90 percent of parolees are males, while only 10 percent are females. Most are white (50 percent), followed closely by African Americans (49 percent). Approximately 21 percent of parolees in 1995 were of Hispanic origin. Among all parolees, 94 percent had been sentenced to more than one year in prison, and 78 percent of them were determined to have an "active" supervision status. Another alarming statistic is the long-term percentage of change in the numbers of offenders on parole. When comparing 1980 to 1995, there was a 218 percent increase in parole supervision in all states.[37] Needless to say, these statistics are alarming and demonstrate the fact that, in the 1990s, more and more individuals were processed in the criminal justice system.

Parole and Sentencing

Parole is not a form of sentencing. The latter is determined by the court and the former by an administrative agency—the parole board. The two practices are, however, closely related. Although parole has increased since 1980, its popularity has been declining slowly. The only explanation of this rare phenomenon is the direct result of the immense overcrowding that is presently experienced by the correctional system. In other words, despite the fact that very few individuals want to release offenders from prisons via parole (due to the belief that once out of prison, they will engage in criminal activity once again), correctional administrators don't have a choice but to release those they consider to be "less harmful" so that others (preferably violent offenders) can occupy their space. Needless to say, sentencing has had an effect on this recent trend.

America has experienced a sentencing movement that has ranged from allowing judges considerable discretion in sentencing decisions, to flat sentencing (in which sentences are established by the legislature), to the indeterminate sentence (often with a minimum and a maximum established by law), to a conservative movement demanding that we return to flat sentencing. Why, at one point in our history, did we believe it important for judges and parole boards to share the determination of the length of incarceration? It was considered important for the inmate to participate in treatment programs and for his or her progress in those programs to be considered in the decision whether to release. No judge at sentencing could possibly predict effectiveness of treatment; the release decision should therefore be left to a later decision-making body. It was also thought that this approach would give the community greater protection. Persons who were "dangerous," who had not yet been "rehabilitated," would not be released into the community. Norval Morris has argued that "It was a fine idea having only the defect that it did not work."[38] Serious abuses of the system resulted in sentencing disparity, with individuals held in prison for long periods of time with little or no treatment.

In the past, well-known individuals have taken a position on the sentencing issue as it relates to parole. In fact, Massachusetts Senator Edward M. Kennedy took the position that sentencing disparity has been compounded by parole. In addition to the abuse of discretion that may occur at the time of deciding parole, Kennedy argued that the very existence of a parole system may encourage judges in their lengthy sentences. Judges may impose harsh sentences to make the community think that they are being tough with offenders—for example, in the case of drug possession offenses—with the expectation that the parole board will release the individuals early. But since judges are not required to state reasons for their sentences, it is possible that parole boards might inadvertently act contrary to the expectations of the judge. Even when the parole board members know what the judge expects, they are not required to follow those expectations.[39] Kennedy concluded that with flat or determinate sentencing, parole release would not be needed. "Under this system of judicially-fixed sentences, parole release would be abolished and whether or not a prisoner has been 'rehabilitated' or has completed a certain prison curriculum would no longer have any bearing on his prison release date."[40]

Organization of Parole

The organization of parole is complex. One reason for this complexity is the variety of sentencing structures under which parole systems must operate. Despite suggestions by the American Bar Association, the President's Crime Commission, the American Law Institute (which proposed a Model Penal Code), and the National Council on Crime and Delinquency (which proposed the Model Sentencing Act), jurisdictions differ in their sentencing structures. The type of sentence is closely related to the parole system. For example, in jurisdictions where sentences are long with little time off for good behavior, parole may involve a long period of supervision. In jurisdictions where sentences are short, parole may be relatively unimportant as a form of release, and supervision will be for shorter periods. Historically, the authority to release prisoners rested on the hands of a state's governor. Today, governors no longer have this power. However, they still influence the process by having the authority to appoint most of the parole board members.

The Advisory Commission recommended eight objectives for a sentencing system consistent with parole objectives. Basically those objectives involve having the legislature and sentencing judges set maximum sentences, but they could not restrict parole-granting authorities in decisions about when to grant parole. Thus, no minimum sentences would exist. In addition, there would be no offenses for which parole was denied by legislation. The commission recommended relatively short sentences with a five-year maximum for most offenses. The purpose of the commission's recommendations appeared to be twofold: to keep offenders from spending long terms in correctional facilities and to give a large degree of discretion concerning their release to parole boards. Abuse of that discretion by parole boards would be limited by the short maximum terms and by the requirement that parole boards give written reasons for refusal to grant parole.

The commission discussed the variety of functions parole boards must perform, in addition to making decisions on parole—from granting pardons in some states to holding clemency hearings and appointing the parole supervision staff. Despite the wide variety of parole programs, the states are equally divided between two models—the independent and consolidated models.

Independent Authority Model

Some parole boards for adult correctional facilities follow the *independent authority model,* establishing the parole board as an agency independent of the institution from which individuals are paroled. This model is supposed to establish a more objective process. Despite this, however, the independent authority model has been severely criticized. The parole board is often composed of people who know little or nothing about corrections. The board is removed from the institution and often does not understand what is taking place there. Decisions may be made for inappropriate reasons, such as the desires of the local police chief. Consequently, parole boards often release those who should not be paroled and reject those who should.

Consolidated Model

The relatively newer *consolidated model* is based on the belief that it is best to consolidate the parole activities within the department of corrections or any other multifunctional department of human services. Under this model, the parole board is able to retain its independent decision-making authority while enjoying the benefit of being organizationally close to the department of corrections in an attempt to be sensitive to the department's needs. Some argue that this model is best since its parole board has more information about the offender (i.e., behavior while in prison, offense committed)—a factor needed in order to grant parole properly.

Parole Board Members: Selection and Qualifications

In most states, a parole board member is appointed by the governor. A department of corrections appoints in whole or in part in some jurisdictions. In some states, members of the board serve part-time; in others, board membership is a full-time position. It has been argued that full-time parole members are mostly well-educated and well-paid individuals who have the "proper training" to successfully conduct parole hearings. Others argue that part-time parole members, although perhaps paid less than full-time members, represent the community more effectively.

What qualifications should parole board members have? Some argue that parole boards should be made up of people who are at least trained in law, the behavioral sciences, and corrections. It has been recommended that they be sensitive to public concerns and willing to challenge the system when necessary. Some boards have too often been rubber stamps of the correctional authorities, thus eliminating the possibility of a check on their abuse of discretion. As can be imagined, parole members vary, in terms of their backgrounds, throughout the United States. For instance, in the state of Mississippi, recent parole members consisted of a businessman, a contractor, a clerk, and a farmer, while the parole board in Washington state was made up of individuals with adequate training in the law, ministry, sociology, and government. This, of course, explains the reason why decisions made by parole boards across the country vary.

Historically, American parole boards have had almost total discretionary power to determine parole. The theory behind this power was that parole is to be regarded as a *privilege* and not a *right*. "The prisoner has no statutory right, even if 'qualified,' to be granted conditional liberty or allowed to remain on parole."[41] Since parole is not to be considered a right, no reasons need be given for denial. Elements of due process are not required at the time the decision is made. As stated by a federal court in 1971,

> the Board of Parole is given absolute discretion in matters of parole. The courts are without power to grant a parole or to determine judicially eligibility for parole. . . . Furthermore, it is not the function of the courts to review the discretion of the Board in the denial of the application for parole or to review the credibility of reports and information received by the Board in making its determinations.[42]

The United States Supreme Court refused to review that case. That opinion was cited with approval by the same court in another case in 1973.[43]

The reasoning of the federal court in ruling that due process is not required at the determination of parole is that the granting of parole is not an adversary proceeding. The granting of parole is a very complicated decision and the board of parole must be able to use evidence that would not be admissible in an adversary proceeding such as a trial.

This general lack of due process at the parole decision stage resulted in bitter complaints from inmates. One described his observations of fellow inmates who went before the parole board:

> They would get their hopes up and do all of the "right things," like going to church and AA meetings and behaving properly. The parole board would encourage them during the hearing. Then they would wait for a long time, sometimes six weeks, before they heard. If their applications for parole were denied, their feelings of despair would later turn to hatred at being rejected with no reasons given for the decisions. This inmate decided not to go for a parole hearing. He did not "wish to go through the very ugly and unpleasant cycles that my fellow inmates have. . . . You, my keepers, have my body, but my mind is somewhat my own. I feel free in the strength of my convictions."[44]

John Irwin discussed some of the ways in which the parole system can be disrupted, resulting in a different set of standards applied at the time of parole

The Parole Granting Decision

hearing than those that existed at the time the inmate was incarcerated. When this happens, says Irwin, a sense of injustice develops in inmates, and this sense of injustice further increases the loss of commitment of the inmate to conventional society.[45] Perhaps Justice Hugo Black best summarized the view of many inmates toward the parole board:

> In the course of my reading—by no means confined to law—I have reviewed many of the world's religions. The tenets of many faiths hold the deity to be a trinity. Seemingly, the parole boards by whatever names designated in the various states, have in too many instances sought to enlarge this to include themselves as members.[46]

The Parole Hearing

The most important stage in the administration of parole is the parole hearing. Until a few years ago, the legal requirements at this stage were unclear and the nature of the hearing differed from state to state. Most states allowed the inmate to be present; some, however, only reviewed the inmate's files. The parole board might hear cases with all members present or may break into panels, with each panel hearing and deciding different cases. The hearings were usually private, attended only by the inmate, members of the board, and a representative of the institution in which the inmate was incarcerated. Reports from family members, from psychology or other treatment personnel, or from institutional staff members might be included. The board might want information on the inmate's plans upon release. Reasons for denial might or might not be given to the inmates considered for parole.

The federal courts were divided over the requirements of due process at the parole hearing, but in a 1979 decision, the United States Supreme Court decided a case on appeal from the U.S. Court of Appeals for the Eighth Circuit. In *Greenholtz v. Inmates of Nebraska Penal and Correctional Complex,*[47] the Court held that due process requirements were met by the Nebraska statute that allowed an inmate, at the time of the first parole release decision in his or her case, an opportunity to be heard and the right to receive a statement of the reasons for a parole denial. The Nebraska statute, said the Court, did create an expectation of parole that must be protected by due process. Whether that expectation exists in other state statutes would have to be determined by examining the statutes in those cases. The Court did not agree, however, that the United States Constitution requires that a parole hearing involve all of the same elements of due process required at the stage of trial. The Court also held that due process at this stage does not require the parole board to specify the "particular" evidence that influenced its parole denial.

Today, the previously held total discretion by the parole board has been limited by the implementation of guidelines. These guidelines are designed to reduce disparities among the times served by individuals who have committed the same or similar crimes. The guidelines are so precise that they give parole board members the specific time the offender will serve, given the nature of the offense and the individual's criminal history. Release is usually granted to individuals who serve the specified time and who have abided by the rules of the institution, to those whose release will not diminish the seriousness of the offense, and to those whose release will not place public safety at risk.

In most states, inmates who are subject to these guidelines are eligible for a release hearing within 120 days after they have been incarcerated. However, the previously held release date may be modified at regularly scheduled parole review hearings. These are held usually every eighteen months.

The existence of the guidelines mentioned in the previous section are particularly important in the scope of numerous allegations claiming that members of parole boards abuse their discretion in deciding parole, with the assumption being that they use "extra-legal" criteria (such as sex, race, socioeconomic status) when making parole-related decisions. What is the empirical evidence on this issue? A classic study on the issue indicated that when differences in kinds of offenders are taken into account, "there is no support for the hypothesis that differences in parole decision outcomes may be partly attributed to the decision-makers rather than to offenders."[48]

Criminologist Joseph E. Scott has conducted several studies on decision making among parole boards. In one study, he analyzed data from the three prisons in a midwestern state, looking at legal, institutional, and personal-biographical factors as each might be related to the decision whether to grant parole. By "legal factors," he meant the seriousness of the crime committed and the individual's prior criminal record. The institutional factor was measured by disciplinary reports that the offender received while in prison and institutional adjustment, which was measured by nine separate factors. Finally, personal-biographical factors were age at the time of release, education, IQ, marital status, race, residence, sex, and socioeconomic status. In general, early parole tended to be granted to those who committed less serious crimes, had fewer disciplinary reports, were younger, had more schooling, had higher IQ scores, were married, were female, and came from higher socioeconomic backgrounds. Basically, the data suggested that the decision whether or not to grant parole was based mainly on the legal factor of the seriousness of the crime.[49]

Leo Carroll and Margaret E. Mondrick found some evidence of racial discrimination in decisions about whether to grant parole. They took the position that discrimination may be found in the "less visible" phases of the criminal justice system. The decisions of parole boards would be less visible than, for example, the actions of the police. "Quite clearly research into agencies that guard the back door of the system is needed every bit as much as research into agencies that keep the front gate."[50] Their finding would be supported by the statistics discussed earlier, which demonstrate that a staggering 49 percent of African Americans were on parole at the end of 1995.[51] This is only 1 percent less than the number of whites released on parole. In other words, the numbers for both African Americans and whites were almost the same despite the fact that African Americans are a minority in the general population.[52]

The Parole Officer and Parole Services

It is important that conditions of parole be reasonable; perhaps more important, however, is the way in which those conditions are enforced. Later in the chapter, we discuss revocation of parole, which may occur when parolees violate its conditions. First, however, it is important to look at the role played by the parole officer, who has considerable power in the determination of parole revocation.

Qualifications of Parole Officers

Parole officers should be highly qualified. In many respects, they should have the same qualifications as those of probation officers. The Advisory Commission, in Standard 12.8, "Manpower for Parole," took the position that by 1975, all states had to "develop a comprehensive manpower and training program which would make it possible to recruit persons with a wide variety of skills, including significant numbers of minority group members and volunteers, and use them effectively in parole programs." The commission specified a bachelor's degree as a

Empirical Evidence on Parole Decisions

minimum requirement for a beginning parole officer, but stated that persons without such a degree should be trained to work with parole officers "on a team basis, carrying out the tasks appropriate to their individual skills." A strong emphasis was placed on the need to utilize volunteers and ex-offenders, combined with "new and innovative training programs in organizational development . . . to integrate successfully the variety of skills involved in a modern parole agency and to deal with the tensions and conflicts which will inevitably arise from mixing such a variety of personnel in team supervision efforts."[53]

Today, the parole officer position requires individuals with many skills. Among these, the individual seeking a career as a parole officer must have skills in working with people and in developing relationships with law enforcement agencies. This person must be able to work under pressure and be able to manage large caseloads.[54] The attitude of the parole officer must always be positive in an attempt to encourage change.[55]

Revocation of Parole

Not long ago, parole could be revoked easily and without due process. Such revocation was justified on the basis of the "privilege versus rights" theory, which we discussed earlier, as well as two other theories: contract theory and continuing custody theory.

The **contract theory** states that the parolee agrees to assume the conditions of release when parole is offered. If those conditions are violated, the contract has been broken, and parole may be revoked. The problem with this theory is that the parolee has little or no bargaining power. He or she has no other alternative by which to obtain early release.[56]

Under the **continuing custody theory,** the parolee remains in the custody of the granting authority, subject essentially to the same rules and regulations governing daily conduct as before he or she was released from prison. That is, the person's daily life is still regulated by authorities who establish rules regarding both the personal and the work life of the releasee. The problem with this theory is that parole is supposed to be rehabilitative and is viewed as a different system from incarceration, so it is irrational to attempt to apply the same rules to parolees and inmates.[57]

Due Process Theory

In the case of parole revocation, a different theory has been applied by the United States Supreme Court. This is the **due process theory,** which embodies the concept that parole is an important phase in the process of rehabilitation. If inmates are to be rehabilitated, they must see the parole system as being fair. It can be argued that fairness demands that an individual be granted due process at the time his or her parole is revoked. The Eighth Circuit did not agree, however. In an early 1970s Iowa case, quoted in Case Study 7.1, the court expressed its fear that allowing due process at parole revocation would endanger the system of parole.[58]

The United States Supreme Court rejected these and other arguments.[59] In summary, the Court said:

1. Parole is an integrative part of the correctional system and its primary purpose is to aid in rehabilitation.
2. The parole system implies that an individual may remain on parole until the rules are violated.
3. Revocation of parole "is not part of a criminal prosecution and thus the full panoply of rights due a defendant in such a proceeding does not apply to parole revocation."

Case Study 7.1

Morrissey v. Brewer

If boards of parole were required to grant hearings, adversary in nature, with the full panoply of rights accorded in criminal proceedings, their function as an administrative body acting in the role of *parens patriae* would be aborted. The probable result of the imposition of such stringent requirements upon their method of operation would actually be to decrease the number of paroles granted due to the heavy burden placed upon the administrative processes of supervision and investigation.

4. Whether parole is a right or privilege is not the crucial question. The issue is the extent to which an individual would be "condemned to suffer grievous loss." The liberty enjoyed by a parolee is important; if terminated, some elements of due process must be involved.
5. The state's interest in protecting society does not preclude or hinder an informal hearing at parole revocation.
6. Society has an interest in not revoking parole unless parole rules have been violated.
7. The requirements of due process fluctuate with particular types of cases.

The elements of due process required at parole revocation were:

1. Written notice of the alleged violations of parole;
2. Disclosure to the parolee of the evidence of violation;
3. Opportunity to be heard in person and to present evidence as well as witnesses;
4. Right to confront and cross-examine adverse witnesses unless good cause can be shown for not allowing this confrontation;
5. Right to judgement by a detached and neutral hearing body;
6. Written statement of reasons for revoking parole as well as of the evidence used in arriving at that decision.

More recently, the Court has heard cases involving revocation of probation as it continues to address issues concerning the due process of correctional clients. These cases—*Bearden v. Georgia*[60] and *Black v. Romano*[61]—have shown that due process must be present in the restriction mechanisms of probation revocation. Specifically, in *Bearden,* the Court held that it was improper to revoke the probation of an indigent who had made an effort to pay the required fine. In *Romano,* the Court held that due process did not mandate that other alternatives be considered before committing the offender to prison on the original sentence.

Prediction of Human Behavior

For centuries, people have been trying to predict human behavior, but only recently have the scientific tools to aid in that prediction been developed. Unfortunately, some researchers have made unfounded claims for the success of their prediction tables, while others have frightened the public with suggestions that all children should be tested for future delinquency. Prediction scares people because of the possibility of control it implies. Suppose, for example, that a causal relationship is found between the presence of the XYY chromosome abnormality and antisocial behavior. Should all male babies be tested at birth to detect those who have the extra Y chromosome? And what would then be done to control the situation? As we have witnessed recently, science has advanced to the point of giving serious consideration to human cloning. Some, in fact, have begun to predict that it won't be long until a gene is identified as being the culprit for aggressive behavior. When and if that happens, what will we do to those who happen to have this gene? Will we modify parole guidelines so they can include a provision for those who have the "aggressive gene"? These are all important questions we must begin to ask ourselves in the wake of a new scientific era.

Parole: Its Present State and Its Future

Today, parole has many faces. These faces vary and are mostly dependant upon the tolerance and imagination of citizens of a particular jurisdiction. In California, for example, a waste recycling plant has been constructed inside the premises of Folsom State Prison. This has been done to enable parole violators to render community service and generate revenues to reduce prison costs while alleviating the city's waste problem. So far, the preliminary reports are favorable and suggest that this program is a success in accomplishing most of its goals.[62]

Also in California, other programs are being implemented for the purpose of determining a more successful way of handling offenders released on parole. In fact, California's Parole and Community Services Division is using state-of-the-art technology to monitor its growing parolee population. Powerful electronic monitors such as ankle transmitters and voice verification systems are only a few of the innovative technological conditions imposed on parolees. Other jurisdictions are considering the use of global satellite positioning, video imaging, and electronic kiosks to enhance parolee supervision.[63]

As these and other programs continue to be implemented, we must ask ourselves, "What will the future hold for parole?" There are those who, after considering this question, claim that parole has to change or it will perish. These critics claim that we should not destroy parole, but should merely attempt to modify its present-day version. It is alleged that one of the modifications needed is to issue "responsibility" back to the offender. In other words, we should shift the personal responsibility to look for a job and find an adequate place to live back to the offenders so they feel they will be at a loss if these goals are not met. To achieve this, it has been proposed that the offender be issued a voucher that could allow him or her to seek a job, education, and drug treatment from a state-selected provider for a specific period of time.[64] This way, the parolee chooses to seek help, while allowing parole officers to conduct other pressing activities.

Despite this previous position, there are those who claim that parole will "continue to fail" as long as it is in existence. These individuals cite Virginia as an example. This particular state has witnessed a 28 percent increase in criminal violence over the last five years. Furthermore, three out of four violent crimes—murder, armed robbery, rape, and assault—are being committed by repeat offenders. As a result, effective January 1, 1995, extremely severe penalties for rape, murder, and armed robbery were imposed.[65] These penalties were implemented at the same time that parole was abolished. The belief is that by enacting these laws, most violent offenders will be in prison, while the state will save revenues and lives. Virginia's plan has been presented by many as an illustration of the future of parole in America. No one really knows what lies ahead for the future of parole. However, one fact remains certain—as citizens become more concerned over the crime issue, there is a strong likelihood that more politicians will begin to consider adopting plans similar to the one implemented in Virginia in which parole was abolished.

WiseGuide Wrap-Up Parole has come under severe attack in the United States. In the early 1970s, the American Friends Service Committee, after its report on the criminal justice system in this country, called for the abolition of parole.[66] The "abolish parole" movement did not, however, gain momentum until the mid-1970s, when some states abolished parole by passing flat sentencing laws. Senator Edward M. Kennedy, one of the writers and sponsors of the bill to revise the United States Criminal Code, Attorney General Griffin Bell, and United States Bureau of Prisons Director Norman Carlson all spoke at hearings on the proposed revision in the summer of 1977, and argued for the abolition of parole.[67] Norval Morris, Dean of the University of Chicago School of Law, in his widely read and provocative book, *The Future of Imprisonment,* called for considerable reduction in the power of the parole board, although he did not call for its abolition.[68]

In this chapter, we looked at the various dimensions of parole as well as other forms of release from prison. We began with a discussion of furloughs and work-release programs, both designed to permit a gradual reentry of the offender back into society. We then looked at attempts to prepare the offender for release through the establishment of prerelease programs. Some of these programs are carried out within the institutions; some involve moving the offenders into halfway programs, another form of "gradual" return to society. We analyzed the major problems that offenders face upon returning to society: financial problems, problems of employment, and finally, social problems.

The major focus of this chapter was, however, on parole, the most frequently used method of release of offenders from incarceration. After distinguishing parole from probation, as well as from other forms of release from prison, we looked briefly at its history. In our discussion of the organization of parole, we looked at two traditional models of parole systems: the independent and consolidation models. A discussion of the process of selection of the parole board, along with a discussion of qualifications for members of the board, set the stage for a detailed discussion of the parole decision.

For years, federal courts took a "hands-off" policy toward parole board decisions, and we analyzed the reasons for that position as well as some of the problems it created. The parole hearing was discussed in light of a Supreme Court case involving the due process issue at this stage. We also looked at some of the empirical studies of parole decisions—how and why they are made. Our attention then turned to parole officers, their qualifications, their functions, and the services that they are expected to provide for parolees.

The important decision of parole revocation was discussed in light of the due process requirements enunciated by the United States Supreme Court. The final portion of the chapter was devoted to the issue of prediction of parole success. This was followed by a discussion on the present and future conditions of parole in the United States.

Notes

1. *Tulsa World.* (October 29, 1977), p. 4, col. 4.
2. Colter, Norman C. "Subsidizing the Released Inmate," *Crime and Delinquency* 21 (July, 1975), 282.
3. Case, John D. "Doing Time in the Community," *Federal Probation* 31 (March, 1967), 9.
4. Markley, Carson V. "Furlough Programs and Conjugal Visiting in Adult Correctional Institutions," *Federal Probation* 37 (March, 1973), 19.
5. Jeffery, Robert, and Woolpert, Stephen. "Work Furlough as an Alternative to Incarceration: An Assessment of Its Effects on Recidivism and Social Cost," *Journal of Criminal Law, Criminology, and Police Science* 65 (September, 1974), 405.
6. Waldo, Gordon P., and Chiricos, Theodore G. "Work Release and Recidivism: An Empirical Evaluation of a Social Policy, reprinted in Marcia Guttentag with Shalom Saar, eds., *Evaluation Studies Review Annual* 2 (Beverly Hills, CA: Sage Publishers, 1977), p. 626, references omitted.
7. Waldo and Chiricos, in Cuttentag and Saar, eds., p. 637. See also Waldo and Chiricos, *Work as a Rehabilitation Tool: An Evaluation of Two State Programs,* U. S. Department of Justice, LEAA, Final Report (Washington, DC: U.S. Government Printing Office, 1974).
8. Elder, John P., and Cohen, Stanley H. "Prediction of Work Release Success with Youthful, Nonviolent, Male Offenders," *Criminal Justice and Behavior* 5 (June, 1978), p. 181.
9. Brookhart, Duane E., Ruark, J. B., and Scoven, Douglas E. "A Strategy for the Prediction of Work Release Success," *Criminal Justice and Behavior* 3 (December, 1976), 324.
10. See Donald Atkinson, C. Abraham Fenster, and Abraham S. Blumberg, "Employer Attitudes Toward Work-Release Programs and the Hiring of Offenders," *Criminal Justice and Behavior* 3 (December, 1976), 335–344.
11. Prison Work-Release Is Assailed by Scopetta Who Cites Escapees, *The New York Times.* (December 27, 1977), p. 24, col. 3.
12. Baker, J. E. "Preparing Prisoners for their Return to the Community," *Federal Probation* 30 (June, 1966), 43.
13. Clark, J. E. "The Texas Prerelease Program," *Federal Probation* 30 (December, 1966), 53, 55.
14. Baker, "Preparing Prisoners," pp. 43–50.
15. Seiter, Richard P. et al., Halfway Houses. National Evaluation Program. Phase I. Summary Report. National Institute of Law Enforcement and Criminal Justice, *LEAA.* (Washington, DC: U.S. Government Printing Office, 1977).
16. The President's Commission on Law Enforcement and Administration of Justice, *Task Force Report: Corrections.* (Washington, DC: U.S. Government Printing Office, 1967), pp. 40–41.
17. Orosz, Connie L. "Laser Treatment Changes Criminal Behavior." (Life, Attitude, Skills, Educational Retraining) (Programs That Work). *Corrections Today* (August, 1996), vol. 58, n.5, 74(4).
18. Orosz, "Laser Treatment," 74(4).
19. Glaser, Daniel. *The Effectiveness of a Prison and Parole System.* (Indianapolis, IN: Bobbs-Merrill, 1964), pp. 317–318.
20. Colter, "Subsidizing the Released Inmate," 285. For a listing of state financial provisions for releasees, see Kenneth J. Kenihan, "The Financial Condition of Released Prisoners," *Crime and Delinquency* 21 (July, 1975), 266–281.
21. Robinson, James W. "Occupational Licensing, the Ex-Offender, and Society," *The Justice System Journal* 3 (June, 1974), 69.
22. *Carter v. Miller,* 98 S.Ct. 786 (1978), affg per curiam, 547 F.2d 1314 (7th cir. 1977). For a discussion, see Dan Fowler, Prisoners' Rights, *American Criminal Law Review* 16 (Summer, 1978), 107.
23. Glaser, *The Effectiveness of a Prison and Parole System,* p. 400.
24. Bakker, Laura J., Morns, Barbara A., and Janus, Laura M. "Hidden Victims of Crime," *Social Work* 23 (March, 1978), 143–148.
25. Schneller, Donald P. "Prisoners' Families: A Study of Some Social and Psychological Effects of Incarceration on the Families of Negro Prisoners," *Criminology* 12 (February, 1975), 402–412.
26. See, for example, Glaser, *The Effectiveness of a Prison and Parole System;* Susan C. Cobean and Paul W. Power, "The Role of the Family in the Rehabilitation of the Offender," *International Journal of Offender Therapy and Comparative Criminology* 22 (No. 1, 1978), 29–38.
27. See Barbara J. Freedman and David G. Rice, "Marital Therapy in Prison: One-Partner-Couple Therapy," *Psychiatry* 40 (May, 1977), 175–183; Florence W. Kaslow, "Marital or Family Therapy for Prisoners and Their Spouses or Families," *The Prison Journal* 58 (Spring-Summer, 1978), 53–59.
28. Friedman, Sidney, and Esselstyn, T. Conway. "The Adjustment of Children of Jail Inmates," *Federal Probation* 29 (December, 1965), 428–437.
29. Waldo, Gordon, and Chiricos, Ted G. "Work Release and Recidivism: An Empirical Evaluation of Social Policy," *Evaluation Quarterly* No. 1, (1986): 87–108.
30. Attorney General's Survey of Release Procedures, *Parole,* vol. 4. (Washington, DC: U.S. Government Printing Office, 1939), p. 4, quoted in Vincent O'Leary, "Parole Administration," Chapter 25 in Daniel Glaser, ed., *Handbook of Criminology.* (Chicago: Rand McNally College Publishing Co., 1974), pp. 909–949; quotation is on p. 909.
31. "The Origins of Parole," in George G. Killinger and Paul F. Cromwell, Jr., eds., *Corrections in the Community: Alternatives to Imprisonment.* (St. Paul, MN: West Publishing Co., 1974), p. 400.
32. The President's Commission, *Corrections,* p. 60. See also O Leary, "Parole Administration," pp. 909–912.
33. Friedman, Lawrence M. *Crime and Punishment in American History.* (New York: Basic Books, 1993), p. 304.
34. U.S. Department of Justice, Bureau of Justice Statistics. *Probation and Parole Population Reaches Almost 3.8 Million.* (June 30, 1996).
35. U.S. Department of Justice, *Probation and Parole Population.*
36. See "Nation's Probation and Parole Population Reached New High Last Year," U.S. Department of Justice, Bureau of Justice Statistics. (August, 1998).
37. U.S. Department of Justice, *Probation and Parole Population.*
38. Morris, Norval. *The Future of Imprisonment.* (Chicago: University of Chicago Press, 1974), p. 47.
39. According to a decision of the United States Supreme Court, "The decision as to when a lawfully sentenced defendant shall actually be released has been committed by Congress, with certain limitations, to the discretion of the Parole Commission. Whether wisely or not, Congress has decided that the Commission is in the best position to determine when release is appropriate, and in doing so, to moderate the disparities in the sentencing practices of individual judges. . . . [T]he [sentencing] judge has no enforceable expectations with respect to the actual release of a sentenced defendant short of his statutory term. The judge may well have expectations as to when release is likely. But the actual decision is not his to make, either at the time of sentencing or later if his expectations are not met." *U.S. v. Addonizio,* 99 S.Ct. 2235, 2242 (1979).
40. Kennedy, Edward M. "Toward a New System of Criminal Sentencing: Law with Order," *The American Criminal Law Review* 16 (Spring, 1979), 361.
41. *Morrissey v. Brewer,* 433 F.2d 942 (8th Cir. 1971), rev'd, 408 U.S. 471 (1972).
42. *Tarlton v. Clark,* 441 F 2d 384, 385 (5th Cir. 1971), *cert. denied,* 403 U.S. 934 (1971).

43. *Scarpa v. U.S. Board of Parole,* 447 F.2d 278 (5th Cir. 1973), vacated, 414 U.S. 809 (1973).

44. Miller, Robert Clarence. "Parole," *Fortune News* (October, 1972), 10.

45. Irwin, John. *The Felon.* (Englewood Cliffs, NJ: Prentice-Hall, Inc., 1970), p. 173.

46. Quoted in Jessica Mitford, *Kind and Usual Punishment: The Prison Business.* (New York: Alfred A. Knopf, 1973), p. 216.

47. *Greenholtz v. Inmates of Nebraska Penal and Correctional Complex,* 99 S.Ct. 2100 (1979).

48. Gottfredson, Don M. and Ballard, Jr., Kelley B. "Differences in Parole Decisions Associated with Decision-Makers," *Journal of Research in Crime and Delinquency* 3 (July, 1966), 119.

49. Scott, Joseph E. "The Use of Discretion in Determining the Severity of Punishment for Incarcerated Offenders," *The Journal of Criminal Law and Criminology* 65 (March, 1974), 214–224.

50. Carroll, Leo, and Mondrick, Margaret E. "Racial Bias in the Decision to Grant Parole," *Law & Society Review* 11 (Fall, 1976), 106.

51. U.S. Department of Justice. *Probation and Parole Population.*

52. For more information, see Ted Gest, "A Shocking Look at Blacks and Crime." *U.S. News and World Report,* (Oct. 16, 1995), vol. 119, no. 15, p. 53(2).

53. The Advisory Commission, *Corrections,* pp. 435–436.

54. Smith, Albert G. "Organizational Skills for Managing Your Probation and Parole Workload," *Corrections Today* vol. 54, no. 5, (July, 1992), pp. 136–142.

55. Nidorf, Barry J. "Probation and Parole Officers: Police Officers on Social Workers?" in *Correctional Issues: Probation and Parole,* p. 73.

56. Palmer, John W. *Constitutional Rights of Prisoners.* (Cincinnati, OH: Anderson, 1973), p. 114.

57. Palmer, *Constitutional Rights,* p. 114.

58. *Morrissey v. Brewer,* 443 F.2d 942 (1971), rev'd 408 U.S. 471.

59. *Morrissey v. Brewer,* 408 U.S. 471.

60. *Bearden v. Georgia,* 461 U.S. 660 (1983).

61. *Black v. Romano,* 471 U.S. 606 (1985).

62. Harrison, Larry, and Lovell, Douglas G. "Inmate Work Program Helps Solve City's Waste Problem," *Corrections Today* (April, 1996). vol. 58, no. 2, 132(3).

63. Morris, Marisela. "Technological Advances in Parole Supervision," *Corrections Today,* (July, 1996) vol. 58, no. 4, 88(3).

64. Dilulio, Jr., John J. "Reinventing Parole and Probation," *Brookings Review,* (Spring, 1997), vol. 15, no. 2, 40(3).

65. Allen, George. "The Courage of Our Conviction: The Abolition of Parole Will Save Lives and Money," *Policy Review,* (Spring, 1995). no. 72, 4(4).

66. American Friends Service Committee. *Struggle for Justice: A Report on Crime and Punishment in America.* (New York: Hill & Wang, 1971).

67. Wilson, Rob. "Parole Release: Devil or Savior?" *Corrections Magazine* 3 (September, 1977), 52.

68. Morris, *The Future of Imprisonment,* pp. 28–50.

The Correctional Client

The Male Inmate

The way prisoners are treated when they enter prison serves as an illustration of society's rejection of those who break the law. They are stripped of most of their personal belongings, assigned a number, examined, inspected, weighed, and documented. These acts represent, to most of them, efforts to deprive them of their true identities. The actions are often conducted in a humiliating way that further advances the prisoners' degrading status. Then they face correctional officers, who have contacts and families in the outside world, but who are there to make sure that inmates conform to the rules of the institution. The guards have the ultimate control over inmates, furnishing "constant reminders of the social degradation to which . . . [they have] been subjected."[1] Gresham M. Sykes has referred to the psychological and social problems that result from the worst punishment—deprivation of liberty—as the "pains of imprisonment." In his classic study of male inmates, Sykes discussed the moral rejection given by the community, which represents a permanent threat to the self-concept of the inmate; the deprivation of goods and services in a society that places a substantial emphasis on material possessions; the deprivation of heterosexual relationships and the resulting threat to the inmate's masculinity or femininity; and the deprivation of security in the inmate population in which the individual is constantly facing threats to his or her safety, health, and life.[2]

The total life of the inmate is regulated by the prison staff, with inmates generally given no opportunities to function in adult roles. This chapter discusses how male prisoners react to all of these regulations and deprivations. We explore the sociological studies of the "prison community," the "inmate subculture," and approaches to an understanding of the ways in which inmates adapt to prison life. The chapter begins with a look at Donald Clemmer's classic study of the prison community, which was published in 1940. We discuss

Key Terms

conjugal visits
deprivation model
furlough
HIV
importation model
segregation

Clemmer's concept of "prisonization." Next we examine the types of social roles that have been analyzed within the prison community. We explore, in detail, the prison community in its roles as an agency of social control. Attention is given to sex roles and sexual behavior in prison, especially homosexuality. Suggested solutions to these problems—conjugal visits and furloughs—are discussed. Finally, we examine the problems associated with prison violence.

Inmate Social Systems in Male Prisons

Some concern over the negative effects that inmates have on one another led the early penologists to either separate prisoners to avoid verbal and physical contact, or to enforce the silent system to avoid verbal contact. With the end of the silent system came the opportunity for inmates to interact verbally. One of the results of this interaction has been the opportunity for inmates to create a prison subculture, or "community." However, this development has not been immune to debate or study. We begin this section with the contributions made by Clemmer.

Prisonization: Socialization into the Inmate System

In 1940, Donald Clemmer published his study of the male prison community at the maximum security prison at Menard, Illinois. This study is now recognized as one of the most important works in the area of inmate socialization. Although this study was conducted in the 1940s, some of its conclusions can be applied in today's prison settings. One of Clemmer's most important contributions was the creation of the concept of "prisonization." Clemmer defined prisonization as "the taking on, in greater or lesser degree, of the folkways, mores, customs, and general culture of the penitentiary." The process starts as the new inmate learns his status as a prisoner. The most important aspects of prisonization are "the influences which breed or deepen criminality and anti-sociality and make the inmate characteristic of the criminalistic ideology in the prison community." The effectiveness of this process on a given inmate is dependant upon several factors: (1) the inmate himself/herself (his/her susceptibility, personality, and so on); (2) the types of relationships the inmate had outside the facility; (3) whether the inmate becomes a member of a primary group in prison; (4) his or her placement in the prison (the specific cell, cell mate, etc.); and (5) the degree to which the inmate accepts the dogmas and codes of the prison culture. However, Clemmer contends that the most important factor is the primary group,[3] although that position has been questioned by later investigators.[4] In short, Clemmer saw prisonization as the process by which new inmates became familiar with and internalize prison norms and values. He argued that once inmates became prisonized, they are, for the most part, immune to the influences of conventional value systems. Today, this notion is widely held by students of prisonization.[5]

Wheeler's Test: The U-Shaped Curved Hypothesis

In the early 1960s, Clemmer's concept of prisonization was empirically tested by Stanton Wheeler in a study at the Washington State Reformatory. Wheeler found strong support for Clemmer's concept of prisonization. However, Wheeler discovered that the degree of prisonization varied according to the phase of an inmate's institutional career, developing along a U-shaped curve. Inmates tended to be more receptive to the institutional values of the outside world during the first period of incarceration (measured at the end of the first six months) and during the last period (last six months prior to release), and less receptive during the middle, or prison career, period (more than six months remaining). In the last six months of incarceration, as the inmate is anticipating release back into society, his main reference group shifts from the inmates within the institution to the society outside. This results in a more conventional, normative orientation similar to that which characterized inmates upon arrival and during the first six months of incarceration. Wheeler concluded that Clemmer's concept of prisonization should be reformulated to include the variable of prison career phase.[6]

Since Wheeler's 1961 publication, numerous investigators have studied the process of prisonization and inmate subculture. Some of them have used Wheeler's methodological approach. An analysis of these studies and theoretical contributions reveals the emergence of two basic models in order to explain the inmate subculture. The models have been given different names, but they may be described as: (1) the **deprivation model,** and (2) the **importation model.** We will examine each model in some detail.

The Inmate Subculture: Two Models for Analysis

Deprivation Model

We made reference earlier to Syke's "pains of imprisonment." Without question, Sykes is the major proponent of the theory that the inmate subculture is the result of the attempt to adapt to the deprivations imposed by incarceration. These include the deprivations of (1) social acceptance, (2) material possessions, (3) heterosexual relationships, (4) personal autonomy, and (5) personal security.[7] The inmate lacks the outlets necessary to deal with the deprivation, loss of status, and degradation that are commonly found behind prison walls. Thus, inmates have few alternatives. Since they seldom escape the realities of prison psychologically, and almost never escape physically, inmates often suffer from these pains of imprisonment. "But if the rigors of confinement cannot be completely removed, they can at least be mitigated by the patterns of social interaction established among the inmates themselves."[8] According to Sykes, the inmate has a choice of either uniting with his fellow captives in a spirit of mutual cooperation or withdrawing to seek only the satisfaction of his own needs. In either case, the inmate's pattern of behavior is an adaptation to the deprivations of the prison environment. In order to understand the inmate's adaptive role, let's examine briefly the adaptation model.

According to the adaptive model, the social system available to inmates is functional for them in that it enables inmates to minimize, through cooperation, the pains of imprisonment. For instance, if inmates cooperate in exchanging favors, it not only removes the opportunity for some to exploit others, but it allows them to more easily accept material deprivation. Their social system redefines the meaning of material possessions. The inmates come to believe that material possessions, so highly valued on the outside, result from "connections" instead of from hard work and skill, which allows them to insulate their self-conceptions from failure in work and skill. In addition, the goods and services that are available to inmates can better be distributed and shared if they have a cooperative social system.

The inmate social system can also help to solve the problem of personal security, to alleviate the fear of further isolation, and to restore the inmate's sense of self-respect and independence.[9] The inmate can begin to recapture his male role in that the characteristics associated with dignity, composure, courage, the ability to "take it" and "hand it out"—traits that are emphasized by the inmate's social system—are regarded by the inmates to be masculine traits.

Support for the adaptation model also comes from a study conducted by Richard A. Cloward.[10] In this study, Cloward examined the "structural accommodation," his term for the situation in which some inmates gain special privileges from the staff by assisting to maintain control and the status quo. The resulting roles develop due to the inmate's need to adapt to the internal character of the prison situation. These analyses are in line with Erving Goffman's discussion of total institutions. Goffman does not deny that individuals bring to their institutions of confinement a background of experiences, but he maintains that the institutional process of mortification and degradation essentially nullifies the impact of those experiences.[11]

It is important to mention that these studies were conducted in all-male institutions. Charles R. Tittle conducted a study in an institution housing both men and women under similar conditions in the late 1960s. Despite the fact that he found some gender differences in inmate social structures, he concluded that generally "the data seem to justify the conclusion that inmate organization is largely a response to institutional conditions," or, in the words of the model, it is an adaptation to the series of deprivations suffered by inmates in formal institutions.[12]

In summary, due to the "pains of imprisonment" and the degradation of inmates, which result in a threat to their self-esteem, inmates repudiate the norms of the staff, administration, and society. In addition, they join forces with each other, developing a social system that enables them to preserve their self-esteem. By doing so, they reject their rejectors—this prevents them from rejecting themselves.

Importation Model

According to John Irwin and Donald R. Cressey, the more traditional approach to an understanding of the inmate subculture is that patterns of behavior are brought with the men to prison.[13] Even Clemmer, despite his theory of prisonization of new inmates, recognized that the prison subculture depended in part on the men's conditions and experiences outside the prison.[14] Clarence Schrag, who collected pre-prison as well as in-prison data, also related prison activities to the broader community.[15]

Irwin and Cressey argued that social scientists have overemphasized inside influences as explanations for the inmate culture. In their argument that most of the inmate subculture is not peculiar to penal institutions, Irwin and Cressey emphasized the need to make a distinction between "prison culture" and "criminal subculture."[16] In order to do this, they postulate three types of prison subcultures, only two of which are criminal.

The first type, the "thief" subculture, refers to the patterns of values that are characteristic of professional thieves and other career criminals. This type is found in the prison setting as well as outside the walls.[17] This type is not restricted to criminals. In fact, it can also be evident among police, correctional officers, college professors, students, and other categories of persons who "evaluate behavior in terms of in-group loyalties."[18]

The second type of inmate subculture is the "convict" subculture, the central value of which is utilitarianism, in which the most "manipulative and most utilitarian individuals win the available wealth and such positions of influence as might exist." This type refers to patterns that can be found anywhere people are incarcerated, and it is "characterized by deprivations and limitations of freedom and in them available wealth must be competed for by men supposedly on an equal footing." Many of the hard-core members of this category of subculture within the prison have spent a great deal of time in juvenile institutions.[19]

Finally, Irwin and Cressey discussed the "legitimate" subculture, which is made up of inmates who isolate themselves or are isolated by other inmates. They make up the largest portion of the inmate population and are of little or no trouble to the staff. They reject both the criminal and the thief subcultures. They are "oriented to the problems of achieving goals through means which are legitimate outside prisons."[20] Clemmer also found that most inmates were not members of inmate groups. According to his study, 40 percent of the interviewed inmates stated that they did not consider themselves as members of any group, while another 40 percent said that they were members only of a "semiprimary group."[21]

Irwin and Cressey indicated that a combination of the convict and the thief subcultures form what is usually referred to as the "inmate subculture." Some conflicts exist between the two groups, but they also share some values. It is not known how much each or both influence the members of the legitimate subculture. Nor is it known what influence the members of the latter have on each other. But Irwin and Cressey hypothesize that all three subcultures bring to the prison patterns of behavior and attitudes from past experience and that the "inmate culture" is really an "adjustment of accommodation of these three systems within the official administrative system of deprivation and control."[22]

Research on these two models was conducted by Charles W. Thomas at a maximum security prison in a southwestern state in 1970. Thomas emphasized the fact that inmates have a past, a present, and a future, and that all are related to the process of prisonization. His research was designed to show the importance of both importation and deprivation variables. When an inmate arrives at prison, both the formal organization and the inmate society compete for his allegiance, and these two represent conflicting processes of socialization. Thomas calls the efforts of the formal organization "re-socialization" and those of the inmate society "prisonization." The success of one requires the failure of the other. The prison is not a closed system, and in explaining the inmate culture, one must examine all of these factors: pre-prison experiences, both criminal and noncriminal; expectations of prison staff and fellow inmates; quality of the inmate's contacts with persons or groups outside the walls; post-prison expectations; and the immediate problems of adjustment that the inmate faces. Thomas found that the greater the degree of similarity between pre-prison activities and prison subculture values and attitudes, "the greater the receptivity to the influences of prisonization." He also found that inmates from the lower as compared to the higher social class are more likely to become highly prisonized and that those who have the highest degree of contact with the outside world have the lowest degree of prisonization. Finally, those with a higher degree of prisonization were among those who had the bleakest post-prison expectations.[23]

Leo Carroll, based on his 1970s study on race relations in an eastern prison, was very critical of the deprivation model, arguing that it "diverts attention from inter-relationships between the prison and the wider society . . . and hence away from issues such as racial violence."[24] Carroll's research generally supported the importation model, but he concluded that the model was incomplete. He extended the importation model in his analysis of racial violence within one prison. Looking at the problem of powerlessness that all inmates face, Carroll analyzed ways in which attempts to cope with this problem might be influenced by the racial identity of the inmate. He then explored "some of the consequences of these differential adaptations in terms of maintaining and perhaps intensifying racial hostility imported into the prison from the community."[25] Recently, scholars have claimed that the importation model holds the "superior explanation for the inmate subcultures found in modern American prisons."[26] This view has been strengthened by correctional reforms and federal court decisions that have eased some of the inmate's pains of imprisonment.[27] According to Carroll and Jacobs, inmates have been enabled to maintain close contact with the outside world by factors such as the liberalization of visitations, telephone and mail privileges, and the permission to wear street clothing.[28]

Toward an Integration of Importation and Deprivation Models

As stated previously, although the integration model has been regarded as the "superior model," some have claimed that the integration of both models is ideal. Barry Schwartz, in his study of a Pennsylvania institution for boys, concluded that pre-prison experiences must be considered, as well as the "functional point of view, which refers such behavior to the system in which it is embedded."[29]

The cross-cultural studies of Akers, Hayner, and Gruninger also supported both models. The functional, or adaptation, model was only partially supported by their data from several countries and from one jurisdiction in the United States. Their data revealed that "the inmate culture varies by whatever differences in organizational environment there are from one institution to the next." But they also found support for the importation view "because it appears that the level of nonconformity to staff norms is more a reflection of the larger culture from which the inmates are drawn than the specific environment of the prison in which they are currently confined."[30]

This integrative approach has been summarized by Thomas. "The existence of collective solutions in the inmate culture and social structure is based on the common problems of adjustment to the institution, while the content of those solutions and the tendency to become prisonized are imported from the larger society."[31]

The integrative approach has also been used in explaining drug use in prison. Akers and his colleagues found that drug use was more or less a function of the adjustment problems individuals faced in prison.[32] A different finding was reached by Thomas and Cage,[33] who discovered that most inmates who used drugs had pre-prison drug experiences. According to the study conducted by Akers, "This suggests that both functional and importation processes are operative, such that the type of prison determines the general level of drug activity which can be expected, but that which inmates will engage in drug use as an adaptation and hence contribute to this level of drug activity depends on which ones have had prior experience with drugs."[34]

Charles W. Thomas, David M. Petersen, and Rhonda M. Zingraff studied inmates in a federal maximum security prison. They concluded that it is not reasonable to argue that either the importation or deprivation model explains the inmate subculture. Variables of each are equally important. "The more relevant issues appear to be how the rather vague propositions associated with each model can be stated more precisely and, more importantly, how they can be merged into a single theoretical framework."[35] Recently, this argument, which is based on the integration of both of these models, has been proposed as a more comprehensive view of the inmate prisonization process.[36]

Having looked at the development of the inmate social system, we now turn to an analysis of the social roles within that system. Gresham Sykes, in his classic study of a maximum security prison, emphasized the social system in the prison and the role that a special vocabulary plays in that system. If prisoners were kept in their cells at all times, an aggregate, but not a society, would exist. In such an aggregate, the officials would merely have to care for the physical needs of the inmates. But inmates leave their cells to eat, to work, to exercise, to attend religious services, to attend prison school, and to watch television. These activities set the stage for the development of a prison social system. Sykes contends that this resulting social system can be mapped by observing the special language that develops.[37]

Sykes holds that the special language is not developed primarily for secrecy or to symbolize the loyalty of the inmates to each other (the guards use the language too) but, rather, as a distinguishing symbol. Special terms designate the social roles played by the inmates. Although these words differ somewhat from institution to institution, the roles they designate remain the same.[38]

An example of the special terminology used by inmates to designate social roles may be seen in Leo Carroll's classic study of a small eastern institution for males.[39] He found that whites had social types similar to those of the whites in Sykes's study; but Carroll's study is particularly important in that he found that African Americans in the institution had a different set of social roles and a different form of organization of their lives while in prison. Their main focus was racial identification. They were, for the most part, united in a solitary group that was based on two ideological perspectives. One, which Carroll calls "soul," emphasizes the historical African American culture and affirms the importance of acceptance and perseverance. The other, "black nationalism," values African culture and emphasizes revolution against racism, colonialism, and imperialism. It was reported that both were imported into the prison from the outside world. In his book, *Life Without Parole,* Victor Hassine (1999) asserted that the tenor of the prison lingo was "generally vulgar and aggressive, expressed with self-important arrogance. Yet, at the same time it exhibited an unbridled honesty that implied a certain unconditional tolerance for the opinions and beliefs of others."[40] Table 8.1 shows some commonly used prison terminology.

Social Roles of the Inmate System

TABLE **8.1** Prison Terminology

Term	Meaning
Fish	New inmate
Get-back	Revenge in prison
Script	Prison money
Shank	A knife
Snitch	A prison informer
Waste	To kill someone
Bug out	To act crazy
Hack	A correctional officer

The Inmate System As an Agency of Social Control

The inmate social system may create problems for guards and other prison personnel. The resulting social roles may also create problems for inmates upon release, and even for society. It is clear, however, that the inmate social system also serves as an agency of social control within the prison. The inmate society becomes a powerful influence over the inmate because it is the only reference group he has. This is enhanced by the fact that the inmate needs status and may be more susceptible than usual to peer-group pressure. Also, the inmate may find social support in the peer group instead of in authority figures.[41] Inmates will therefore allow themselves to be controlled by the social system of their peers—a form of social control that is functional to the prison since it maintains order within the institution. To understand this system of control, we must examine more carefully the problems of control faced by the institution.

There are two powerful groups that seek control within the correctional facility—the correctional officers, who are mainly interested in custody and security, and the inmates, who are interested in escaping as much as possible from the pains of imprisonment. One of the most cited studies was that of Richard Cloward, who examined the power struggle between these two groups; we will summarize his approach.[42] Finally, we will look at two recent approaches to the explanation of the relationship between social control and the inmate social structure.

Cloward notes that in most institutions, force can be converted into authority because people recognize the legitimacy of authority and are motivated to comply. However, in prison, inmates have rejected the legitimacy of those who seek to control them, and a real problem of social control is the result. In many ways, the job of the custodian is a very difficult one. He or she is expected to maintain control and security within the institution, but has to give up the traditional method of doing so—force. The liberal philosophy of treatment and rehabilitation, with its accompanying policy of granting the inmates more input into the regulation of prison life, has become less popular in recent years, but continues to present problems for guards who wish to exercise more social control of inmates.

Forms of Social Control

Segregation

One of the forms of social control that is used by various correctional institutions is **segregation**—expulsion from the group—although the success of this method is questionable. In fact, the worse the behavior, the more prolonged is the inmate's probable stay in the institution. The inmate may be transferred to a more secure institution, which only relocates but does not solve the problem. At some point, officials must come to terms with the problem of controlling the inmate, since he or she cannot "be expelled from the system as a whole."[43] Another form of segregation is solitary confinement, which is usually imposed for extreme behavior. With the overcrowding problems in correctional facilities in the 1990s, there is limited space in which to implement this method. Also, it must be noted that courts have placed some restrictions on the use of solitary confinement.

Incentives

If they cannot use physical force or segregation, how are correctional officers to control inmates? The use of incentives, embodied in the practice of granting good time and parole, has developed. First, there is an emphasis on voluntary isolation. Correctional officers often tell inmates to watch out for other inmates, do their own time, and not get involved with others. At times, parole may be recommended for those inmates who do not participate in certain primary group activities. Not too long ago, an incentive philosophy developed that is based on rehabilitation and social reintegration. Cloward describes this incentive system as a "functional equivalent of the historic separate and silent systems."[44] His thesis is that the system does not work because the goals for which inmates are told to strive are really not available to them.

It has been claimed that the goal in prison is to rehabilitate the inmate by helping him or her reintegrate into society. It has long been recognized that any inmate cannot be forced to reform. Therefore, the application of negative sanctions will only antagonize the inmate. Inmates must voluntarily participate in their own rehabilitation; the modern prison programs have been devised to secure this goal. Yet rates of recidivism are high and prisons are characterized by pressures toward deviant, not conforming, behavior. Cloward argues that these results are brought about by a system that promises rehabilitation and provides inmates incentives to strive toward that goal, but then turns them out into a society that will not let them achieve that goal. "Thus the society itself bars access by legitimate means to socially approved goals the prisoner has been led to covet," and the presence of recidivists in prison undermines the rehabilitative goal for new inmates. The recidivists, by their presence, are making the statement that "you cannot make it legitimately on the outside."[45] This then undermines the effectiveness of the incentive system for those inmates who might be inclined to cooperate.

Illegitimate Opportunities

What about the inmates who will not cooperate with the incentive system? Some argue that they must be controlled, and Cloward suggests that this is done by providing them with illegitimate opportunities to satisfy certain needs and desires. Cloward explained how this system leads to social control. Despite the fact that correctional officers have more power than do inmates, they cannot control inmates without inmate support. Physical force is no longer an acceptable weapon, segregation is limited, and incentives do not always work. "Limitations on power in the one system therefore compel adaptive or reciprocal adjustments between the two systems. In effect, concessions must be made by the officials to the inmates." A system of accommodation develops. The correctional officers provide the inmates with illegitimate ways to fulfill their needs and, in return, those inmates exert social control over other inmates. The system provides that all parties fulfill their roles. If the inmates do not perform, the correctional officers can threaten to withdraw and establish relationships with other inmates. If correctional officers do not perform, inmates can organize other inmates in a way to embarrass them. "Each is captive and captor of the other," and this results in stability within the prison. As inmates become upwardly mobile, they become more conservative because they do not want to upset their positions in the system. Thus, the accommodative system leads toward inmate passivity and docility, and the inmate elites "constitute the single most important source of social control in the prison." They are against the official value system, but they avoid unnecessary conflict with that system. They play an integrating role between the inmate system and the official system. "They mediate and modify the diverse pressures emanating from each system. They bring order to an otherwise strifeful situation."[46]

Social Control: An Original Approach

John Irwin[47] published his original analysis of the inmate social structure in men's prisons in 1977. The following sections examine Irwin's contribution.

Irwin's Approach

Irwin pointed out that there is currently more conflict among inmates and staff members in prisons than has historically been the case. He attributes this to the increasing conflict in our society.

Irwin traced the development of theories about the prison community, demonstrating how the general theories prevalent in sociology permeated such studies. The earlier findings about inmate social roles took place in a social system that was made up of those whose duty was to maintain order and those who had to adapt to the "pains of imprisonment." The result was a system of accommodation. Some prison leaders would receive special privileges in exchange for assisting guards in maintaining order. The various social roles reflected the functions within the accommodative system.

In the 1960s, however, the climate of the prison began to change. The inmate population shifted to minorities, mainly African Americans and Puerto Ricans, who brought with them the African American nationalistic and militant organization from the society outside the prison. The rising development of racial pride and activism among Hispanics spread to prisons. For instance, in the state of California, Hispanic inmates became more hostile to whites and developed closer relationships to African American inmates. In the meantime, white inmates were developing a deep sense of the injustices of prison conditions, especially with regard to the indeterminate sentence. "In 1969 the 'political' activities in the prisons were fused with the outside radical movement, and the 'prison movement' came into being."[48]

In the 1970s, inmates began to organize and demand improvement in their living conditions. Administrators reacted with fear and hostility. They attempted to identify the "revolutionaries" and transfer them to other institutions. While all of this was taking place inside prisons, social scientists were launching their attacks on the rehabilitative ideal. Some argued that treatment had failed and, in addition, treatment was being applied in a discriminatory manner. A new ideology of community corrections was substituted, but it too was criticized.

How has all of this affected the inmate social code? According to Irwin, no single inmate culture, system, or code has emerged. Such a culture precluded by the variety of ethnic, class, and criminal elements within the prison, the variety of experiences the inmates have had outside the prison, and the open hostility within the prison. Having said that, today's correctional system is overrepresented with African American and Hispanic inmates,[49] which is beginning to create a predominate inmate code that is formed along racial and ethnic lines.

The Small Clique

The small clique is the major component of the prison social world. It ranges from a group of two or three, to a large organization such as the CRIPS (Common Revolution in Progress—a known gang in the United States). The small cliques have very little or nothing to do socially with other groups in the correctional facility. With a few exceptions, inmates confine their interactions to their own cliques. Most of these cliques form their own gangs in prison, predominantly along racial, ethnic, and demographic lines. With the emergence of gangs, prisons have become much more complex settings. Some of these gangs include, but are not limited to, the White Mafia, Black Muslims, Mexican Mafia, and the Aryan Brotherhood. It is important to note that the diversity that exists in gangs intensifies power struggles within the institution and generates a "cycle of violence and vengeance."[50]

The Sub-Rosa Economic Life

According to Irwin, the prison community is also characterized by the sub-rosa economic life. In almost every prison, there is an economic system that is legal. For instance, inmates may earn money on prison farms or in industries, although their wages are severely limited and they are not completely free to spend the money in any way they choose. Irwin is, however, referring to an informal, secret economic system, which is usually illicit although it may be generally tolerated.[51]

Irwin argued that this sub-rosa economic system has also undergone changes in the near past. Affluence has increased in prison, as it has in society. Inmates are not allowed to have cash, but many acquire it, smuggled in by friends on the outside. They have more contraband (illegal drugs, alcohol, and so on) than ever before. Gambling and distributing contraband are the main forms of economic activity. "Wheeling and dealing" is frequent and extremely important because goods are still relatively scarce in prison. To acquire scarce goods, inmates interact with others whom they would otherwise avoid. Rules for wheeling and dealing develop, which are violated frequently, thus increasing hostilities. Stealing and cheating are acceptable under the theory that "might makes right." An inmate has to be able to protect himself/herself if there is some contact with these sub-rosa economic activities. Because individuals cannot usually protect themselves on their own, gangs and cliques develop.

Effect on Correctional Officers and Administrators

These changes in the inmate prison community have affected guards and the administrative officials. Prison guards are becoming more professionalized, even developing unions. Conflicts have developed between the "old" and the "new" officers. The nature of this conflict is, at times, rooted in the fact that "old" correctional officers may be "fixed" in their ways and resist the proposed changes often suggested by the "new" personnel. The inmates know this and use the conflict to their advantage. "These divisions are going to remain and continue to play an important role in shaping the prison social world. They must be included in any sociological examination of the contemporary prison."[52]

Finally, the violence associated with the sub-rosa economic activities is easier for the administration to accept, despite the fact there is often more of it than there was in former times when the violence was directed against the administration. This violence does not threaten the moral values or self-concepts of the administration and is therefore not as disturbing to them psychologically. Also, it lends itself to lock-ups and other repressive control measures. However, the lives of the administrators are not easier. They constantly face increasing demands and organization by guards and a loss of the underlying philosophy of rehabilitation that was used to justify the practices of the institution. In addition, administrators have to face the public's demand to be tough on inmates while considering the rehabilitative potential of inmates.

The System Aspects of the Sub-Rosa Economy

Williams and Fish, in their extensive discussion of the sub-rosa economic system in prisons, have argued that administrators must look at the illicit economic transactions as a network—a system—not as individual acts. For instance, suppose a guard finds out that inmate John, who wanted to change his cell assignment, made an illicit arrangement with inmate Steve, who was in a position to influence the change. John "paid" Steve two cartons of cigarettes for this transaction. The guards probably would react only to this transaction and not consider the total economic system. But if John and Steve were not caught, the transactions in the following scenario might result: Steve gives the cigarettes to Paul, to whom he owes a debt for another illicit activity. Paul has an outstanding bad debt, and he uses the cigarettes to "hire" Roger to beat up Dick, who owes the debt. The transactions can continue, with the same two cartons of cigarettes involved as "payment" in each transaction, perhaps eventually being returned to the first inmate in the series of transactions.

It is important, both to the goals of custody and of treatment, that correctional officers understand the system's nature of these illicit economic transactions. With regard to custody, correctional officers must maintain peace among inmates, keep contraband out of prisons, and prevent escapes, all of which may be related to the illicit transactions. As inmates gain power through these illicit economic transactions, they may gain access to contraband, facilitate escapes, and gain power over other inmates. Any one or all of these activities may lead to violence within the prison. Treatment may be affected in those cases in which inmates engaging in illicit activities are motivated primarily by their rebellion against society, rather than by their desire to solve an immediate economic need. For those types of inmates, success in illicit prison ventures may serve to convince them that such activities are worthwhile and should be continued in society upon release.[53]

Sexual Problems in Prison

There are two problems of extreme concern both to prison officials and to inmates—these are the sexual adjustment of the inmate within the institution and the maintenance of the inmate's emotional ties with family and friends outside the prison. These ties are extremely important if the inmate is to be rehabilitated. In the past, studies have shown that "those inmates with strong family ties, and who have maintained those ties during incarceration, are more successful on release than those offenders without such ties."[54] Isolation from family and friends, indeed from all members of the opposite sex, can be the more severe punishment an inmate faces. Absence from his family means an absence of responsibility and the probable loss of sight of the everyday problems of the outside world. It means the lack of an opportunity to support and care for the family.

Isolation from the opposite sex implies abstinence from the satisfaction of heterosexual relationships at a time when, for many inmates, sex drives are quite strong. Many may turn to homosexual behavior, not because of a preference, but because they need some sexual outlet.

Homosexuality

It is virtually impossible to obtain accurate data on the degree to which homosexual acts take place within a prison or jail due to secrecy and also because some prison administrators contend that homosexuality is not a problem within their institutions. Clemmer found that 40 percent of the men in his prison study had some homosexual experiences while in prison. Sykes reported 35 percent, and Joseph Fishman, in a 1934 study, estimated the percentages to be between 30 and 45.[55] These estimates were discussed at a conference on prison homosexuality in the early 1970s. Peter C. Buffum wrote a synthesis of the five working papers presented at that conference, and he concluded that the evidence suggests that many of the "beliefs" about prison homosexuality are myths. Among the important myths are that there is a high incidence of homosexual rape in prisons, and that rape is the main form of prison homosexuality. Finally, the belief that we can solve the problem by establishing outlets for sexual drives is also a myth.[56] Others have not agreed with this position since they argue it is impossible to retrieve the total number of homosexual acts that may have been diverted through the implementation of adequate sexual outlets.[57]

In a discussion of prison homosexuality, it is important to understand prisoner sexual problems in light of the experiences of those people before they entered prison. Correctional facilities merely present situations in which people must make a sexual adjustment.[58] The fact that, in some cases, the adjustment appears to be made in terms of sociological sex roles is quite interesting.

Male Homosexuality: Findings of Earlier Studies

All sexual assaults that take place within the confinement of prisons and jails cannot be categorized as homosexual attacks.[59] Instead, most of these attacks are made for political reasons in order to demonstrate dominance over some individuals. In some cases, a male who is particularly vulnerable to homosexual attacks will enter into a relationship with another male who agrees to "protect" him from the attacks of others.[60] Earlier studies found that the homosexual acts of male prisoners seemed to be a response to their sexual needs coupled with their background of socialization. Men are taught to be aggressive and it has been argued that, for some, playing the male role (the wolf) in a homosexual act enables them to retain this self-concept. Such men are usually from a background in which a man's masculine self-concept is based more on sexual activity than on any other characteristic (in contrast to males who gain masculinity from job status or family or both). It is very important to his self-concept that he retain the only measure of masculinity he has. Playing the male role allows him to continue thinking that he is "masculine" because he is the aggressor and the penetrator. Although he may also be looking for a meaningful emotional relationship to replace those he had outside the prison, he is more likely to be looking for the release of physical tension. Thus, many inmates see the relationship as "little more than a search for a casual, mechanical act of physical release. Unmoved by love, indifferent to the emotions of the partner he has coerced, bribed, or seduced into a liaison, the wolf is often viewed as simply masturbating with another person."[61]

Carroll's Study: Homosexuality and Race Relations

Leo Carroll's study of male inmates is consistent with prior findings that emphasize the sometimes violent and mainly physical nature of the sexual relationships in men's prisons, as opposed to the predominant family nature of such relationships in women's prisons. Carroll also found that prostitution is the most frequent type of homosexual relationship and that it is usually an intraracial relationship. However, he found that aggressive and violent sexual behavior was often explained not in terms of an attempt to prove one's masculinity, but as the result of racial problems.

Carroll reviewed the historical existence of tension regarding sexual relations between African Americans and whites. White men have often had access to African American women as well as white women, but white women have been almost totally inaccessible to African American men. If an African American man did gain such access, even with the consent of the woman, he faced great trouble, even death by lynching. African American men were also criticized for not being able to protect their women from white men. According to Carroll, this background influences prison sexual relationships between African Americans and whites. Sexual assaults of African American prisoners on whites may be partially explained by the lack of female sexual partners and the greater solidarity of African Americans within the prison, "but the motive force behind them has its roots deep within the entire socio-historical context of black-white relations in this country. The prison is merely an arena within which blacks may direct aggression developed through 300 years of oppression against individuals perceived to be representatives of the oppressors."[62]

Carroll observed that, traditionally in our society, African Americans have not had the ways of proving their masculinity that are available to white men. In prison, an African American has a chance, as one inmate said, to show that he is a man "by making a white guy into a girl." Beginning a sexual assault upon a white "is to some extent an imitation rite by which black prisoners demonstrate their manhood and blackness to their peers." African Americans rationalize this behavior as retaliation for the way the white man has treated them in our society. "He's been raped—politically, economically, morally raped," said an African American.[63] They pick victims who are higher educated than they and who lack criminal identity. That may be because they see those persons as being middle class, the class they perceive as the main oppressor. Another reason is that "their isolation precludes retaliatory responses."[64]

The African Americans often harass and threaten their victims prior to the attack. In addition to heightening the activity, such harassment serves other purposes. The aggressor may find out whether the young man has friends who will come to his aid, and he may use the harassment to gain the trust and confidence of the victim and thus manipulate him. Sexual assaults are called "train jobs" because several inmates are involved. In most interracial assaults, the white victim will be subjected to the sexual attacks of several African Americans, although the composition of the African American group will change from time to time.[65]

One final point refers to the question—why do not other white inmates protect the young and physically small from such attacks by African Americans? According to Carroll, the stronger whites use the situation. After African American inmates seem to be through with the victim, the white inmates who want sexual relationships come along, are kind to him, and in a real sense, "seduce him." After the treatment a white victim has received from the African American inmates, "it ain't nothing for him to take care of me and a coupla of others, he's glad to do it."[66]

This discussion of male homosexuality and the forms it takes in prison should be considered in light of our previous discussion of the importation-versus-deprivation theories advanced to explain the inmate community. Clearly, prison represents the inmate with a problem of sexual deprivation, but according to Buffum (speaking of the options the inmate faces—nocturnal sex dreams, masturbation, and sexual contact with the same sex), "the meaning, amount, and character of these adjustments will be strongly dependent on the meaning that these same behaviors had for the inmate before he or she was incarcerated."[67] It is important to mention here that although Carroll's study focused on black-on-white violence, white-on-black assaults do occur and have been the source of much attention recently.

Recent Issues Affecting Prison Homosexuality

The issues affecting prison homosexuality discussed earlier are augmented in today's correctional facilities by the presence of the **HIV** virus. This crude reality of today's correctional system has made matters more complex for prison administrators and guards. The "safe-sex" campaigns launched via mass communication have had little effect inside prisons. This is mostly due to the fact that inmates do not have access to condoms and other means of protection against the HIV virus. Thus, the deprivation of heterosexual activity in addition to the lack of availability of condoms increase the chances of inmates being infected by the HIV virus. The problem is so serious that in states such as Texas, acquired immune deficiency syndrome (AIDS) was the leading cause of death among its inmates in 1994—it left a toll of 138 deaths. To address this, the Texas Department of Criminal Justice (TDCJ) uses "protective custody" if contact with an HIV-positive inmate poses a threat to other inmates. In addition, "special housing" may be used if a warden perceives an inmate's violent behavior as a threat to the safety of others.[68] Although it is known that homosexual acts take place in today's prison facilities, their frequency and nature are unclear. The general misunderstanding that exists among the general population in regard to the frequency of homosexual acts in prison has been augmented in recent years by the media. Just recently, a sex scandal in a Georgia prison involving fourteen employees, including a deputy warden, took center stage in most newspapers. These individuals were indicted for having sex with female inmates—an episode of prison misconduct in which force of a psychological rather than a physical nature powered the abuse.[69] Another incident that received national attention involved Marion Barry, mayor of Washington, D.C., who was alleged to have engaged in oral sex in a crowded prison visiting room while serving time for possession of cocaine. In this incident, it was alleged that Barry's visitor was a prostitute.[70] These incidents are usually regarded by the public as occurring frequently inside prisons. For instance, in 1993, the *New York Times* published an article titled "The Rape Crisis Behind Bars," which discussed the entrenched tradition of rape in prison and went on to regard prison as a training site for most rapists.[71] Unfortunately, these assumptions remain unchallenged for the most part.

The consensual sexual activity among inmates has been examined less frequently than has coerced sex. Studies of sex between "homosexuals" in correctional facilities have taken the perspective that this type of sex is either an asocial problem or is a result of being institutionalized. Recent studies argue that inmates often "improvise" while in prison, mostly due to the fact that heterosexual contact is nonexistent.[72] However, few researchers have examined male-to-male sexual relationships between caring sexual partners, perhaps because there is thought to be little to no violence in this type of sexual contact. Thus, consensual sex in prison is viewed by many as being less threatening to the inmate or institutional security than is rape. In fact, it has been reported that this type of sexual encounter occurs more frequently than rape in today's prisons.[73]

Homosexual Rape in Prisons

Susan Brownmiller supported the importation theory of homosexual rape. Brownmiller argued that rape in prison is a power play. She analogized homosexual rape in a male prison to the rape of a female by a male in society—it is the result of a need to dominate, control, and conquer. "Prison rape . . . is an acting out of power roles within an all-male, authoritarian environment in which the younger, weaker inmate, usually a first time offender, is forced to play the role that in the outside world is assigned to women."[74]

Other studies have suggested that rape in prisons is "rampant,"[75] and that sexual assaults are "epidemic."[76] Despite this, some studies have suggested that consensual sex in prison seldom happens and that sexual assaults are extremely rare. In these studies, it is reported that numbers of males admitting to being raped in prison range are less than 1 percent.[77] Due to the differences of opinion in regard to prison rape, a study was conducted in 1994 at a Delaware prison. Its purpose was to explore the nature and frequency of sexual contact between male inmates. The authors of this research administered a survey of sexual behavior to respondents who were questioned extensively about the sexual activity they engaged in, observed directly, and heard about "through the grapevine" before their entry into the prison treatment program. The findings of this study suggested that (1) although sexual contact is not widespread, it nevertheless takes place; (2) the preponderance of the activity is consensual instead of forced; and (3) inmates themselves perceive the myth of pervasive sex in prisons, often contradicting their own realities.[78]

Despite the finding made by the previously mentioned study, there is an increasing concern over the rights of inmates not to be the victim of sexual assaults. A new approach to inmate rape is represented by the Prisoner Rape Education Project (PREP), a pioneering team effort led by survivors and professionals. This approach was issued in 1993 by the Safer Society project of the New York State Council of Churches. PREP aims at providing practical information and advice to inmates and staff on avoidance and survival; it consist of two audiotapes that are custom-made for prisoners and a manual for staff. Aside from this new approach sponsored by private organizations, the courts are also rendering some attention to the issue of rape in prisons. In July 1993, the Federal Court of Appeals (Eleventh Circuit) affirmed a state-wide prison training program on rape. This program was ordered in 1990 by Florida district court judge James C. Paine, who stated in *LaMarca v. Turner,* that "rape is one of the most degrading events, short of death, that can occur in prison."[79] In 1994, the U.S. Supreme Court, in *Farmer v. Brennan,* reinstated an inmate's right to claim for money damages from prison officials for failing to render protection from rape.[80] It is only safe to assume that rape will continue to take place in prisons as the incarceration rate grows to unprecedented proportions.

Alternatives to Prison Homosexuality

What can be done to decrease prison homosexuality short of solitary confinement for all inmates? Several suggestions have been made. In this section, we discuss the two most frequently mentioned—conjugal visits in prisons and home furloughs—and then analyze these measures with regard to their potential for reducing prison homosexuality.

Conjugal Visits   Administrators in some jurisdictions permit **conjugal visits.** This system provides prisoners with opportunities for sexual and social contacts with their spouses in a relaxed, unsupervised special area of the prison community. During the visits, the couple may engage in sexual intercourse, may just be alone together, or may use the time in any other way they choose. In some cases, the visit has been expanded to include the entire nuclear family, not just the spouse. Some involve a live-in weekend instead of just a few hours on visiting day.

One of the first institutions in the United States to permit conjugal visits was the Mississippi State Prison at Parchman. Parchman, an old plantation converted into a penal farm, consisted of 21,000 acres of rich delta land and sixteen inmate camps. Each camp had a residence building and a camp sergeant. Parchman was largely self-sufficient and the buildings and grounds were maintained by prison labor.

Parchman has no record of when or how the first conjugal visits were started, although it is said that they can be traced as far back as 1918, when African Americans were allowed to take their wives or girlfriends to their rooms. For privacy, they hung towels up around their beds. Later, the inmates built what came to be known as the "red houses." These separate buildings were used for private visits of inmates with their wives. These visits were not guarded, and the inmate and his visitors were free to stroll anywhere on the 21,000 acres. Only married couples were permitted to use the conjugal visiting facilities, which consisted of rooms that were 8 by 10 feet in size, furnished with mirrors, beds, and tables. "About one-fourth of Parchman's 1,700 inmates have access to these rooms: the three-fourths who do not include disciplinary cases, condemned prisoners, unmarried men and all women."[81]

This is only one example of the conjugal visits that are presently taking place in prisons throughout the United States. In fact, conjugal visits are allowed in only seven states despite the fact that there is a growing number of groups that advocate the implementation of this program in all states. One of the negative effects of conjugal visits involves the humiliation that some women have to endure from guards as they are escorted to a room to meet with their spouse. It is often reported that guards make fun of and reprimand these women while they are being searched. Most prison wives struggle with decisions concerning their sexual lives. Some of them believe that they should be celibate until their husbands are released, while others agree with their spouses that extramarital sexual encounters will be acceptable until the inmate is released from prison. However, it is important to note that it is not sex that most prison wives miss the most, but rather they long to be held in the privacy of a home. This has led to the formation and continuing growth of support groups across the nation that advocate for the creation of improved visitation conditions, including special playrooms where fathers can spend time with their children. This is particularly important since it has been estimated that 80 percent of all women and 50 percent of all men in prison have children. Furthermore, statistics show that more than 1.5 million minors have a parent behind bars. It is important to note that 43 percent of these children are under the age of seven, while 45 percent are between the ages of seven and twelve.[82] Most studies suggest that the closer the ties of the incarcerated inmate with his family, the less likely the inmate will commit crimes once released.

Furloughs   Mississippi was the first state to allow inmates to take leave from prison to visit their families. In 1918, ten-day holiday leaves were allowed for minimum custody inmates. In 1922, Arkansas instituted a **furlough** program, but for the next thirty-two years, no additional jurisdiction adopted the furlough. In the 1960s, several states and the entire federal prison system began furlough programs.[83] In the 1988 presidential elections, furloughs became an issue as Vice-president Bush raised the issue with regard to Willie Horton. Mr. Horton was released on furlough in Maryland, which was being governed at the time by Michael Dukakis. When on furlough, Horton raped a woman twice and then stabbed her husband. At the time, voters saw furloughs as part of Dukakis's "liberal" policy toward inmates—this damaged Dukakis's credibility as a presidential candidate and assisted George Bush in winning his presidential bid. The publicity given to Horton affected furloughs to the extent that they declined in number in 1988. This took place despite the fact that evidence suggests that inmates commit few crimes while they are on furloughs.[84] However, the number of furloughs increased in some areas of the country in the 1990s, as suggested by a survey conducted by the American Correctional Association (ACA). One of these states, Florida, experienced a 73 percent increase in furloughs over the previous year.[85] In addition, several states have recently reported a success rate of 95 to 100 percent in their furlough programs.[86]

Advocates of furlough programs argue that they encompass conjugal visiting but eliminate the "possibility of degradation" and allow sexual relations to occur in normal circumstances and surroundings. Furloughs are broader than conjugal visits because they allow the inmate to leave the institution in order to perhaps look for a job or attend a funeral. A study of California inmates in 1969 indicated that "82 percent . . . looked for, confirmed, or secured a job for parole. The responses of the families, in turn, suggest strong support and a positive beginning. An independent rater listed 86 percent as having accomplished 'most' of the things planned."[87] Another study indicated that inmates who receive furloughs before they are released from the prison on parole are better parole risks than those who do not receive furloughs.[88]

It is important to note that furlough programs will, of course, involve risks. Additional children may be born, illegal offenses may be committed, and inappropriate behavior short of illegal offenses could occur. But such risks exist any time an inmate is released from prison. Since most inmates are eventually released, the challenge is to find ways to help them readjust to the community.

Violence in Prisons

One final subject of importance in looking at the prison community is the violence that takes place. We have already discussed the violence involved in homosexual rape. However, other forms of violence occur in prison. Recently, the television network HBO created a program called "Oz," which depicts some of the violence that takes place inside prison.[89] The reaction by many viewers is of shock and disbelief that such incidents of violence can take place inside a controlled facility such as a prison. In fact, statistics suggest that the annual number of assaults by inmates rose 20 percent—from 21,590 in 1990 to 25,948 in 1995. Also, assaults on staff grew by one-third, from 10,731 in 1990 to 14,165 in 1995. However, despite this trend, fewer inmate violations unrelated to assault were reported in 1995 than in 1990.[90] In the next section, we look at inmate self-inflicted violence, assaults and batteries, prison homicides, and finally, riots.

Inmate Self-Inflicted Violence

According to Hans Toch, the most frequent form of violence in prisons is inmate self-inflicted violence. Little attention is paid in the press to such violence, if indeed it is even reported outside the prison walls. Such violence at times results in the death of the inmate.[91]

One of the reasons why we do not hear about inmate self-inflicted violence is that it is downplayed by inmates. "Inmates see it as an unmanly and weak thing to do unless it is blatantly manipulative."[92] Such violence is also downplayed by staff who may see publicity on inmate self-inflicted violence, especially when a weapon is used, as an indication that the prison is lax on security.

Assaults, Batteries, and Prison Homicides

James B. Jacobs, in his study of the Stateville Prison, pointed out that although the "most distinctive manifestation of prison violence is homosexual rape,"[93] there are other types of violence. It is very hard to define violence, but we can argue that it must include verbal threats (technically, these are called assaults), batteries (the actual offensive touching of a person), and in the extreme, homicide. An inmate describes the condition of a fellow inmate after being the victim of a violent episode, referring to the fellow inmate as having "his intestines spilling out from a razor slash across his stomach. We had to keep pushing his entrails back into place as we raced the gurney down the corridor."[94] Prison violence may consist of any combination of these forms, involving inmates against guards, guards against inmates, or inmates against each other. We confine our discussion here to one of the most serious crimes inside correctional facilities—prison homicide.

In 1977, Sawyer F. Sylvester, John H. Reed, and David O. Nelson published *Prison Homicide,* the result of their 1973 study on prison data from all states as well as from federal jurisdictions. The work has been described by criminologist John C. Ball, former president of the American Society of Criminology, as the most extensive work on prison homicide. We will look briefly at the findings of the classic study.

The investigators found that, as expected, there are more prison homicides in maximum security prisons among inmates who have a history of violence, but they were surprised to find that the main factors in such homicides were not gang conflicts and racial tensions. They found that in order to understand the prison homicides, it was necessary to look at the relationship of the murderer to the victim. Most prison homicides, like those outside prison, involve the more violent-prone members of society. However, a distinction must be made between those murders involving one assailant and those involving multiple assailants. Multiple assailants seem to be more rational and take more effort to plan their homicides than do single assailants, who are more emotional or episodic. For example, the latter may kill as a result of a homosexual relationship, whereas the former might kill those who violate the inmate code as punishment. Multiple assailants are usually younger, more intelligent, and more often from urban environments. They are more likely to have committed another homicide while in prison and they, like all assailants, have prior records of violence outside the prison, although those acts of violence were usually serious personal crimes and burglary, but not homicide. Single assailants, on the other hand, "seem to have a less patterned criminal career. If not serving sentences for homicide, they are usually serving shorter sentences than assailants in multiple-assailant homicides."[95]

What explains rates of violence in prisons? Sylvester, Reed, and Nelson concluded that size, not density, of the prison is an important variable, but quickly noted that large prisons may have a selective population of persons most likely to engage in homicide. It may also be that it is more difficult to control the population in large rather than in small prisons. They found no evidence of a relationship between the existence of recreational facilities and homicide rates but warned that they had no measure of the quality or the use of these facilities and no indication of their value for reasons other than possibly preventing homicide. They found no evidence of an interracial nature of conflict when looking at prisons nationwide, although there was some evidence that it might be a factor in state prisons. On the whole, African Americans and whites were victims in proportion to their numbers in the general prison population.

> Given the fact that young blacks outside prison walls are twelve times as likely to be victimized by homicide, the racial parity of victimization within prison walls is striking. Anything that might be construed to be a "subculture of violence" among blacks outside prison appears to be ameliorated by conditions inside prison walls.

They warned, however, that one must be cautious in interpreting the data and that their study should not serve "as a justification for what is, but a call to further responsibility and action."[96]

Statistics show us that a total of 314 correctional officers at the federal, state, and local levels have been killed in the line of duty by inmates. One of the first recorded incidents involved the death of Andrew F. Turner, a correctional officer at the Leavenworth Federal Penitentiary in Kansas. He was killed by inmate Robert Stroud with a homemade knife, as a result of a disciplinary report Turner filed a day earlier. As a result of this incident, President Woodrow Wilson commuted Stroud's sentence to life imprisonment. To help fill some of the long days behind bars, Stroud developed a fascination with birds, and soon after his death he became known as "The Birdman of Alcatraz." All totaled, twenty-one members of the Federal Bureau of Prisons have been killed in the line of duty. One of the most recent deaths took place in December 1994, when D'Antonio Washington, age thirty-one, was viciously assaulted by an inmate who beat him to death with a hammer. This attack took place at the U.S. Penitentiary in Atlanta, Georgia.[97] Among inmates, violence seems to also be a predominant phenomenon. Between 1990 and 1995, a total of 410 inmates were killed by other inmates in both state and federal prison facilities.[98] This figure is not inclusive of homicides that took place in jails, suicides, or aggravated assaults. In addition, we must consider the fact that these statistics only include "reported" crimes, therefore ignoring the criminal incidents that occur and are not reported. The lack of reporting may occur because the victim may fear retaliation or may feel correctional staff will not take any action to punish the offender.

Prison Riots

The historical occurrence of riots in this country is interesting and also important to the sociological analysis of the causes of riots. In 1969, thirty-nine riots were reported; in 1970, fifty-nine occurred, an increase over 1969 of 51 percent. Recently, riots at Santa Fe in 1980 and Atlanta in 1987 have received public attention. According to the book *Prison Violence in America,* a total of 260 riots were reported in the United States between 1971 and 1983. The primary cause of these riots was racial problems, while the second was inmate dissatisfaction with rules or privileges. It has also been reported that most of these inmate riots usually involved twenty-five to forty-nine inmates, while only eighteen of them involved 500 inmates or more. It is also important to note that riots occur in series. The Jackson, Michigan riot of 1952 was followed by more than twenty-five riots through 1953. The 1955 riot in Walla Walla, Washington was followed by a long series of riots, as was the Attica riot in September 1971. In contrast, studies reveal that only one riot occurred in this country between 1884 and 1888 and that in no decade prior to the 1920s did we have more than a total of five riots reported.[99]

An important feature of these earlier riots is that they apparently were isolated incidences, unrelated to influences outside the institution.[100] In their 1956 analysis of riots, sociologist Frank E. Hartung and psychologist Maurice Floch classified riots as (1) brutal, or (2) collective. Most of the early riots were brutal in nature, triggered mainly by complaints about harsh conditions—poor, insufficient, or contaminated food; inadequate, unsanitary, or dirty housing; sadistic brutality by prison officials; or some combination of these factors.[101] According to Hartung and Floch, prisoners would complain to officials about these conditions, officials would get defensive and resort to disciplinary measures, prisoners would complain and violate internal prison rules, assault others or themselves, and occasionally riot.

The second type of riot, the collective riot, first took place in 1952, according to Hartung and Floch. This type of riot differs sociologically and psychologically from the brutal type. In the 1960s, riots in American prisons took a dramatic shift, analogous to the civil rights protests and student protests on campus. Prisoners still demanded medical, recreational, and educational improvements, but it was increasingly common for inmates to question the legitimacy of their incarceration and to claim that they were political prisoners of an unjust and corrupt political system. Although all prison riots are unique, they usually take place in stages. Spotlight 8.1 explains the five stages of prison riots.

Some inmates contend that their crimes are a justifiable retaliation against a society that denies them the opportunity for social and economic gain. Denial of basic rights in prison, cruel punishment, racial prejudice, and other violations of the system make inmates one of America's most deprived minorities.[102] There is a development of political protest in prisons; prisoners, like members of labor unions and African American civil rights organizations, can be viewed as a group of individuals searching for an effective way of expressing demands and achieving results from the political system. Their attempts have gained more public reaction, although that reaction has not been reflected in substantial prison reform. Prisoners have also formed unions in an attempt to improve their bargaining power. Hartung and Floch theorized that the collective riot results from the combination of three sociological and social psychological components: (1) the nature of the maximum custody prison; (2) the aggregation of different types of inmates within one prison; and (3) the destruction of semiofficial, informal inmate self-government by a new administration.[103]

Spotlight 8.1

Stages of Prison Riots

1. **Initial Explosion:** The sudden (or planned) uprising in which inmates gain partial control of the institution.

2. **Organization:** The emergence of leadership among inmates. This takes place as correctional personnel mobilize to respond.

3. **Confrontation:** Inmates are confronted by force. This can vary from long discussions to the issuance of quick warnings.

4. **Termination:** Custodial control is regained. This is done through firepower, nonlethal force, or an agreement.

5. **Explanation:** The incident is investigated with the intent of identifying the cause of the disturbance while providing public assurances that all necessary remedies have been implemented.

Source: *Correctional Institutions* by Fox, © 1983. Adapted by permission of Prentice-Hall, Inc., Upper Saddle River, NJ.

Most inmates, historically and at the time Hartung and Floch were writing, were incarcerated under conditions of maximum security. Most inmates do not need that type of security, yet they live in confined quarters where almost every detail of their lives is monitored and ordered, leaving them with little to do except plan to escape. Hartung and Floch claimed that incarceration under such conditions leads to emotional problems. That, combined with the second reason —the mingling of different types of inmates—gives aggressive inmates an even greater advantage over the more passive types. The aggressive inmates, which include the predatory habitual criminals, take over the leadership of the inmate groups. With the lack of sufficient numbers of guards, some of the administrative functions of the prison are given over to the inmates; they then develop considerable power over other inmates and even over the administration. It is the inmates and not the officials who are in a position to control other inmates and maintain order and discipline within the prison. Those inmates in control are thus able to "obtain a great deal of self-expression" and are in a sense "elevated to semiofficial self-government." They are in control of those few things that make prison life tolerable, and in return for this power, they keep other inmates under control, thus pleasing the officials. Hartung and Floch contended that when such inmate control was removed during periods of reform, and not replaced with other avenues for inmate self-expression, problems resulted. The aggressive inmates then became a destructive force. This is still the case in today's prisons.

Recent attempts have been made to prevent prison riots from taking place. However, they vary from institution to institution. Studies on the "lessons of prison riots" have suggested that correctional institutions can help prevent riots by making sure their emergency response teams are fully functional; by taking aims to prevent illegal drugs from entering prisons; by improving communication with inmates; by creating intensive training for prison officers; and by establishing various inmate programs.[104] In some cases, such as that of the State Correctional Institution at Huntington, Pennsylvania, conflict resolution programs have been implemented to reduce prison violence by teaching inmates the skills and resources to handle their own and other inmates' anger. This program also teaches correctional officers the communication skills necessary for positive interaction with inmates.[105] However, it is important to note that the implementation of these programs does not guarantee a riot-free environment. Some have argued that as long as we have overcrowded prison facilities in the United States, we better get used to paying the price associated with the increasing number of prison riots.

WiseGuide Wrap-Up In this chapter, we discussed the inmate community, or subculture, with its various social roles. Starting with Clemmer's concept of "prisonization," we traced the development of the theories and studies of inmate subculture. We examined the views of various sociologists who have argued that the inmate subculture is the result of adaptation as well as importation. Inmates do make certain adjustments in prison because of the "pains of imprisonment"—the deprivations imposed by prison life. But those adjustments are influenced by the background experiences of inmates, as well as by their current contacts with the outside world and their expectations for the future.

We discussed the specific problems associated with prison homosexuality, and examined conjugal visits and furloughs as possible solutions to some forms of prison homosexuality. If the analyses are correct, and prison homosexuality fulfills more than purely physiological needs, it is quite possible that neither conjugal visits nor furloughs will have a great impact in reducing prison homosexuality. If aggressive male homosexuality is the result of the aggressor's need to be dominant and to show his masculinity, or if it represents racial tension, homosexuality will not significantly decrease by programs aimed only at opportunity for sexual release. Finally, we discussed prison violence and analyzed the patterns of such violence, especially prison riots, and considered several suggestions for preventing prison violence.

The discussions in this chapter make it clear that we cannot ignore the problems that individuals face when they are incarcerated. The ways in which inmates adapt to prison life have implications not only for the security of the institution and of society, but for the future of the inmates and society when the incarcerated individuals are released. As Justice Marshall once said with regard to prison life,

> When the prison gates slam behind an inmate, he does not lose his human quality; his mind does not become closed to ideas; his intellect does not cease to feed on a free and open interchange of opinions; his yearning for self-respect does not end; nor is his quest for self-realization concluded. If anything, the needs for identity and self-respect are more compelling in the dehumanizing prison environment.[106]

Notes

1. Trasler, Gordon. "The Social Relations of Persistent Offenders," in Robert M. Carter, Daniel Glaser, and Leslie T. Wilkins, eds., *Correctional Institutions.* (Philadelphia: J.P. Lippincott and Company, 1972), p. 207.

2. Sykes, Gresham M. *The Society of Captives.* (Princeton, NJ: Princeton University Press, 1958), pp. 63–83.

3. Clemmer, Donald. *The Prison Community.* (1940; reprint ed., New York: Rinehart and Winston, 1958), pp. 298, 300, 301.

4. See, for example, Barry Schwartz, "Peer Versus Authority Effects in a Correctional Community," *Criminology* 11 (August, 1973), 233–257.

5. Adams, Kenneth. "Adjusting to Prison Life," in Michael Tonry, ed., *Crime and Justice: A Review of Research,* vol. 16, (Chicago: University of Chicago Press, 1993), pp. 275–359.

6. Wheeler, Stanton. "Socialization in Correctional Communities," *American Sociological Review* 26 (October, 1961), 697–712.

7. Sykes, *Society of Captives,* p. 82, emphasis deleted.

8. Sykes, *Society of Captives,* p. 82, emphasis deleted.

9. Sykes, Greshan M., and Messinger, Sheldon L. "The Inmate Social System," in Richard A. Cloward et al., eds. *Theoretical Studies in Social Organization of the Prison.* (New York: Social Science Research Council, 1960), p. 17.

10. Cloward, Richard A. et al. *Theoretical Studies in Social Organization of the Prison.* (New York: Social Science Research Council, 1960), pp. 21, 35–41.

11. Goffman, Erving. "On the Characteristics of Total Institutions," chapter 2 in Donald R. Cressey, ed., *The Prison: Studies in Institutional*

Organization and Change. (New York: Holt, Rinehart and Winston, 1961), pp. 22–47.

12. Tittle, Charles R. "Inmate Organization: Sex Differentiation and the Influence of Criminal Subcultures," *American Sociological Review* 34 (August, 1969), 503.

13. Irwin, John, and Cressey, Donald R. "Thieves, Convicts and the Inmate Culture," *Social Problems* 10 (Fall, 1962), 143.

14. Clemmer, *Prison Community,* pp. 229–302.

15. Schrag, Clarence C. *Social Types in a Prison Community,* unpublished master's thesis, Seattle: University of Washington, 1944.

16. Irwin and Cressey, "Thieves, Convicts and the Inmate Culture," p. 142.

17. See, for example, Walter C. Reckless, *The Crime Problem,* 2d ed. (New York: Appleton, 1945), pp. 144–145; 148–150; Edwin H. Sutherland, *The Professional Thief.* (Chicago: University of Chicago Press, 1937).

18. See, for example, William Foote Whyte, "Corner Boys: A Study of Clique Behavior," *American Journal of Sociology* 46 (March, 1941), 647–663.

19. Irwin and Cressey, "Thieves, Convicts and the Inmate Culture," p. 148.

20. Irwin and Cressey, "Thieves, Convicts and the Inmate Culture," p. 148.

21. Clemmer, *Prison Community,* p. 130.

22. Irwin and Cressey, "Thieves, Convicts and the Inmate Culture," p. 153.

23. Thomas, Charles W. "Prisonization or Resocialization: A Study of External Factors Associated with the Impact of Imprisonment," *Journal of Research in Crime and Delinquency* 10 (January, 1975), 13–21.

24. Carroll, Leo. "Race and Three Forms of Prisoner Power: Confrontation, Censoriousness, and the Corruption of Authority," in C. Ronald Huff, ed., *Contemporary Corrections: Social Control and Conflict.* (Beverly Hills, CA: Sage Publications, 1977), p. 40.

25. Carroll, "Race and Three Forms," in Huff, ed., p. 41.

26. Wright, Richard, A. *In Defense of Prisons.* (Westport, CT: Greenwood, 1994). (For a different view, see Geoffrey Hunt, Stephanie Riegal, Tomas Morales, and Dan Waldorf, 1993. "Changes in Prison Culture: Prison Gangs and the Case of the Pepsi Generation." *Social Problems* 40: 398–410.

27. Carroll, Leo. *Hacks, Blacks, and Cons: Race Relations in Maximum Security Prison.* (Prospect Heights, IL: Waveland, 1988).

28. Carroll. *Hacks, Blacks, and Cons.* See also Jacobs, James, B. *Stateville: The Penitentiary in Mass Society.* (Chicago: University of Chicago Press, 1977).

29. Schwartz, Barry. "Pre-Institutional vs. Situational Influence in a Correctional Community," *The Journal of Criminal Law, Criminology and Police Science* 62 (Winter, 1971), 542.

30. Akers, Ronald L., Hayner, Norman S., and Gruninger, Werner. "Prisonization in Five Countries: Type of Prison and Inmate Characteristics," *Criminology* 14 (February, 1977), 538.

31. Quoted in Akers, Hayner, and Gruninger, "Prisonization," p. 548.

32. Akers, Ronald L., Hayner, Norman S., and Gruninger, Werner. "Homosexual and Drug Behavior in Prison: A Test of the Functional and Importation Models of the Inmate System," *Social Problems* 21 (No. 3, 1974), 410–422.

33. Thomas, Charles W., and Cage, Robin J. "Correlated of Prison Drug Use," *Criminology* 15 (August, 1977), 193.

34. Akers, Hayner, and Gruninger, "Prisonization in Five Countries," 548. For another study on drug use among inmates, see Charles Tittle, "Inmate Organization: Sex Differentiation and the Influence of Criminal Subcultures," *American Sociological Review* 34 (August, 1969), 492–505.

35. Thomas, Charles W., Petersen, David M., and Zingraff, Rhonda M. "Structural and Social Psychological Correlated of Prisonization," *Criminology* 16 (November, 1978), 390–391.

36. Lawson, Darren P., Segrim, Chris, and Ward, Theresa D. (Sept. 1996). "The Relationship Between Prisonization and Social Skills Among Prison Inmates." *Prison Journal,* vol. 76, no. 113, p. 293 (17).

37. Sykes, *Society of Captives,* pp. 5–6, 84.

38. For discussions of the special vocabularies utilized in men's prisons, see Clemmer, *The Prison Community,* pp. 89–90; Clarence Schrag, "A Preliminary Criminal Typology," *The Pacific Sociological Review* 4 (Spring, 1961), 11–16.

39. Carroll, Leo. *Hacks, Blacks, and Cons: Race Relations in a Maximum Security Prison.* (Lexington, MA: D. C. Heath and Co., 1974).

40. Hassine, Victor. *Life Without Parole,* 2nd ed. (Los Angeles, CA: Roxbury Publishing Co., 1999).

41. Trasler, "Social Relations of Persistent Offenders."

42. Cloward, "Social Control in the Prison," p. 22.

43. Cloward, "Social Control," p. 23.

44. Cloward, "Social Control," pp. 27–28.

45. Cloward, "Social Control," p. 31.

46. Cloward, "Social Control," pp. 35, 42, 48.

47. Irwin, John. "The Changing Social Structure of the Men's Prison," chapter 1 in David F. Greenberg, ed., *Corrections and Punishment,* vol. 8. Sage Criminal Justice System Annuals (Beverly Hills, CA: Sage Publications, 1977), pp. 21–40.

48. Irwin, "The Changing Social Structure of the Men's Prison," p. 27.

49. See Theodore G. Chiricos and Charles Crawford, "Race and Imprisonment: A Contextual Assessment of the Evidence," in *Ethnicity, Race and Crime: Perspectives Across Time and Place,* ed. Darnell F. Hawkins, (Albany, NY: State University of New York Press, 1995).

50. Clarke, Harold. "Gang Problems: From the Streets to Our Prisons," *Corrections Today,* vol. 54, no. 5 (July, 1992), p. 8.

51. For a detailed discussion of the inmate sub-rosa economy, see Vergil Williams and Mary Fish, *Convicts, Codes and Contraband.* (Cambridge, MA: Ballinger Publishing Company, 1974).

52. Irwin, "The Changing Social Structure of the Men's Prison," p. 37.

53. Williams, Vergil L., and Fish, Mary. *Convicts, Codes, and Contraband: The Prison Life of Men and Women.* (Cambridge, MA: Ballinger, 1974), pp. 137–142.

54. Markley, Carson W. "Furlough Programs and Conjugal Visiting in Adult Correctional Institutions," *Federal Probation* 37 (March, 1973), 19–26.

55. Fishman, Joseph. *Sex in Prison.* (New York: National Library Press, 1934), cited in Peter C. Buffum, *Homosexuality in Prisons.* (U.S. Department of Justice, et al., Washington, DC: U.S. Government Printing Office, 1972), p. 13.

56. Buffum, *Homosexuality in Prisons,* p. 2.

57. For a discussion on the myths of sex in prison see "Sex in Prison: Exploring the Myths and Realities," Christine A. Saum; Hilary L. Surratt; James A. Inciardi; Rachael E. Bennett. *Prison Journal,* December, 1995, vol. 75, no. 4. p. 413 (18).

58. Gagnon, John, and Simon, William. "The Social Meaning of Prison Homosexuality," *Federal Probation* 32 (March, 1968), 24.

59. Eigenberg, Helen. "Homosexuality in Male Prisons: Demonstrating the Need for a Social Constructionist Approach," *Criminal Justice Review* 17: 2 (1992): 219–234.

60. For more information see "The Deal Behind Bars," Stephen Donaldson, *Harper's Magazine,* (August, 1996), vol. 293, no. 1755, p. 17 (2).

61. Sykes, *Society of Captives,* p. 97.

62. Carroll, *Hacks, Blacks, and Cons,* p. 184.

63. Carroll, *Hacks, Blacks, and Cons,* p. 185.

64. Carroll, *Hacks, Blacks, and Cons,* p. 186.

65. Carroll, *Hacks, Blacks, and Cons,* p. 183.

66. Carroll, *Hacks, Blacks, and Cons,* p. 186.

67. Buffum, *Homosexuality in Prisons,* p. 9.

68. Editors, Managing Infectious Diseases (Bulletin), Texas Department of Criminal Justice, 1995.

69. Curriden, M. "Prison Scandal in Georgia: Guards Traded Favors for Sex." *National Law Journal,* (September 20, 1993) p. 8.

70. Nichols, B. "Barry Denies Sex-In-Prison Allegations." *USA Today,* (January 6, 1992), p. A3.

71. Donaldson, S. "The Rape Crisis Behind Bars." *The New York Times,* (December 12, 1993), p. A11.

72. Irwin, J. *Prison in Turmoil.* (Boston: Little, Brown, 1980).

73. See Nacci, P. L., and Nkane, T. R. "The Incidence of Sex and Sexual Aggression in Federal Prisons," *Federal Probation* 7, (1983) 31–36.

74. Brownmiller, Susan. *Against Our Will: Men, Women and Rape.* (New York: Simon and Schuster, 1975), p. 258.

75. Weiss, C., and Friar, D. J. *Terror in Prisons: Homosexual Rape and Why Society Condones It.* (New York: Bobbs-Merrill, 1974).

76. Davis, A. J. "Sexual Assaults in the Philadelphia Prison System and Sheriffs Vans," *Trans-Action,* (December, 1968), pp. 8–16.

77. Lockwood, D. *Prison Sexual Violence.* (New York: Elsevier, 1980); also Tewksbury, R. "Measures of Sexual Behavior in an Ohio Prison," *Sociology and Social Research* 74, (1989b), 34–39.

78. Saum, Christine A., Surratt, Hillary L., Inciardi, James A., and Bennett, Rachel E. "Sex in Prison: Experiencing the Myths and Realities," *Prison Journal* (December, 1995), vol. 75, no. 4. p. 413 (18).

79. Donaldson, Stephen. "Can We Put an End to Inmate Rape?" *USA Today* (Magazine). (May, 1995), vol. 123, no. 2600, p. 40(3).

80. Donaldson, "Can We Put an End?," p. 13.

81. "Only on Sunday," *Time* (August 18, 1967), 49. For a detailed study of the Parchman program of conjugal visiting, see Columbus B. Hopper, "The Conjugal Visit at Mississippi State Penitentiary," *The Journal of Criminal Law, Criminology, and Police Science* 53 (September, 1962), 340–343.

82. Dallao, Mary. "Coping with Incarceration—From the Other Side of the Bars," *Corrections Today* (October, 1997), vol. 59, no. 6. p. 96(3).

83. Markley, "Furlough Programs," pp. 20–21.

84. "Study of 53,000 Inmates on Furlough in '87 Finds Few Did Harm," *The New York Times.* (October 12, 1988), p. 12; "Tough Talk Cuts Prison Furloughs," *Tampa Tribune* (November 27, 1988), p. 12.

85. "Prison Furloughs Up 73 Percent From Last Year," *Tallahassee Democrat* (November 12, 1990), p. 2c. For a discussion and evaluation of the Florida Community Control Program (FCCP), see Dennis Wagner and Christopher Baird, "Evaluation of the Florida Community Control Program," Bureau of Justice Statistics, (Washington, DC: U.S. Department of Justice, January, 1993).

86. "Number of Prison Furloughs Increases," *On The Line,* 15 (March, 1992): 5.

87. Serrill, Michael S. p. 25., citing study by Norma Holt, *California Pre-Release Furlough Program for State Prisoners.* (Sacramento, CA: California Department of Corrections, 1969).

88. Holt, quoted in Serrill, *California Pre-Release Furlough Program,* p. 25.

89. Silver, Marc. "This is Not 'I Love Lucy'" (Violent Graphic Depiction of Life on the Home Office Series "OZ"), *U.S News and World Report* (July 14, 1997), vol.123, no. 2. p. 8 (1).

90. Chaiken, Jan M. *Census of State and Federal Correctional Facilities, 1995.* (Washington, DC: Bureau of Justice Statistics. U.S. Department of Justice, August, 1977).

91. Toch, Hans. *Peacekeeping: Police, Prisons, and Violence.* (Lexington, MA: D.C. Heath and Company, 1976), p. 61.

92. Toch, Hans. "A Psychological View of Prison Violence," in Albert K. Cohen, George F. Cole, and Robert G. Bailey, eds., *Prison Violence.* (Lexington, MA: D.C. Heath and Company, 1976), p. 49.

93. Jacobs, James B. "Prison Violence and Formal Organization," chapter 6 in Cohen et al., eds., *Prison Violence,* p. 79.

94. Hassine, *Life Without Parole,* p. 13.

95. Sylvester, Sawyer F., Reed, John H., and Nelson, David O. *Prison Homicide.* (New York: Halsted Press, 1977). p. xxii.

96. Sylvester, Reed, and Nelson, *Prison Homicide,* pp. 75, 82.

97. Floyd, Craig W., (Feb. 1997). "Violence Behind Bars." (Prison Officers Killed in The Line of Duty) (In The Line of Duty), *Corrections Today,* Feb. 1997. v59, n1, p. 64 (1).

98. Bureau of Justice Statistics. *Correctional Population in the United States, 1995.* (Washington, DC: U.S. Department of Justice, 1997), p. 18.

99. For a discussion of the patterns of riots, see the following source: G. David Garson, "The Disruption of Prison Administration: An Investigation of Alternative Theories of the Relationship Among Administrators: An Investigation of Alternative Theories of the Relationship Among Administrators, Reformers, and Involuntary Social Service Clients," *Law and Society Review* 6 (May, 1972), 531–561.

100. Most of the analysis of prison riots has consisted of reporting after the fact of a particular riot. See, for example, *Attica: The Official Report of the New York State Special Commission on Attica.* (New York: Bantam Books, 1972); and Tom Wicker, *A Time to Die.* (New York: Ballantine Books, 1975).

101. Hartung, Frank E., and Floch, Maurice. "A Social-Psychological Analysis of Prison Riots: An Hypothesis," *Journal of Criminal Law, Criminology, and Police Science* 47 (May-June, 1956), 51.

102. Atkins, Burton M., and Glick, Henry R. *Prisons, Protest, and Politics.* (Englewood Cliffs, NJ: Prentice-Hall, 1972), pp. 1–2.

103. Hartung and Floch, "A Social-Psychological Analysis of Prison Riots," 52.

104. Montgomery, Jr., Reid H. "Bringing the Lessons of Prison Riots into Focus" (includes related article on the fearful future of prison riots due to increasing prison populations), *Corrections Today* (February, 1977), vol. 59, no. 1, p. 28 (5).

105. Love, Bill. (August 1994). "Programs Curbs Prison Violence Through Conflict Resolution," (State Correctional Institution of Huntingdon, Pennsylvania) (includes related article, "Stemming the Violence"), *Corrections Today* (August, 1994), vol. 56, no. 5, p. 144 (3).

106. *Procunier* v. *Martinez,* 416 U.S. 396, 428 (1974) (Justice Marshall, with whom Justice Brennan joins, concurring).

The Female Inmate

Until recently, females were seldom studied either as offenders or as victims in the system of criminal justice. Various "reasons" have been given for this neglect: Women have constituted a much smaller percentage of total offenders than their proportion of the population; their crimes have generally been of the kind that do not seriously threaten society, except perhaps its moral fiber, as in the case of prostitution; and women arrested for violations of the law are usually first-time offenders.

Key Terms

battered woman syndrome
chivalry hypothesis

In general, women offenders have not been seen as a grave social problem. They have not presented the serious problems of violence in prison that we have experienced in men's prisons. As inmates, they have been considered easier to manage than male inmates, resulting in less security in women's institutions. The early view on female criminality was based on the notion that police were less likely to arrest women, while juries were less likely to convict them due to a general attitude of protectiveness and benevolence toward them. This became known as the **chivalry hypothesis**. Consequently, the fact that women are generally considered to have been better treated is exemplified by frequently made comments regarding correctional facilities for women as "country clubs" when compared to those for men.

Recently, however, some of these widely held beliefs have been challenged as scholars have begun to take a serious look at the female in the criminal justice system. This chapter focuses on the female offender in the correctional system. To gain some background for our discussion of the differences in institutions for adult males and females, we begin with a brief history of females in the correctional system as well as a comparison of male and female arrest rates. We analyze the profile of the female offender and then return to our discussion of institutions for female offenders. After a brief introduction to the emergence of the separate institution for females, we examine the reasons why so little empirical research has been conducted on these institutions and their occupants. Finally, we learn about the new generation jails for female offenders.

History

Until the late nineteenth century, male and female inmates occupied dungeons, almshouses (poorhouses), and jails. Usually women and children were not segregated from men, resulting in many instances of sexual abuse. Institutions were plagued with physical and sexual abuses and exploitation as well as the inevitable corruption that might be expected when there is no classification of inmates.

Elizabeth Gurney Fry, a middle-class Quaker, was the first person in the United States to fight for changes in the treatment of sentenced children and women. In fact, when Fry and other fellow Quakers visited London's Newgate Prison in 1813, they were shocked by the conditions surrounding women in this institution. This so affected Fry that she began to push for separate institutions for women, to be staffed by women, while offering a domestic environment. Due to Fry's efforts, a parliamentary committee heard about the conditions in which female offenders were incarcerated and, in 1918, ordered reforms to be implemented immediately.

As prison reform began in this country, the practice was to segregate women into corners of existing institutions, which were usually modeled after the penitentiary system. There were few women inmates, a fact that was used to "justify" not providing them with even a matron. Vocational training and educational programs were not even considered.[1] In 1873, the first separate prison for women, the Indiana Women's Prison, was opened. Its emphasis was on rehabilitation, obedience, and religious education. Other institutions followed—a facility in Framingham, Massachusetts in 1877; a reformatory for women in New York in 1891; the Westfield Farm in 1901; and an institution in Clinton, New Jersey in 1913. Separate institutions for women continued to be the basic pattern of incarceration for women until the first coed prison of modern times was established in the United States in 1971. Gradually, other states built facilities for women. However, recent statistics show that female offenders are incarcerated in only fifty-three institutions for women, twenty-nine coed facilities, and approximately 3,500 local and county jails.[2]

Little attention has been given to the female offender until recently. The lack of attention was dramatically illustrated in the 1967 report of the President's Crime Commission, which, in its 222-page report, contained no references to the female offender.[3] This paucity of data is particularly interesting in light of the fact that "women's reformatories were among the very first to involve themselves in research." The Bedford Hills Reformatory for Women in New York employed a psychologist in 1910 and, in 1912, opened a Laboratory of Social Hygiene for research. At about that same time, a Massachusetts reformatory for women established a research department. These developments came well before research departments in prisons for men. However, most of the early efforts were abandoned because of financial problems and apathy of prison officials. When research on inmates began, it was usually conducted on male populations.[4]

In the 1960s, there was a significant emphasis placed on the rights of female offenders in the United States. This, of course, was aided by the political climate the country was experiencing at the time. Soon after, with a Republican administration, the "mood" toward female inmates began to change once again. The growing, punitive drug-related laws of the 1980s, accompanied by a rising fear of crime, led to a "no tolerance" approach toward offenders in general. This approach has had a negative impact on female inmates because it has led to the existing lack of concern over the special needs of female offenders. Some of these needs include, but are not limited to, the emotional trauma of weakening the ties with their children, loss of financial assets, and uncertain relationships with husbands and other loved ones. These needs, when not properly addressed, result in an almost unbearable prison environment in which radical measures such as suicide or escape become feasible options.

The Female in the Criminal Justice System

In a provocative article on the female offender, Ray R. Price, after noting some of the changes the women's liberation movement has created in our society, summed up the position of women in the criminal justice system:

> Probably no part of our society has been so exclusively a male domain as the criminal justice system. The criminal law has been codified by male legislators, enforced by male police officers, and interpreted by male judges. Rehabilitation programs have been administered by males. The prison system has been managed by men, primarily for men.[5]

This lack of attention to women and crime has been particularly noticeable in the literature on the female offender. Before looking at the characteristics of the female offender, however, it is important to note some of the differences in the data on arrests of males and females. This brief overview may help explain the differences in the correctional facilities for each, as well as the various ways in which male and female inmates react to imprisonment.

Data on Arrests of Males and Females: A Comparison

Crime data must be analyzed carefully. An extensive discussion of the problems of interpreting data from the *Uniform Crime Reports*, the basic source of data on crime, cannot be undertaken here.[6] It should be noted, however, that the Federal Bureau of Investigation, which compiles data, warns that one should be careful interpreting the data.

Arrest rates of males and females differ significantly. Although males constitute roughly 50 percent of the population in the United States, they account for 81 percent of all of the arrests made in the United States in 1991. Twelve percent of all male arrests were for driving under the influence, the crime for which men were most often arrested. Women were most often arrested for larceny-theft, which accounted for 76 percent of all arrests of women for serious crimes.

The arrest rates for both males and females have changed in recent years. Interestingly, the number of female arrests increased 24 percent between 1986 and 1991, while the number of male arrests increased only 13 percent in this same period.[7] Women accounted for 19 percent of adult arrests in 1991—this constitutes an increase of 17 percent in 1986. Table 9.1 shows the number of arrests in 1986 and 1991.

The impact of these changes on corrections has been and will continue to be significant. The Bureau of Justice Statistics of 1989 indicated that for the ninth consecutive year, the rate of female incarceration rate surpassed that of men.[8] The 1988 to 1989 increase was 22 percent, while the increase from 1980 to 1984 doubled, with 40,000 females incarcerated.

TABLE **9.1** **Number of Arrests in the United States during 1986 and 1991**

	1986	1991	Percent Change
Female	1,805,422	2,230,417	23.5%
Male	8,582,422	9,667,402	16.7%

Source: Bureau of Justice Statistics, U.S. Department of Justice, "Women in Prison" (March, 1994).

If the present trend of arrest rates of adult women and female juvenile offenders continues to rise, we will be forced to increase the use of probation, develop more opportunities for diverting offenders out of correctional facilities, or increase the capacity of correctional institutions. The increasing cost associated with the physical facilities will be compounded by the need for increased medical, psychological, and psychiatric personnel and services as well as for educational, recreational, and vocational opportunities. If trends continue, female correctional facilities may face some of the same problems that we have witnessed in male institutions in recent years, such as overcrowding.

Interpretation of Data on Female Arrests

The dramatic increase of female arrests may be due to the fact that women are gaining a more equal standing with their male counterparts in society. Thus, one can make the educated guess that their role in criminal behavior has changed from being passive to aggressive in recent years. Also, because drug-related laws carry long prison terms, it can also be speculated that today more women are being sentenced for drug-related offenses than in the past. In fact, in a recent survey, one-third of female offenders, compared to one-quarter of male inmates, were reported to have used a needle to inject illegal drugs.[9] It can only be speculated that the number of female arrests will continue to grow at a faster rate than male arrests due to the increasingly participatory role of women at all levels of society, including criminality.

However, even if we were to accept some of the previously mentioned explanations, there would still be unanswered questions. For instance, why have arrests of women risen so much faster for property crimes but more slowly for violent personal crimes (such as murder and non-negligent manslaughter) than have the percentages of arrests for men? In one of her earlier examinations of female criminality, Freda Adler suggested that since the latter are mainly crimes of passion involving interpersonal relationships, the lower rate of increase for women in this area may indicate that women are more interested than men in improving their financial status.[10]

Other explanations may be more plausible. Normally, cultural changes take place faster in economic than in other areas; women may be trained to restrain their emotions and violence to a greater extent than are men, and that training might be easier to overcome in areas other than domestic. It might be that men who are attacked by women are less likely to report such assaults, or if they are reported, police are less likely to arrest than in cases in which men assault women. Support for the economic reasons comes also from an analysis of crime data from other countries. According to Adler, when the economic disparity between men and women decreases, there is a corresponding increase in rates of female criminality.

Joseph Weis emphasized that when close attention is paid to the official crime rates in the United States, the increases in rates of female criminality are not so surprising. He looks at the dramatic increases in larceny, mainly shoplifting, a crime for which most arrests have traditionally been of women.[11] These crimes are tied to the traditional female roles "in the legal and illegal marketplaces; they move from shopper to shoplifter, from cashing good checks to passing bad ones, from taking aspirins to popping bennies and barbs, from being a welfare mother to being accused of welfare fraud, and so on."[12]

Weis's position is that the image of the new female criminal is a myth based on pop criminology and too much reliance on official crime data. After studying self-reports of middle-class delinquency, he argues that these data reflect gender-role opportunities. Weis concludes that the alleged relationship between female liberation and the emergence of a new type of female criminal is a social invention, not a reality. "Women are not more violent today than a decade ago and the increase in property offenses suggests that the sexism which still pervades the straight world also functions in the illegal marketplace."[13]

Another scholar who has written extensively about women and crime, Rita James Simon, states that "women are committing those types of crimes that their participation in the labor force provides them with greater opportunities to commit than they had in the past." The propensities of men and women to commit crimes are not basically different; the difference has been in opportunities.[14]

Darrel J. Steffensmeier has brought many of these explanations together in his evaluation of trends in female criminality from 1960 to 1990. He indicates that much of the change in both male and female criminality is similar and reflects the social and legal forces that impact both, but that, indeed, there are several differences. Using official data, confirmed by both the National Crime Victimization Survey (NCVS) and self-report data, Steffensmeier notes that women show a much greater involvement in property crimes, especially the minor offenses of larceny-theft, fraud, forgery, and embezzlement and in the typical sex-related offenses, primarily prostitution.

He describes several factors that he believes account for these differences. First, society has different norm expectations for women. Women are expected to be care-givers. They are socialized to be wives and mothers, which leaves very little time for a criminal lifestyle. Even with many women choosing a career path, this socialization factor remains strong. Women also are affected by their sexual/physical attractiveness. Fathers and husbands tend to be protective of women and girls and create a double standard for their behavior. It is acceptable for males to be aggressive and engage in rough and wild behavior, but the expectation is not the same for females. The criminal justice system often reinforces this standard by giving more latitude to males and restricting the behavior of females. In addition, society's value on femininity makes it difficult for a female to violate this stereotype and act in nonfeminine ways that would lead her into criminal opportunities.

Second, the moral development of men and women is such that women are more likely to make moral choices that would not hurt others while men tend to be more aggressive. For women, this means they are less likely to engage in violence and in behaviors that could result in harm to others.

Third, physical strength and aggression are key qualities of criminal offenders and women are either less strong and aggressive, or at least perceived to be so. This means they are not likely to be accepted in criminal subcultures, much less valued, and when they are included, it is as a female, either as someone's "woman" or as property in the pimp-prostitute relationship.

Finally, many women lack access to criminal opportunity. Not only are they perceived to be less qualified for criminal behavior, but they have limited accessibility to the types of jobs that provide an opportunity for criminal behavior. Jobs such as truck driver and laborer often provide opportunities for theft and other crimes not associated with typical "female" jobs.[15]

After looking at the studies of female criminality, we can conclude that female criminality is a complex phenomenon that deserves more attention. The studies discussed here suggest several variables that might be influential. Although scholars do not agree on why male and female arrests rates are changing, a look at the traits of female offenders may present some insight.

Profile of Female Offenders

The typical female inmate is best portrayed by the 1994 Bureau of Justice Statistics Survey of state female prisons. This survey indicates that female inmates resemble, for the most part, male inmates in terms of race and ethnic background. However, women are substantially more likely than men to be serving time for a drug-related offense and less likely than men to be serving time for a violent crime. According to the 1994 survey, female state prison inmates were most likely to be African American, between the ages of twenty-five and thirty-four, unemployed at the time of arrest, high school graduates or holders of a GED (or with some college), and unmarried. Furthermore, nearly six in ten female inmates were raised in a household with at least one parent absent, while half reported that an immediate family member had also served time. Four in ten survey respondents reported they had been victims of prior sexual or physical abuse.[16]

Most of the female inmates who belonged to a racial or ethnic minority had unique characteristics—they were unmarried, mothers of children under age eighteen, and daughters who had grown up in homes where both parents were absent. The explanation for the over-representation of minority groups in female prisons may rest on the fact that racism played a significant role at the time of arrest and conviction, and in sentencing. Furthermore, the explanation may also be found in the differences that exist in socioeconomic class and position occupied by white and African American women throughout history. It may be that African American women have experienced more need, encouragement, and a greater opportunity to engage in criminal behavior than their white counterparts. More women of African American descent have had complete responsibilities for taking care of their families while being emancipated for over a century through necessity. Because she has frequently lacked institutional support or role models, the African American woman has found herself looking after a large number of children and, in many cases, having to support them financially in a world that constantly seeks candidates with training and/or a formal education, both of which are seldom present among African American women. Some argue that there is very little doubt that it was out of necessity, and not preference, that the African American woman developed traits, such as toughness and aggressiveness, that were conducive to the types of crimes she is often accused of committing.[17]

In the 1990s, a different type of female offender is arriving at the footsteps of prison. She is called the battered woman. These women often find themselves in a correctional institution because they resorted to violence to end their victimization after enduring long periods of abuse by their husbands. Statistics suggest that female offenders who committed homicide were almost twice as likely as a relative, such as a parent or sibling, to have killed an intimate (husband, exhusband, or boyfriend).[18] Unfortunately, for many of them, their action is not considered an act of self-defense. This is because in most cases, they are not being

T A B L E **9.2** **Most Serious Offense of State Prison Inmates,
by Sex, 1991 and 1986**

| | Percent of Prison Inmates | | | |
| | 1991 | | 1986 | |
Most Serious Offense	*Female*	*Male*	*Female*	*Male*
All offenses	100.0%	100.0%	100.0%	100.0%
Violent offenses	32.2%	47.4%	40.7%	55.2%
Murder[a]	11.7	10.5	13.0	11.2
Negligent manslaughter	3.4	1.7	6.8	3.0
Kidnaping	.4	1.2	.9	1.7
Rape	.4	3.7	.2	4.5
Other sexual assault	1.3	6.2	.9	4.7
Robbery	7.8	15.2	10.6	21.3
Assault	6.2	8.3	7.1	8.1
Other violent[b]	1.1	.5	1.2	0.8
Property offenses	28.7%	24.6%	41.2%	30.5%
Burglary	4.5	12.9	5.9	17.0
Larceny/theft	11.1	4.5	14.7	5.6
Motor vehicle theft	.7	2.3	.5	1.4
Arson	1.0	.7	1.2	.7
Fraud	10.2	2.4	17.0	3.2
Stolen property	1.0	1.4	1.6	2.0
Other property[c]	.1	.5	.4	.5
Drug offenses	32.8%	20.7%	12.0%	8.4%
Possession	11.8	7.3	4.0	2.9
Trafficking	19.8	13.0	7.3	5.3
Other/unspecified	1.3	0.4	0.7	0.2
Public-order offenses	5.7%	7.0%	5.1%	5.2%
Weapons	.5	1.9	.9	1.5
Other public-order[d]	5.1	5.1	4.3	3.7
Other offenses	.6%	.4%	.9%	.7%
Number of inmates	38,462	665,719	19,761	430,151

Source: U.S. Dept. of Justice; Office of Justice Programs; Bureau of Justice Statistics, "Women in Prison: Survey of State Prison Inmates, 1991."

Note: Excludes an estimated 7,462 inmates in 1991 and 505 inmates in 1986 for whom offense was unknown. Detail may not add to total because of rounding.

[a] Includes non-negligent manslaughter.

[b] Includes blackmail, extortion, hit-and-run driving with bodily injury, child abuse, and criminal endangerment.

[c] Includes destruction of property, vandalism, hit-and-run driving without bodily injury, trespassing, and possession of burglary tools.

[d] Includes escape from custody, driving while intoxicated, morals and decency, and commercialized vice.

threatened at the time the offense takes place. However, due to recent events that have publicized the long, painful agony of these women (i.e., the O.J. Simpson criminal trial), a new line of defense based on the **battered woman syndrome** has been created. Thus defense attorneys now often rely on the claim that long periods of abuse result in a woman's empowerment as she takes action against her aggressor. Despite the fact that some of these abused women often receive commuted sentences, many remain in prison facilities serving long sentences after being convicted of homicide. Table 9.2 shows the distribution of the most serious offenses of state prison inmates by gender. As is evident in this table, the greatest percentages of female inmates are in prison for drug-related offenses. This is followed closely by acts of violence and property offenses. Of the drug offenses, trafficking seems to be the most frequent offense committed by women that leads to their incarceration. Among violent offenses, murder was, by far, the offense most frequently committed by female offenders. This is an interesting phenomenon in light of the preceding discussion. Finally, in the property offense category, larceny/theft was the offense most often committed by women.

Research on Women's Prisons

Several explanations have been advanced for the lack of study, until recently, of women's prisons. In the first place, women constitute roughly only 5 percent of the state correctional population, and at least half of that number have been found to reside in jails, not prisons. Presumably those women in jails are incarcerated for lesser offenses than committed by those in prisons. Consequently, it is not unreasonable to assume that researchers have paid little attention to female inmates since they are not considered to constitute the serious problems created by male inmates, most of whom reside in prisons as opposed to jails.

Second, the relatively smaller population of women makes research difficult. Samples are not as large; it is therefore not as easy to generalize as it is with data on male inmates, and it is difficult to compare the various studies that are conducted.

Third, the lack of research on women prisoners may be a function of who conducts the research. Most of the studies on the female offender have been conducted by women, and until recently, large numbers of women have not been trained in social science research methodology.

Fourth, some past studies have indicated that administrators of correctional facilities for women are more reluctant than those in men's prisons to allow researchers to enter their institution.

However, it is important to note that the combination of the women's rights movement, the rise of feminist scholarship, and the noted increase in female criminality have begun to reverse the long-standing neglect of research on women's prisons. In direct response to these factors, a rich and complex literature that examines the treatment of women by criminal justicians has begun to emerge.[19] It can only be speculated that this trend will continue to take its course and we will continue to benefit from it by learning more about the complexities involving the incarceration of female offenders.

Centralization and Decentralization: A Comparison

Most of the early analyses conducted on the construction of women's prisons revealed a process of centralization by various states. In fact, from 1930 to 1959, only two or three prisons were constructed for female offenders in each decade. Most of these were built in the South and West because prison construction for women in these regions was lagging. Despite this, in the 1960s, several more female prisons were built in the South and West, with seventeen more constructed in the 1970s. Furthermore, two more female prisons were built in the Northeast during the 1970s. However, it was not until the 1980s that the biggest growth took place, with the construction of more than thirty-four new prisons for female offenders.

Despite this trend, the process of centralization of women's facilities has begun to reverse. Even though one study indicated that by 1988, forty-four states were housing all-female inmates in one or two facilities, several states had made arrangements for the extensive expansion of facilities for women. In fact, some consider the expansion, or decentralization, as a positive factor for female inmates. It is clear that the potential exists for the reversal of the current trend regarding inmate isolation and inferior programs offered in female facilities. Interestingly, some believe that this will only increase the potential for women to be sent to custodial institutions unnecessarily.

At the turn of a new millennium, most facilities for women are situated in rural areas of the United States. Their location creates a further hardship on female inmates as it moves them farther away from their families and familiar environments. In some cases, this isolates female inmates to such a degree that they often lack visitors for months. Many inmates who are also mothers suffer from an increasingly weak relationship with their children. This isolation is often augmented by the lack of services that female prisons provide. The remote locations of female prisons make it very difficult for volunteers to travel. This results in the lack of adequate staffing for programs and services often offered in male correctional institutions.[20]

Architecture

The architecture of female institutions was classified in an LEAA survey into four categories. In the first category was the *complex*, featuring a group of buildings, usually built around the administration building, and including several living units as well as buildings for vocational, educational, and other types of programs. Second was the *single building*, with all functions housed in one building. Third was the *campus design*, which is similar to a college campus. In this design, there is a large area with trees and shrubs and a group of buildings placed throughout the grounds, each usually with a special function. Finally, the *cottage* design contains small buildings resembling multifamily homes. "Each cottage is designed to be self-sufficient and contains individual rooms, as well as kitchen facilities. This design is intended to replicate, to the extent possible, a homey atmosphere."[21] Some institutions have variations on these designs—for example, a cottage within a complex.

Of the institutions that were built between 1930 and 1966, most have followed the traditional style, which is the cottage or modified cottage. This style has been found to be the most appropriate since most female prisons have small inmate populations. These institutions have put into practice only simple classification techniques. A study by Strickland in 1966 suggested that most of these female facilities were custody-oriented; the rest were either custodial, treatment-oriented, or treatment facilities. Despite the fact that the number of female prisons is increasing, the total number constitutes only a small percentage of all prisons in the United States. In fact, the 1993 American Correctional Association's directory listed seventy-five female correctional institutions in the United States.[22]

In contrast to institutions for adult males, institutions for adult women are generally more aesthetic and have a less secure environment. Female inmates are, for the most part, not regarded as high security risks since they have not proven to be as violent as male inmates. Despite the fact there are some exceptions, on the whole, institutions for female offenders are built and maintained with the view that the occupants are not great risks to themselves or to others. This is evidenced by the architecture of most female correctional facilities. It is interesting to note that some of these facilities have rooms, and not the open cells or dorms of the male facilities. Many facilities also allow curtains and bedspreads and cooking areas, creating an almost home-like environment. Some even allow female inmates to wear their own clothing and to have greater latitude with commissary items (i.e., cosmetic products).

Security Levels

Currently, most women's prisons are designated as medium security facilities. As in the past, there are few custody-graded facilities because there are fewer female inmates. Because the whole range of security-graded females must be housed in the same facility, all females are incarcerated either in medium or maximum security prisons regardless of their need for it.

Personnel

The administration of female correctional facilities has changed dramatically in recent years. In 1966, only ten of the female institutions were headed by female correctional administrators, whereas in 1993, the picture was much different—237 of the 1,653 correctional administrators were females.[23]

Educational and Vocational Programs for Women

One of the advantages of the relatively smaller population in female prisons (as opposed to male prisons), is that there is greater opportunity for the inmates to have some contact with the staff. There is also a chance for greater innovation in programming. On the other hand, the smaller number of female inmates has been used to "justify" lack of funding for educational and vocational programs as well as the lack of research on the effectiveness of such programs.

Traditionally, and to a great extent even today, correctional institutions for women reflect the expected role that women play in our society. In the late nineteenth century, when reformers advocated separate institutions for women, the emphasis was on reformatories, not prisons, where women were to learn the behaviors appropriate for the female role in society. They lived in cottages that were like "homes," not in large institutional-type structures characteristic of prisons for men.

In earlier times, for example, women prisoners were trained to milk and care for cows. As Joy Eyman so "aptly" states the situation,

> Dairymen are turning to women to help ease the labor shortage. Those dairymen who have tried women in milking operations are pleased with the results. Women are proving to be better milkers than men and understand the problems of swollen udders, mastitis, and other mammary infections.[24]

Some programs for women have been designed to reflect the same traditions. Many are determined by federal funding that supports the programs. At the national level, the transfer of programs from one area to another has often failed to take into account local differences that might impede such transfers. In the past, an LEAA study suggested that we should "focus on the female offender as a woman, and examine how her needs relate to those of other women on the outside," not on how she may differ from male offenders or on traditional concepts of causation of crime among women.[25]

Although there have been attempts in recent years to address the particular needs of some incarcerated women, many of today's vocational and technical programs are far behind what they should provide. In general, most, if not all, programs for women fall into five major categories. These include:

1. Institutional maintenance, including clerical work, food service for the institution, and general cleaning and maintenance of the grounds;
2. Education, which is mostly remedial;
3. Vocational training, most often geared toward stereotypical jobs (cosmetology, sewing, food service and clerical skills);
4. Treatment (including Alcoholic Anonymous, Narcotics Anonymous, etc.); and
5. Medical care.[26]

Martha Wheeler, past president of the American Correctional Association (ACA), however, warned about designing programs for female inmates on the assumption that they will not play the traditional female role in society. She indicated that in her work, many female inmates indicate that they prefer the traditional role. When some of these inmates at the parole stage are asked about getting jobs, their response is that they want to get a man. Wheeler raised the important issue of whether our role is to prepare these women for new roles in society or to meet them where they are and help them with programs that enable them to become more secure with the world in which they expect to live. Wheeler concluded by stating that "at the risk of contradicting NOW (National Organization of Women), I really have to say that we should let our women say something about where they are and where they want to be and where they want to go."[27]

Wheeler missed the point, however, which is not to force all women to assume nontraditional roles, but to make available to all female inmates educational and vocational training that would enable them to assume such roles if they so choose. The fact is that training programs in women's prisons are not as extensive as those in men's prisons. Those that are available still emphasize the traditional female roles in society and do not adequately prepare women for employment outside the home. Educational facilities are usually inferior to those of men's prisons. This is particularly distressing in light of the findings that female inmates want more training than is available to them and that many do expect to work and to support dependents when they are released. The variety of educational courses from which they may choose is considerably limited compared to those offered to men. The same is true of the industries that exist within prisons. In short, "although women are much less likely to be sent to prison than are men, once there, the opportunities afforded to women for rehabilitation and vocational training are much less than are those for men."[28]

The National Advisory Commission on Criminal Justice Standards and Goals recommended that in institutions for women:

> Appropriate vocational training programs should be implemented. Vocational programs that promote dependency and exist solely for administrative ease should be abolished. A comprehensive research effort should be initiated to determine the aptitudes and abilities of the female institutional population. This information should be coordinated with labor statistics predicting job availability. From data so obtained, creative vocational training should be developed which will provide a woman with skills necessary to allow independence.[29]

A recent survey conducted among state prisons for women indicated that some of the problems facing vocational programs in these institutions include aging equipment, limited funding, and lack of competent civilian staff.[30] This survey was mailed to all state prisons for women, thus, it can be regarded as being highly precise in its findings. Some of the other problems reported in this survey included inconsistent attendance (inmates enter mid-course and leave prison or are transferred to other units before completing the training program), a low inmate pay scale (female inmates are paid on a lower scale than their male counterparts, at times receiving only half the amount paid to men), and low inmate self-esteem. Survey respondents not only highlighted the problems with these programs, but they also made several recommendations to improve the existing services. These include:

1. Certifying programs by the appropriate industry or state board and allowing inmates to take required exams while still incarcerated.
2. Equal pay for women and men in comparable inmate jobs.

3. New and/or updated equipment in instances where existing machines and equipment are no longer adequate (e.g., sewing machines and computers).
4. Increased interaction with employers in the community.
5. A stronger partnership between the department of corrections and the department of education or other educational suppliers.
6. Encouraging women to enroll in nontraditional programs.
7. Coordinated moves and transfers in states that have multiple facilities, enabling inmates to complete training courses.[31]

Recently, an educational training program was the subject of media attention due to its high "success rate." The program, established in Oklahoma prisons, was used to teach female inmates the basic concepts of preventing the transmission of sexually transmitted diseases (STDs). The program is so popular among inmates that it has a continuous waiting list. In 1996, eighty-five women completed the program. Nearly 125 women were expected to complete the program by the end of 1997. The program is believed to be highly beneficial to female inmates because, according to Melanie Spector, a health department counselor, "women incarcerated are among the highest risk for HIV and STDs." She added that "The same behavior and psychological issues that have put them in jail can put them at risk for HIV."[32] According to Spector, "They are a forgotten population, a disenfranchised population, and a population where the disease manifests itself . . . that's where we need to be—in the prison. I know it's not as nice as being at a university, but that's where the prevention efforts need to be."[33] The program, which started in 1995, is a collaborative effort among several institutions, including the HIV Resource Consortium, the Oklahoma State Department of Health, Tulsa Community AIDS Partnership, Tulsa City-County Jail, Tulsa Community College, and the Oklahoma State Department of Corrections. It is worth noting that inmates who complete the sixteen-hour program also have the option of receiving one college credit through Tulsa Community College.[34]

Other programs in female correctional facilities have been addressing issues of parenthood, specifically, issues that arise when female inmates, probationers, and parolees give birth while under some form of supervision or confinement. Among the many programs that have been developed to address this particular issue are the Program for Caring Parents at the Louisiana Correctional Institute for Women; Project HIP (Helping Incarcerated Parents) at the Maine Correctional Center; Neil J. Houston House, a substance abuse program for female nonviolent offenders in Massachusetts; and the Nursery Program at Taconic Correctional Facility in New York.[35] Although each of these programs is based on a unique approach, they all share the same quality of service that is designed to strengthen the bonds between parent and child, while improving the parenting skills of the offenders who are enrolled in the programs. This is definitely crime prevention in the making.[36] These programs are primarily concerned with the offenders in their role as mothers, but they also aim at the proper nurturing of a child during the first year of life. This, of course, is based on the findings made in various studies that link a lack of love and nurturing by a mother during the first year of a child's life with that child's inability to develop compassion and empathy for others later in life.

Medical Treatment of Female Inmates

Many of the new facilities for female inmates have begun to address the major medical and treatment programs necessary to meet the special needs of women. The small number of female inmates and their frequent, expensive medical needs have made their treatment problematic in both the state and federal systems. The two major areas of medical treatment for women are, and have been, obstetrics and gynecology. Not only are some women pregnant when they enter the system, but many women's lives are threatened by their reproductive problems. In 1992, the lawyer of several female inmates who filed suit against the state of Georgia over sexual abuse discovered during his investigation several cases of women with breast lumps who had not been treated properly. As it turned out, these lumps were cancerous.

Another similar instance took place in April 1995, when the two largest women's prisons in California were sued in federal court by female prisoners who alleged that inmates suffer terribly from conditions such as tuberculosis (TB), AIDS, and cancer.[37] They also claimed that in some cases, inmates died due to inadequate medical care. In their twenty-one-page complaint, lawyers representing the female inmates told of long delays in obtaining care for life-threatening illnesses, disruptions in administration of desperately needed medications, and frequent misdiagnoses of cancer, meningitis, and other serious illnesses. Among the cases cited is one in which an inmate in one of these institutions had legs so swollen that she could barely walk. Despite her condition, the prison personnel required her to walk to the dining hall when she wanted to eat. The inmate was found frequently outside the prison medical clinic lying on the ground and crying in pain. It is reported that for months, she begged medical doctors for help, without success. Finally, to add insult to injury, although the doctors found she had cancer, little medication was given to her. Inevitably, this lack of care resulted in her death nine months later.

Another case cited by the women's attorneys involved an inmate with HIV at the other correctional facility in question. The inmate tested positive for TB, but was taken off preventive medication because she was pregnant. She soon developed full-blown TB during her pregnancy. Despite the fact that she later contracted pneumonia, the inmate was not diagnosed until she was sent to an outside hospital to deliver her baby. According to the complaint, the inmate was sent back to prison only one day after her baby was born.[38]

Drug treatment is another weakness of female prisons. It is often the case that female inmates find these programs insufficient to meet their needs. This is especially problematic because, as stated earlier, growing numbers of female inmates are being incarcerated for drug crimes or drug-related property crimes. Current drug treatment is an adaptation of those programs designed for male correctional facilities. These programs neglect the special problems of abuse and lack of self-esteem that characterize many of the women in prison on drug-related charges.[39] Despite this, however, there are drug treatment programs that work. In the state of Michigan, programs are offered that address the special health care needs of its female inmate population. Specifically, Michigan's substance abuse program called Njideka ("survival is paramount") has received a great deal of attention for its alleged effectiveness.[40] The program's focus is HIV intervention and it is designed specifically for women engaged in high-risk behaviors. In order to fulfill this purpose, ten weekly HIV empowerment workshops are conducted. The content of the workshops is presented and discussed from a culturally relevant perspective so that women can identify with the HIV-prevention messages and effectively perceive their risk for acquiring HIV via drug use and other related behaviors.[41]

Earlier in the text, we discussed how male offenders adjust to the pains of imprisonment. We analyzed the development of the inmate community and considered the source and importance of this phenomenon. An inmate community develops

The Female Prison Community

in women's prisons, too, although as this discussion indicates, its nature and purpose differ from those of the male inmate community.

Less has been written on the female inmate community, and most of the literature in this area was written by prison administrators or other personnel, or by former or current inmates, and is not systematic or scientific. We now consider some of the few systematic studies.

Source of Female Inmate Societies

In the discussion of the male prison community, we considered two theories concerning the source of the inmate culture—*importation* and *deprivation.* These theories have also been applied in an analysis of the source of female inmate societies. Rose Giallombardo concluded that deprivation theory alone cannot explain inmate social systems, although deprivation may precipitate its development. "The evidence reported thus far indicates that the adult male and female inmate cultures *are* a response to the deprivations of prison life, but the *nature* of the response in both prison communities is influenced by the differential participation of males and females in the external culture."[42] The latter refers to the concept of importation. Giallombardo illustrates her point primarily by looking at gender roles within penal institutions for women and girls. Those gender roles reflect the roles that women play in our society. Roles and statuses are imported into prison, along with attitudes and values. The deprivations of prison life provide the structure in which these roles may be played.

When we compare the inmate systems of men and women, the evidence seems to suggest that the roles within those systems differ, and they reflect the traditional differences in attitudes, values, and roles that have distinguished men and women in this culture.

Pains of Imprisonment

In his study of male inmates, Sykes suggested that loss of security is the greatest problem that the male inmate faces. Female offenders appear to be more concerned with the loss of liberty and autonomy. They miss the lack of freedom to come and go and resent the restrictions on communications with family and friends. They may be frustrated because they have no control over things that happen in the outside world—their children may be neglected, a loved one may become sick or die, their husbands may become unfaithful, and so forth. In the institution, everything is planned for them. They must walk by twos to meals and cannot be late. They may be locked in their rooms at night if they do not want to sit in the living room with the other inmates. They cannot use the telephone to call relatives, and many of their actions are controlled by the sounding of a bell. They cannot change these rules, and they are not allowed to voice opposition.

For some female offenders, depending on their lives outside, the prison is a deprivation of goods and services to which they are accustomed. As soon as they enter the institution, they are stripped of most of their worldly possessions. "In this single act, a kind of symbolic death of the individual takes place. In the performance of this stripping and mortifying process, the prisoner is brought to terms with society's rejection of the criminal."[43]

Pollock-Byrne has reviewed the studies that analyze the sex differences in prisonization by focusing on the influence of deprivation and importation. She concludes that these early studies are wrong in their assumption that women do not form a subculture like men do. The problem of these earlier studies is that they attempt to measure prisonization using concepts adapted to the male institution, not the female. Consequently, Pollock-Byrne argues that these studies miss the different needs of female inmates who do form a subculture.

Regarding importation factors, female inmates are characteristically different from males. For the most part, female inmates are less likely to be violent, to have a professional involvement in crime, and to have extensive criminal histories than their male counterparts. Most female inmates, unlike the majority of males, are most likely to have been the subject of exploitation and abuse. In fact, many females are likely to have committed their crimes out of economic necessity in support of their dependent children.[44] Female inmates are also less likely to fight against one another on the basis of race as male inmates are.[45]

The deprivation factors facing women result from not being able to visit with their children and the rest of their families. In all likelihood, prison life likely bores most women, not only those with children and families. In fact, it places them in a situation where they have to be around people they may have never chose to strike a conversation with in the outside world. To add insult to injury, female inmates lose much of their privacy. Inevitably, this creates a severe tension for many of the female inmates for whom close, personal relationships are so critical.

As a result, many female inmates engage in homosexual activities and create pseudo-families and friendships to deal with the "pains of imprisonment."[46] Consequently, homosexuality may not be a lifestyle for many of these women, but a response to the human need for affection and the attention often missed. Interestingly, pseudo-families evolve to replace familial relationships in the real world, most commonly the mother-daughter relationship. These family units are used in female institutions to control inmates just as the gang units are used in male facilities. These pseudo-families are not as strong today as they were a decade ago because of family programs and furloughs that have served to alleviate some of the deprivations of imprisonment.[47]

A major reason that women experience prisonization differently than men has to do with their role as mothers. The loss of the parental role creates a tension for many of these female inmates. It is estimated that between 70 and 80 percent of incarcerated women are mothers. Thus, we can conclude while the pains of imprisonment for men may seem to be a much tougher experience, the overall prison experience is believed to be more difficult for women.[48]

Social Roles of Female Inmates

Like male prisoners, female inmates develop a special language to designate social roles. Although some of the same social roles are designated, the language differs from that of the male prisons. The language differences, however, relate mainly to the different function that the inmate subculture seems to serve for female as compared to male inmates. For females, the inmate subculture serves mainly as a substitute for the family. Women take on special family roles for which they have special prison argot. For example, the woman who plays the male role in the family is called the *stud,* as contrasted to the "female," who is called the *femme.* They may refer to each other as *daddy* or *mommy.* Their family relationship takes on not only sexual dimensions, but also an economic dimension. For female inmates, the "family" is also the basic socioeconomic unit. The members of the family share legal and illegal goods. The economic and sexual relationships are closely related. In fact, some women may become involved in homosexual relationships for economic reasons. The femme may become involved in homosexuality so that the stud may get items for her, or the latter may "seduce" the former with economic goods and services. Gifts are given to show fidelity, love, and concern.[49]

Parity Issue

Aside from their unique subculture and the predicaments it brings, female prisons are currently facing other challenges. One of these challenges is the "parity issue." Most reform efforts for female inmates are based on the assumption that women should receive the same treatment as men do while incarcerated. To ensure this equality, litigation is often used to bring female institutions into compliance. However, such litigation has not always provided the services often needed in female correctional institutions. Although the "reasons" provided by states for lack of equal services vary, most claim that they cannot provide equal services because females make up a smaller proportion of the total inmate population. In addition, some claim that they do not have the necessary resources to provide equal services for both male and female inmates. The courts have stated this is not justifiable reason, but many states still have yet to comply.[50]

The parity of treatment issue is, however, not so simple. Equality of service delivery is not what equal treatment means when one understands the differences in prisonization for males and females. As mentioned previously, females have radically different needs than males have. A male correctional officer working in a female facility makes it very clear how important it is to understand these differences. Men are more concerned with their macho images, power, and control, while women are more concerned with their children, their relationships, and their economic situation.[51]

There is a need to understand these differences and use this knowledge to influence policy. Providing parity for women does not mean giving equal treatment, but just treatment based on the needs of female offenders.[52] Many women end up being over-incarcerated because state departments of corrections over-restrict low-risk inmates. They have a small number of females so it is easier to restrict them in existing facilities than to provide appropriate ones.

An understanding of the major needs of female offenders is necessary. Correctional administrators must understand the problems that motherhood places on female inmates and must direct prison policy to meet the programming needs of females in today's society.

The New Generation Jails

It is no secret that due to the fast-growing number of inmates, facilities are being built in all regions of the country to house female offenders. What type of facilities are these? Will women's facilities offer the same services offered in male prisons? Having explored the parity issue, it should not be surprising to find out that some of the new generation jails aim at offering the same services to women that are available to their male counterparts. It is important to study these new jails because statistics show us that a great deal of female offenders either serve their time or await trial in jails as opposed to prisons.

Today, there are more than 100 facilities in the United States that can be categorized as podular direct or new generation jails. It is important to note that most of these have emerged during the past decade. One of the many reasons why these facilities have grown is because they offer a different relationship between inmates and their keepers. In fact, the podular direct facilities "substitute the coercion represented by steel bars, environmental irritants, intermittent supervision, and violence of older jails with individual rooms, carpeting, and a relatively safer, quieter, and directly supervised situation."[53]

Recently, a study was conducted to find out how male and female prisoners adapted to these new facilities.[54] The findings of this study suggested that female inmates experienced the conditions of confinement at the podular direct supervision in a very different way than did their male counterparts. There is a pattern of improvement in the perception of the jail experience by males, while there is an increased dissatisfaction among female offenders. The authors of this study are careful to conclude that the findings of this study are not final. In fact, they finish their conclusion with a statement regarding the further need to conduct research on these new facilities and their impact on female offenders.[55] This will be necessary if we expect to house a great majority of female offenders in these new generation jails.

WiseGuide Wrap-Up This chapter analyzed adult female offenders in corrections. For most of our history, female offenders were simply ignored. Scholars concentrated their attention on males and juveniles. With the increasing crime rates among women, however, scholars have turned their attention to the subject, although they are not in agreement on the "causes" of these increased rates. Increased opportunities in the marketplace compete with women's liberation as the main explanations.

In addition, we discussed the interpretation of data on female offenders while studying the profile of female offenders. We examined the centralization and decentralization of women's prisons, the architecture of female correctional facilities, security levels of these institutions, the personnel and location of female prisons, educational and vocational programs offered to female offenders, and the pains of imprisonment that are often part of the female experience behind bars. We finalized our discussion with a brief look at the new generation jails, which aim at offering the same services for both male and female offenders.

One of the major challenges for corrections at the turn of the century is to recognize that equal treatment for women in corrections does not mean receiving the same treatment that men receive. The needs of female inmates are unique and, if they are not met, none of the outcomes envisioned for these women can take place. Thus, rehabilitation cannot work, recidivism will continue, and other victims, primarily the children of these women, will continue to suffer.

Notes

1. Ross, J.G. et al. National Evaluation Program, Phase 1 Report, *Assessment of Coeducational Corrections,* National Institute of Law Enforcement and Criminal Justice (Washington, DC: U.S. Government Printing Office, 1978).
2. U.S. Department of Justice. Bureau of Justice Statistics. "Women in Prison." (March, 1994).
3. President's Commission on Law Enforcement and Administration of Justice. *Task Force Report: Corrections.* (Washington, DC: U.S. Government Printing Office, 1967).
4. Rasche, Christine E. "The Female Offender as an Object of Criminological Research," in Brodsky, Annette M., *The Female Offender.* (Beverly Hills, CA: Sage Publications, 1975), p. 10.
5. Price, Ray R. "The Forgotten Female Offender," *Crime and Delinquency* 23 (April, 1977), 101–102.
6. For a discussion of the criticisms of this source of data on crimes, see Sue Titus Reid, *Criminal Justice,* 5th ed. (Madison, WI: Coursewise, 1999).
7. U.S. Department of Justice, "Women in Prison."
8. U.S. Bureau of Justice Statistics. *Sourcebook of Criminal Justice Statistics,* 1989. (Washington, DC: U.S. Department of Justice, 1990).
9. U.S. Department of Justice, "Women in Prison."
10. Adler, Freda. *Sisters in Crime: The Rise of the New Female Criminal.* (New York: McGraw-Hill, 1975), p. 16.
11. Weis, Joseph G. "Liberation and Crime: The Invention of the New Female Criminal," *Crime and Social Justice* 6 (Fall-Winter, 1976), 19.
12. Weis, "Liberation and Crime."
13. Weis, "Liberation and Crime," p. 24, See also Gary J. Jensen and Raymond Eve, "Sex Differences in Delinquency: An Examination of Popular Sociological Explanations, *Criminology* 13 (February, 1976), 427–449.
14. Simon, Rita James. *Women and Crime.* (Lexington, MA; D.C. Heath, 1975).
15. Steffensmeier, Darrel. "National Trends in Female Arrests, 1960–1990; Assessment and Recommendations for Research," *Journal of Quantitative Criminology* 9:413–441.
16. Snell, Tracy L. "Women in Prison." U.S. Department of Justice. Bureau of Justice Statistics. (March, 1994).

17. Adler, *Sisters in Crime,* pp. 140–142.

18. Snell, "Women in Prison."

19. Nagel, Ilene H., and Johnson, Barry L. "The Role of Gender in a Structured Sentencing System: Equal Treatment Policy Choices and the Sentencing of Female Offenders Under the U.S. Sentencing Guidelines," *Journal of Criminal Law and Criminology,* (Summer, 1994), 85, no. 1, pp. 181–221.

20. Church, George. "The View from behind Bars," *Time,* (Fall, 1990), pp. 20–21.

21. Glick, Ruth M., and Neto, Virginia V. *National Study of Women's Correctional Programs.* (Washington, DC: Department of Justice, Law Enforcement Assistance Administration National Institute of Law Enforcement and Criminal Justice, 1977), p. 20.

22. American Correctional Association. *ACA Directory 1993.* (Laurel, MD: American Correctional Association, 1993), p. xvii.

23. American Correctional Association, *ACA Directory.*

24. Eyman, Joy. *Prisons for Women.* (Springfield, IL: Charles C. Thomas, 1971), p. 60, quoted in Glick and Neto, *National Study,* p. xxxiv.

25. Glick and Neto, *National Study,* p. xxv.

26. Wilson, Christine Ennulat. "Women Offenders: A Population Overlooked." In *Higher Education in Prison: A Contradiction in Terms?* Miriam Williford, ed. (Phoenix, AZ: American Council on Education and the Oryx Press, 1994).

27. Wheeler, Martha. "The Current Status of Women in Prisons," in Brodsky, *The Female Offender,* p. 85.

28. Simon, Rita James. *The Contemporary Woman and Crime.* (Rockville, MD: National Institute of Mental Health, 1975), p. 76.

29. The National Advisory Commission on Criminal Justice Standards and Goals. *Corrections.* (Washington, DC: U.S. Government Printing Office, 1963), p. 378, emphasis deleted.

30. Winifred, Mary. "Vocational and Technical Training Programs for Women in Prison," *Corrections Today,* (August, 1996), vol. 58, no. 5, p. 168(3).

31. Winnifred, "Vocational and Technical Training," p. 168.

32. "Inmate Program Chosen for National Recognition," (for teaching the prevention of sexually transmitted diseases among female inmates), *AIDS Weekly Plus* (June 30, 1997), no. 9, p. 26(1).

33. "Inmate Program Chosen," p. 26.

34. "Inmate Program Chosen," p. 26.

35. Scheridan, John J. "Inmates May Be Parents, Too" (Programs that work), *Corrections Today* (August, 1996), vol. 58, no. 5, p. 100(3).

36. Scheridan, "Inmates May Be Parents," p. 101.

37. "Female Inmates Sue California Prisons, Neglect of TB, AIDS, Cancer Care Cited." (Tuberculosis), *AIDS Weekly* (April, 1995), p. 16(2).

38. "Female Inmates Sue," p. 17.

39. Church, George. "The View from behind Bars," *Time,* (Fall, 1990), pp. 20–21.

40. Epp, Jann. "Exploring Health Care Needs of Adult Female Offenders," *Corrections Today,* (October, 1996), vol. 58, no. 6, p. 96(4).

41. Epp, "Exploring Health Care," p. 99.

42. Giallombardo, Rose. *The Social World of Imprisoned Girls: A Comparative Study of Institutions for Juvenile Delinquents.* (New York: John Wiley and Sons, 1974).

43. Giallombardo, Rose. *Society of Women: A Study of a Woman's Prison.* (New York: John Wiley and Sons, 1966), p. 96.

44. Pollock-Byrne, Joycelyn. *Women, Prison, and Crime.* (Pacific Grove, CA: Brooks/Cole Publishing, 1990), pp. 129–160.

45. Church, George. "The View from behind Bars," *Time,* (Fall, 1990), pp. 20–21.

46. Ibid.

47. Pollock-Byrne, *Women, Prison, and Crime,* pp. 129–160.

48. Harris, Jean. "Comparison of Stressors Among Female versus Male Inmates," *Journal of Offender Rehabilitation* 19 (1993), pp. 43–56.

49. Williams, Vergil L., and Fish, Mary. *Convicts, Codes, and Contraband: The Prison Life of Men and Women.* (Cambridge, MA: Ballinger Publishing Co., 1974), pp. 99–122.

50. Muraskin, Roslyn, and Alleman, Ted. "Disparate Treatment in Correctional Facilities," *It's a Crime: Women and Justice.* (Englewood Cliffs, NJ, Regents/Prentice-Hall, 1993), pp. 211–225.

51. Whittaker, Richard. "Working in Women's Prisons—A Male Perspective," *Corrections Today* 52 (1990), pp. 58–159.

52. Chesney-Lind, Meda. "Patriarchy, Prisons, and Jails: A Critical Look at Trends," *Prison Journal* LXXI (Spring-Summer, 1991), pp. 51–67.

53. Jackson, Patrick G., and Stearns, Cindy A. "Gender Issues in the New Generation Jail," *Prison Journal* (June, 1995), vol. 75, no. 2, p. 203(19).

54. Jackson and Stearns, "Gender Issues," p. 213.

55. Jackson and Stearns, "Gender Issues," p. 213.

The Juvenile Offender

As this text was written, several incidents of school-related violence captured national attention. In Jonesboro, Arkansas, a couple of kids, ages eleven and thirteen, pulled the school fire alarm and began shooting at students and teachers as they exited the school. Several individuals, including a school teacher, died. A few days later, in Springfield, Oregon, a young man began shooting at random in his school cafeteria. This incident left a couple of students dead and a few others wounded. Recently, two students opened fire on their peers at Columbine High School in Littleton, Colorado. The death toll reached fifteen, including the two offenders who committed suicide after the incident.[1] Thus, there is very little doubt that the timing of these events makes the study of juvenile offenders in the correctional system particularly relevant. What is society to do with children who kill other children? To answer this question and others that may come to mind, we need to analyze the various issues involving juvenile offenders in today's correctional system.

The year 1979 was officially designated the "International Year of the Child," focusing on the needs and rights of children. The year was also characterized by continually rising rates of crime among juveniles, with considerable attention focused on the involvement of children in violent crimes. It was noted that elementary and high school teachers and students were victimized to such an extent that the 1955 best-selling book by Eva Hunter, *The Blackboard Jungle,* seems mild in comparison.

Data made available in the late 1970s led a popular magazine writer to conclude, "It would appear we have met the enemy—and he is our child."[2] Many people, at the time, explained the juvenile crime by criticizing the juvenile court system, called by some *the failed system.* According to one article, the juvenile justice system, a sieve

Key Terms

beyond a reasonable doubt
double jeopardy
gangs
obedience/conformity model
parens patriae
reeducation/development
    model
status offenders
treatment model

through which most of these kids come and go with neither punishment nor rehabilitation, has become a big part of the problem.[3]

Today, the juvenile court is under serious attack by conservatives who argue that we must punish juveniles as adults. In fact, the Texas legislature is considering the execution of eleven-year-olds. Many have claimed that recent changes in the juvenile justice system have been caused by the nature and extent of the juvenile crime problem. Thus, in order to assure a more comprehensive understanding of this complex topic, this chapter focuses on the juvenile offender in historical and modern contexts.

The discussions in this chapter focus on juveniles who are considered to be delinquent or criminal. That is, they have been brought to the attention of law enforcement officials because it has been alleged that they have violated the criminal law, or because it was thought that they engaged in noncriminal behaviors that are considered serious enough for juvenile court adjudication. Juvenile courts today have jurisdiction over those juveniles who run away from home, who are considered by their parents as incorrigible, who are truant from school, and so on. These behaviors, if displayed by adults, are not criminal. In fact, adults who engage in these types of behaviors are not processed in criminal courts. However, because such acts may bring juveniles under the jurisdiction of the juvenile court, they are called *status offenses;* the juveniles who engage in these offenses are called **status offenders.** The term *status offenders* includes juveniles who are brought under the jurisdiction of the juvenile court due to their neglect or dependancy. These juveniles will not be the focus of this chapter.

In earlier chapters we discussed some elements of due process as they apply to criminal trials while analyzing the adversary system. We looked at the role of the police, and prosecuting and defense attorneys, as well as the function of the criminal courts. All of those procedures and structures were developed to protect the rights of adult defendants and to provide them with the opportunity for a fair trial. In the late 1800s, this system of criminal justice was, however, considered too harsh for some special cases, mostly notably those of juveniles.[4] As a result, a special system was created for these special cases. The following section focuses on the system designed for the special handling of juveniles—a system that was not even considered a part of the criminal justice system, but was originally perceived as a separate system.

The juvenile court was developed as an alternative to the criminal court. After a brief review of some of the events that preceded the development of the juvenile court, we carefully examine that particular philosophy. Finally, we look at the most significant legal developments that have affected the court while paying close attention to their implications for the future of the juvenile court.

Background and History

The first recorded discussion of juvenile problems dates back some 3,700 years,[5] but the first juvenile code was the Biblical code. It provided, for example, that stubborn and rebellious children could be taken by their parents into the city to be stoned to death by the city's elders. Other provisions allowed the death sentence for children who cursed or killed their parents. The philosophy of punishment was "an eye for an eye, tooth for tooth, hand for hand, foot for foot, burning for burning, wound for wound, stripe for stripe."[6] No distinctions were made between punishment for acts committed by children and those committed by adults.

In England, under the common law, a child under seven was considered incapable of committing a crime. A child between seven and fourteen years was presumed incapable, but that was a *rebuttable presumption.* A child over age fourteen was treated as an adult. Thus, at the age of seven, a child could be found "guilty" of a felony and punished as an adult. A 1961 study noted that within the prior 100 years in England, children were hanged for offenses that would now be considered trivial. "And at a somewhat earlier period, there were two hundred capital offenses with the law making little or no distinction between child and adult offenders."[7]

In colonial America, children were treated like adults, and in the nineteenth century, a thirteen-year-old boy was hanged in New Jersey. Children who escaped the death penalty often faced corporal punishment and deprivation. Prior to 1899 in the United States, "boys and girls were sadistically punished by private and public floggings, deprived food, lodged in dungeons and cells along with adults, forced to do cruelly hard labor, and otherwise abused and neglected."[8]

The first attempt at specialized treatment for children occurred in the English court of chancery. It applied the doctrine of **parens patriae,** which was interpreted to mean that the sovereign had the power to oversee any children in his kingdom who might be neglected or abused by their parents. The court exercised this duty only when it was thought necessary for the welfare of the child, and that rarely occurred. Protection of society and punishment of parents were not considered to be sufficient reasons to invoke the power. Both in the English system and the system adopted during the early period of American history, the doctrine applied only to children who were in need of supervision or help because of the actions of their parents or guardians—not because the children themselves were delinquent. The extension to the juvenile court of jurisdiction over delinquent children was an innovation adopted in Illinois in 1899.[9]

Prior to 1899, special institutions existed for juveniles that were developed to segregate juvenile delinquents from other criminals. The New York House of Refuge, established in 1824, was the first of these juvenile institutions and served as a model for others. These institutions were an improvement over the previous conditions, but they handled children *after* they commited crimes and placed little emphasis on prevention and rehabilitation. Furthermore, they apparently represented society's desire to get the delinquents out of sight, for they were really prisons that emphasized hard work and discipline and not rehabilitation. At least they were moving in the right direction and did eliminate some of the evils of imprisoning children with adult criminals.

By the middle 1800s, the United States established probation for juveniles and built separate detention facilities for them. The 1800s also saw the evolution of progressive ideas in the care and treatment of dependent and neglected children. The creation of protective societies, such as the Society for the Prevention of Cruelty to Children developed in New York in 1875, paved the way for the juvenile court. However, Illinois gets credit for the establishment of the first juvenile court in 1899. Other states quickly followed the lead. In fact, by 1925, all but two states had followed the Illinois model. Consequently, all states, with no exception, had a juvenile code in place by 1945.

The growing dissatisfaction with the treatment of juveniles and the increasing emphasis on humanitarianism encouraged the reformers to press their advocacy of a system that would emphasize treatment rather than punishment. Their major focus was on individualized handling and treatment of the juvenile offender. Although, in theory, the treatment of offenders seems to be the goal of today's juvenile courts, in practice, the advocacy for punishment is ever increasing.

The Juvenile Court

Doctrine of *Parens Patriae*

Before a court can dispense individualized treatment, it must acquire jurisdiction over the child. This is easily done, as the philosophy of the juvenile court is based on the doctrine of *parens patriae*. Under this doctrine, the state delegates to parents the care of their children. If parents violate that trust in their guardianship, the state may take custody to achieve the ultimate goal—the welfare of the child.

The doctrine of *parens patriae* became firmly established in early case law. A Pennsylvania court ruled that although the parents are usually the best guardians of their children, their right to rear them is not inalienable. If parents neglect their responsibility, the public has an interest in protecting their children.

The establishment of the juvenile court in 1899 extended the doctrine of *parens patriae* to delinquent children. The doctrine assumes that the state is "the ultimate parent of the child," and the proceeding of the juvenile court was to be one by which the state "reaches out its arm in a kindly way and provides for the protection of its children."[10] Figure 10.1 illustrates today's procedures for the handling of a juvenile offender case. Although this information is accurate and describes most jurisdictions, some may process juvenile cases somewhat differently.

Contrast with Criminal Court

The juvenile court, with its emphasis on individualized treatment, was originally visualized as a social agency or clinic, not a court of law. That vision was later to encounter much criticism. The court was to be a social institution designed to protect and rehabilitate the child, not a court designed to try the child's guilt. The purpose was to treat, not to punish. Clearly, then, the juvenile court was to differ from the criminal court. In fact, the basic purpose of the juvenile court was to protect the child from the stigma attached to the proceedings in a criminal court. Even the vocabulary of the courts differed. Children would not be "arrested," but "summoned"; they would not be "indicted," but a petition would be filed on their behalf. If detention was necessary, children would be detained in facilities separate from adults, but not in jails. They would not have a "trial," but a "hearing," which would be private and in which juries and prosecuting attorneys would rarely, if ever, be used. Nor would they usually have counsel. The hearing would be informal, for the ordinary trappings of the courtroom would be out of place. Judges would not act as impartial observers, as was their function in the criminal court. Rather, they would act as wise parents disciplining their children in love and tenderness, deciding in an informal way what was best for those children.

Juveniles would not be "sentenced" as the concept is known in the criminal court. Rather, after the hearing they would be "adjudicated." A disposition would be made only after a careful study of the juvenile's background and potential, and the decision would reflect the best interests of the child. The relationship between the child and the judge was seen as that of a counselor-patient or doctor-patient relationship.

The juvenile court hearing differed from the criminal court in procedure as well as in theory. Rules of evidence that characterize the criminal court were not applied to the juvenile court. For example, the juvenile did not have the right to cross-examine his or her accusers. Indeed, there was no need for that safeguard since everyone was assumed to be acting in the best interests of the child. *Hearsay evidence,* which would be excluded from the criminal court, would be admitted in the juvenile court. Judges needed all of the information they could get for an adequate disposition of the case, and it was not contemplated that the information might be false. The emphasis in the juvenile court was not on what the child did,

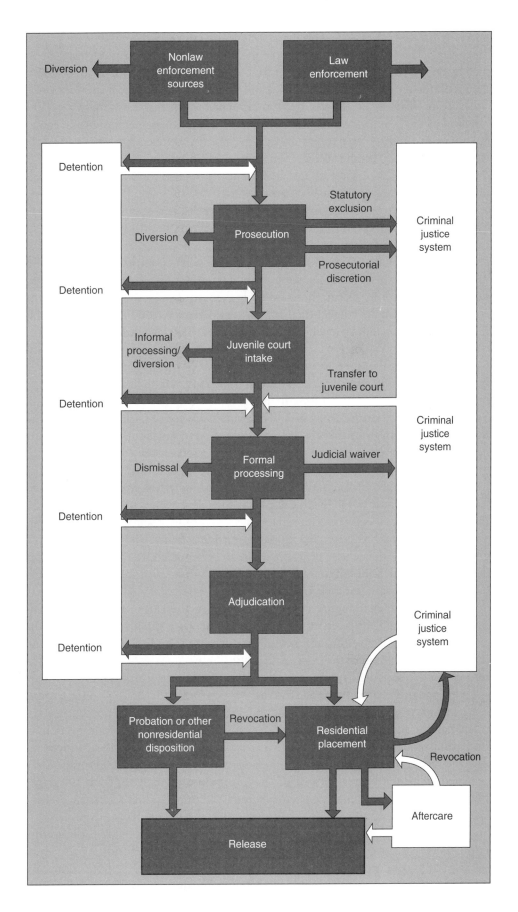

Figure 10.1

The Stages of Delinquency Case Processing in the American Juvenile Justice System

Note: This chart gives a simplified view of case-flow through the juvenile justice system. Procedures vary among jurisdictions. The weights of the lines are not intended to show the actual size of caseloads.

Source: Howard Snyder et al. *Juvenile Offenders and Victims: 1996 Update on Violence* (Washington, DC: U.S. Department of Justice, 1996), p. 76.

but on what the child was. The court was to be concerned mainly with a total diagnosis of the child that would enable the judge to "save" the child from a criminal career through proper treatment, in contrast with the criminal court's concern with the narrow issue, during trial, of the guilt or innocence of the accused.

The juvenile court was to be treatment, not punishment, oriented. The purpose of the court was to prevent children from becoming criminals by catching them in the budding stages and giving them the love and protection that would be provided by parents who believe their children are salvageable.

The early advocates of the juvenile court believed that law and humanitarianism were not sufficient for treatment of the juvenile. They expected the court to rely heavily on the findings of the physical and social sciences. It was expected that these research findings would be applied scientifically in the adjudication and disposition of juveniles, and this was the first attempt to utilize the social sciences in law. The failure of the social sciences to develop sufficient research to implement this philosophy adequately, the failure of the legal profession to recognize and accept those findings that would be of assistance, and the abuse of discretion by correctional officials are perhaps responsible for the tensions that have developed over the lack of procedural safeguards in the juvenile court.

Procedural Safeguards

Because the juvenile court would be acting as a wise parent, "the historic leaders of the juvenile court movement firmly believed that formal procedure . . . [would be] at best, excess baggage and, at worse, positively harmful."[11] Therefore the procedural safeguards of the criminal court were not applied. The founders believed that justice is cold and often cruel. It is based on the concept of punishment—people "get what they deserve," and the founders wanted more for the juvenile. They apparently actually believed that the system they devised would go "beyond justice" and not give children what they deserved, but what was best for them in the way of treatment and rehabilitation.[12] Some scholars claimed that this approach was meant to safeguard *supraconstitutional* rights. That is, children were given more rights than those given to adults in criminal court. The juvenile court did not take away rights, it added to them. It gave greater protection to children than they could get in the criminal court.[13]

Not all scholars agree with this attitude of the early juvenile court. For instance, Anthony Platt refers to the early proponents of the juvenile court as the *child savers*. Platt argues that the juvenile court diminished the civil liberties and privacy of juveniles and that the child-saving movement was prompted by the middle class to support its own interests in dominating the lower class.[14]

Pisciotta notes the less-than-benevolent attitude of the court toward females and African Americans. In the early 1800s, African American youths were often held in adult facilities while white youths were sent to juvenile residential institutions. These African American youths received little education or other specialized programming compared to their white counterparts. Females were reported as having been deprived of this programming as well. Their programming was directed at reforming their religious and moral values and their domestic skills.[15]

The courts emphasized that the procedural safeguards of the criminal court were set aside in the interest of treatment and the welfare of the child because they were incompatible with those interests. Since the state, in recognizing its duty as "parent," was helping, and not punishing the child, no constitutional rights were violated. The child is legally a ward of the state and has no

Case Study 10.1

Commonwealth v. Fisher[16]

[The juvenile court] . . . is not for the punishment of offenders but for the salvation of children . . . No child under the age of 16 is excluded from its beneficent provisions. Its protecting arm is for all who have not attained that age and who may need its protection. It is for all children of the same class . . .

To save a child from becoming a criminal, or from continuing in a career of crime, to end in maturer years in public punishment and disgrace, the Legislature surely may provide for the salvation of such a child, if its parents or guardian be unable or unwilling to do so, by bringing it into one of the courts of the state without any process at all, for the purpose of subjecting it to the state's guardianship and protection . . .

It is for their welfare and that of the community at large . . . Every statute which is designed to give protection, care, and training to children, as a needed substitute for parental authority and performance of parental duty, is but a recognition of the duty of the state, as the legitimate guardian and protector of children where other guardianship fails.

"constitutional" rights that the courts must respect. This philosophy of the juvenile court was summed up in an early court decision, part of which follows in Case Study 10.1. Note the clear indication that the juvenile court was perceived as an institution far more humane than the adult criminal court, always acting in the "best interests of the child."

The dream of the "rehabilitative ideal" of the founders of the juvenile court has not been realized. Although "the rhetoric of the juvenile court movements speaks of assistance, treatment, friendly concern; the reality reflects the hardness of the criminal process."[17] Or, in the blunt words of former Supreme Court Justice Abe Fortas, "There may be grounds for concern that the child received the worst of both worlds: that he gets neither the protections accorded to adults nor the solicitous care and regenerative treatment postulated for children."[18]

In reality, the juvenile often receives punishment, not treatment. Being processed through the juvenile court rather than the criminal court does not remove the stigma of being labeled a "criminal." "Despite all protestations to the contrary, the adjudication of delinquency carries with it a social stigma. This court can take judicial notice that in common parlance 'juvenile delinquent' is a term of opprobrium and it is not society's accolade bestowed on the successfully rehabilitated."[19] The label of being "delinquent," which is often given to juvenile offenders, is most prevalent in instances when the former offender is attempting to seek a different lifestyle. In particular, when the former offender tries to seek employment, he or she often encounters questions pertaining to his or her past behavior (i.e., number of times arrested, convicted, and/or sentenced). It is often difficult to successfully find a job while answering positively to the questions mentioned. This labeling also extends to loan applications, organization membership requests, and others.[20]

Adjudication as a juvenile delinquent may and usually does destroy a child's reputation in his or her home community, and "the stigma of conviction will reflect upon him for life."[21] Children are always delinquents or "former delinquents," and most people will never allow them to forget that fact. That is particularly tragic since the juveniles might have been adjudicated for relatively minor offenses—for example, truancy or insubordination. But for a child, "Any brush

The Reality of the Juvenile Court System

with the law can leave indelible blots on . . . [his] record and life course, and cannot be treated lightly."[22]

In reality, the juvenile did not receive "more than justice," as the juvenile court founders promised. In many cases, the state failed to act in the best interests of the child, with the result that "American juveniles . . . exchanged the precious heritage of individual freedom under law for the tyranny of state intervention whenever the state considers that its interests are affected."[23]

Judicial Changes in Juvenile Court Philosophy

In 1967, the U.S. Supreme Court declared that changes had to take place in the juvenile court system. Other cases followed that historic decision and extended to juveniles many of the constitutional protections already recognized for adults.

In re Gault

In re Gault was the first juvenile case from a state court to be heard by the United States Supreme Court. A brief look at the facts of the case indicates the seriousness of the lack of due process in the juvenile court at that time.

The events that led to *Gault* began on June 8, 1964, when fifteen-year-old Gerald Gault and a friend were taken into custody in Arizona. A Mrs. Cook had complained that the boys were making lewd phone calls to her. Gault's parents were not notified that their son had, in effect, been arrested. When they returned home from work that evening and found that Gerald was not there, they sent his brother to look for him and eventually got the information that he was in custody. The parents were never shown the petition that was filed the next day. At the first hearing, attended by Gerald and his mother, Mrs. Cook did not testify; no written record was made of the proceedings. At the second hearing, Mrs. Gault asked for Mrs. Cook to appear, but the judge said that would not be necessary. The judge's decision was to commit Gerald to the State Industrial School until his age of majority.

When the judge was asked on what basis he adjudicated Gerald delinquent, he said he was not sure of the exact section of the code. The section of the Arizona Criminal Code that escaped his memory defined as a misdemeanant a person who "in the presence or hearing of any woman or child . . . uses vulgar, abusive, or obscene language." For this offense, a fifteen-year-old boy was committed to a state institution until his majority. The maximum legal penalty for an adult was a fine of $5 to $50 or imprisonment for a maximum of two months. An adult would be afforded due process at his trial, but a juvenile was not so entitled.

The judge also said, based on his recollection that Gerald had been before the juvenile court in the past, that Gerald was "habitually involved in immoral matters." He had once stolen a baseball glove and then refused to tell the police department the truth about the incident, and he had also admitted making nuisance phone calls. There had, however, been no adjudication of delinquency in those incidents.

The case was appealed to the United States Supreme Court, which reversed the decision. Justice Fortas delivered the opinion for the majority. Counsel had raised six basic rights: notice of charges, right to counsel, right to confrontation and cross-examination, privilege against self-incrimination, right to a transcript, and right to appellate review. The Supreme Court ruled only on the first four of these issues. The court limited the extension of procedural safeguards in the juvenile court to those proceedings that might result in the commitment of juveniles to an institution in which their freedom would be curtailed. Justice

Fortas clearly excluded from the Court's decision the preadjudication and the postadjudication, on dispositional stages.

Justice Fortas reviewed the philosophy of the juvenile court, noting as we have, that the founders were acting in what they thought to be a humanitarian and benevolent fashion. But, he said, the reality of the juvenile court is that the dream has not materialized. Lack of procedural safeguards had in many instances resulted in an adjudication of delinquency based on inaccurate facts. What was designed to be a court that would always act in the best interests of the child had become an institution that was often arbitrary and unfair. It was therefore necessary to inject some procedural safeguards into the juvenile court.

Many questions regarding elements of due process and juveniles were not answered by the Supreme Court in *Gault.* Most of these issues have been considered by lower courts.

Kent v. United States

The *Kent* case was decided a year before *Gault.* Although it was decided by the U.S. Supreme Court and thus carries some weight with other courts, technically it dealt with the interpretation of a Washington, DC statute and not a federal constitutional issue.

Kent, a sixteen-year-old, was arrested and charged with rape, housebreaking, and robbery. In accordance with a Washington, DC statute, jurisdiction over Kent was waived from the juvenile to the criminal court. Kent's requests to see his social service file and to have a hearing on the waiver issue were denied despite the fact that the statute required a full investigation prior to waiver. In denying Kent's requests, the judge did not give any findings of fact or state any reasons for the transfer.

Kent was indicted by a grand jury and tried in criminal court, where he was found not guilty by reason of insanity on the rape charge, but guilty of the other charges. He received a total of thirty-to-ninety years in prison. His case was affirmed on its first appeal, but the U.S. Supreme Court reversed the decision. The Court acknowledged the doctrine of *parens patriae* and the need for flexibility in juvenile court proceedings, but emphasized the need for procedural protections when acts with such serious consequences are taken. The Court concluded that "there may be grounds for concern that the child receives the worst of both worlds, that he gets neither the protection accorded to adults nor the solicitous care and regenerative treatment postulated for children."[24]

Other Supreme Court Decisions

Not all aspects of procedural process have been extended to juveniles by the Court, but a few decisions have extended some of the basic rights of juvenile defendants. In *In re Winship,* the Court extended the standard of proof of **beyond a reasonable doubt** to juvenile court cases.[25] The Court has refused to extend the right to a trial by jury to juveniles, reasoning that to do so might put an end to "what has been the idealistic prospect of an inmate, informal protective proceeding."[26] The Court recognized the freedom of states to provide jury trials for juveniles, and some have done so. As of 1987, twelve states granted the right to trial by jury for juveniles.[27]

In 1974, the Supreme Court considered the issue of **double jeopardy,** which is a second prosecution after a first trial for the same offense. The Court ruled that there could not be an adult criminal trial after a juvenile court hearing in which an offender was found to be delinquent. The juvenile has a right to a transfer hearing to determine whether he or she should be tried in adult court before any delinquency hearing is held.[28]

In 1984, the Supreme Court reiterated its commitment to the *parens patriae* doctrine in the juvenile court and refused to rule invalid the New York preventive detention statute for juveniles. The Court reasoned that preventive detention protects society from dangerous juveniles in addition to protecting those juveniles from themselves. The Court upheld the statute in *Schall v. Martin* because the juveniles were apprehended for serious crimes; they were detained briefly, and their detention followed proper procedural safeguards.[29]

Perhaps the most controversial area of concern regarding juveniles is whether they should be subjected to capital punishment. The Supreme Court has considered the issue. In *Eddings v. Oklahoma,* the Court considered the imposition of the death sentence on Monty Lee Eddings, who was sixteen when he killed an Oklahoma highway patrol officer. The issue was not decided in this case, however. The Court remanded the case for resentencing, noting that mitigating factors had not been considered in the original sentencing. Those factors were considered, and Eddings was again sentenced to capital punishment, but before his case reached the U.S. Supreme Court again, the Oklahoma Court of Criminal Appeals changed the sentence to life imprisonment.[30]

In *Thomson v. Oklahoma,* the Court reversed the capital sentence of William Wayne Thomson, who was fifteen when he committed a heinous capital crime.[31] But in 1989, the Court upheld the capital sentences of two youths, ages sixteen and seventeen years. In *Stanford v. Kentucky,* the Court emphasized that whether a punishment is cruel and unusual and thus forbidden by the Eighth Amendment is determined in part by the attitude of society. The Court concluded,

> We discern neither a historical nor a modern societal consensus forbidding the imposition of capital punishment on any person who murders at 16 or 17 years of age. Accordingly, we conclude that such punishment does not offend the Eighth Amendment's prohibition against cruel and unusual punishment.[32]

Legislative Changes in the Juvenile Court Philosophy

It is clear from some of the Supreme Court decisions that the court does not consider that all elements of due process are *constitutionally* required in juvenile court hearings. This does not, however, preclude states from passing statutes that require, for example, a trial by jury, in juvenile hearings. Some states have enacted statutes changing the sentencing of juveniles. Briefly, the trend in sentencing juveniles involves: (1) the removal of status offenders from the jurisdiction of the juvenile court; (2) harsher sentences for violent and persistent juveniles; and (3) proportionality—a greater emphasis on tailoring the punishment of the juvenile to the seriousness of the offense committed. The changes have led some to refer to the "second revolution" in juvenile justice.[33] The first of these changes is discussed here, while the second and third are examined in the following section.

The first major change, removing status offenders from the jurisdiction of the juvenile court, received impetus from the Juvenile Justice and Delinquency Prevention Act, passed by Congress in 1974 and subsequently amended.[34] Although we cannot detail the numerous provisions of the act here, the thrust of it is toward finding alternatives to incarceration for juveniles, especially status offenders. Before states can receive federal funds, they must meet several requirements, one of which is to "provide within three years after submission of the initial plan that juveniles who are charged with or who have committed offenses that would not be criminal if committed by an adult, or such nonoffenders as dependent or neglected children, shall not be placed in juvenile detention or correctional facilities." Further, states must provide that neither status offenders nor "juveniles alleged to be or found to be delinquent" may be confined or detained "in any institution in which they have regular contact with adult persons incarcerated because they have been convicted of a crime or are awaiting trial or criminal charges."[35]

One of the most comprehensive legislative changes of the state statutes regarding juveniles took place in the state of Washington in 1977, when the Juvenile Justice Act became effective.[36] That act defines "juvenile," "youth," and "child" as "any individual who is under the chronological age of eighteen years and who has not been previously transferred to adult court, or who is over the age of eighteen years but remaining under the jurisdiction of the court as provided [in another section of the Act]." A "juvenile offender" is "any juvenile who has been found by the juvenile court to have committed an offense." An offense is defined as "an act designated a crime if committed by an adult under the law of this state, under any ordinance of any city or county of this state, under any federal law, or under the law of another state if the act occurred in that state."[37]

It is due to the apparently increasing violent nature of juveniles, however, that legislators are calling for changes in the juvenile court philosophy. The nature of today's violent juvenile offender deserves further attention.

Violent Juveniles and Society's Reactions: Recent Changes

According to the Office of Juvenile Justice and Delinquent Prevention, during the period from 1973 through 1988, the number of juvenile arrests for Violent Crime Index offenses (including murder, and non-negligent manslaughter, forcible rape, robbery, and aggravated assault) varied with the changing size of the juvenile population. However, in 1989, the juvenile violent crime arrest rate broke out of this historic range. Specifically, the years between 1988 and 1991 experienced a 38 percent increase in the rate of juvenile arrests for violent crimes. The rate of increase then diminished, with the juvenile arrest rate increasing very little between 1991 and 1992. This rapid growth over a short period of time moved the juvenile arrest rate for violent crimes in 1992 far above the rate for any other year since the mid-1960s.[38]

But these are only the numbers. Who are the violent juvenile offenders? A profile of violent juveniles arrested over the years indicates that most of these juveniles are young males from socially or economically disadvantaged minority groups who reside mostly in inner cities.

As the number of violent juveniles has increased and the media and politicians have sensitized the American people to the nature of their crimes, public fear and public policy have developed at an alarming rate. The major reaction has been a "get-tough" stance regarding juvenile crime.

This reaction directly opposes the tradition of the juvenile court to treat the juvenile's problems using the philosophy of *parens patriae*. The public has increasingly argued against what they feel to be the "permissiveness" of the juvenile justice system. Many feel that violent juveniles should be treated as adults, as the national commissions on violence and crime of the 1960s and the presidential commissions of the 1980s documented.

A great deal of the existing research indicates that most of the violent crime is committed by a small portion of juvenile offenders. However, the public still feels that the system should be changed to react to their violence.[39] These juveniles have been regarded as "the violent few." Such juveniles are believed to be the ones most in need of a response by the system. The system's current failure to stem the tide of growing juvenile violence is the result of its failure to provide that response. It can only be asserted that once the system responds, the faith of the public can be restored.

This response should be more comprehensive than originally envisioned by the founders of the juvenile justice system. Instead of continuing to utilize the resources of the juvenile system for the purpose of handling this growing problem, there should be a range of options available—including options in the juvenile justice system, the criminal justice system, a combination of the two, and the use of specialized components from both the juvenile and criminal justice systems. If this is not accomplished, violent juveniles will continue to be handled by the juvenile system, which means they will be handled much like nonviolent offenders or they will be sent to the criminal justice system where they usually receive more lenient treatment due to age.

Some have suggested that the resources of both systems be expanded in order to respond to the violent juvenile problem. In the past, specialized components, such as programs designed for the sole purpose of dealing with violent juveniles, have been rare. Hamparian makes several suggestions of the components that each of these programs should contain. Law-abiding and safe programming, staff-intensive security programming, close ties to the community, contracting with private community agencies, juvenile involvement in choice and decision making, and group therapeutic programs illustrate a systematic, comprehensive approach in dealing with violent juvenile offenders.[40]

The Nature and Type of Juvenile Offenders

While it would appear that most of the offenses committed by juveniles are violent in nature, an analysis of data from 1992 reveals that this is not necessarily the case. In 1992, there were 2,296,000 juvenile arrests. Of these, 1,456,500 arrests were for nonindex offenses,[41] 709,800 were for property crimes, 129,600 were for violent offenses, 145,300 were for vandalism, and so on.[42] When compared to the number of arrests for property crimes, juvenile violence-related arrests were obviously low. However, violent offenses committed by juveniles continue to be on the rise. In fact, the same 1992 source reveals that from 1988 to 1992, the percentage of violence-related arrests increased 44 percent among juveniles. During this same period, property-related arrests increased only 8 percent among juveniles.[43] This alarming trend has been the source of public concern as citizens are becoming increasingly aware, via the media, of the outbursts of violence in all settings, especially those that juveniles frequent (i.e., schools, malls).[44]

According to a report released by the Office of Juvenile Justice and Delinquency Prevention, three-quarters of the more than 36,000 juveniles held in public, long-term facilities in 1991 were held in institutional facilities. For the most part, these facilities were training schools. Of the roughly 34,000 juveniles held in privately operated, long-term facilities, 80 percent were held in facilities with open environments.[45] Most of these facilities were halfway houses. Moreover, the majority of youths in private institutional facilities were in training schools. Interestingly, minorities constituted more than two-thirds of all residents in public, long-term facilities. In addition, this report concluded that private, long-term facilities also housed a disproportionate number of minorities.[46] When attempting to analyze these statistics, it is important to keep in mind that states with older youths under juvenile court jurisdiction may experience higher juvenile custody rates. This must be taken into account when comparing juvenile offender statistics from state to state.

The problems that are caused by gang activity in adult correctional institutions have been well documented.[47] However, very little is known about the difficulties posed by **gangs** in juvenile correctional institutions. To better understand these difficulties, we refer to a national study conducted in 1990 of 155 state juvenile institutions.[48] This study estimated that gang-related affiliation in juvenile correctional facilities ranged from zero percent in about 22 percent of the institutions to 97 percent in the institutions located in large urban areas in the Midwest. One out of every four inmates was identified as a gang member in approximately 30 percent of the institutions surveyed. The rate was 50 percent or higher in 12 percent of the institutions.

As anticipated, the study also showed that the number of female gang members in these institutions was lower than that of males. Over half of the institutions surveyed did not identify any female gang members. Clearly, race also played a role in juvenile gang activity. Twenty-two percent of the institutions reported having a separate white gang. Gangs formed along racist and ethnic lines are more likely than not to engage in behavior that oppresses a specific group of individuals that may belong to another racial or ethnic group.

One of the greatest problems for juvenile correctional institutions is the growing gang violence. The study mentioned previously showed that 28 percent of the institutions reported an assault on a correctional official by a gang member during the past year. One-third of these assaults resulted in hospitalization. Over 50 percent of the institutions reported that gangs were responsible for some amount of damage to government property. In addition, juvenile prison gangs are responsible for most of the drug consumption and distribution within the correctional institution. This represents a security nightmare to prison administrators.

The methods for dealing with gang violence demonstrated the growing need to react to the problem. The institutions reported the use of transfers, informers, segregation, isolation of leaders, lockdown, prosecution, interruption of communications, dealing with gang members on a case-by-case basis, ignoring their existence, infiltration, displacement of members to different institutions, cooption of prisoners to control gangs, meeting with gang leaders on as-needed basis, and joint meetings between various gang leaders.

The study also asked administrators for their recommendations concerning gang control within the institution. Many of the administrators felt that staffing and training were weak in the gang area. In fact, they suggested more formal training on gangs. In conjunction, the hiring of specialized staff was thought to be of assistance. Staff members who reflect the cultural backgrounds of the juveniles, and who specialize in youth problems, social issues, and counseling were believed to be the most beneficial additions in confronting the gang problem. The primary issue was less hiring of security staff and more recruitment of counseling staff; in other words, more rehabilitation and less punishment and social control.

Of the administrators surveyed, most stated that there needed to be a consistent effort to define gang activity and to identify gang members. This effort would require the involvement of the staff members, who would be encouraged to increase their understanding of gangs.

Administrators also cited the prevention and elimination of gangs as a goal. It was sustained that if juvenile detention facilities provided more counseling, they could increase the self-esteem necessary to stop gang involvement. The use of a speaker bureau of ex-gang members was recommended as a method of deterrence to potential gang members.

Juvenile Gangs

In addition, procedural recommendations aimed at a get-tough policy with juvenile gang members. One method suggested the simple separation of gang members. More extensive measures involved the development of statutory law, thus making it a violation to engage in gang-related activities within the detention facility. A final measure involved the transfer of juveniles identified as gang members to adult institutions. The bottom line was not to tolerate gang activity within the correctional institution.[49]

Gender Differences

Traditionally, female juvenile offenders have been committed to juvenile facilities less frequently than their male counterparts. In fact, data on children in custody in 1989 revealed that males accounted for 88 percent of commitments and 81 percent of detentions, but females made up only 48 percent of all voluntary commitments. Recent data (1995) on arrests show a changing scenario as far as arrests are concerned. Specifically, these data show that between 1985 and 1994, the percentage of growth in female arrests was greater than the increase in male arrests for most offense categories.[50] This later trend is in direct contradiction to the prior literature that shows the juvenile system as being traditional in terms of its unwillingness to deal with most female offenders. Some have explained the latest rise of arrests among female juvenile offenders as a reflection of the changing social roles in our society. Regardless of which explanation is correct, the fact remains that the face of the juvenile offender is changing to one that the system may not be ready to host. Despite this, as will be evident in the following discussion, administrators are addressing the frequent violent incidents that take place in juvenile institutions.

Waiver to Criminal Court

With the increasing violence associated with juveniles in correctional facilities, one option that has emerged has been to transfer them out of the juvenile system altogether. In one of the few national studies of juvenile waivers to date, Hamparian and her colleagues describe the major reasons for judicial waiver—minors being waived their right to be treated as juvenile offenders and consequently sent to adult courts. One reason is media and community reaction. The crimes committed by some juveniles are so violent that public sentiment pushes the system to find a more severe alternative for such children. Since the adult system is based on punishment and not benevolence, the better choice appears to be the adult system. This can be clearly illustrated in the recently publicized cases in which juveniles, who have killed fellow school classmates, have been immediately treated by the criminal justice system as adult offenders after their arrest.

A second reason why juveniles are sent to adult courts is to find a viable option for chronic violent offenders. With the juvenile court's attitude of benevolence and treatment, there comes a point at which the court no longer has any resources to deal with a repeat violent offender.

Another reason is to remove juveniles who act like adults in their commission of a crime. These juveniles are so violent and street-smart that no amount of remediation from the juvenile court can work.

Lastly, many believe that by waiving the juvenile to adult court, the juvenile has a better chance of receiving a longer sentence than those imposed by the juvenile court. Such people believe that the juvenile is too far gone for any assistance by the juvenile court.[51]

Of these reasons, the primary purpose is thought to be the possibility of receiving a more severe sentence in the adult court.[52] As the number of violent offenders increases, the use of waiver should become a primary tool for dealing with a system that does not have the options for dealing with violent criminals. In fact, many have suggested that judicial waiver should be used more for violent offenders and not property offenders.[53]

Some jurisdictions have enacted harsher sentences for juveniles who commit violent offenses, while others have looked at the overall issue of whether the punishment for juvenile offenses is appropriate (that is, proportional) to the type of offense committed.

Harsher Legislative Sentences for Violent Juveniles

Using juvenile justice records from ten states on their handling of violent offenders between 1985 and 1989, and adult court data from fourteen states, the juvenile court's handling of violent offense cases involving sixteen- and seventeen-year-olds was compared with violent case dispositions in the criminal (adult) courts.[54] Despite the fact that adult court defendants were expected to have lengthier criminal records, the study showed that violent juvenile offenders were more likely to receive sanctions in juvenile court than were adult violent offenders in criminal court. In fact, this study found that criminal courts were more likely (32 percent) than juvenile courts (24 percent) to incarcerate violent offenders. The findings of the study further suggested that juvenile courts made greater use of formal probation than did criminal courts (25 percent compared with 9 percent).

One of the states that has responded to the growing juvenile crime rate is Texas. In 1987, Texas enacted a law that allows the court to transfer cases to adult court when the juvenile is thirteen or fourteen years of age—below the minimum of fifteen years old. The law affects juveniles thirteen or fourteen years of age who have committed either capital murder; murder; aggravated sexual assault; aggravated kidnapping; deadly assault of a law enforcement officer, correctional officer, or a court participant; and attempted murder. The juvenile can be sentenced up to thirty years. The first phase of the sentence will be served in a Texas juvenile facility. If the child is not paroled by age eighteen, he or she will be moved to the adult system for incarceration.[55] As can be expected, other states have enacted similar laws.

Juvenile Corrections

In the 1700s and early 1800s, it was thought that the family, the church, and other social institutions should handle juvenile delinquents. Jail was the only form of incarceration, and that was usually only for the purpose of detention pending trial. From 1790 to 1830, the traditional forms of social control began to break down as mobility and town sizes increased. Belief in "sin" as the "cause" of delinquency was replaced by a belief in community disorganization. Some method was needed whereby juveniles could be put back into an orderly life. It was decided that the institution—the house of refuge, the "well-ordered asylum," patterned after the family structure—was the answer. The model was used for juveniles, adult criminals, the aged, the mentally ill, orphans, unwed mothers, and vagrants. By institutionalizing these persons, their lives could become once again ordered as they were removed from the corruption of society. Life in the total institution was characterized by routine, head counts, bells to signal the beginning and the end of activities, marching to all activities, and so on.

By the 1850s, many were admitting that custody was all that the institutions offered. Overcrowding, lack of adequate staff, and heterogeneous populations all led to the realization that institutionalization was not accomplishing its purpose. The next concept for juveniles was the training school, which was often built around a cottage system. It was thought that cottage "parents" would create a "home-like" atmosphere. Hard work, especially farm work, was emphasized. In the past seventy years, few changes have occurred in that pattern, although the number of institutions has increased and some new types have evolved. We now have honor farms, vocational and educational training schools, forestry and honor camps, as well as a number of new treatment techniques.

Short-Term Incarceration

The overall number of juveniles in jails has increased significantly. In 1993, there was an average of 3,400 jail inmates—this constitutes a substantial increase since 1983.[56] The use of jail for juveniles is called "detention." This concept is described as the temporary care and maintenance of children, held for the court, who are pending adjudication of their cases.

Not all children who are arrested actually end up in detention. The primary reasons for detention include seriousness of the charge, prior record, failure to appear, no adult supervision, unavailability of a judge, and to teach children a lesson. In 1984, the case of *Schall v. Martin* was upheld by the Supreme Court. This case supports the use of preventive detention in cases in which it is believed the child is likely to commit another crime before the next court date that is serious enough to be considered an adult crime.[57]

The low number of jail facilities for juveniles has meant that some juvenile offenders are often sent to adult jails. In these adult facilities, they are often not separated from the view or sound of adult inmates. This is still true even though the Federal Juvenile Justice and Delinquent Prevention Act, which was amended in 1980, requires all states to remove such juveniles from the adult jail system. In some facilities where juveniles are separated, correctional officers have been known to await the eighteenth birthday of a particular "unruly" juvenile offender with the "gift" of being immediately escorted to a jail cell housing adult offenders.

Many of the juvenile offenders detained are not held on delinquency charges, but for status offenses, because they are victims of abuse and neglect, and because they need foster care. The number of detained juveniles is overrepresented by low-income and minority children.[58]

Types of Correctional Facilities for Juveniles

Most of the correctional facilities for juveniles may be classified as one of three types. The first, the *training school*, houses the majority of confined juveniles—generally, this is the largest of the types of facilities. It was the first type of widely accepted facility for the confinement of juveniles, and it is the most secure. Some jurisdictions operate other types of facilities that are less secure, such as ranches, forestry camps, or farms. These are generally located in rural areas and permit greater contact with the community than is the case with the training school. The least physically secure facilities are halfway houses and group homes.

Generally, halfway houses and group homes for confinement of juveniles, compared to those for adults, are less secure, have been more recently constructed, and are designed to accommodate a much smaller population. Like many of the adult facilities, however, they are often located in rural environments. In many institutions for the confinement of juveniles, an attempt has been made to make the facility as home-like as possible. Campus-like environments or cottage-type settings are not uncommon, with a small number of juveniles housed in each building along with cottage or house "parents."

Despite these efforts, the architecture of many of the facilities for juveniles reflects the premise that all who are confined therein must face the same type of security as those few who actually need the secure environment.[59] Security is important, but security needs may vary. According to the juvenile corrections mandate, institutions should "seek the least restrictive alternative type of institution for each of its inmates." This reflects the public's concern for enhancing the juvenile's contact with the outside world.

But community and facility security are also important. The goal is to develop alternatives that are the least restrictive as possible, but at the same time protect the community.[60] The American Correctional Association (ACA) speaks to the concern over facility security. The ACA acknowledges the individual rights of the juvenile, but feels these rights should be balanced with facility security.

According to the ACA, this balance can be achieved by focusing on size, organization, and location of juvenile facilities. Smaller facilities increase staff contact with juveniles, which means that the personal needs of the juveniles are more likely to be met. Organizational procedures designed to meet the needs of the inmate, the institution, and the public are more likely to benefit all. Location is perhaps the most critical factor. If contact with the outside is to be maintained, then juvenile facilities must be located near community resources that can be used to assist the juvenile.[61]

The administration and operation of juvenile correctional facilities differ in various aspects from the administration of adult facilities. It is best to discuss administration and operation in terms of institutional models, the executive who heads the institution, the staff, and the programs in juvenile corrections.

Administration and Operation of Juvenile Correctional Facilities

Institutional Models

Juvenile correctional institutions can be analyzed according to their two basic goals—treatment and custody. In a classic analysis of six institutions, investigators developed three organizational models on the treatment-custody-treatment continuum: obedience/conformity, reeducation/development, and treatment.

The **obedience/conformity model** emphasizes habits, respect for authority, and training in conformity. "Conditioning" is the main technique used in this model. All inmates are expected to conform to external controls immediately. This process is pursued with strong staff control and many negative sanctions. Today, this model represents most of the custodial-type institutions for juveniles.[62]

The **reeducation/development model** places emphasis on changing inmates via "training." Characterized by closer inmate-staff relations than those of the obedience/conformity model, this approach emphasizes changes in attitudes and social behaviors, the acquisition of skills, and the development of personal resources.

Compared to the other two models, the **treatment model** seeks greater personality changes in inmates. The focus in the treatment institution is on the psychological reconstitution of the inmate. Punishments are seldom utilized and, when used, are not severe; varied activities and gratifications are emphasized; great emphasis is placed on self-insight and the development of self-esteem. "In the milieu treatment-variant, attention is paid to both individual *and* social controls, the aim being not only to help the inmate resolve his personal problems but also to prepare him for community living."[63]

Why are these models important? The goals of an institution, as reflected in the models, affect the organization in many ways. They affect the way that staff members perceive their responsibilities and carry out those perceptions, the perceptions of the inmates, and in general, the entire day-to-day operation of the institution. The goals of the organization are operationalized through the executive who has the responsibility of planning for the translation of those goals into realistic programs. The structure of power and authority, the nature of programs offered, the level of conflict in the organization, the interaction of staff and inmates, the interaction among inmates themselves—all are affected by the organizational type, and the executive plays a key role in the organization.

The Executive

The executive of the juvenile correctional institution may be viewed as the one who "formulates specific goals and policies that give meaning and direction to the enterprise," who "is the link between the organization and its environment," and who "establishes the structure of roles and responsibilities within the organization that enable it to pursue its goals."[64] The role is an extremely important one and requires well-qualified personnel. This individual, who is often called a superintendent, has the difficult task of providing leadership to those overseeing juvenile offenders while assuring the public that punishment is being carried out. The executive of a juvenile facility must also face the challenges of limited funding, which restricts the implementation of rehabilitative programs in the juvenile correctional institution. Thus, it is clear that the job of the executive can be both frustrating and challenging.

Staff

In addition to the executive, there are several other levels of staff in juvenile correctional institutions. These levels include other top administrators, treatment personnel, academic and vocational teachers, custodial staff, and persons who provide indirect services. The executive often has an assistant or deputy superintendent, or several persons at that level—for example, an assistant superintendent in charge of indirect services, of social services, of residential environment, and so on—depending on the total size of the institutional staff. Likewise, the number of teachers, both academic and vocational, as well as the number of treatment personnel, will vary with the size and funding of the institution.

Nonprofessional personnel are also employed at juvenile institutions. In the past, parents, usually a husband and wife team, lived in small cottages with the youths. However, in today's correctional facilities, it is common to find individuals who work eight-hour shifts and live in the community. These individuals have different titles: youth counselors, group counselors, group supervisors, cottage supervisors, and so on. Indirect services are provided by individuals occupying such positions as business director, superintendent of buildings and grounds, and secretaries, among others.

In general, individuals occupying these various positions in juvenile correctional facilities, when compared with those who occupy comparable positions in adult institutions, are better educated; are predominantly male, young, white, and married; and have served in juvenile corrections for several years. However, those who are employed in residential institutions, as compared to community facilities, tend to be older and less educated. Many are kind and caring persons who are sincerely interested in the welfare of children. However, lack of resources for hiring the most qualified persons has been a problem, as well as the insufficient number of employees, especially in the areas of psychological and psychiatric treatment.[65]

It is without question that staff is an essential element in all juvenile institutions. In an earlier study of male juveniles in an Ohio residential institution, investigators found that staff members frequently used their power to their own advantage to the extent of victimizing the inmates. They found that staff members' reactions to the boys depend in part on their previous work experience and on the length of time they have worked with juveniles. During their careers, staff members go through "plateaus," or stages, and their relationships with inmates vary in terms of these plateaus. There was some evidence of physical brutality against inmates, sexual exploitation of the boys, staff members aiding in escapes, staff members neglecting their responsibilities, and various forms of deception of inmates. Administrators were reported as having the need to keep the hard-core youths under control, and to develop a "punishment-centered" and repressive atmosphere. This atmosphere affected staff and inmate morale, with the result that "[r]elationships among staff members are characterized by high intraorganization conflict. Organizational processing of boys, in addition, creates an environment which is antitherapeutic at best and only a step from the chain gang at worst."[66]

Programs and Treatment

Special facilities for juveniles were originally established to isolate them from the harmful effects of society and from incarcerated adults. Later, with the development of the juvenile court, the philosophy of treatment rather than punishment—of "salvaging" the juvenile—became predominant. Various commissions during the past century have, however, pointed out the failure of juvenile corrections to provide adequate services and programs to enable the implementation of this treatment philosophy. During the last two decades, courts have entered the picture and required not only some elements of due process in the adjudication of juveniles, but also changes in the disciplinary handling of institutionalized juveniles as well as in the degree and kinds of services provided in those institutions.

Today, there are numerous programs in place throughout the many juvenile facilities in the United States. Thus, it would be impossible to discuss all of these in this text. However, we will make reference to a few of these programs that have made recent claims of being highly successful.

The first of these programs is called "Youth as Resources" (YAR). This program, which is implemented in the Indiana Department of Corrections, has been regarded as being highly successful in its efforts to give juveniles a sense of belonging, self-worth, responsibility, and community connection.[67] YAR was created by the National Crime Prevention Council in 1986 with funding from the Lilly Endowment. It is based on the premise that youths are resources, and when treated as such, they can make a difference in their local communities. As part of the program, more than 1,500 young people in state and regional Indiana youth correctional facilities have designed and implemented a variety of projects, ranging from violence prevention to educating children about the harmful effects of drugs and gangs. In 1995, YAR was evaluated and the following findings were made:

- Many of the participants grew excited about the possibility of building communities.

- Adult leaders claimed that 78 percent of youth participants in the program learned about working together.

- Many of the young people in correctional settings stated that YAR gave them a sense of belonging.[68]

Due to the high success claimed by participants of this program, other states are being encouraged to implement similar programs in their juvenile facilities. This campaign is being aided by the creation of a document that highlights the work of the YAR program in Indiana. It is hoped that this document will serve as the framework for how YAR can work in any juvenile correctional setting nationwide.

Another program established in Delafield, Wisconsin aims at developing juvenile sex offenders into responsible individuals equipped to meet life's challenges.[69] The program, Stout Serious Offender Treatment Program (SSOP), claims that less than 50 percent of its participants have returned to an institution. Currently, SSOP staff includes two full-time social workers, a group facilitator, seven youth counselors, six teachers, and a section manager. The program is based on an intensive six-phase group therapy approach aimed at addressing juvenile sex offender dynamics.

SSOP also uses a behavioral level system through which each offender is expected to progress, with Level I indicating minimal cooperation with rules and responsibilities, and level IV representing the maximum level of adherence to rules.[70] It is expected that SSOP will be replicated in other jurisdictions, much like the previously mentioned program.

These two programs illustrate the many programs that are being implemented throughout the United States. It is often the case that some of these programs do not last a long time due to budgetary constraints, or perhaps due to bad publicity in regard to their alleged "failure" to rehabilitate notorious juvenile offenders. Regardless of the situation, it is expected that new programs will be implemented in the near future as innovative ideas are put into practice.

Juvenile Inmate Social System

In earlier chapters, we discussed male and female inmate social systems. We looked at the theories concerning the origin of inmate social systems, considering whether they are imported into prison or whether they represent an adaptation to the pains of imprisonment. We also noted the differences in the inmate social system of women as compared to that of male inmates. One could conclude from those discussions that the development of the inmate culture might indeed be a reaction to the deprivations of prison life, but that the nature of that response—that is, the differences in the social systems of male and female offenders—is strongly influenced by the cultural differences that males and females experience outside prison. Thus, female offenders develop a system that simulates the family while men develop one that allows them to be aggressive and domineering. The differences were even seen in the nature of homosexual relationships.

Studies have revealed that inmate social systems develop among institutionalized juveniles. There are not a great many of these studies, but a few should be noted. An earlier survey of juvenile correctional facilities studied the differences between "veterans," juveniles who had been at the institutions the longest periods of time, and "newcomers." The study revealed that a hard core of veterans tended to emerge, that they reinforced each other, and that reinforcement "sets the tone" for the entire program. They are also extremely influential on the impressionable newcomers. A social climate, controlled and dominated by the veterans, develops and has a far greater influence than does the staff.[71]

A study of male juvenile offenders in a public training school found an informal inmate code that served to legitimate to the stronger inmates their exploitation of the weaker ones. The code is functional for some of the aggressive inmates. It provides them with a sense of dignity, confidence in their achievements, and a way to develop self-esteem, as well as a reason for avoiding the "people-changing" techniques of the correctional staff. The code victimizes the weak and the white, who are in the minority. These inmates are considered "losers" in the inmate social system and are further ostracized by their peers. "Therefore, the code clearly works to the disadvantage of the weak by increasing both their exploitation by peers and their isolation from staff." The investigators concluded that the inmate social code was the result of both importation of norms from the outside as well as the result of attempts to adjust to the deprivations of institutional life.[72]

An earlier study examined the inmate social system of a private training school. This study also revealed the presence of a strong inmate social system in which boys gained power and status through interaction with their peers. Violence, scapegoating, ranking, and manipulation were found to be the "underlying mechanisms of social control" and they were "patterned into roles which intermesh in a stable pecking order." The deviant values of the inmates were sustained by relationships with their peers within the cottage. Weaker inmates were exploited by the stronger; the social exchanges of peers were "institutionalized and taught to new members as the 'law' of the cottage." The aggressive, manipulative, and exploitative values of the boys were far more powerful in the socialization process than were the values of the correctional staff.[73]

An analysis of the female juvenile inmate social system of three institutions, found that in all of the institutions, the inmate social system simulated the family life of women outside of institutions. The inmates referred to their relationships as "marriages," with the traditional roles of mothers, fathers, and children. Even divorce was mentioned. In this study, it was determined that the "informal social system is functional in that it provides substitute relationships for the community ties that were severed, and it enables the inmates to experiment in new social roles." The problem, however, is that in time, the female juvenile inmates view the "new roles" as reality. We do not know the extent to which these adaptations affect the ability of the offender to adjust to, establish, and maintain meaningful heterosexual relationships after release from confinement.[74]

Deinstitutionalization

Dissatisfaction with the closed institution (highly guarded and isolated facilities) in the twentieth century has led to several movements—diversion (divert the juvenile offender away from prison), community corrections, and deinstitutionalization. The latter began with an emphasis on probation, foster homes, and community treatment centers for juveniles. The California Youth Authority established in the early 1960s, and the closing of the institution for juveniles in Massachusetts in 1970 and 1971, have given impetus to the movement.[75]

Some say the movement toward deinstitutionalization for juveniles began in the early 1960s when the government began granting money to localities to improve conditions in the field of delinquency. Others say it began when social scientists began to assume roles that clinicians had been playing and became involved in policy decision making at the local and federal levels. Still others point to the interest of lawyers in reforming the juvenile court in the 1960s and 1970s. It has been argued that the movement toward decarceration was motivated primarily by a desire to save the cost of constructing new facilities and repairing existing institutions.[76]

Whatever the reasons, it is clear that the movement toward deinstitution-alization is unlike most others in the field. It involves a major change: abandoning large institutions and replacing them with a different concept of corrections. The process has been described as follows:

> [T]he penal institution has been dissected like a cadaver in a morgue. No organ, no angle, no aspect has defied scrutiny and commentary. The net result of these analyses has been a literature which has hardened attitudes toward the institution as a snake pit; as a demonic invention conceived with the best of intentions but which, like so many other innovations grounded in the blind zeal of reformers, turn out to be as bad as or worse than the practices they replace. The pendulum has swung to the point that modern reformers—both lay and professional—would demolish the institution stone by stone.[77]

Jerome G. Miller advocated deinstitutionalization in Massachusetts. In 1969, he took charge of the state's Department of Youth Services. He first attempted reform of the system, but "after 15 months of bureaucratic blockades, open warfare with state legislators, and sabotage by entrenched employees, Miller abandoned reform and elected revolution."[78] Between 1969 and 1973, Miller closed the state institutions for juveniles, placing the juveniles in community-based facilities. It is significant that this radical approach first occurred in the state of Massachusetts, for it was in that state that the first training school for boys was established in 1846, and the first for girls in 1854.

The procedures used by Miller are interesting. When he decided to close the oldest training school for boys, he decided to move all of the boys on the same day. They were screened carefully, and those who qualified were sent home. The rest were taken to the University of Massachusetts. The program there involved four factors: placement, advocacy, group leaders, and a national conference on delinquency prevention and treatment programs:

1. In terms of "placement," the university was seen only as a buffer. The goal was to place individuals back in the community as soon as possible, in a viable living situation with job and education opportunities and a method for follow-up study of the youths while they were in the community.
2. Each boy from the institution had an "advocate," a student who was responsible for daily and hourly supervision during the month and for assisting the boy in integrating back into the community.
3. Group leaders, selected from the staff of one of the detention centers, led group discussions of juveniles and advocates.
4. The themes of social problems, education and employment, and family and alternative placement models were discussed at the "national conference," which featured discussion groups and nationally known speakers and leaders.[79]

The Massachusetts experiment with deinstitutionalization has been evaluated by a team of social scientists from Harvard University. In the early stages of evaluation, they concluded, guardedly, that the experiment was a success. In 1977, however, this tentative conclusion was questioned. Although the recidivism rates of the youths had not increased or decreased, and it might be concluded that deinstitutionalization, although no better, was no worse than institutionalization and certainly was more humane, the evaluators pointed out that there was a crisis in the reaction of the public, the courts, and the police. The concern was over the need for more secure facilities. A task force was appointed to consider the issue. At the same time, the evaluators conducted their final survey of staff connected with the programs for youth in that state. They concluded, "we are left with a picture of the reformed agency showing clear signs of difficulty and crisis in the political structure that supports it, and some suggestions of difficulty in its actual operations." The evaluators were looking specifically at the effects of the use of extreme tactics in effecting reform.[80]

Miller left the Massachusetts Department of Youth Services in 1973 for a similar position in Illinois. He has been attacked as a poor administrator who spent money without legislative approval:

> Hubbub follows him like a swarm of hornets. When he left Massachusetts to head the Illinois department of child welfare, he soon alienated the state's social workers, put the child welfare system into a swivel, and was forced to resign. But Pennsylvania quickly hired him.[81]

Another critic of Miller's actions in Massachusetts stated that "with quiet reformist satisfaction, he left the state to its own devices and went elsewhere . . . Massachusetts is sending so many youthful offenders to training schools in nearby states that its neighbors are beginning to complain."[82]

The deinstitutionalization efforts in Massachusetts have been criticized specifically because Miller closed the juvenile institutions without first providing reasonable alternatives for handling the confined juveniles. "More generally, the massive expansion of the population on probation and parole has not been accompanied by extensions in the degree and scope of outside supervision," with the result that probation and parole supervision were meaningless in many cases.[83]

In evaluating deinstitutionalization, it is important to consider the issue of whether the negative effects of institutionalization will occur also in community treatment centers or other forms of handling juveniles. Consider that large institutions for juveniles house primarily those offenders who were in smaller institutions previously. Thus, the smaller institutions or those involved primarily in community corrections must take responsibility for at least part of the failure of the correctional system to rehabilitate juveniles. It may be that replacing large institutions with smaller facilities may not have a significant impact on juvenile offenders.[84] If juveniles who already have a strong orientation toward crime are confined together, they may continue to infect and teach each other as well as the new recruits.

The movement toward deinstitutionalization or decarceration might encourage some youths to commit crimes or to continue committing crimes, on the basis of their belief that they will not be punished. The movement toward removing status offenders from the juvenile justice system should not be confused with a continued need to confine more serious offenders.

A recent study on the effects of deinstitutionalization confirms the results of the Massachusetts study on deinstitutionalization. This study found that those juveniles assigned to alternatives other than training school had higher rates of recidivism than those who completed the training school experience. The results of this study contrast with those of another study conducted in 1990 that claimed that community alternatives were at least as effective as institutionalization.

The conclusion drawn from this inconsistency is that "neither institutional programs nor community-based programs are uniformly effective or ineffective."[85] It appears that the design of the program is the critical factor. For the design of the program to be effective, it must be related to a plausible theory of delinquency, it must be implemented correctly, and it must be carefully evaluated.

Deinstitutionalization is not the sole answer. Arguments on either side of the debate are not so simple. Reduction in recidivism among juveniles will involve a more informed policy concerning what works.[86]

WiseGuide Wrap-Up The study of the handling of juveniles in this country is perhaps one of the most discouraging of all phases of the criminal justice system, for it has been in this area that unattainable goals of rehabilitation, reformation, and reintegration have been the highest. This is clear in our discussion, at the beginning of this chapter, as we learned that the juvenile justice system based its philosophy on the concept of *parens patriae* since its creation in Cook County, Illinois.

In this chapter, we studied various aspects of juvenile offenders including, the major Supreme Court cases affecting juvenile offenders, society's reaction to the juvenile crime problem, the nature and type of juvenile offender, juvenile gangs, the rendering of harsher sentences to juvenile offenders, and the institutional models in existence today. The examination of these topics was aimed at helping us achieve a better understanding of the complexities involving the incarceration of juvenile offenders in the United States today.

Recent juvenile crimes in school settings have made a substantial impact on the public, leaving many with the fear that they can no longer regard schools as being safe. This frenzy has been aided by the media, who seem eager to cover any incident that may involve school-related violence for the purpose of increasing ratings. This has raised many issues concerning the existing policies in regard to juvenile offenders. We can make the educated guess that existing juvenile crime policies will become more punitive as Americans demand a "safer" environment for their children.

Notes

1. CNN. April 28, 1999.
2. Cronley, Connie. "Blackboard Jungle Updated," *TWA Ambassador* (September, 1978), 25; See also R. J. Rubel, *Violence in Schools—Implications for Schools and School Districts.* (College Park, MD: Institute for Reduction of Crime, Inc., 1978).
3. *Time* (July 11, 1977), 25, 27.
4. Flicker, Barbara. "History of Jurisdiction Over Juveniles and Family Matters," in *From Children to Citizens,* Francis X. Hatmann, ed. (New York: Springer-Verlag, 1987), p. 237.
5. Kramer, S. *History Begins at Sumer.* (Toronto: Doubleday, 1959), p. 12.
6. See Deut, 2:18–21; Prov. 20:20; Exod. 21:15–16, 24–35, and Lev. 21:9.
7. Nicholas, F. "History, Philosophy, and Procedures of Juvenile Courts," *Journal of Family Law* 1 (Fall, 1961), 158–159.
8. Reed, A. "Gault and the Juvenile Training School," *Indiana Law Journal* 43 (Spring, 1968), 641.
9. Ketchman, Orman. "The Unfulfilled Promise of the American Juvenile Courts," in Margaret Keeny Rosenheim, ed., *Justice for the Child.* (New York: Free Press, 1962), p. 24.
10. *Statr v. Scholl,* 167 N.W. 830, 831 (1918).
11. Paulsen, Monrad. "The Constitutional Domestication of the Juvenile Courts," in Philip B. Kurland, ed., *Supreme Court Review.* (Chicago: University of Chicago Press, 1967), p. 239.
12. The benevolent attitude has been questioned by some social scientists, for example, Anthony Platt, who refers to the early proponents of the juvenile court as the 'child savers.' Platt takes the position that the juvenile court diminished the civil liberties and privacy of juveniles and that the child-saving movement was promoted by the middle class to support its own interests. See Anthony Platt, *The Child Savers.* (Chicago: University of Chicago Press, 1969).
13. Alexander, P. "Constitutional Rights in the Juvenile Court," in Rosenheim, Margaret K., ed. *Pursuing Justice for the Child.* (Chicago: The University of Chicago Press, 1978), pp. 89–92 (emphasis added).
14. Platt, *Child Savers.* p. 13.
15. Pisciotta, A. W. "Race, Sex and Rehabilitation: A Study of Differential Treatment in the Juvenile Reformatory, 1825–1900." *Crime and Delinquency* 29 (1983), 254–269.
16. *Commonwealth v. Fisher,* 62 At. 198, 199, 200 (S. Ct. Pa. 1905).
17. Paulsen, Monrad. "Role of Juvenile Courts," *Current History* 53 (August, 1967), 240.
18. *Kent v. United States,* 383 U.S. 541, 556 (1966).
19. *Winburn v. State,* 32 Wis. 2d 152, 162 (1966).
20. For a discussion on labeling theory, see Vold, George, B., Bernard, Thomas, J., and Snipes, B. Jeffrey, *Theoretical Criminology,* 4th ed. (New York: Oxford University Press, 1998).

21. *Jones v. Commonwealth*, 38 S.E. 2d 444, 447 (1946).

22. Fisher, B. C. "Juvenile Court: Purpose, Promise, and Problems," *Social Service Review* 34 (March, 1960), 78.

23. Ketchman, "The Unfulfilled Promise of the Juvenile Court," p. 38.

24. *Kent v. United States*, 383 U.S. 541, 554-555 (1967).

25. *In re Winship*, 397 U.S. 358 (1970).

26. *McKeiver v. Pennsylvania*, 403 U.S. 528, 543 (1971).

27. Rossum, R. A., Koller, B. J., and Manfredi, C. P. *Juvenile Justice Reform: A Model for the States.* (Claremont, CA: Rose Institute of State and Local Government and the American Legislative Exchange Council, 1987).

28. *Breed v. Jones*, 421 U.S. 519 (1974), remanded, 519 F. 2d 1314 (9th Cir. 1975).

29. *Schall v. Martin*, 467 U.S. 253 (1984).

30. *Eddings v. Oklahoma*, 455 U.S. 104 (1982).

31. *Thomson v. Oklahoma*, 470 U.S. 830 (1988).

32. *Stanford v. Kentucky*, 492 U.S. 361 (1989).

33. Hellum, Frank. "Juvenile Justice: The Second Revolution," *Crime and Delinquency* 25 (July 9, 1979), 299–317.

34. U.S. Code, Title 42, Section 5601 et. seq. See also Barbara Flicker, "History of Jurisdiction over Juvenile and Family Matters" in Francis Hartmann, ed., *From Children to Citizens.* (New York: Springer-Verlag), pp. 232–233.

35. 42 U.S. Code & 5633 (12) (A), (13). The proposed juvenile justice standards would remove noncriminal behavior from the jurisdiction of the juvenile court and it is this proposal that has been the most controversial. See *The New York Times* (February 5, 1980), p. A18, col. 1.

36. Wash. Rev. Code Ann. & 13.40.020 (10), (11), (14).

37. Wash. Rev. Code Ann. & 13.40.020 (10), (11), (14).

38. Snyder, Howard N., and Sickmund, Melissa. Office of Juvenile Justice and Delinquency Prevention. *Juvenile Offenders and Victims: A Focus on Violence* (May, 1995), p. 6.

39. Fagan, Jeffery. "Treatment and Reintegration of Violent Juvenile Offenders: Experimental Results," *Justice Quarterly* 7 (1990): 233–263.

40. Hamparian, Donna. "Violent Juvenile Offenders," in *From Children to Citizens*, Francis X. Hartmann, ed. (New York: Springer-Verlag, 1987), pp. 128–142.

41. For a list of nonindex offenses, see Cole, George and Smith, Christopher, *The American System of Criminal Justice*, 8th ed. (West/Wadsworth, Belmont: CA, 1998), p. 60.

42. Snyder and Sickmund, *Juvenile Offenders and Victims*, p. 13.

43. Snyder and Sickmund, *Juvenile Offenders and Victims*, p. 13.

44. For the latest polls on juvenile violence, go to http://www.gallup.com

45. Snyder and Sickmund, *Juvenile Offenders and Victims*.

46. Snyder and Sickmund, *Juvenile Offenders and Victims*. p. 14.

47. Crouch, Ben, and Marquart, James. *An Appeal to Justice.* (Austin, TX: University of Texas Press, 1989).

48. Knox, George W. "Gangs and Juvenile Correctional Institutions," in *An Introduction to Gangs* (Berrien Springs, MI: Vande Vere Publishing, 1991), pp. 301–309.

49. Knox, *Introduction to Gangs.* p. 301.

50. Snyder and Sickmund, *Juvenile Offenders and Victims*, p. 14.

51. Hamparian, Donna et al. *Major Issues in Juvenile Justice Information and Training: Youth in Adult Courts: Between Two Worlds.* (Columbus, OH: Academy for Contemporary Problems, 1982), p. 12.

52. Champion, Dean, and Mays, Larry. *Transferring Juveniles to Criminal Courts: Trends and Implications for Criminal Justice.* (New York: Praeger, 1991).

53. Fagan, Jeffery, and Deschenes, E. P. "Determinants of Judicial Waiver Decisions for Violent Juvenile Offenders," *Journal of Criminal Law and Criminology* (1981), 314–347.

54. Snyder and Sickmund, *Juvenile Offenders and Victims*, p. 14.

55. Act of 17 June 1987, Ch. 385, Tex. Sess. Law Serv. 3764 (Vernon) (effective 1 September 1987). For a detailed discussion of the legislative history of this statute and the implications of the statute, see Robert O. Dawson, "The Third Justice System: The New Juvenile Criminal System of Determinant Sentencing for the Youthful Offender in Texas," *St. Mary's Law Journal* 19, no. 4 (1988): 943–1016.

56. *Bureau of Justice Statistics Sourcebook*, 1996, Table 6.13, p. 511.

57. *Schall v. Martin*, 467 U.S. 253 (1984).

58. Schall, Ellen. "Principles for Juvenile Detention," in Hartmann, ed. pp. 349–361.

59. For a discussion of the negative impact that secure facilities might have on some juveniles, see Theodore M. Newcomb and Rhea Kish, *Time Out: A National Study of Juvenile Correctional Programs*, National Assessment of Juvenile Corrections (Ann Arbor: University of Michigan Press, 1976), pp. 122–124. The chapter on control in juvenile institutions concludes with this sentence: "Perhaps it's time to reassess the degree to which the delicate balance of control in correctional programs is tipped in the direction of custody." (p. 124).

60. Cook, Phillip. "Notes on an Accounting Scheme for a Juvenile Correctional Association," in Hartmann, ed. pp. 365, 367.

61. American Correctional Association. *Standards for Small Juvenile Detention Facilities.* (Laurel, MD: American Correctional Association, 1991), pp. 31, 43, 58.

62. Street, David et al. *Organization for Treatment.* (New York: Free Press, 1966).

63. Street, *Organization*, p. 21, emphasis in the original.

64. Street, *Organization*, p. 45.

65. Sarri, Rosemary C., and Vinter, Robert D. "Justice for Whom: Varieties of Juvenile Correctional Approaches," in *The Juvenile Justice System*, Malcolm W. Klein, ed. (Beverly Hills, CA: Sage, 1976), pp. 181–183.

66. Bartollas, Clemens et al. *Juvenile Victimization: The Institutional Paradox.* (New York: John Wiley & Sons, 1976), p. 232.

67. Nagorski, Maria. "Volunteer Program Empowers Youths," *Corrections Today* (August, 1996), vol. 58, no. 5, p. 171(2).

68. Nagorski, "Volunteer Program," p. 171.

69. "Workshop Tackles Tough Issues," ACA 1996 Winter Conference, *Corrections Today* (April, 1996), vol. 58, no. 2, p. 60(1).

70. "Workshop Tackles Tough Issues," p. 60.

71. Vinter, Robert D., ed., with Theodore M. Newcomb and Rhea Kish. *Time Out: A National Study of Juvenile Correctional Programs.* National Assessment of Juvenile Corrections (Ann Arbor: University of Michigan Press, 1976).

72. Bartollas et al., *Juvenile Victimization*, p. 69.

73. Polsky, Howard W. *Cottage Six: The Social System of Delinquent Boys in Residential Treatment.* (New York: John Wiley & Sons, 1967), pp. 168–169. For a discussion of the social system, by type of institutional model (obedience/conformity; reeducation/development, and treatment) discussed earlier, see the work of Street et al., *Organization for Treatment*, pp. 222–254.

74. Pollock-Byrne, Joycelyn. *Women, Prison, & Crime.* (Pacific Grove, CA: Brooks/Cole Publishing Company, 1990), pp. 145–147. See also Rose Giallombardo, *The Social World of Imprisoned Girls: A Comparative Study of Institutions for Juvenile Delinquents.* (New York: John Wiley & Sons, 1974), pp. 244–245.

75. Bartollas et al., *Juvenile Victimization*, pp. 7–8.

76. Scull, Andrew T. *Decarceration: Community Treatment and the Deviant: A Radical View.* (Englewood Cliffs, NJ: Prentice-Hall, 1977), pp. 140–141.

77. Bartollas et al., *Juvenile Victimization*, pp. 262–263.

78. *Time* (August 30, 1976), p. 63.

79. Dye, Lary L. "The University's Role in Public Service to the Department of Youth Services," in *Closing Correctional Institutions: New Strategies for Youth Services.* (Lexington, MA: D.C. Heath, 1973), pp. 120–121.

80. Miller, Alden D. et al. "The Aftermath of Extreme Tactics in Juvenile Justice Reform: A Crisis Four Years Later," in *Corrections and Punishment,* David F. Greenberg, ed. (Beverly Hills, CA: Sage, 1977), p. 245. See also R.B. Coates et al., *Diversity in a Youth Correctional System—Handling Delinquents in Massachusetts.* (Cambridge, MA: Ballinger Publishing, 1978); and "The Legacy of Jerome Miller," *Corrections Magazine* 3 (September, 1978): 12–18.

81. *Time* (August 30, 1976), p. 63. Subsequently Miller became president of the National Center for Action on Institutions and Alternatives.

82. Miller, Harry L. "The 'Right to Treatment': Can the Courts Rehabilitate and Cure?" *Public Interest* 46 (Winter, 1977): 97.

83. Scull, *Decarceration,* pp. 101–102.

84. Erickson, Maynard L. "Schools for Crime?" *Journal of Research in Crime and Delinquency* 15 (January, 1978): 32–33.

85. Gottredson, Denie, and Barton, William. "Deinstitutionalization of Juvenile Offenders," *Criminology* 31 (1993), 591–611. See also William Barton and Jeffery Butts, "Viable Options: Intensive Supervision Programs for Juvenile Delinquents," *Crime and Delinquency* 36 (1990), 238–255.

86. Gottredson and Barton, "Deinstitutionalization."

Chapter

11

Probation

WiseGuide Intro

Due to the existing overcrowded conditions of prisons, more attention is being given to alternatives and modifications to confinement sentences. It has been long recognized that crime and delinquency are failures of the community as well as of the individual offenders. Thus, the task of corrections has been regarded as one of reintegrating the offender into the community, of restoring family ties, of educating or employing the offender, and in general, of securing for him or her a place in the normal functioning of society. According to recent statistics, the most frequently used method of attempting such reintegration is probation. In fact, nearly 3.1 million adults in the United States were on probation on December 31, 1995. This constituted 58 percent of all adults under correctional supervision in 1995. These statistics further suggest that approximately 21 percent of the probationers were women, a larger portion than for any other correctional population. In 1995, about 66 percent of adults on probation were white, while 32 percent were African American. The probation population grew by more than 1.1 million from 1985 to 1995—this constitutes an annual average of 4.6 percent.[1]

Probation can be defined as a sentence granted by a judge, in which the offender is not confined to an institution but must fulfill some condition(s) imposed by the court. The offender must remain in the community and must be under the supervision of a probation officer, who is usually a court-appointed official. The original sentence imposed on the offender remains in force and can be invoked at any time should the provisions of probation be violated. Probation differs from parole in that the latter requires the offender to serve a portion of his or her sentence in an institution before being released to the community, whereas an individual being sentenced to probation is, in most cases, released to the community at once.[2]

Key Terms

intermittent incarceration
modification of sentence
probation officers
PSI (Presentence Investigation Report)
shock incarceration
split sentence

Ideally, the decision of allowing a convicted person to live in the community under supervision is to be made after careful study of the person's background, behavior, and potential for success. The decision is supposed to be based on the philosophy that the rehabilitation of some individuals might be hindered by imprisonment and will be aided by supervised "freedom." Recently, probation has been imposed on prominent members of society such as Michael Brown (son of the late U.S. Commerce Secretary Ron Brown).[3]

We begin this chapter with a brief historical overview of probation before looking at recent data on the use of probation as an alternative to prison. The purposes of probation are then discussed, followed by a discussion of its organizational system, including supervision as well as the conditions of probation. Considerable attention is given to the decision to grant probation as well as to revoke it. Variants of traditional forms of probation, such as shock probation, are discussed. Finally, our discussion turns to an evaluation of probation, including an analysis of its future.

Historical Overview

Scholars often disagree on the origins of probation, but its use is often traced to English common law. The earliest use of a system that resembled probation was the concept of "benefit of clergy." The church maintained that it was the only organization to have jurisdiction over members of the clergy. Thus, if clergy members committed crimes, they would not be subjected to the criminal courts. Instead, they would be handled by the church courts. Henry II objected to this system, however, and insisted that clerics suspected of crimes be tried in secular courts. The resulting compromise provided that clergy accused of crimes would be tried in secular courts but with "benefit of clergy." This meant that their bishops could claim dispensation for them. The charge would be read, but the "state" would not present evidence against the accused cleric. Instead, the accused would be allowed to give his view of the accusation and bring witnesses. With the only "evidence" coming from witnesses selected by the accused, most cases resulted in acquittals. Later, benefit of clergy was extended to all church personnel as protection against capital punishment, and eventually to all people who could read. The ability to read signified a person's association with the church. To test the clerical character, the individual accused of a crime was given a psalm, usually the fifty-first, to read. If he demonstrated an ability to read, he was released from secular court and turned over to the ecclesiastical courts. The device was used to mitigate the harsh sentences of the criminal law. But because of its severe abuse, it fell into disfavor. Parliament later declared that certain acts would be felonies "without benefit of clergy" and finally abandoned the use of the device.[4] In addition to benefit of clergy, the English also released people on their own recognizance and used a device called "judicial reprieve," which was a forerunner to the suspended sentence.[5]

In the United States, probation can be traced to John Augustus, a prominent Boston shoemaker. In 1841, Augustus, who is now considered to be the "father of probation," became the first probation officer when he encountered a man who was going to be sentenced in the Boston courts. Augustus bailed the man out of jail and succeeded in getting his sentence reduced. From that day forward, he would often petition the Boston courts to suspend an individual's sentence and grant the accused conditional liberty under his supervision.[6] The people who Augustus bailed out and supervised varied in terms of their backgrounds. He first started with drunkards, then with women and children, and later with offenders of all types. He would find them shelter, food, clothing, and a place to work.[7] In fact, records indicate that between 1841 and 1859, judges released almost 2,000 offenders into Augustus's custody instead of incarcerating them.[8]

Due to the high degree of success enjoyed by Augustus, the state of Massachusetts legislated an official, localized trial of his practices. This resulted in the official hiring of the state's first probation officer. In 1880, the Massachusetts legislature approved the nation's first statewide hiring of probation officers.[9] The Massachusetts law required that officers "carefully inquire into the character and offense of every person arrested for crime . . . with a view to ascertaining whether the accused may reasonably be expected to reform without punishment."[10] The popularity of the Massachusetts law gave rise to the enactment of similar laws in other states. In fact, by 1925, every state had some type of probation for juveniles, and by 1939, at least thirty-nine states had laws for adult probation. By 1967, every state had adult probation laws.[11] Unlike the individual states, the federal government lagged behind in its implementation of probation laws, and it was not until 1925 that the Federal Probation Act was passed.

The Impact of Probation on the System of Justice

In late 1976, the Criminal Justice Directory Survey of Probation and Parole agencies was conduced by the Bureau of the Census for the Law Enforcement Assistance Administration. It was the first systematic effort to collect data on probation and parole on a large scale. The survey revealed that on September 1, 1976, almost 1.5 million men, women, and children were on probation and parole in state and local systems. The study also revealed the existence of 3,868 state and local probation and parole agencies in the United States, employing 55,807 persons, of whom 60 percent were involved in counseling clients. An additional 20,263 volunteers were involved in probation and parole programs.[12]

In the 1970s, probation was imposed in as high as 70 percent of the sentences in some states and 54 percent in the federal system.[13] In 1967, the President's Commission on Law Enforcement and Administration of Justice concluded that the "best data available indicate that probation offers one of the most significant prospects for effective programs in corrections." However, the commission also noted that in most jurisdictions, probation fell short of meeting the two basic requirements for success: a system that facilitates the accurate selection of persons to receive probation, and adequate community resources for probationers.[14] In 1973, the National Advisory Commission on Criminal Justice Standards and Goals predicted that probation would "become the standard sentence in criminal cases" and took the position that, as compared to incarceration, probation "offers greater hope for success and less chance for human misery."[15] That commission also emphasized the importance of adequate and fair administration of probation in order to attain the predicted success.

In 1995, a national survey was conducted on all adults on probation under the supervision of state and local agencies. This survey used a nationally representative sample and was administered in two parts. The study consisted of a review of the administrative records of 5,867 adult probationers, providing detailed information on current offenses and sentences, criminal histories, levels of supervision and contacts, participation in treatment programs, and disciplinary hearing outcomes. Administrative records were obtained from 167 state, county, and municipal probation agencies nationwide. Systematic samples of probationers were drawn from rosters prepared by each of the participating probation agencies. The response rate was 87.4 percent.[16] Spotlight 11.1 presents some of the main findings of this study.

Spotlight 11.1

Highlights of the Characteristics of Adults on Probation in 1995

- An estimated 1.5 million felons and 1 million misdemeanants were under the supervision of state and local probation agencies.

- Drug trafficking (15 percent) and possession (13 percent) were the most common offenses among felons; driving while intoxicated (35 percent) and assault (11 percent) among misdemeanants.

- Half of all probationers had a prior sentence to probation or incarceration—30 percent to jail or prison and 42 percent to probation.

- Drug or alcohol treatment was a sentence condition for 41 percent of adults on probation; 37 percent received treatment. Drug testing was required of 32 percent.

- About three-quarters of the felons and two-thirds of the misdemeanants were contacted by a probation officer in the prior month.

- Since entering probation, nearly one in five offenders had a disciplinary hearing. Of these, 38 percent were arrested or convicted for a new offense, 41 percent failed to report or absconded, and 38 percent failed to pay a fine or restitution.

Source: Bureau of Justice Statistics. U.S. Department of Justice. *Characteristics of Adults on Probation, 1995.*

The results of this survey further suggest that in 1995, 58 percent of adults who were on probation under the supervision of state and local agencies had been convicted of a felony; 39 percent of a misdemeanor, and a 3 percent of other infractions. At the time the survey began in 1995, more than 453,000 adults were on probation for a violent offense; 757,000 for a property offense; 561,000 for a drug offense, and 815,000 for a public order offense.[17] Other sources suggest that in 1996, 515,600 women were on probation. This number accounted for 21 percent of all adults on probation—an increase from 18 percent in 1990 and from 16 percent in 1985.[18] It has been speculated that as women's roles in society become more dominant, their participation in the criminal justice system—especially in regard to being sentenced to probation—will increase.

Purpose of Probation

The purpose of the federal probation system was described by the Federal Judicial Center as follows:

> The central goal of the Probation System is to enhance the safety of the community by reducing the incidence of criminal acts by persons previously convicted. The goal is achieved through the counseling, guidance, assistance, surveillance and restraint of offenders to enable their reintegration into society as law abiding and productive members.[19]

In 1970, the American Bar Association approved a set of standards in support of more extensive use of probation. The standards are presented in Spotlight 11.2.

How are these purposes listed in Spotlight 11.2 carried out? To answer this question, we look first at the organization of probation departments and then at the functions of the probation officer.

Organization and Conditions of Probation

As mentioned earlier, probation originated in a Boston courtroom. Thus, the first probation agencies were part of the judicial branch of government. This was the case in the eastern states. As the idea of probation moved west, variations in its organizational structure began to take place. Today, probation is not only part of

Spotlight 11.2

Desirability of Probation

1. It maximizes the liberty of the individual while at the same time vindicating the authority of the law and effectively protecting the public from further violations of law;

2. It affirmatively promotes the rehabilitation of the offender by continuing normal community contacts;

3. It avoids the negative and frequently stultifying effects of confinement which often severely and unnecessarily complicate the reintegration of the offender into the community;

4. It greatly reduces the financial costs to the public treasury of an effective correctional system;

5. It minimizes the impact of the conviction upon innocent dependents of the offender.[20]

the executive branch of government, but also has statewide unification. This was brought about at a time when the pros and cons of each organizational system were considered. In fact, the Advisory Commission examining this issue made the statement that probation services should be located within the executive branch of government: "Such placement would facilitate a more rational allocation of probation staff services, increase interaction and administrative coordination with corrections and allied human services, increase access to the budget process and establishment of priorities, and remove the courts from an inappropriate role."[21] The commission noted that when the probationers are located within the judiciary, they are often required to perform functions that are not only unrelated to probation supervision, but that may also be detrimental to that function, as, for example, serving summonses.

Today, probation has changed not only in its organizational structure but also in the way it is administered. In fact, for the most part, probation is seldom issued as a single punishment aimed at replacing incarceration. Judges, who are under constant pressure by the public to act "tough" on criminals, are sentencing offenders to probation along with some other type of sanction. The modern forms of sentencing in which probation is issued along with other sanctions are as follows:

- **Split sentence:** An individual is sentenced to a specific period of incarceration. This is usually followed by a period of probation.

- **Shock incarceration:** An offender who has been sentenced to prison is released and resentenced to probation. The prison time was supposed to "shock" the individual offender.

- **Intermittent incarceration:** An offender who was sentenced to probation spends weekends or nights in a local jail. The idea is that the offender is part of the community while still being supervised in a controlled correctional facility.

- **Modification of sentence:** An individual's original sentence is reconsidered within a limited time frame. The sentence is modified to include probation.[22]

Most of these types of probation sentences include specific restrictions or conditions that vary from jurisdiction to jurisdiction. However, some of these conditions are common to all regions. For instance, probationers are required in most cases to report to an officer periodically, at specified times and places; the officer may also visit the client. Probationers may change residence only with the permission of the supervising officer. They must work (or attend school or some other approved activity); if those plans change, such changes must be reported. In some cases, they are not allowed to make changes without prior permission of the supervising officer or court. Probationers are often required to submit periodic reports of their activities and progress. In many cases, they are restricted in the use of alcoholic beverages and appearance in bars or other "questionable" places. In some jurisdictions, they are not allowed to drink any alcoholic beverages or liquors. In most places, probationers are not permitted to own, possess, use, sell, or have under their control deadly weapons or firearms.

Probationers' associations are restricted. Normally, they are not allowed to associate with former inmates, although in some jurisdictions this is allowed as long as it is approved by the supervising officer. In fact, some jurisdictions forbid probationers from associating with people with "bad reputations," a vague requirement that is hard for them to interpret.

For the most part, probationers are not allowed to leave the country or, in some cases, the state, without the permission of an official. Such permission is granted infrequently and only for extraordinary reasons. They are, of course, required to refrain from violating laws and must cooperate with their supervising officers. In some cases, curfews or restrictions on where they may live may be imposed. Finally, the civil rights of probationers are affected. Probationers are sometimes not allowed to engage in businesses or sign contracts without the permission of their probation officer.[23]

Other conditions of those being sentenced to probation in the 1990s have been examined. In fact, recent statistics show that in 1995, nearly 100 percent of "current drug users" (defined as those who reported drug use in the month before the offense) reported having some kind of special condition included in their probation sentence. The most common punitive condition imposed on offenders was monetary (82 percent) in nature—including fees, fines, and court costs. A majority of drug users also reported restrictions as stipulated in their probation sentence against the use of alcohol and drugs (56 percent). Half of the current drug users received a sentence that required them to attend some kind of substance abuse treatment, and 42 percent reported receiving drug treatment on their current sentence.[24] It is estimated that this trend will continue as long as individuals convicted for drug-related offenses are being sentenced at disproportionate rates to either prison or probation.

It should be clear, then, that probation has changed since the time of Augustus due to the changing needs of the correctional system. Today, as the correctional population is growing beyond expected proportions, there is a greater need to issue probation. However, the growing fear of crime among the citizenry has created public pressure to sentence individuals to probation along with some other sanction.

After having examined the organizational structure and forms of probation, it is important to look at the activities conducted by those who enforce the conditions of probation. Some have argued that the role of the probation officer should be studied in an attempt to understand the complexities surrounding modern-day probation sentences. Thus, we now turn our attention to the study of probation officers.

Probation officers, since the years of John Augustus, aimed at the rehabilitation of the offender. However, the role of the probation officer has changed somewhat. The challenges of bigger caseloads and limited powers make the duties of a probation officer very hard to achieve. Every state prescribes a unique mission for its probation officers.

For the most part, probation officers are asked to perform two functions—investigation and supervision of offenders. The investigative function involves the preparation of the Presentence Investigation Report (**PSI**), which is often used in the sentencing of the individual offender. In addition, the supervisory role involves the close control of the offender's actions. We will examine both of these functions, starting with the creation of the PSI.

The functions of a probation officer begin before the individual under consideration by the court is actually placed on probation. The probation officer usually prepares the **Presentence Investigation Report (PSI),** which is based on the social work concept of looking at the individual's total life history. The PSI can be of invaluable assistance to the sentencing judge, who decides what methods of treatment should be used with the offender. In cases in which the accused is actually committed, the PSI may be helpful to personnel in charge of inmate classification at the correctional facility, as well as to the parole board at the time of parole decision. The report also aids the probation officer if the accused is placed on probation. Finally, such information may even be helpful to researchers who may seek data on those sentenced to probation.

The content of the PSI has changed since its original form. During the early years of the PSI, the belief was that the more information it contained, the more comprehensive it was. The thought was that in order to effectively rehabilitate an offender, the courts and probation personnel needed to know as much as possible about the offender. Over time, PSI reports have changed in length. The belief today is that short PSI reports are just as effective as the long reports of the early days of probation. Due to the growing amount of cases, judges used to simply skim through long PSI reports looking for specific information that would assist them in their sentences. Thus, most of those involved in the process of creating and interpreting these reports unanimously agreed that shorter was better.

The new PSI is not only short, but also standardized. Questions pertaining to the offender's background and habits are almost always asked. These questions are often verified by other sources. When a probation officer asks an offender if he or she has a drug problem and the answer is no, the probation officer will usually verify this information by asking family members or friends of the inmate if this is true. If it turns out that the offender was telling the truth, the probation officer will write in the PSI report that there is no apparent drug problem.

In addition, the PSI report usually includes information regarding the impact the crime committed by the offender had on the victim. This addition is the direct result of the victim's rights movement of the 1970s. The probation officer usually interviews the victims and asks a series of questions about their perception of how much and what type of damage was created as a result of the criminal incident. When this new line of questioning was introduced, there was a concern among many that victims would often exaggerate the harm caused by the offender in an attempt to seek retaliation. However, studies have suggested that this is not the case at all. Spotlight 11.3 shows the information requested in a "typical" PSI report.

The Probation Officer

The Presentence Investigation Report

After preparing the Presentence Investigation Report, the probation officer may also be expected to make a presentence recommendation to the judge, which may or may not be followed. In the past, however, some studies have shown that in making such recommendations, probation officers do not consider all of the data in the Presentence Investigation Report, but rely very heavily on the offense committed and on the prior record of the offender in question.[25]

Supervision of Probationers

Clearly one of the primary functions of the probation officer is to supervise probationers. However, the type and degree of supervision will vary. In some probation departments, it is the probation officer's job to counsel probationers, particularly when they are juveniles. In other departments, the probation officer is only expected to supervise the activities of his or her probationers, and that supervision may be extremely limited. The choice of these models may depend on the availability of resources, the caseload of probation officers, their professional training, the needs of probationers, and many other factors. Essentially, the officer's basic function is to assist the probationer in making important transitions—from law-abiding citizen to convicted offender and from free citizen to one under supervision.

Many probation officers prefer to have a close interpersonal relationship with the client whom they are assisting.[26] This is probably because the role of most probation officers—advocacy of due process and enforcement of the law—is successfully achieved by relying heavily on an interpersonal interaction with the offender. The literature contains numerous articles discussing ways in which probation officers may improve their supervisory relationships with their clients. Many articles also discuss the expectation that probation officers go beyond supervision and actually serve as treatment agents for their clients.[27] Treatment of probationers can be multidimensional. Probably the greatest need of the probationer is to learn the social skills involved in successful interpersonal relationships. In one sense, criminality may be seen as the result of the failure to relate to other people successfully. The offender does not have command of the tact, insight, and judgement needed to relate to others. Most offenders have long histories of personal failures, and the probation officer is a key person in helping them to build up their self-confidence and to acquire the social skills and habits necessary for successful interpersonal relationships.

Claude Mangrum discussed the importance of what he calls "the humanity of probation officers." He argued that people live in an environment that creates inhumanity, manifested in poverty, violence, and crime. People no longer take time to relate to other human beings as people; they feel little commitment to each other and to the community.[28] Probationers may feel this most; they have often been the victims of social injustice, social rejection, and social stigma. It is therefore important that probation officers not "put them down" by questioning their essential dignity and worth as human beings.

Probation officers must be genuine in their relationships with clients. They must be sensitive to their clients' needs and relate to them as people, not simply as cases. This does not mean that probation officers cannot be firm. "There is nothing necessarily incompatible between warmth and acceptance and firm enforcement of the laws of the land. We must take whatever corrective measures are necessary; but these must not permit us to demean the dignity of the individual."[29] Probation officers must be effective in their communication with offenders, talking *with* them, not *to* them. Above all, the client must be treated with dignity and made to feel that he or she is important, at least to the probation officer.

Spotlight 11.3

Presentence Investigation Report

Basic Information Regarding the Following:

Date
Name
Address
County
Court number
Offense
Class
Custody status
Maximum penalty
Detainers or pending charges
District attorney
Presiding judge
Counsel
Plea
Verdict
Birth date
Height
Eye color
Age
Weight
Hair color
Race
Sex
Marital status

Education
Citizenship
Employment status
Concerned agencies
Place of birth
Distinguishing marks
Number of dependents

A More Detailed History of the Following:

Offense summary
Plea bargain/negotiations and stipulations
Official version
Defendant's version
Accomplices/codefendants
Victim's statement/damages
Prior record
Arrests not resulting in conviction
Driving record
Prior parole, probation, and institutional
  performance
Family history
Marital history
Education
Health

When probation officers go beyond supervision of their clients and begin a treatment process, however, some problems may occur. Three potential problems have been discussed by Shelle G. Dietrich in a classic article on probation.[30] The first major problem that may occur when probation officers try to serve as therapists stems from their lack of qualifications. Many, if not most, officers are not specifically trained as treatment personnel. According to Dietrich, "this lack of specialized training is rarely addressed and seems to be frequently forgotten."[31] The second major problem arises when probation officers are given short-term, simplistic advice that may have potentially harmful consequences. Dietrich quoted as an example some of the comments of Mangrum. For instance, probation officers are told to treat their clients with dignity, to be honest with them, to be concerned and genuine. Dietrich characterized such suggestions as "descriptive generalities, leaving the reader with "the feeling that the advice has evaporated into amorphous, vague directives which are frequently contradictory and difficult to apply to specific situations." When specifics are given, the advice is often "questionable and reflects cognitive, simplistic conceptions of human relationships."[32] In some cases, the advice, if taken, may have a harmful effect on the client. Dietrich concludes, the "assumption of responsibility for being 'helpful' in untrained areas should be soberly reconsidered."[33]

Finally, Dietrich argued, even if the probation officer is trained and skilled in treatment techniques and is licensed in such work, the very nature of the position precludes some kinds of treatment. Because of the legal nature of probation work, the probation officer can never promise the confidentiality that an effective treatment relationship requires. In reality, the probation officer has a conflict of interest. The officer represents the interests of the state in violations of the probation agreement or the law, as well as the interests of the client in treatment and supervision.

Dietrich proposed that the probation officer be seen not as an agent of change, but as a "case manager." With his or her knowledge of community agencies and resources, the function of the probation officer could be to "make such possibilities available to the probationer." It would not be the function of the probation officer to engage in therapeutic treatment, but to refer the probationer to qualified treatment personnel in the community, as well as to introduce the client to vocational, educational, and other resources.[34] This position received some support from the Advisory Commission, which clearly rejected the traditional concept of one person—a probation officer—as the sole treatment agent of a probationer. The commission characterized the probation officer as a community resource manager. In that capacity, the officer would "utilize a range of resources rather than be the sole provider of services—his role until now and one impossible to fulfill." Having said that, it must be noted that Dietrich and his comments have come under heavy criticism by some who argue that probation officers serve as therapists and perform as such in a successful manner.

One of the problems associated with the supervision of offenders in today's correctional system is that due to overcrowding, more and more judges are sentencing some violent offenders to probation. Thus, it is necessary for most probation officers, who are often overworked with large caseloads, to take some steps to ensure their personal safety. Some have recommended that probation officers attain the mental preparedness needed to ensure their safety through rigid training. This training should include crisis rehearsals as well as crisis identification.[35]

Recently there has been a trend of large numbers of probationers—specially those of violent backgrounds—violating their probation condition. This is the case mostly among offenders who have been sentenced to intensive supervision. Specifically, statistics from the National Institute of Justice show that an average of 65 percent of intensive supervision probationers and parolees violate their sentences, compared to 38 percent for traditional programs. It is worth noting that many of the violations are for special conditions of supervision that apply only to intensive supervision probation.[36]

Due to the problems currently facing probation officers, technology is being used as a method to assist probation officers in conducting their supervisory role effectively. In Westchester County, New York, cameras have recently been used to supervise probation offenders more closely. Rocco Pozzi, probation commissioner of Westchester County, proudly announced that his probation agency developed an aggressive enforcement program that would keep a closer watch on 1,800 probationers who had been charged with driving while intoxicated or while ability was impaired. The agency had set up a "sting" operation that began by inviting 172 probationers to meet with probation officers to review their cases over a three-day period. At the location where the probationers were meeting with their probation officers, surveillance units were in position. When the probationers left, officers followed them to see whether they used public transit or taxis or drove away in their own vehicles. If the latter, they were videotaped and the licenses of the vehicles were noted. The testimony made by each officer and the videotape evidence were used to secure arrest warrants. The subsequent arrests were announced publicly and attracted extensive local media attention. The message was that Westchester County took probation seriously.[37]

Recruitment of Probation Officers

In the 1970s, the Advisory Commission pointed out that probation officer salaries must be high enough to attract qualified applicants. The committee suggested that the baccalaureate degree should be considered the basic educational requirement, but greater efforts should be made to create opportunities for those who have not completed that degree. The commission went on to say that such persons, with proper training, could carry out some of the activities of probation officers. In addition, it was recommended that special attention be given to the recruitment and training of persons who are from the socioeconomic and minority groups from which most probationers come, as well as to the recruitment of women.

National studies have been conducted in an effort to resolve staffing problems. In the past, states and local governments have attempted to solve the problem by raising the salaries of probation officers, making an effort to recruit minorities while reducing workloads and providing greater opportunities for education and training. However, these attempts have been curtailed somewhat by the overwhelming amount of cases processed each day in the criminal justice system and the attempts to abolish affirmative action programs, which are expected to reduce the number of minority members hired as parole officers.

The commission concluded that a more effective approach would be for states to develop staffing programs that include effective job classification. The commission recommended that "each state immediately should develop a comprehensive manpower development and training program to recruit, screen, utilize, train, educate, and evaluate a full range of probation personnel, including volunteers, women, and ex-offenders." Included in that program should be "effective utilization of a range of manpower on a full or part-time basis by using a systems approach to identify service objectives and by specifying job tasks and range of personnel necessary to meet the objectives. Jobs should be re-examined periodically to insure that organizational objectives are being met."[38]

The commission further recommended that after personnel are employed in probation services, continuing education and training should be made available. Personnel should be able to choose one of two tracks: "direct service to probationers or administration. Each track should have sufficient salary and status to provide continuing job satisfaction."[39]

Services Provided to the Probationer

If the purpose of probation is to assist the probationer in his or her adjustment problems, serious consideration must be given to the individual needs of that person. The Advisory Commission pointed out that too often probationers are considered a homogeneous group in that they all need treatment. In reality, their needs are quite varied. Attention should be given to those needs and to the possibility of letting the individual participate in the treatment program designed for him or her. In addition, probation officers need to know what it means to be a probationer and what problems the individual faces as a consequence of his or her status under the law.

The commission recommended classification of probationers and identification and classification of their needs. To implement effective delivery of the services that probationers need, the commission said it would be necessary to:

1. Develop a goal-oriented system.

2. Identify service needs of probationers systematically and periodically, and specify measurable objectives based on priorities and needs assessment.
3. Differentiate between those services that the probation system should provide and those that should be provided by other resources.
4. Organize the system to deliver services, including purchase of services for probationers, and organize the staff around workloads.
5. Move probation staff from courthouses to residential areas and develop service centers for probationers.
6. Redefine the role of probation officers from caseworkers to community resource managers.
7. Provide the services to misdemeanants.

The Advisory Commission concluded that probation services should be goal-oriented. The eventual goal should be the reintegration of the probationer into society so that he or she can manage without outside assistance. In addition, probationers can help determine what their own needs are; the priorities can be established and problems identified. Objectives must be specified before one can judge whether those objectives have been accomplished.

A great deal of probation programs are drug-related. Statistics suggest that in 1995, nearly 70 percent of probationers reported they used drugs in the past. This frequency of drug use presents a problem to probation officers in their attempt to rehabilitate offenders. Thus, drug treatment programs are frequently offered to probationers who are regarded as having had a drug-related problem. When it comes to attendance at drug treatment programs, statistics suggest that in 1995, nearly one-third of alcohol- or drug-involved probationers were currently enrolled in an alcohol or drug treatment program. As shown in table 11.1, half of alcohol- or drug-involved probationers said they had received treatment on their current sentence to probation, and about one-third had been treated at some time in their lives.[40] Thus, it is clear from the statistics cited previously that today's probation services are geared, in great part, toward offenders who abuse drugs frequently. This is a direct response to the overwhelming number of drug users who have entered the correctional system in the past few years. There are those who argue that as long as we have severe punishments attached to drug-related laws, the correctional system will continue to be overwhelmed with its admission of drug offenders. This, as expected, will also have a negative effect on probation in the near future.

Court Limitations

In the past, the courts generally would not interfere with the administration of prisons or probation systems. Consequently, conditions for probation, once established, were not disturbed by the courts unless such conditions were illegal, immoral, or impossible for the individual to fulfill. However, courts have since abandoned this hands-off concept. We now look at a few classic cases. But first, let us consider *People v. Blankenship*, in which the court upheld the requirement that a defendant undergo a vasectomy as a prerequisite to probation. The case was decided in 1936 and probably would not be decided the same way today.

The defendant, male, was twenty-three years old and pleaded guilty to the rape of a thirteen-year-old girl. Both had syphilis, although there was no evidence that he transmitted the disease to her. The court recognized that syphilis can be cured, but "it was not so much concerned with curing the disease with which appellant was afflicted as it was with preventing appellant from transmitting the disease to his possible posterity."[41]

T A B L E **11.1** Treatment History of Alcohol- or Drug-Involved Probationers, 1995

Participated in an Alcohol or Drug Treatment Program	Percent of Alcohol- or Drug-Involved Probationers
Ever	64.2%
While incarcerated	10.2
Before current sentence	39.8
During current sentence	53.6
Currently in program	30.1
Number of probationers	1,390,572

Source: *Substance Abuse and Treatment of Adults on Probation, 1995.* Bureau of Justice Statistics. U.S. Department of Justice (March, 1998).

Note: Probationers may have received treatment at multiple times in the past.

In *People v. Dominguez,* the defendant was a twenty-year-old mother of two illegitimate children who was convicted of armed robbery. The trial court imposed as a condition of probation that she not become pregnant out of wedlock again. She did, and the court revoked the probation. On appeal, the case was reversed. The court noted that while the trial court has wide discretion in setting the terms of probation, that discretion in determining probation "must be impartial, guided by 'fixed legal principles, to be exercised in conformity with the spirit of the law.'" The court said that when the condition of probation has no relationship to the crime for which the probationer was convicted or to future criminality, and which is not in itself criminal, it is invalid. "Contraceptive failure is not a indicium of criminality."[42]

In *Irman v. State,* an appeals court ruled that requiring a young man to cut his hair for two years as a condition of probation was unconstitutional. The court recognized that a probationer occupies a special status and that, as a result, the court may require conditions that it could not impose on free persons. Such conditions, as refraining from associating with immoral persons, abstaining from alcohol or drugs, and even holding an approved job, all fall within the category of "no temptation" conditions. These conditions are intended to assist a person in avoiding temptations that might be related to law-breaking behavior. These conditions are, then, designed to help the individual become a law-abiding citizen. In another case, the court ruled that requiring as a condition of probation that a person undergo psychiatric care at his own expense with a psychiatrist approved by the court, was unreasonable.[43]

The probationer's right to marry was questioned in a 1968 case. A defendant pleaded guilty to selling marijuana and was placed on probation. Before that sentence was decided, she married. She did not tell her attorney because he had advised her that at the sentencing hearing she should not mention the name of the fellow she was "dating" because he had been arrested on a drug charge. She was given a short jail sentence and was placed on probation with stipulations, one of which was that she live with her parents. Later, in order to get the probation order changed, she claimed that the conditions of probation denied her the right of cohabitation with her husband. The court said it would decide such cases on a case-by-case basis and that it was not suggesting that probation would normally separate husband and wife. But due to the circumstances in this case, the probation order was not only upheld, but made more stringent. The court noted that probation is not a right but an act of "grace and clemency" and that the "judge is vested with a wide discretion, which will not be disturbed in the absence of abuse."[44]

Finally, in the case of a woman convicted of child abuse, the lower court ordered as a condition of probation that she have no children during the five-year probationary period. The appellate court struck that order, ruling that it was an unconstitutional violation of the right to privacy and an abuse of judicial discretion.[45]

The American Bar Association has suggested, in the past, the following restrictions on the conditions of probation: Generally, every probationer should be required to lead a law-abiding life, but no other conditions should be required by statute. Additional conditions of probation should be made by the sentencing court on an individual basis, according to the needs in each case. It is appropriate to develop standards for such conditions "as long as such conditions are not routinely imposed." The conditions imposed in each case should be for the purpose of assisting the probationer to lead a law-abiding life. "They should be reasonably related to his rehabilitation and not unduly restrictive of his liberty or incompatible with his freedom of religion. They should not be so vague or ambiguous as to give no real guidance." The ABA proposal then lists areas in which conditions might be appropriately made:

1. Cooperating with a program of supervision;
2. Meeting family responsibilities;
3. Maintaining steady employment or engaging or refraining from engaging in a specific employment or occupation;
4. Pursuing prescribed educational or vocational training;
5. Undergoing available medical or psychiatric treatment;
6. Maintaining residence in a prescribed area or in a special facility established for or available to persons on probation;
7. Refraining from consorting with certain types of people or frequenting certain types of places;
8. Making restitution of the fruits of the crime or reparation for loss or damage caused thereby.[46]

The Decision to Grant Probation

Technically, the granting of probation, which may be done only by the court, is a form of sentencing. In reality, however, it is usually considered to be a disposition in lieu of sentencing. In some cases, the court will sentence a defendant to a term of incarceration, but suspend the sentence for a specified period of time during which the offender will be on probation. If the offender does not violate the terms of probation for that period of time, the sentence will never be imposed; if violations occur, the offender will be incarcerated. Because of the close relationship of probation to sentencing, which the Supreme Court considers to be a crucial stage in the criminal justice process, the defendant is entitled to due process at the probation hearing. The fundamental idea of due process under the United States Constitution is that a person should not be deprived of life, liberty, or property without reasonable and lawful procedures. This means, among other things, that the judge may not be unreasonable, arbitrary, or capricious in the decision whether to grant probation. The defendant is entitled to an attorney at this stage, as well as when the probation is revoked and the suspended sentence is imposed.[47]

Recently, several questions have been raised about disparity in probation sentences. In fact, a study was conducted in 1995 that aimed at measuring the differences that exist among rural and urban adult probation admissions. Interviews were conducted on 3,698 adult offenders on probation in Illinois. The questions were based on the probationer's supervision and treatment experiences. It was found that offenders in nonmetropolitan counties were much less likely to be on probation for drug offenses and much more likely to be on probation for other offenses. However, there were some similarities. In fact, it was determined that the average length of probation was the same in both metropolitan and nonmetropolitan counties—20 months. This was the case for various categories of offenses, including violent offenses, property offenses, drug offenses, and DUI (driving under the influence).[48] From the findings of this study, we can only assume that differences do exist in the manner in which probation is administered. These differences exist from jurisdiction to jurisdiction, depending on the area of the country, or even within a state.

Historically, probation could be easily and quickly revoked, and without due process. However, not too long ago, the United States Supreme Court handed down cases that indicate a requirement of some elements of due process at the revocation of probation. This approach is based on the belief that probation is an important phase of the rehabilitation process, and that if offenders are to be rehabilitated, they must see the system as being fair. If the system is arbitrary, offenders will lose respect for it and may be more likely to repeat crimes. It is therefore in the interest of society as well as the probationer or parolee that they be treated fairly.[49]

Revocation of Probation

In *Morrissey v. Brewer,* the U.S. Supreme Court enunciated the due process requirements for revocation of parole[50]; we will look at that decision when we discuss parole. In a later case, *Gagnon v. Scarpelli,* the Supreme Court extended those rights involving revocation of parole to revocation of probation, indicating that, in general, parole and probation revocation are the same for purposes of due process. The Court stated "probation revocation, like parole revocation is not a stage of a criminal prosecution, but does result in a loss of liberty."[51] The Court therefore held that a probationer, like a parolee, "is entitled to two hearings": a preliminary hearing at the time of arrest and detention for the purpose of determining whether there is probable cause to believe that the terms of probation were violated; and a second, more comprehensive hearing when the final revocation decision is made.

The "success" of probationers is usually measured by their degree of recidivism (habitual criminality) compared to the rate of recidivism of persons who had been incarcerated. Recidivism may be measured by violations of law or merely by violations of one or more of the conditions of probation. Technically, then, a probation "failure" could result if a probationer marries without the consent of the supervising officer. Such a measure of "success" is crude and does not necessarily measure rehabilitation. It really measures only whether or not a person is caught violating another law or probation rule. The measure cannot reach those who do not possess the proper skills and mature judgement that are considered essential to rehabilitation.

Measuring the Success of Probation

Comparison of "success" from jurisdiction to jurisdiction is also difficult. The types of persons placed on probation differ, as do the definitions of probation violation utilized in the collection of data. Jurisdictions that place a small percentage of persons on probation may have fewer violations than those that place a larger percentage because the former do not grant probation to anyone who might be a "risk." To add insult to injury, probation's success is subject to a critical public that constantly demands quick, inexpensive solutions to major predicaments such as crime.

Empirical Evidence

In the late 1980s, a study of adult felons on probation examined the enforcement of sanctions that were part of the probation sentence. The analysis was conducted from results of a follow-up survey of convicted adult felons placed on state probation in 1986. The survey tracked 12,370 probationers for three years, from 1986 to 1989. Results indicated that sizable numbers of offenders were discharged from probation before having fully complied with the conditions of their sentences. In fact, among those released without compliance were 24 percent ordered to participate in alcohol treatment, 20 percent in mental health counseling, 32 percent in a drug treatment program, 25 percent ordered to reside in a residential facility, 33 percent ordered for drug testing, 33 percent ordered to house arrest, 35 percent for day reporting, 21 percent ordered to perform community service, 69 percent ordered to pay supervision fees, and 40 percent ordered to make restitution.[52] These results suggest that sanctions that are imposed along with probation are not rigorously enforced. A possible reason for this may be that there are inadequate resources in place to enforce and monitor drug tests, house arrests, community service, payment of fines, and treatment participation. This lack of resources may be a result of the growth of incarceration rates in the past years, with prisons and jails benefitting the most from state and local budgets (average of two cents for every dollar spent in most states). At the same time, spending on probation and parole has been limited (average of two-tenths of one cent of every dollar spent in most states).[53]

Consequently, it is equally important to mention that the recidivism rates of those who attend treatment programs, are lower when compared to the rates of those who do not attend. In fact, the state of New York is hosting a program targeted at probationers who have been convicted two or more times of driving while intoxicated and are not presently receiving any treatment service. This program melds probation with the treatment of these offenders at facilities such as the Hudson Mohawk Recovery Center and Seton Addiction Services for one or two years. In 1996, a ten-year study of the program was concluded. This study compared outcomes for participants to those for a control group of probationers not offered formal treatment.[54] The results of this study suggest that:

1. Program graduates were arrested 40 percent fewer times for DWI offenses and two-thirds fewer times for non-DWI offenses;
2. On average, a person in the treatment program went nineteen months longer before being rearrested for any crime;
3. Program participants were only one-fifth as likely to violate probation as were members of the control group.[55]

Thus, it can be argued that the program has been effective in lowering the recidivism rates of probationers who had been convicted of DWI offenses. However, we must be careful in making concrete assumptions or generalizations about the effectiveness of this program when considering its implementation in another jurisdiction.

Unfortunately, unlike the New York program previously mentioned, recent studies have indicated that probation in the 1990s (as a whole) is a failure and that the only option we have is to reinvent it. Joan R. Petersilia, former director of RAND's criminal justice research program, calculated that we currently spend about $200 per probationer for supervision. She notes that "it is no wonder that recidivism rates are so high."[56] A recent study argues that it should be no surprise that probationers have a high recidivism rate when we consider the problems facing probation officers.[57] These include being underpaid, overworked, and having scores of cases to manage. This same study suggests that we must reinvent probation by investing more money, allocating more agents, and maintaining a closer supervision of offenders. It is also argued that probation should be teamed with police agencies as part of a larger crime prevention initiative.[58] Thus, the collective effort of all of the social control agencies in the criminal justice system is put to work. It is not clear whether the suggestions made by this study will work once implemented—however, we are certain that the number of probation studies will grow as correctional administrators and the general public explore alternatives to incarceration.

No one really knows what future awaits probation. However, some jurisdictions have already taken the initiative in implementing different modernized versions of probation, which they claim to be highly successful. For instance, in 1995, probation departments in Oklahoma, Utah, Oregon, and Texas began to test telephone reporting programs to monitor low-risk offenders. Probationers are asked to call a 900 number once a month to answer a number of computerized questions.[59] This approach aims at reducing paper reporting—both mail-in and office reporting. This program has been praised by most of the agencies presently using it. In fact, Patty Davis of the Oklahoma Department of Corrections stated that this was one way "to work smarter and free up officers for more meaningful contact with offenders who really need intervention activity."[60] Davis added that the program is "used with more than low-risk cases, that is, if you have to report and pay fees, then the offender is eligible."[61] Everyone involved in this new approach to monitor the activities of probationers cautioned that this was not the solution—just one approach toward the improvement of probation.

The Future

In other jurisdictions, probation and police executives are establishing partnerships that highlight information-sharing and joint supervision projects to improve the efficiency of community safety services. Most of these community justice programs involve high-risk offender monitoring and the creation of police, citizen, and corrections and human service provider networks. Some of these jurisdictions include Redmond, Washington's high-risk offender monitoring program, Boston's Night Lite and Tracker programs, and Knoxville, Tennessee's network of citizens, police, corrections and human service providers working together to reduce crime.[62] The outcome of these programs is yet to be measured. However, the preliminary results are positive and several probation agencies have recently expressed interest in adopting similar programs in their particular jurisdiction.

In a recent article, Charles J. Kehoe holds that in the next six to eight years, technological advances will directly affect probation, especially juvenile probation.[63] Kehoe predicts that soon centralized probation offices will be virtually extinct. Communication technology will enable probation officers to do their jobs without ever having to report to an office. Thus, by logging into a home computer and modem, officers will be able to check a daily schedule, send and receive documents, and communicate with co-workers and supervisors.[64]

Kehoe adds that in the near future, court hearings will be held on closed circuit television, which will minimize the risk of violence and escape attempts when transporting offenders to and from court. In fact, the state of Florida is already implementing this approach. The satellite usage will also be implemented to educate all probation personnel more effectively. It is believed that probation officers will enjoy the benefit of video conferences that will be transmitted live via satellite. This will hopefully allow unlimited access to training and other programs by probation staff all over the country and the world. At the end of the article, Kehoe warns about the "dangers" associated with the use of this new technology. One of these dangers is the sacrifice that will obviously be made on our privacy. The following question is asked: How far are we willing to go to reduce crime and at what cost?[65]

WiseGuide Wrap-Up   In this chapter, we reviewed the history and practice of probation, one of the most controversial and frequently used practices in the entire criminal justice system. We considered the purpose of this form of sentencing and looked at the problems, both legal and sociological, of the decision to grant and revoke probation. We examined previous and current empirical evidence of the success or failure of probation, with the conclusion we reach so often in an analysis of social science research: We really have not measured effectiveness. Maybe it will be impossible to measure the effects of probation, but social scientists should continue their efforts to do so.

Despite the cries of leniency and the trend toward harsher reactions to those who have been convicted of crimes, probation continues to be the most frequently used form of sentencing. More attention should be given to the goals of probation in given cases and to the conditions imposed on particular probationers. Are the conditions really related to the goals of probation? Probation is intended and should be a flexible form of reaction to the convicted person, a method by which the court can devise an individualized sentence. This is especially important in cases in which incarceration appears to be unnecessary for the safety of society and in which it would perhaps be detrimental for the offender. As the correctional population grows to unprecedented proportions, probation will be even more important in our system of criminal justice.

Notes

1. Bureau of Justice Statistics, U.S. Department of Justice. Correctional Population in the United States, 1995. (June, 1997).
2. The Columbia Encyclopedia, Edition 5. "Probation." p. 30172. (New York: Columbia University Press, 1993).
3. Brown, Michael. "Probation for Illegal Contribution," *Jet* (December 15, 1997), vol. 93. no. 4, 36 (1).
4. For a more detailed discussion of benefit of clergy, see David Dressler, *Practice and Theory of Probation and Parole*, 2nd ed. (New York: Columbia University Press, 1969), pp. 16–18.
5. "The Origins of Probation: From Common Law Roots," in George G. Killinger and Paul F. Cromwell, Jr., *Corrections in the Community: Alternatives to Imprisonment.* (St. Paul, MN: West, 1974), pp. 159–160.
6. Montgomery, Reid, Jr., and Dillingham, Steven N. *Probation and Parole in Practice* (1983).
7. Montgomery and Dillingham, *Probation and Parole.* p. 13.
8. Champion, Dean. "Felony Plea Bargaining & Probation: A Growing Judicial & Prosecutional Dilemma," *Journal of Criminal Justice* (1988), vol. 16, no. 4, p. 291.
9. See Act of Mar. 22, 1880, cah. 129, 1880 Mass. Acts 87.
10. Act of Mar. 22, 1880, cah. 129, 1880 Mass. Acts 87.
11. Montgomery and Dillingham, *Probation and Parole,* Supra note 25, at 24.
12. U.S. Bureau of the Census, National Criminal Justice Information and Statistics Service. *State and Local Probation and Parole Systems.* (Washington, DC: U.S. Government Printing Office, 1978), pp. vii, 1.
13. Carlson, Norman A. "The Future of Prisons," *Trial* 12 (March, 1976), 32.
14. The President's Commission on Law Enforcement and Administration of Justice. *Task Force Report: Corrections.* (Washington, DC: U.S. Government Printing Office, 1967), p. 27.
15. National Advisory Commission on Criminal Justice Standards and Goals. *Corrections.* (Washington, DC: U.S. Government Printing Office, 1973), p. 159.
16. Bonczar, Thomas P. *Characteristics of Adults on Probation, 1995.* Bureau of Justice Statistics. U.S. Department of Justice. (Washington, DC: U.S. Government Printing Office, December, 1997).
17. Bonczar, *Characteristics of Adults,* p. 13.
18. U.S. Department of Justice. "Percentage of Women on Probation and Parole Rising." *Jet,* (September 8, 1997), vol. 92, no. 16, 40(1).

19. The Federal Judicial Center. *An Introduction to the Federal Probation System.* (Washington, DC: U.S. Government Printing Office, 1976), p. 1.
20. American Bar Association Project on Standards for Criminal Justice. *Standards Relating to Probation.* (Approved Draft, 1970), p. 27.
21. National Advisory Commission on Criminal Justice Standards and Goals. *Corrections.* (Washington, DC: U.S. Government Printing Office, 1973), p. 159.
22. Clear, Todd, and Cole, F. George. 4th ed. *American Corrections.* (Albany, NY: Wadsworth Publishing Company, 1997).
23. For a listing of conditions of parole, by states and designations, see *The Sourcebook of Criminal Justice Statistics, 1996.* (Washington, DC: U.S. Government Printing Office, 1996).
24. Bureau of Justice Statistics. U.S. Department of Justice. *Substance Abuse and Treatment of Adults on Probation, 1995.* (March, 1998).
25. See James Robinson, Leslie T. Wilkins, Robert M. Carter, and Albert Wahl. *San Francisco Project,* Research Report No. 14. (Berkeley: University of California School of Criminology, 1969).
26. See, for example, the earlier work of Daniel Glaser, *The Effectiveness of a Prison and Parole System.* (New York: The Bobbs-Merrill Co., 1964).
27. The literature is discussed in Shelle G. Dietrich, "The Probation Officer as Therapist; Examination of Three Major Problem Areas." *Federal Probation* 43 (June, 1979), 14–19.
28. Mangrum, Claude T. "The Humanity of Probation Officers," *Federal Probation* 36 (June, 1972) 47–50.
29. Mangrum, "Humanity," p. 48.
30. Dietrich, "Probation Officer as Therapist," p. 15.
31. Dietrich, "Probation Officer as Therapist," p. 15.
32. Dietrich, "Probation Officer as Therapist," p. 15.
33. Dietrich, "Probation Officer as Therapist," p. 18.
34. Dietrich, "Probation Officer as Therapist," p. 19.
35. Brown, Paul W. "Probation Officers Need to Rely on More Than Luck to Ensure Safety," *Corrections Today* (April, 1994), vol. 56, no. 2, 180(2).
36. Morrison, Richard D. "The Risk of Intensive Supervision." In *Complete Control: Correctional Security* (July, 1994), vol. 56, no. 4, 118(3).
37. Evans, Donald G. "Probation Undercover: Westchester County's DWI," *Drinking While Impaired* (August, 1996) vol. 58, no. 5, 172(2).
38. National Advisory Commission on Criminal Justice Standards and Goals, *Corrections,* p. 337. For a critique of the use of volunteers as probation officers, see David A. Dowell, "Volunteers in Probation: A Research Note on Evaluation," *Journal of Criminal Justice* (Winter, 1978), 6:9 357–361.
39. Advisory Commission, *Corrections,* p. 338.
40. Bureau of Justice Statistics. U.S. Department of Justice, *Substance Abuse and Treatment of Adults on Probation, 1995.*
41. *People v. Blankenship,* 61 P.2d 352, 353 (1936).
42. *People v. Dominguez,* 64 Cal. Rptr. 290, 293 (1967).
43. *In re Bushman,* 463 p. 2d 727 (1970).
44. *In re Peeler,* 72 Cal. Rptr. 254, 258 (1968).
45. *Ohio v. Livingston,* 372 N.E.2d 1335 (1978).
46. American Bar Association, *Standards Relating to Probation,* p. 45.
47. *Mempha v. Rhay,* 389 U.S. 128 (1967).
48. Ellsworth, Thomas, and Weisheit, Ralph A. "The Supervision and Treatment of Offenders on Probation: Understanding Rural and Urban Differences," *The Prison Journal,* (June, 1997), vol. 77, no. 2, 209 (20).
49. Plamer, John W. *Constitutional Rights of Prisoners.* (Cincinnati, OH: Anderson, 1973), p. 114.
50. *Morrissey v. Brewer,* 408 U.S. 471.
51. *Gagnon v. Scarpelli,* 411 U.S. 778, 782 (1973).
52. Langan, Patrick A. "Between Prison and Probation: Intermediate Sanctions," *Science,* (May 6, 1994), vol. 264, no. 5160, 791(3).
53. Langan, "Between Prison and Probation," p. 792.
54. "New York Program That Merges Treatment, Probation Gets Results." (Rensselaer County Probation Alcohol Treatment). *Alcoholism and Drug Abuse Week* (February 5, 1996), vol. 8, no. 6, 6(1).
55. "New York Program That Merges Treatment, Probation," p. 6.
56. Dilulio, John J. Jr. "Reinventing Parole and Probation" *Brookings Review* (Spring, 1997), vol. 15, no. 2, 40(3).
57. Dilulio, "Reinventing Parole," p. 40.
58. Dilulio, "Reinventing Parole," p. 41.
59. Evans, Donald G. "Four States Experiment with Telephone Technology" (Telephone-Reporting Technology to Monitor Offenders). *Probation and Parole Forum* (December, 1995), vol. 57, no. 7, 170.
60. Evans, "Four States Experiment," p. 170.
61. Evans, "Four States Experiment," p. 170.
62. Evans, Donald G. "Probation and Police Collaboration: Promoting Public Safety," *Corrections Today,* (June, 1997), vol. 59, no. 3, 126(2).
63. Kehoe, Charles J. "Dramatic Changes in Store for Juvenile Probation Agencies" (Juveniles: A Generation at Risk), *Corrections Today* (December, 1994). vol. 56, no. 7, 96(3).
64. Kehoe, "Dramatic Changes in Store," p. 98.
65. Kehoe, "Dramatic Changes in Store," p. 97.

Alternatives to Prison

12

Community Corrections and Intermediate Sanctions

A philosophy of *revenge,* followed by the dominant theme of *restraint,* characterized early penal institutions. In the United States, a humanitarian effort strongly influenced early correctional philosophy, with an emphasis on *reformation* of the individual. The Quakers thought this could be accomplished by giving the offender time to think and reflect, through religious training, and by isolating the offender from the harmful influence of questionable people. The emphasis was on the "total institution," resulting in the removal of the individual from home and society. In that atmosphere, it was thought, the person could be *rehabilitated.*

The philosophy of rehabilitation has come under challenge, however, resulting in a variety of "trends" in corrections. A return to *retribution* in sentencing, at least for adults, and more recently for violent juvenile offenders, has been one of the results. Another has been the emphasis on community-based treatment. One of the key words in corrections today appears to be *reintegration.* Institutionalization has not been effective and, in many cases, has created more serious problems for offenders; thus, some argue that the emphasis should be on keeping as many offenders as possible in the community. "It is believed that reintegration of the offender with the law-abiding community . . . cannot be accomplished by isolating the offender in an artificial, custodial, setting."[1] This mentality has led to the creation of penalties considered to be less harsh than prison but more stringent than probation. These are often known as **intermediate sanctions.** They include, but are not limited to, fines, parole, house monitoring, halfway houses, day treatment centers, boot camps, and intensive supervision probation (ISP). The sanctions will be discussed in this chapter as part of the broader idea of community corrections.

Key Terms

boot camps
community-based corrections
deinstitutionalization
intermediate sanctions

This chapter explores the trend toward community-based corrections. We begin with a historical view of community corrections and note the position taken by previous national commissions. Because there are a variety of approaches to community corrections, and some confusion about those approaches, we then consider the meaning of the term *community-based corrections.* Various models, legislation, and recent trends in community corrections are discussed.

In addition, we examine the compliance of those who are sentenced to community-based corrections programs. As part of this discussion, we look at the findings of recent studies that have attempted to evaluate the effectiveness of intermediate sanctions imposed by the judicial system. Finally, we examine the need for research, and explore major perceptions and recommendations regarding intermediate sanctions.

Overview of Community-Based Corrections

History

The concept of **community-based corrections** has existed for centuries, but the organized approach to this form of handling offenders is very recent. In the United States, this approach can be traced from the first halfway house in 1887 in New York City, to a highly complex array of current programs. The major impetus for the movement, however, was the Federal Prisoner's Rehabilitation Act of 1965 and the President's Crime Commission Report of 1967. The Prisoner's Rehabilitation Act provided for furloughs, work release, and community treatment facilities for federal inmates. In addition, the President's Crime Commission Report stated that the new direction in corrections recognizes that crime and delinquency are failures of the community as well as of the individual offenders. The commission saw the task of corrections as one of reintegrating the offender into the community, restoring family ties, getting the person an education or employment, and in general, securing for the offender a place in the normal functioning of society. That, said the commission, requires changes in the community as well as in the offender. The commission described the traditional method of institutionalizing offenders as a "fundamental deficiency in approach." The commission concluded that reintegration is "likely to be furthered much more readily by working with offenders in the community than by incarceration."

In 1973, the National Advisory Commission on Criminal Justice Standards and Goals called for an increased emphasis on probation, already the most frequent form of sentencing. The commission concluded, "The most hopeful move toward effective corrections is to continue and strengthen the trend away from confining people in institutions and toward supervising them in the community."[2]

Why this movement? The National Advisory Commission stated the reasons:

First, state institutions consume more than three-fourths of all expenditures for corrections while dealing with less than one-third of all offenders. Second, as a whole they do not deal with those offenders effectively. There is no evidence that prisons reduce the amount of crime. On the contrary, there is evidence that they contribute to criminal activity after the inmate is released.

Prisoners tend to dehumanize people. . . . Their weaknesses are made worse, and their capacity for responsibility and self-government is eroded by regimentation. Add to these facts the physical and mental conditions resulting from overcrowding and from the various ways in which institutions ignore the rights of offender, and the riots of the past decade are hardly to be wondered at. Safety for society may be achieved for a limited time if offenders are kept out of circulation, but no real public protection is provided if confinement serves mainly to prepare men for more, and more skilled, criminality.[3]

The importance of integrating or reintegrating the offender into the community was emphasized by Paul C. Friday and Jerald Hage. After a brief look at the approaches generally used by sociologists to explain delinquent behavior, Friday and Hage used those approaches to develop an integrated perspective. "The objective is to indicate what factors influence youth reliance on groups supporting delinquent values by considering the patterns of role relationships." They base their approach on the social integration theory of Durkheim, especially his work on suicide.[4] Noting the importance of role relationships, Friday and Hage point out that for adolescents in our society, the development of an integrated role pattern is greatly hindered by the social structure of society, which often isolates them from basic social institutions. "When adolescents have meaningful kin, educational, work, and community relationships, they are more likely to become socialized to the dominant norms of society. Integration is facilitated by interaction across all role patterns." When these do not exist, a young person is more likely to move into deviant behavior, with the youth group being "the only meaningful role relationship."[5]

Reintegration of the offender into the community is not, however, a one-way process. Lloyd E. Ohlin, Alden D. Miller, and Robert B. Coates, in their evaluation of deinstitutionalization in Massachusetts, emphasized the need for the community to take an active role in the process of treating the offender—a strategy they call advocacy—which goes beyond reintegration. They maintained that it might not be sufficient to try to reintegrate the offender into the community; the latter may need to change more than does the offender. For example, if resources for reintegration are not available, they must be developed. The advocacy approach involves getting the community to provide the resources for offenders.[6]

Definition of Community-Based Programs

Ohlin, Miller, and Coates emphasized that the words "'community-based' focus attention on the nature of the links between programs and the community." When determining which programs are the least community-based and which are the most, one looks to the *extent* and *quality* of the relationships between those involved in the program—both clients and staff—and the community. For example, the old chain gangs (which incidently are being reintroduced in some states), work(ed) in the community, but are not what we mean by community-based corrections.[7] "Generally, as the frequency, quality, and duration of community relationships increase, the program becomes more community-based."[8]

Community-based treatment should be distinguished from diversion, a term that is often used to refer to community-based corrections. Technically, diversion means to turn the offender aside *from* the criminal (or juvenile) justice system. It should not be used to refer to "a different routing *within* the correctional component of this system." The appropriate term to use for the process of the "development and use of community-based correctional programs as alternatives to institutions," is the term **deinstitutionalization**.[9] Diversion is an important process that has implications for improvement of the system of corrections. This is especially true today, with the incarceration rate at an all-time high. With the present "catching up" state of most constructions of correctional facilities, diversion of inmates may be the only option that some correctional administrations have.

The concern over the definition of community corrections continues to haunt correctional administrators. In fact, in January, 1995 during the Winter Conference in Dallas, the president of the American Correctional Association charged a Community Corrections Committee to prepare a statement describing the purpose and mission of community corrections. The committee, in response to the president's charge, decided that it would be necessary to develop a definition of community corrections before creating a mission statement and supporting principles.[10] However, the committee quickly realized that the task of defining community corrections was not an easy one. In fact, it was full of obstacles—in the past most practitioners who attempted to define it have always concentrated on the factors that do not make a program part of the community corrections family. David Duffee, co-author of *Community Corrections: A Community Field Approach,* noted that "while it may be difficult to derive an authoritative definition of community corrections, it is important to understand that simple definitions are becoming increasingly more difficult to sustain."[11] The committee found Duffee's statement truthful as members debated over a "simple" definition of community corrections—this was made increasingly difficult as the committee began to consider the inclusion of some forms of intermediate sanctions.

The committee continued to work on the challenge of defining community corrections at an all-day meeting at the headquarters of the American Correctional Association (ACA) in Maryland on May 10, 1996. In arriving at the proposed definition, the committee made note of the fact that there were some elements of a definition that needed to be taken for granted. These included the following:

- Community corrections is part of the justice system, which involves both adults and juveniles, and also includes a broader context containing elements of social justice.

- Community corrections agencies are involved in administering sanctions and providing services. Services are provided to victims, defendants, and offenders.

- Community corrections agencies acknowledge that they exist to enhance public safety.

- Community corrections is effective and efficient when it works in partnership with local communities and other agencies interested in safer communities and justice.[12]

Finally, the committee agreed that community corrections can be defined as the "part of the justice system providing sanctions and services to enhance public safety and maintain offenders/defendants within the community. These goals are accomplished by selecting appropriate participants, holding offenders accountable, repairing the harm done to victims and the community, supervising and treating offenders/defendants, involving citizens, and maintaining positive ties between the community and the offender."[13] Supporters of this definition argue that the most important of its components is the fact that it acknowledges that community corrections is part of the broader justice system. Furthermore, this definition is also praised by many since it specifies the mechanisms that can be implemented to achieve the specified goals while acknowledging that the work of community sanctions is accomplished by keeping offenders within the community. The latter will continue to challenge corrections administrators as the citizenry demands more severe sanctions, most of which include long prison sentences.

Even though the idea of sexual predators on conditional release in the community is unthinkable to many, recently published statistics suggest that these types of offenders are less likely than any other offender to be placed in community release programs. On the average, the ratio of all offenders sentenced to probation or parole to those incarcerated in jail or prison is nearly three to one. However, the numbers change dramatically for those convicted of rape or any other sexual assault. For these offenders, the ratio is much lower: 1.4 to 1.[14]

> Sex offenders represent 4.7 percent of the 5 million convicted offenders serving time at both federal and state correctional facilities, and those on parole and probation. Bureau of Justice Statistics studies of sex offenders discharged from prison or sentenced to probation showed that sex offenders are more likely than other violent offenders to be rearrested for a new, violent sex offense.[15] Thus, it is not surprising that with the growing concern over crime, citizens are less willing to tolerate a sexual predator being part of their community—even if the sex offender is fulfilling all aspects of the sentence imposed by the courts. Evidence of this can be traced to the passage of Megan's Law. This particular law mandates public notification of the whereabouts of dangerous sex offenders. Although this law prohibits neighbors of sex offenders from seeking retribution against them, it enhances the possibility of labeling to take place. It is important to note that there are usually some sanctions that accompany the conditional release of offenders into the community. As mentioned earlier, these are called intermediate sanctions.

Sex Offenders Sentenced to Community Corrections: Recent Trends

Intermediate Sanctions

The Major Forms

The demand for more intermediate sanctions comes from judges, correctional administrators, and at times, even the general public. As explained earlier, most intermediate sanctions aim at punishing the offender while keeping him or her in the community. The advantages of this approach are numerous. For instance, the offender may be able to keep his or her job and thus be able to support any dependants. This will prevent the dependant family from drawing welfare or some other type of social benefit. In addition, the community will benefit from these sanctions by not being forced to pay for the incarceration of the inmate. As more people are being supervised by the department of corrections, intermediate sanctions continue to be justified. This is particularly true in jurisdictions where overcrowded prison conditions are forcing correctional administrators to take extraordinary measures (i.e., contracting out with a private prison facility, transferring inmates to other states). Overall, then, the benefits of intermediate sanctions are numerous, and they vary according to the type of sanction being imposed. Spotlight 12.1 shows each of the major forms of intermediate sanctions in place today.

The Four Major CCA Models

In the early 1970s, the states of Minnesota, Iowa, and Colorado adopted Community Corrections Acts (CCAs) that were to serve as models for many aspects of community corrections programming and financing in the following years. The implementation of these acts was largely a result of the efforts of concerned professionals and community groups. These acts have been implemented with the aim of bringing funding to local and county agencies for the planning, development, and delivery of correctional services and sanctions at the local level.[16] Two decades

Spotlight 12.1

Major Forms of Intermediate Sanctions

1. **Fines** These are issued by the courts with a high degree of frequency. In fact, statistics suggest that over $1 billion in fines are collected every year by U.S. courts. For the most part, fines are usually issued along with another type of sanction. For instance, a judge may impose one year of probation and a fine of $300.

2. **Community Service** This specific condition usually requires the accused to give a determined number of hours of free labor in public service. This includes, but is not limited to, cleaning a park, repairing an old house, or painting over a graffiti-covered wall. The idea is that the offender will be able to repair some, if not all, of the damage that has been committed against the community. Some go as far as arguing that this condition is beneficial psychologically to offenders, who begin to take pride in their community and are less likely to commit another crime.

3. **Restitution** This condition requires the offender pay a specific sum of money to the victim, the victim's family, or perhaps even a crime victim support fund. Again, the assumption is that the offender will repair the wrongdoing via a financial contribution.

4. **Intensive Supervision Probation (ISP)** These programs target offenders who are subject to incarceration, and require a more intensive supervision of probationers. This attention is allowed, in part, by the smaller caseload of each ISP officer.

5. **Home Confinement** Offenders under this program are sentenced to incarceration. However, their sentence is served in their homes. The terms of home confinement vary from state to state. In some cases, home confinement programs allow offenders to leave their home for specific periods of the day. Others, however, are more restrictive and do not allow the offender to leave the home at any time. The benefits of home confinement are numerous. It reduces or eliminates the cost associated with incarceration, allows the offender to maintain a job (in some cases), and does not break up the family composition.

6. **Shock Incarceration** These programs are based on the notion that the offender is sentenced to a jail or prison term for a specific amount of time. After the offender serves thirty to ninety days in jail or prison, a judge reduces the sentence and then releases the offender to the community under a probationary status. The idea is that the offender will be shocked after the "prison experience" to such an extent that he or she will be unlikely to engage in criminal activity in the future.

7. **Boot Camps** Offenders usually serve a short sentence and are then sent to a rigorous, military-like regimen. This program is aimed at developing discipline and respect for the law—it targets first-time juvenile offenders. **Boot camps** usually last up to four months and contain routines full of physical training (PT), marches, drills, and hard labor. The success of these programs is currently being debated. Some argue that they offer a wonderful way to discipline those who are thought of as being "impressionable," while others believe that these programs legitimize violence and make offenders more physically and emotionally fit to enhance their criminal careers.

later, almost half of the American states have implemented laws that are patterned after these early acts. Thus, it is imperative that we examine the evolution, commonalities, differences, and various traits of these acts in an attempt to identify their influence on the creation of what is now known as *intermediate sanctions*.

In 1973, Minnesota was the first state to adopt a CCA. State officials were interested in reducing fragmentation in service delivery, controlling costs, and redefining the population of offenders. At the time, local officials were willing to assume increased correctional responsibilities for less serious offenders as long as they were also given state subsidies.[17] Soon after, Iowa and Colorado followed the example set forth by Minnesota. All of the CCAs in these states reflected the characteristics, values, and attitudes of Midwestern people. In fact, all of these acts placed a strong emphasis on "doing the right thing" while developing rational policies and humane practices. An additional model, which incorporated characteristics of the Minnesota and Colorado CCAs but also included unique elements, can be characterized as a "southern" model that began with the Virginia Community Diversion Incentive Act and later assumed a form that would be followed by the Tennessee CCA.

All four of these models shared a number of characteristics that have been replicated by other states. The original four Community Corrections Acts:

- Were legislatively authorized: Statues provided the framework and authority for the other defining features of CCAs.

- Were authorized statewide: CCAs mandated or authorized all localities, individually or in combination, to take advantage of the funds and authority granted.

- Provided for citizen participation: CCAs provided for citizen involvement and specified roles that citizens played.

- Defined an intergovernmental structure: CCAs delineated the roles to be performed and the power and authority to be exercised by involved state and local agencies or units of government.

- Required local planning: CCAs provided that local planning would precede and serve as the basis for the development, implementation, and modification of local correctional sanctions and services.

- Provided for state funding: CCAs provided for state subsidies to support local correctional programs and services.

- Called for decentralized program design and delivery: CCAs provided for local control of the processes employed to assess local needs, to establish local priorities, and to plan local programs.

- Endorsed locally determined sanctions and services: CCAs provided resources and authority for sanctions and services to be developed and delivered at the local level.[18]

Some argue that the original implementation of CCAs contributed to the creation of what is now known as "intermediate sanctions." Others have claimed that, at the very least, we must regard CCAs as the equivalent of intermediate sanctions. Which one of these two positions is correct? First, let us examine the definition of intermediate sanctions. These sanctions are generally defined as "dispositional options that lie between traditional probation and total confinement in state prisons on a spectrum of intrusiveness, level of punishment, and control."[19] Interestingly, most of the literature suggests that the development of CCAs that took place in the 1970s influenced the creation of the first intermediate sanctions in the mid-1980s. It is argued that CCAs gave acceptance to the notion that sanctions needed to be implemented at the intermediate level. In regard to the question posed earlier of whether or not CCAs are equivalent to intermediate sanctions, we must agree that it depends upon the state implementing the CCA. For instance, the early models were inclusive of all or most local correctional programs and services, including probation and parole. Hence, in the states that utilized these early models, CCAs included intermediate sanctions, but were not limited to midrange options. However, in other states such as Kansas and Indiana, the CCAs that were adopted did not provide for the integration of probation and parole services. Thus, it must be maintained that some CCAs have focused largely on intermediate sanctions but others have included probation, parole, and other services along with a broad array of intermediate sanctions. Some of the other areas in which CCAs are different include the extent of decentralization of correctional services, the nature of citizen participation, the relative emphasis on deinstitutionalization, and the level of focus on rehabilitation of offenders through community-based approaches.[20]

The contribution of CCAs toward the development of intermediate sanctions is unprecedented. In fact, many have argued that without CCAs, no state would have ever implemented what is now known as intermediate sanctions. Thus, it is imperative to understand the benefits and lessons taught by the creation and implementation of the original four CCA models in order to better understand the function of community corrections. In light of this, we have looked at the commonalities, differences, and some of the alleged contributions of these four original CCA models. The original four CCAs have served as models to other states that have since enacted legislation for the purpose of modifying or, in some instances, creating community corrections programs. Although it would be impossible for us to study all of the states that have enacted CCAs, we will examine, in detail, one of the original CCA models (Minnesota) as well as the implementation of the first CCA in the state of Michigan. Hopefully, both of these will serve as an illustration of both the original and more recent cases in which CCAs were implemented. We now turn our attention to the study of the CCAs in the states of Minnesota and Michigan.

CCAs: The Minnesota and Michigan Experiences

Minnesota

Kenneth F. Schoen, Commissioner of the Minnesota Department of Corrections, gave his opinion of Minnesota's statutory response to the move toward community-based corrections:

> Incarceration is extremely expensive and it does not affect crime rates. The Minnesota Community Corrections Act changes the role of corrections. Instead of serving to cage society's rejects, corrections becomes a joint effort by the community and the offender to reintegrate that offender into society. If we want a more realistic approach to correction, this act represents an option well worth considering.[21]

For each offender committed to a Minnesota state facility, a "charge-back" from the state subsidy was given to the community, which served as a powerful incentive against state commitment. If a county wished to participate in the Community Corrections Act, it had to select a local advisory board for corrections, composed of local citizens and persons from the local criminal justice system. The board had to devise a plan for community corrections and then submit the plan to the county commissioners. If approved, the plan then had to be submitted to the State Commissioner of Corrections. If the latter thought the plan workable, the subsidy from the state began. The amount that each county received in state subsidy was determined by a formula based on the correctional needs, population, and financial resources of the county, minus projected costs for the number of people the county committed to state institutions, as well as any other state subsidies received by the county.[22]

Did the plan achieve its goals? The first goal, reduction of state commitments, occurred. The second goal, increased cost-effectiveness, was more difficult to measure. Schoen said that in the long run, the second goal was probably reached, but in the short run, the state had to operate parallel systems of corrections. The third goal was to decrease the demand for state institutions, which would eventually be phased out. That did not happen, because when the plan was implemented in about 1973, the demand for increased incarceration began.

Critics of the Minnesota plan have pointed out that there has been no indication that serving time in jail is more therapeutic for inmates than serving time in prison, and that the inclusion of jails in the program is therefore questionable. The formula used for determining the subsidy has also been the source of criticism, especially for not sufficiently taking into consideration the greater needs of high-crime urban areas. Criminologist David Ward gave his view:

> [I]t has yet to be proven to me that local communities can do a better job at providing services or that program interest is high at the community level. I think these people have good intentions, but it has been my experience with community groups that they're not sophisticated enough to stick with programs, and in the end they wind up being taken over by professionals. I'm skeptical that communities can be made to become more responsive and effective.[23]

Michigan

In Michigan, probation first became viable in the early twentieth century. In fact, it was not until the early 1900s that the state assumed some responsibility for offenders other than those who were committed to state prisons. In 1937, the Model Corrections Act created the Michigan Department of Corrections (MDOC).[24] This same act provided state-funded probation services for the first time in the state. However, no other community alternatives were offered until the 1960s when the MDOC implemented a work pass/release program for state prison inmates. In 1975, Governor William Milliken officially acknowledged the problem of prison overcrowding and requested that the leadership to deal with the problem come from other agencies of government. The director of corrections at the time, Perry Johnson, implemented the Probation Incentive Program, through which the state reimbursed counties that diverted offenders to local intermediate sanctions programs. This was later aided by the funds that became available by the Law Enforcement Assistance Administration.

Due to the request made by director Johnson, the Michigan legislature funded two community corrections programs and a residential probation program in Detroit in 1977. In that same year, the Michigan State Senate introduced the first formal legislation aimed specifically at subsidizing local community-based programs. In 1981, after a series of prison riots, community corrections legislation was reintroduced in the state of Michigan. This legislation proposed subsidies to counties as well as legislation allowing two-year jail sentences. Finally, in 1989, the Michigan Community Corrections Act (Public Act 511) became law. Not only did the CCA create an autonomous agency, but it also required that advisory boards be established for the purpose of developing and implementing community corrections plans. The CCA also had specific language regarding the aims of diverting sentences: "The plan shall include . . . provisions that detail how the city, county, or counties plan to substantially reduce, within one year, the use of prison sentences for felons for which the state felony sentencing guidelines upper limit for the recommended minimum sentence is 12 months or less."[25]

According to reports, Michigan's CCA is regarded as an enormous success. Since the act was enacted, seventy-nine of Michigan's eighty-three counties have voluntarily formed local advisory boards, which are made up of local corrections officials, judges, prosecutors, law enforcement agents, and local government representatives. Michigan's CCA has also expanded the use of intermediate sanctions in local jurisdictions. As a proportion of all sentences, it is reported that prison dispositions have decreased from 37.2 percent in 1989 to 29.3 percent in 1993. Data from 1994 suggested that this trend has continued.[26] In addition, as expected, the implementation of Michigan's CCA, community service work, electronic monitoring, day reporting, employment, and drug testing and treatment programs have been expanded in most communities in the state. These programs are helpful to corrections officials in the monitoring of offenders in the community—this enhances public safety and increases the accountability of Michigan's criminal justice system. However, it must also be noted that the reported success has been overshadowed by the continued growth of the state's inmate population. This growth, as is the case in many other states, can be attributed in part to the passage of more than 100 state statutes that have increased penalties and the use of prison sentences. In Michigan, these laws include prison sentences for third-offense drunk driving and for those found guilty of possession of 50 grams or less of a controlled substance.[27]

The Classification Process

Because we have already studied the process of classifying inmates and facilities within the correctional system, we will not discuss this topic in great detail here. However, it is important to mention that any inmate who faces the possibility of being sentenced to an intermediate sanction has to undergo a classification process. Needless to say, this process is different in every jurisdiction. Recently, however, many jurisdictions have begun to classify their inmates inside jail facilities. This is particularly important for correctional administrators who claim to have the advantage of placing low-risk offenders in intermediate sanction programs by classifying inmates early in the process. It must be noted here that the intermediate sanction sentence is influenced by both the classification process and judicial discretion.

As you may have guessed, correctional administrators are not the only group that classifies inmates. Those who make policy also frequently need to select "target" populations as they "test" new programs. This is especially true of new programs in the area of community corrections. Recently, many policymakers have begun to use solid data on jail populations as they consider implementing new, innovative programs in the area of community corrections. These data often include admission date, pre/post-sentence, primary offense severity, classification level and date classified, and release reason and release date. Breaking down these data can often lead policymakers to not only target a particular group, but also to gain insight into the two main factors driving jail populations: admissions and length of stay.[28]

A data-driven policy approach to selecting target populations for intermediate sanctions and community corrections must begin with an understanding of the individual passing through the jail facility. Two of the most frequently selected inmate populations targeted for diversion from jail are those placed on pre-trial status as well as minimum security inmates.[29] Inmates who have not yet faced trial (especially if they are nonviolent and have no prior assault record, no escape history, no warrants, and no institutional problems) are prime candidates to be placed on some type of intermediate sanction. Consequently, low-risk offenders who have similar characteristics may also be subject to participation in these programs. If available, these data could also be beneficial to judges and prosecutors in their decision-making process. As Americans become more conscious of the prejudices that exist in the criminal justice system, it can only be speculated that more and more classification procedures will be adopted by jail and prison administrators in their attempt to make the process as "objective" as possible. This, of course, will always be the subject of criticism as it is often argued that the basis used to send an individual to either prison or some form of intermediate sanction is biased and unfair to the "disadvantaged."

Effectiveness?

Now that we understand the history of CCAs as well as the classification methods used when considering who will be sent to an intermediate sanction, it is important to examine the effectiveness of these programs. Do they reach the goals set out by legislators, correctional administrators, and citizens at large? To answer this question, we will review the findings of several studies, starting with a survey that was conducted on convicted adult felons placed on state probation in 1986.[30] The survey tracked 12,370 probationers for a period of three years, from 1986 to 1989, for the purpose of finding out the "effectiveness" and compliance of some forms of intermediate sanctions. Statistically weighted, the sample of 12,370 represented 79,000 probationers. Some of the sanctions that were considered included the following:

- Alcohol treatment
- Counseling
- Drug treatment
- Residential placement
- Drug testing
- House arrest
- Day reporting
- Intensive supervision
- Split sentence
- Community service
- Supervision fees
- Victim restitution[31]

The preliminary results indicated that sizable numbers were discharged from probation before having fully complied with their specific condition. These included 24 percent of those ordered to participate in alcohol treatment, 20 percent ordered for mental health counseling, 32 percent ordered for drug treatment, 25 percent ordered to be placed in residential facilities, 33 percent ordered for drug testing, 31 percent ordered for house arrest, 35 percent ordered for day reporting, 21 percent ordered to perform community service, 69 percent ordered to pay supervision fees, and 40 percent ordered to make restitution. When considered together, 49 percent of those sanctioned were found to have

Effectiveness
and Enforcement
of Intermediate
Sanctions

Spotlight 12.2

Characteristics of Successful Intermediate Sanction Programs

1. Services are intensive and last three to nine months. These services are based on cognitive and social learning behavioral/psychological theories and are used for higher risk offenders.

2. Services target criminological needs. These include antisocial attitudes and values.

3. The style and mode of treatment is matched to the learning style and personality of the offender.

4. The behavior exhibited directly influences the reinforcement of the program. Contingencies are enforced in a firm, but fair, manner. Positive reinforcement (e.g., tangible rewards, activities, social reinforcers) is used much more frequently than punishment (e.g., fines and restitution). The reported ratio is four to one.

5. Most therapists relate to offenders in sensitive and constructive ways and are trained and supervised appropriately.

6. The structure of programs and their activities disrupt the criminal network by placing offenders in situations in which pro-social activities predominate.

Source: Paul Gendreau (February, 1995), "Examining What Works in Community Corrections." *Corrections Today,* vol. 57, no. 1. p. 28(3). Reprinted with permission of the American Correctional Association, Lanham, MD.

been in noncompliance by the time of their probation discharge. Further analysis indicated that of those who did not comply, only 21 percent had been punished with jail confinement for their noncompliance.[32]

The author of this study argued that there may be several reasons why intermediate sanctions are not working or are not being enforced. He suggested that it could be due to lack of adequate resources for enforcing and monitoring drug tests, house arrests, community service, payment of fines, and treatment participation. Although budgetary restrictions are not the sole reason for the high incidence of noncompliance of intermediate sanctions, they can take some of the blame. In fact, the budgetary situation is so bad that, according to the author of this study, prison, jail, parole, and probation populations all nearly tripled in size from 1977 to 1990. Yet, only spending for prisons and jails had increased. Specifically, "In 1990, prison and jail spending accounted for two cents of every state and local dollar spent, twice the amount spent in 1977. Spending for probation and parole accounted for two-tenths of one cent of every dollar spent in 1990, unchanged from what it was in 1977."[33]

Despite the criticisms mentioned previously, there are those who argue that some forms of intermediate sanctions are effective in reducing recidivism rates while alleviating the prison population. Approximately two dozen major reviews of the existing literature that explored "what works" have been conducted in the last fifteen years.[34] Although the items mentioned in each study vary from program to program, there are some common characteristics shared by most of the intermediate sanction programs that have been regarded as successful (usually determined by low recidivism rates). These characteristics are listed in Spotlight 12.2.

In contrast to successful programs, services offered in programs that have been regarded as unsuccessful usually target low-risk offenders, and non-criminological needs such as anxiety, depression, and self-esteem. Some of these unsuccessful programs have also relied on Freudian psychodynamic and Rogerian nondirective therapies. In fact, they have frequently used medical model approaches such as drug treatments and "punishing smarter" approaches such as Intensive Supervision Probation (ISP) and boot camps.[35]

The success rate of modern intermediate sanction, boot camps, is also being questioned. The main goal of boot camps is to develop discipline and respect for authority through a military-like regimen. Consequently, they have been the subject of criticism due to increasing incidents involving the abuse of power. In fact, a clear example of this can be found in the boot camps in the states of Wisconsin and Oklahoma, which recently have come under investigation by their respective state legislatures for allegations of abuse.[36] To add insult to injury, some of these boot camps are reportedly not doing what they are supposed to do. The most cited criticism comes from criminologist Doris MacKenzie of the University of Maryland, who recently completed a study of boot camps. She found that boot camp graduates had the same rate of recidivism as did felons released from traditional prisons (approximately 30 to 40 percent).[37] Her conclusion was that boot camps just do not work. In part, this is because the offender, upon successful completion of the boot camp program, is released to the same crime-ridden neighborhood that he or she came from. These criticisms, although growing, are still meeting resistance by those who are true believers in the "effectiveness" of boot camps. Supporters of these camps argue that MacKenzie's figures are not accurate because she ignores the fact that every boot camp is run differently. Some operate strictly on a military format, while others offer more integrated programs. Furthermore, supporters add that most recidivists who had successfully graduated from boot camps are being sent back to prison for technical parole violations. Regardless of which position is accurate, the effectiveness of this form of intermediate sanctions will continue to be questioned as plans to establish more of these programs are carried forward.

Enforcement

What are the negative ramifications for the system as a result of the large number of individuals who do not comply with the conditions set forth by intermediate sanctions? It is estimated that each of the offenders who does not comply with these conditions will require at least one court hearing. At the national level, this means that up to 1.5 million offenders require at least one more additional court hearing and modification of their sentence.[38] Needless to say, this noncompliance adds significantly to the current budgetary and personnel burden experienced by the criminal justice system. As a way to address this, in the last several years, some parole and probation agencies have begun to examine the processes with the goal of increasing compliance and reducing the amount of violations. Most of these agencies have started to focus on policies and practices within probation and parole services to improve offender accountability and agency response. A researcher of criminal justice policies, Peggy Burke, pointed out:

> We realized that it was not simply a revocation decision that was the issue—but rather how the system responded to violations. We began seeing revocation as only one piece of a process that began with release and the setting of conditions, involved the supervision process in its entirety, and focused particularly on how the system responded to violation behavior, even short of the issuance of a formal violation report or a revocation. . . . There is something that lies between benign neglect, or "letting it slide" on the one hand, and revocation and reincarceration on the other for parole violators. Their behavior presents a range of severity or danger to the

community. Surely probation and parole agencies' responses to these behaviors might well be structured along some continuum of intermediate sanctions, in much the same way that an initial sentencing decision might be made. And this might well yield supervision of offenders, more responsible use of resources, and perhaps even better outcomes with offenders.[39]

Many agencies are realizing that not all noncompliant behavior deserves the same attention. Thus, the type of noncompliant behavior is assessed and then ranked according to its level of seriousness. This ranking usually determines how the probation agency will respond. In most cases, the more serious behavior is forwarded to the court, while the less serious is handled by the probation agency. The state of South Carolina is one of the jurisdictions that has developed guidelines for the purpose of ranking violators. Its program is nothing less than a very aggressive attempt to formalize responses to noncompliant behavior. In South Carolina, violation behavior is categorized on the basis of the offense and risk imposed. The following categories are included:

- **Category A**   This category usually involves the most serious violations, with the agent issuing a warrant or citation. These violations include convictions for a new offense, a second violation of home detention, the failure to report within thirty days, the possession of a weapon, the failure to pay financial penalties within six months, or termination from community service due to unsatisfactory performance.

- **Category B**   The violations that occur in this category indicate the offender is unwilling to cooperate or is demonstrating signs of community instability, such as unacceptable employment and residence patterns. The agent has the choice to place the offender in an intermediate sanction program or to simply refer the entire case to a hearing officer.

- **Category C**   The types of violations that take place within this category include minor violations that the agent can usually resolve at the supervisory level.[40]

In South Carolina, the violation process begins once an offender violates any of the conditions of release prescribed by the courts. At that time, the agent has a series of options, including reprimands, counseling, treatment referrals, day care placement, restructured supervision plans, increased drug testing, and increased supervision contacts. If the agent is not fully satisfied with the response, he or she still has other options. These include placing the offender in a halfway house for up to seventy-five days, increasing the number of public service hours, and imposing other unlimited conditions.[41] If the offender continues to violate his or her conditions of release, a warrant is usually issued. Once this takes place, the offender is mandated to appear before an administrative hearing officer who usually determines if incarceration is necessary given the severity of the offense and the potential risk the offender poses to the community. The role of the hearing officer is important in that he or she can determine whether a partial or full revocation from probation is appropriate. In some cities, such as Seattle, an individual who does not appear before a hearing officer is considered to be a fugitive. In that regard, the individual is apprehended immediately, thus limiting the individual's freedom for the sake of protecting the community. In Seattle, a Fugitive Apprehension Team has recently been created for the purpose of tracking down fugitives[42] (including those who have violated some term of their intermediate sanction). It is important to note that we have described the enforcement process in South Carolina as an illustration of the many systems that are currently in place throughout the United States.

Although there is some research available on intermediate sanctions, there is still a need for further information regarding these alternative programs. The need for further research is enhanced by the present state of overcrowding facing most correctional institutions. Also, it is thought that more detailed research in the area could assist policymakers in determining appropriate sanctions for offenders. According to Lawrence Bennett, "Research has provided a good deal of information that can benefit administrators in planning intermediate sanction and community correction programs. However, it is obvious that more research needs to be done to help practitioners determine not only what programs work but also which aspects of each program play critical roles in observed outcomes."[43]

The Need for Further Research

Supporters of intermediate sanctions have become increasingly concerned over the perception of sanctions as a form of punishment. This is particularly relevant in our current society in which political figures are constantly basing their stance on a particular issue on public opinion polls. There are those who argue that intermediate sanctions have the same punitive effect as prison sentences. However, there is very little research in this area that would suggest a verdict one way or another. In Minnesota, a groundbreaking study was conducted to explore the perceptions of intermediate sanctions as a form of punishment.[44] Specifically, the study was designed to measure how offenders and staff in Minnesota rank the severity of several criminal sanctions and which specific sanctions they judge as being equivalent in punitiveness.

Perceptions of Intermediate Sanctions

The study offered various results. First, it was discovered that there are intermediate sanctions that equate, in terms of punitiveness, with prison. For instance, inmates viewed one year in prison as "equivalent" in severity to three years of intensive probation supervision or one year in jail, while at the same time, they viewed six months in jail as equivalent to one year of intensive supervision. Despite the fact that inmates and staff ranked most sanctions in the same way, the staff ratings were higher for three and six months in jail and lower for one and five years of probation. These two groups differed on the difficulty of complying with individual probation conditions. For instance, the staff judged most probation conditions as being harder for offenders to comply with than did inmates. The findings of this study also suggested that it is no longer necessary to equate criminal punishment with prison alone.[45] The findings determined conclusively that at some level of intensity and length, intensive probation and prison are equally severe, and that probation may actually be the least desirable form of punishment.[46] These findings are important, and should represent a warning sign to political figures who pride themselves in their belief that the longer they incarcerate offenders, the more effective they are in reducing the fear of crime among the citizenry.

During the 125th Congress of Corrections, which was held on August 9, 1995 in Cincinnati, the American Correctional Association's executive committee approved nine legislative position statements. Of these, one pertained to community corrections and intermediate sanctions.[47] During this meeting, it was asserted that support needed to be given to community corrections while increasing the use of intermediate sanctions. The American Correctional Association (ACA) made a statement supporting a balanced approach to crime reduction that

Recommendations

included a range of criminal justice services. These included confinement in prison or jail, community corrections, intermediate sanctions, and other nonincarcerative options for nonviolent offenders. One of the most important recognitions made by the ACA pertains to the combination of incarceration with other effective programs aimed at prevention, policing, punishment, treatment, restitution, reparation, and education. The ACA statement concluded by making a strong statement calling for adequate funding to federal, state, and local governments for construction and operation of correctional facilities and programs for a complete range of effective interventions.[48]

Others argue that correctional intervention at the community level needs to have a more restorative perspective. They feel that "restorative justice":

- Holds the offender directly accountable to the individual victim and the community affected by the criminal act.

- Requires the offender to take responsibility to "make things whole again," to the degree that it is possible.

- Provides victims purposeful access to the court and correctional processes, which allows them to shape offender obligations.

- Encourages the community to become involved in supporting victims, holding offenders accountable, and providing opportunities for offenders to reintegrate into the community.[49]

It is proposed that in order to bring about the restorative perspective, the Community Corrections Acts should be amended. Despite the fact that CCAs provide states with a subsidy and an authority to plan and implement correctional programs, they have not achieved a satisfactory level for victims. In fact, victims are often revictimized by the criminal justice system by being "forced" to reenact or relive the traumatic criminal episode that led them to their victimization. Thus, it is further recommended that in order for the system to be successful, it must include the protection of fundamental rights.[50] It is not clear if these recommendations will find an echo. However, what is clear is the fact that community corrections and intermediate sanctions will continue to change as they become one of the preferred methods of punishment at the dawn of the new era of corrections in the United States.

WiseGuide Wrap-Up In 1972, the National Advisory Commission Progress Report stated that "the thrust towards community-based corrections supports the most significant philosophical trend corrections has experienced in years."[51] In this chapter, we examined this trend, beginning with a brief discussion of the historic concept of community-based corrections. We noted that although the concept has been around for centuries, the organization and systematization of community-based corrections in this country is a relatively recent phenomenon, gaining its greatest impetus from the 1967 President's Crime Commission Report. The major emphasis then became *reintegration* of the offender, replacing the emphasis on rehabilitation, which in turn suspended the philosophies of revenge, restraint, and reformation. A growing awareness that traditional institutionalization of offenders was not achieving the goal of rehabilitation, and that such institutionalization was extremely costly, along with the increasing evidence of the harmful effects of imprisonment, fueled the movement.

After examining the meaning of community corrections, we discussed the major forms of intermediate sanctions being implemented today, including fines, community service, restitution, intensive supervision probation (ISP), home confinement, shock incarceration, and boot camps. In addition, we also examined the various community corrections systems that were implemented in four states—these were to serve as models for other states in their attempt to establish community correctional programs. Our discussion also focused on the legislative movement and its influence on the creation and implementation of community corrections acts (CCAs) throughout the country, as well as a brief explanation of the classification process in which offenders are determined to be "fit" to participate in intermediate sanction programs. Finally, we examined various issues pertaining to the effectiveness, enforcement, and perception of intermediate sanctions, while the case was made that further research in this area is greatly needed. The discussion ended with a series of recommendations to improve the quality of intermediate sanctions in the near future.

The movement toward community-based treatment may represent a desperate attempt to do something without knowledge of its impact. Disillusionment over attempts at rehabilitation through institutionalized treatment has led to the current trend toward harsher sentencing for serious offenders, decriminalization of juvenile status offenders, and the increased use of community-based treatment. The major problem, however, is that when we adopt a new approach, we burden that approach with the responsibility of reducing the crime rate. Consequently, we rush to evaluate the approach in terms of recidivism, and if those rates are not reduced, we conclude that the program has failed. It may be that the burden of reducing recidivism is too great for any treatment method or approach to handle and that we should look to other measures of success or failure.

Notes

1. Klapmuts, Nora. "Community Alternatives to Prison," Chapter 15 in *Community Health and the Criminal Justice System,* John Monahan, ed., (New York: Penguin Press, Inc., 1976), p. 206.

2. National Advisory Commission on Criminal Justice Standards and Goals. *A National Strategy To Reduce Crime.* (Washington, DC: U.S. Government Printing Office, 1973), p. 121.

3. *A National Strategy To Reduce Crime.* p. 121.

4. Durkheim, Emile. *Suicide.* (New York: Free Press, 1951).

5. Friday, Paul C., and Hage, Jerald. "Youth Crime in Postindustrial Societies: An Integrated Perspective," *Criminology* 14 (November, 1976), 347–367; quotations are on pp. 348–349, 365, 366.

6. Ohlin, Lloyd E., Miller, Alden D., and Coates, Robert B. *Juvenile Correctional Reform in Massachusetts. A Preliminary Report of the Center for Criminal Justice of the Harvard Law School.* National Institute for Justice and Delinquency Prevention, LEAA (Washington, DC, 1997).

7. Ohlin, Miller, and Coates, *Juvenile Correction Reform,* p. 23.

8. Rutherford, Andrew, and Bengur, Osman. *Community Based Alternatives to Juvenile Incarceration.* National Evaluation Program; Phase I, Summary Report. National Institute of Law Enforcement and Criminal Justice, LEAA. (Washington, DC: U.S. Government Printing Office, 1976), p. 11.

9. Vinter, Robert D., Downs, George, and Halls, John. "Juvenile Corrections in the States: Residential Programs and Deinstitutionalization: A Preliminary Report" (Ann Arbor: University of Michigan Press, 1975).

10. Evans, Donald G. "Defining Community Corrections," *Corrections Today,* October, 1996) vol. 58, no. 6, 124 (2).

11. Duffee, David and McGarrell, Edmund F. *Community Corrections: A Community Field Approach.* (Cincinnati: Anderson Publishing Co., 1990).

12. Evans, "Defining Community Corrections," 124 (2).

13 Evans, "Defining Community Corrections," 124 (2).

14. McMurry, Kelley. "Fewer Sex Offenders on Community Release Programs than Other Criminals," *Trial* 33, (April, 1997), no. 4, 88–89.

15. McMurray, "Fewer Sex Offenders," 88–89.

16. Harris, Kay. "Key Differences Among Community Corrections Acts in the United States: An Overview," *The Prison Journal* 76:2 (1996), 192–238.

17. Harris, M. Kay. "Key Differences Among Community Corrections Acts in the U.S.: An Overview," *Prison Journal* (June, 1996), vol. 76, no. 2, 192(47).

18. Harris, "Key Differences," 192(47).

19. Harris, "Key Differences," 192(47).

20. Harris, "Key Differences," 192(47).

21. Schoen, Kenneth F. "The Community Corrections Act," *Crime and Delinquency* 24 (October, 1978), 464.

22. Minn. Stat. Ann. & 401.01 et seq. (West).

23. Quoted in "Minnesota's Community Corrections Act Takes Hold," *Corrections Magazine* 4 (March, 1978), 54.

24. Clark, Patrick M. "The Evolution of Michigan's Community Corrections Act" (Michigan Community Corrections Act), *Corrections Today* (February, 1995), vol. 57, no. 1, 38(3).

25. Clark, "Evolution," 38(3).

26. Clark, "Evolution," 38(3).

27. Clark, "Evolution," 38(3).

28. Wells, David, and Brennan, Tim. "Jail Classification: Improving Link to Intermediate Sanctions," *Corrections Today* (February, 1995), vol. 57, no. 1, 58(4).

29. Wells and Brennan, "Jail Classification," 58(4).

30. Langan, Patrick A. "Between Prison and Probation: Intermediate Sanctions," *Science* (May 6, 1994), vol. 264, no. 5160, 791(3).

31. Langan, "Between Prison and Probation," 791(3).

32. Langan, "Between Prison and Probation," 791(3).

33. Langan, "Between Prison and Probation," 791(3).

34. Gendreau, Paul, and Paparozzi, Mario A. "Examining What Works in Community Corrections," *Corrections Today* (February, 1995), vol. 57, no. 1, 28(3).

35. Gendreau and Paparozzi, "Examining What Works," 28(3).

36. Sileo, Chi Chi. "Abuse, Absolution Found at Boot Camp" (Failure of Alternative Prisons that Provide Discipline and Training in Behavior Modification), *Insight on the News* (June 27, 1994), vol. 10, no. 26, 6(5).

37. Sileo, "Abuse, Absolution," 6(5).

38. Taxman, Faye S. "Intermediate Sanctions: Dealing with Technical Violators," *Corrections Today* (February, 1995), vol. 57, no. 1, 46(7).

39. Taxman, "Intermediate Sanctions," 46(7).

40. Taxman, "Intermediate Sanctions," 46(7).

41. Taxman, "Intermediate Sanctions," 46(7).

42. Olsson, Kurt S. "CCO Leaves No Stone Unturned in Tracking Down Fugitives" (Seattle Fugitive Apprehension Team Corrections Officer Sean Zelka), *Corrections Today* (June, 1996), vol. 58, no. 3, 88(1).

43. Bennett, Lawrence A. "Current Findings on Intermediate Sanctions and Community Corrections," *Corrections Today* (February, 1995), vol. 57, no. 1, p. 86(4).

44. Petersilia, Joan, and Piper Deschenes, Elizabeth. "Perceptions of Punishment: Inmates and Staff Work the Severity of Prison versus Intermediate Sanctions," *Prison Journal* (September, 1994), vol. 74, no. 3, 306(23).

45. Petersilia and Piper Deschenes, "Perceptions of Punishment," 306(23).

46. Petersilia and Piper Deschenes, "Perceptions of Punishment," 306(23).

47. Smith Ingley, Gwyn. "Position Statements Released" (Legislative Priorities on Corrections) (Legislative Issues), *Corrections Today* (April, 1996), vol. 58, no. 2, 206(3).

48. Smith Ingley, "Position Statements," 206(3).

49. Carey, Mark. "Restorative Justice in Community Corrections," *Corrections Today* (August, 1996), vol. 58, no. 5, 152(4).

50. Carey, "Restorative Justice," 152(4).

51. U.S. Department of Justice. *Progress Report of the National Advisory Commission on Criminal Justice Standards and Goals.* (Washington, DC: U.S. Government Printing Office, 1972), p. 32.

Inmates' Legal Rights

Most of us feel comfortable discussing the various aspects of corrections until we consider the topic of "inmate rights." In fact, many would regard the notion that correctional inmates have rights as "offensive." Despite this, as a college student who is becoming acquainted with the correctional system, you must consider the notion that inmates deserve the protection of the U.S. Constitution although they have committed a criminal act. In this chapter, we review the history of inmate rights, and provide an overview of the First, Fourth, Eighth, and Fourteenth Amendments of the U.S. Constitution. We examine prison programs and legal rights and, finally, prison overcrowding.

Recognition of inmates' legal rights has a short history. The earlier position of courts on inmates' rights was expressed in an 1871 case in which a federal court declared bluntly that the convicted felon:

> Has as a consequence of his crime, not only forfeited his liberty, but all his personal rights except those which the law in its humanity accords to him. He is for the time being the slave of the state.[1]

More recently, the U.S. Supreme Court has taken another view on inmates' rights, as expressed by this 1974 statement:

> But though his rights may be diminished by the needs and exigencies of the institutional environment, a prisoner is not wholly stripped of constitutional protections when he is imprisoned for crime. There is no iron curtain drawn between the Constitution and the prisons of this country.[2]

Before 1974, lower federal courts began looking into prisoners' claims that they were being denied basic constitutional rights during confinement. By the 1980s, numerous lawsuits had been filed by inmates, and federal courts scrutinized prison conditions, particularly regarding overcrowding. Entire prison systems were placed under federal court orders to reduce populations and make other changes in prison conditions. By the 1990s,

Key Terms

conditions of confinement
cruel and unusual punishment
deliberate indifference
double celling
habeas corpus
hands-off doctrine
inquisitory system

extensive jail and prison overcrowding resulted in an explosion of federal lawsuits concerning conditions of incarceration.

No attempt can be made in an introductory book to cover the vast body of law on inmates' legal rights. It is possible, however, to get a very good overview of the ways that courts have responded to the issues raised by inmates. A few words of warning are in order.

It is important to understand that the decisions of courts in one jurisdiction do not apply to courts in other jurisdictions. Courts faced with similar facts may, and often do, decide issues differently. Only when the U.S. Supreme Court decides the issue is the case binding on all courts, and the Supreme Court has not decided many inmates' rights cases.

Another important point is that the law of inmates' rights is changing rapidly. In all probability, some of the cases discussed in this chapter will be altered or over-ruled while the book is in production. Because the law changes so rapidly, many of the cited cases are recent decisions. Exceptions are Supreme Court cases that are important regardless of their date of decision (if they have not been changed by later Supreme Court cases), and lower federal court cases that are important for historical reasons or because they are critical cases in a particular area and are still good law. All cases are checked up to press time to ascertain whether changes have occurred, such as a higher appellate court's decision to alter or overrule a cited case.[3]

Historical Overview

In the United States, administration of state prisons has historically been considered off limits to federal courts. Federal courts would not hear cases from state courts because no federal rights were considered to be involved. In addition, federal courts observed a hands-off doctrine toward federal prisons, reasoning that prison administration is a part of the executive, not the judicial, branch of government.

Likewise, state courts traditionally have not heard complaints from inmates concerning conditions within state prisons. State courts have heard cases involving mainly post-conviction remedies that attacked the confinement itself, as opposed to the **conditions of confinement.** Conditions were considered to be within the realm of prison administration and thus were not a proper sphere for judicial interference.

This unwillingness of federal courts to interfere with the daily administration of prisons is called the **hands-off doctrine.** The general reluctance of courts to interfere in the daily administration of prisons is seen in federal court decisions. In 1950, the Seventh Circuit stated that, "The Government of the United States is not concerned with, nor has it the power to control or regulate the internal discipline of the penal institutions of its constituent states. All such powers are reserved to the individual states."[4]

In 1979, in *Bell v. Wolfish,* the Supreme Court emphasized that prison administrators should be accorded wide-ranging deference in the adoption and execution of policies and practices that in their judgement are needed to preserve internal order and discipline and to maintain institutional security.[5]

If federal courts defer to prison officials for the daily administration of prisons, on what basis are those courts involved today? What brought inmates to their attention? Among other issues, the civil rights activism of the 1960s included the treatment of inmates, and during that period, federal courts began to look at what was happening inside prisons. Many of the earlier cases involved allegations of physical brutality as well as questionable living conditions.

One of the most publicized of the earlier accounts of corporal punishment within a modern prison came from two Arkansas prisons. Among other punishments was the inflicting of electric shock through a device wired to the genitals and to one of the big toes of the inmates. Arkansas inmates alleged that inmates had been murdered at the prison and buried in the prison yard. In 1967, the Arkansas governor released a prison report that had been ordered and then suppressed by the former governor. That report:

> Painted a picture of hell in Arkansas. To maintain discipline, prisoners were beaten with leather straps, blackjacks, hoses. Needles were shoved under their fingernails, and cigarettes were applied to their bodies."[6]

In January 1968, Thomas O. Murton, Arkansas prison system superintendent appointed by the governor of Arkansas, exhumed the bodies of three inmates who allegedly had been murdered by inmates or prison officials. National attention to this process was too much for the governor, and Murton was fired. A movie, *Brubaker,* portrayed the attempts of Murton to reform the Arkansas prison system. His own accounts are found in his book, *The Dilemma of Prison Reform.*[7]

The federal district court heard evidence on the prison conditions in Arkansas and concluded that inmates were living under degrading and disgusting conditions. The court found the prison system unconstitutional. The need for judicial intervention into the administration of prisons was stated emphatically by the federal court. "If Arkansas is going to operate a Penitentiary System, it is going to have to be a system that is countenanced by the Constitution of the United States."[8]

Modern Litigation

An Introduction

Since the 1970s, federal courts have heard many cases on prison conditions. Federal intervention has been extended to jails as well. Some prison officials have been ordered to close facilities until conditions are corrected; others have been ordered to change specific conditions. Officials who have defied these orders have been held in contempt of court. Judges continue to defer to prison authorities concerning day-to-day prison operations, but they intervene when federal constitutional rights are violated. It is important to look at those rights more closely.

In analyzing inmates' rights historically, prison officials spoke of the difference between *rights* and *privileges.* Rights require constitutional protection; privileges are there by the grace of prison officials and may be withdrawn at the discretion of officials. In 1971, the Supreme Court rejected the position that "constitutional rights turn upon whether a governmental benefit is characterized as a 'right' or a 'privilege.'"[9]

It is clear, however, that a hierarchy of rights is recognized. Some rights are considered to be more important than others and therefore require more extensive due process before they may be infringed upon. An inmate's right to be released from illegal confinement is more important than the right to canteen privileges. Some of the other rights that are ranked high in the hierarchy are the right to protection against willful injury, access to courts, freedom of religious belief, freedom of communication, and the right to be free of cruel and unusual punishment.

The recognition of inmates' rights and of the hierarchy of rights does not mean that the government (or prison officials acting as government agents) may not restrict those rights. Rights may be restricted if prison officials can show that the restriction is necessary for security or for other recognized penological purposes such as discipline and order.[10]

In analyzing whether prison officials have shown one or more of these purposes, the Court uses a reasonableness test. "When a prison regulation impinges on inmates' constitutional rights, the regulation is valid if it is reasonably related to legitimate penological interests."[11] The reasonableness test is not as strict as the closer analysis that the Court applies to basic constitutional rights. A less stringent test is used in prison because the Court recognizes that "limitations on the exercise of constitutional rights arise both from the fact of incarceration and from valid penological objectives—including deterrence of crime, rehabilitation of offenders, and institutional security."[12]

How do we know what is reasonable? In *Turner v. Safley*, the Supreme Court suggested several factors that should be considered when analyzing whether infringements on individual rights are appropriate within a prison:

1. Whether there is a logical connection between the regulation and the legitimate interest it is designed to protect;
2. Whether inmates have other means of exercising that right;
3. The impact that accommodating the right in question would have on other inmates, correctional officers, and prison administration and staff;
4. The absence of readily available alternatives that fully accommodate the prisoner's rights at little or no cost to valid penological interests.[13]

Substantive Legal Rights

Our individual constitutional rights come from the Bill of Rights to the federal Constitution, as applied to the states through the Fourteenth Amendment. Those rights, known as substantive legal rights, include the right to counsel, the right to be free of unreasonable searches and seizures, the right to a public trial by a jury of one's peers, and the right to be confronted by witnesses. Courts have held that some, but not all, of these rights apply to inmates. One very important area of rights is the basis for considerable litigation on prison issues—First Amendment rights, including freedom of speech, assembly, the press, and religion and the right to address the government when rights are violated. Another important source of rights is the Eighth Amendment, the right to be free of unreasonable searches and seizures.

The Fourteenth Amendment right to due process and equal protection is crucial to an understanding of inmates' rights. Certain elements of due process must accompany disciplinary decisions, such as rescinding an inmate's acquired good time or placing inmates in solitary confinement. Equal protection becomes an issue in our discussion of the differences in treatment, work opportunities, and medical care provided for male, as compared to female, inmates. Due process and equal protection are the foundations for enforcing all rights, and thus need further explanation.

Due Process and Equal Protection

The criminal justice systems in the United States are adversary, in contrast to the **inquisitory system** characteristic of some other countries. The two approaches may be distinguished in several ways. The adversary approach assumes that the accused is innocent until proven guilty. The accused does not have to prove his or her innocence; that burden lies with the state (or the federal government in a federal trial). In contrast, the inquisitory system assumes guilt, and the accused must prove that he or she is innocent. This difference between the two approaches is related to another basic contrast: The inquisitory approach places a greater emphasis on conviction than on the *process* by which that conviction is secured. The adversary approach, however, requires that proper procedures be followed, procedures designed to protect the rights of the accused.

In the United States, the adversary system embodies the basic concepts of *equal protection* and *due process*. These concepts are considered necessary to create a system in which the accused has a fair chance against the tremendous powers of the prosecutor and the resources of the state. Theoretically, the protections prevent the prosecutor from obtaining a guilty verdict of an innocent defendant. In reality, justice does not always prevail.

The impossibility of explaining exactly what is meant by due process is illustrated by this comment of a former U.S. Supreme Court justice:

> "Due Process" . . . cannot be imprisoned within the treacherous limits of any formula. Representing a profound attitude of fairness between man and man, and more particularly between the individual and government, "due process" is compounded of history, reason, the past course of decisions, and stout confidence in the strength of the democratic faith we possess. "Due process" is not a mechanical instrument. It is not a yardstick. It is a process.[14]

In a 1994 case, the Second Circuit defined substantive due process as a process that "protects individuals against government action that is arbitrary, conscience-shocking, or oppressive in a constitutional sense, but not against government action that is 'incorrect or ill-advised.'"[15]

The basis for the right to due process and equal protection comes from the Fourteenth Amendment to the Constitution, which guarantees that we shall not be deprived "of life, liberty, or property, without due process of law." Also, we may not be denied "the equal protection of the laws."

The concept of due process means that those who are accused of crimes and are processed through a criminal justice system must be given the basic rights guaranteed by the Constitution. For example, defendants may not be subjected to unreasonable searches and seizures by the police. When questioned about acts that, upon conviction, may involve a jail or prison term, defendants do not have to answer questions by the police until they have an attorney present. If they do not wish to talk even with an attorney present, they may remain silent. If defendants cannot afford an attorney, the state must provide one for them. They do not have to testify against themselves at trial. Certain rules of evidence must be observed during the trial.

Defendants may not be tried twice for the same offense; once a judge or jury has decided that the defendant is innocent, the state may not bring those same charges again in an effort to wear down the defendant. In short, the state must conduct the criminal trial and the processes preceding and following that trial by the rules embodied in the Constitution, as interpreted by the Supreme Court of the United States, and according to the established procedural statutes.

The equal protection clause of the Fourteenth Amendment is the focus of frequent lawsuits. That clause declares that the state may not attempt to enforce statutes against persons solely because of specific characteristics such as race, age, or gender. The state or federal government, however, may enact statutes that distinguish between men and women if there are legitimate reasons for doing so, and this may become a key matter in prison issues.

The brief excerpt in Case Study 13.1 from *Liberta v. Kelly*, a case arising under New York statutes and decided by a federal court, indicates the reasons why the federal court upheld the state's exclusion of women as defendants from its rape and sodomy statutes. According to the federal court, the New York statute did not violate the equal protection clause of the federal Constitution.[16]

Case Study 13.1

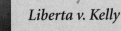

Liberta v. Kelly

[Briefly, the facts are as follows: Mario Liberta and Denise Liberta were separated, and Denise had obtained two protective orders that required Mario to live apart from Denise and their young son but that granted him visiting privileges with the child. Mario had a history of abusing his wife physically. On the occasion in question, he persuaded her to let him see the child in her presence, indicating that he would bring a friend with him. The friend left quickly, however, and Mario forced Denise to perform oral sex on him while the child watched, after which he raped Denise. After a long discussion of other issues in this case, the court focused on the defendant's argument that he had been denied equal protection of the law because the New York sodomy and rape statutes included only men as defendants.]

Women and men thus are not similarly situated with regard to rape. Rape is unquestionably a crime that requires male participation as a practical matter, and only male rape of a female can impose on the victim an unwanted pregnancy. These facts provide an "exceedingly persuasive justification" for a statute that provides heightened sanctions for rapes committed by men. Moreover, it cannot be contended that a rape statute punishing only men "demean[s] the ability or social status" of either men or women, particularly in the context of a penal code that prohibits coercive sexual conduct by women. The exclusion of women from [the New York statute] therefore, does not deny men equal protection of the laws.

In recent years, several states have changed their rape and sodomy statutes to include women as perpetrators, but the point of this case is that it is not necessarily a violation of equal protection to define these crimes as crimes that may be committed only by men.

The equal protection clause, like the due process clause, must be examined in the context of the facts of a given case. This is why it is impossible to state "the law" on most issues. Such elasticity of American constitutional provisions is important, but at times frustrating, to one who wants an immediate, definitive answer. The issues in this text must be understood in the context of this flexibility.

Procedural Issues

The enforcement of inmates' legal rights requires an understanding of the difference between criminal and civil cases. Not all constitutional rights that exist at the pretrial, trial, and appellate stages of criminal cases apply to civil cases, and some of the rules of evidence differ. This is mostly due to the fact that criminal cases are considered to carry a heavier burden of responsibility than civil cases since the accused of a criminal charge may even face death as a probable punishment. The distinction between criminal and civil cases is important for another reason. The number of civil cases filed in the past two decades has increased even more dramatically than the number of criminal cases. Inmates have accounted for many of these filings. The resulting backlog in civil courts means that inmates (and others) may face a long wait before a case is decided. Furthermore, it is argued that many of the cases that inmates file are frivolous and should not be consuming the time of already overcrowded courts.

Most civil actions brought by inmates are over confinement conditions or prison officials' actions. They involve one of two types of legal actions: *habeas corpus* or a Section 1983 action.

Habeas Corpus

Habeas corpus means "you have the body." There are numerous types of *habeas corpus* actions, but the most relevant to this chapter is the action brought by the correctional client who is requesting that the court grant a *writ* of *habeas corpus,* directing prison officials to release a particular individual.

When inmates request a writ of *habeas corpus,* they argue that they are illegally confined. Inmates may make this argument because prison conditions are alleged to be unconstitutional, or they may have been disciplined without observance of proper procedures. The *habeas corpus* action holds that, "I am being held illegally in this prison because my rights have been violated. Therefore, I should be released." Historically, only a few inmates have been successful in their *habeas corpus* petitions, but multiple petitions are filed by numerous inmates.

Supreme Court Chief Justice William Rehnquist, a committee he appointed to study the issue of *habeas corpus,* and the Bush administration sought measures to curb abuse of this process of challenging prison conditions. More recently, Congress has considered legislation to limit *habeas corpus* petitions, but at the time of this writing, the legislation has not passed. Proponents of these efforts argue that finality in the law is important and that in capital cases in particular, the delays created by subsequent *habeas corpus* petitions are too long. Continuous appeals cost the government money and question the legitimacy of the justice procedure. Opponents argue that as long as inmates have a legal issue, especially if they are under death sentences, a court should hear their arguments.

The April 1991 Supreme Court decision in *McCleskey v. Zant* imposed new limits on death-row inmates' filings of *habeas corpus* petitions. The Court had recognized previously that *habeas corpus* petitions may be denied for inmates who have abused the process. For example, an inmate might have several issues to appeal, but may bring only one; if that one is denied, the inmate might try to file another petition for a writ of *habeas corpus,* and that subsequent petition may be denied if it could have been filed with the earlier writ. In *McCleskey,* the Court admitted, however, that it had not defined clearly the criteria to be used for holding that an inmate has abused this appeals process. In this case, the Court said that "a petitioner may abuse the writ by failing to raise a claim through inexcusable neglect."[17]

In his second *habeas corpus* petition, McCleskey claimed that he was convicted of murder as a result of evidence obtained in violation of his constitutional rights when the government planted an informant in the jail to get information from him. McCleskey showed that for almost a decade, the government had concealed the evidence that the "inmate" was an informant. McCleskey argued that he could not have brought up this information in his first petition for *habeas corpus* because the information was not available to him at that time. The Court disagreed and held that he should have brought up this ground for appeal in his first petition. Since he did not do so, he was not entitled to a second chance.

As a note of interest, McCleskey's first petition concerned the argument that he was convicted unfairly because of racial discrimination. He cited evidence that he and other African American men whose alleged victims were white were four times more likely to be convicted of murder than African American men convicted of murdering nonwhite victims. The Court questioned the evidence and upheld the conviction. McCleskey was executed in the fall of 1991. In May 1992, the Court limited *habeas corpus* proceedings further by holding that no longer are federal courts required to conduct hearings on the petitions of state inmates challenging their convictions. This is true even if those inmates can show that their attorneys had not presented facts crucial to their cases or had not presented the facts properly at their trials.[18]

Despite this, in 1995, the U.S. Supreme Court facilitated the possibility that inmates may win new trials on some *habeas corpus* writs. In *O'Neal v. McAninch,* the Court concluded that offenders deserve the benefit of the doubt if the federal courts are not certain if mistakes committed by the trial court were harmless. By

Spotlight 13.1

Enforcing Inmate Rights through Civil Cases

In 1989, a New York court awarded a total of $1.3 million in seven lawsuits brought by inmates on their estates for damages caused by the actions of police in the 1971 Attica prison riots. These awards were granted to inmates who did not participate in the riots but who were victimized by excessive force by authorities attempting to regain control of the prison. Police efforts during that uprising were described by a state investigating committee as constituting the "bloodiest encounter between Americans since the Civil War." Individual damage awards ranged from $35,000 to $473,000.[1]

Larger damage awards have been made in more recent cases in which individuals have sued police for violating their civil rights. Rodney King, who suffered permanent injuries as a result of force used on him by Los Angeles police officers, was awarded $3.8 million in damages by a jury that heard his case against the Los Angeles Police Department, but a jury refused to award King punitive damages from the individual officers. Two of the officers were convicted of violating King's civil rights and were sentenced to serve time in prison.[2]

[1] "Court Awards $1.3 Million to Inmates Injured at Attica," *New York Times* (October 26, 1989), p. 14.

[2] "Rodney King Gets $4 Million in Compensation for Beating," *New York Times* (April 20, 1994), p. 1; "Rodney King Jury Refuses to Award Punitive Damages," *New York Times* (June 29, 1994), p. 1.

concluding this, the Court made it harder for judges to dismiss the mistakes made by the trial courts.[19]

Section 1983 Actions

A second and more frequently used method by inmates in their petition to federal courts is a Section 1983 action. This is usually filed for monetary damages to compensate for illegal actions taken by prison (or police) officials against inmates. The name is derived from the section number of the federal statute under which the action may be brought. As a section of the Civil Rights Act, it is provided that:

> Every person who, under color of any statute, ordinance, regulation, custom, or usage, of any State or Territory, subjects or causes to be subjected, any citizen of the United States or the person within the jurisdiction thereof to the deprivation of any rights, privileges, or immunities secured by the Constitution and laws, shall be liable to the party injured in an action at law, suit in equity, or other proper proceeding for redress.[20]

In order to come under the jurisdiction of this statute, inmates must show that prison officials deprived them of their rights as protected by the U.S. Constitution or by a federal statute. Moreover, Section 1983 claims may encompass almost any aspect of an inmate's life.

If an inmate succeeds in a Section 1983 action, he or she may be awarded damages for the deprivations, as described in Spotlight 13.1. The federal court can mandate prison officials to modify the prison conditions that led to the constitutional violation. In cases of extreme violations, courts have closed jails or prisons until conditions were corrected. In cases of overcrowded facilities, judges can order prison officials to reduce the inmate population.[21]

Tests of Civil Liability

The Supreme Court has developed tests for determining whether inmates' constitutional right to be free of the Eighth Amendment's ban against **cruel and**

Case Study 13.2

Wilson v. Seiter

The complaint alleges overcrowding, excessive noise, insufficient locker storage space, inadequate heating and cooling, improper ventilation, unclean and inadequate restrooms, unsanitary dining facilities and food preparation, and housing with mentally and physically ill inmates. Petitioner sought declaratory and injunctive relief, as well as $900,000 in compensatory and punitive damages. . . .

Petitioners . . . charged that the authorities, after notification, had failed to take remedial action. Respondents . . . denied that some of the alleged conditions existed, and described efforts by prison officials to improve the others. . . .

[The Court reviewed prior cases, concluding the following:]

These cases mandate inquiry into a prison official's state of mind when it is claimed that the official has inflicted cruel and unusual punishment. Petitioner concedes that this is so with respect to *some* claims of cruel and unusual prison conditions. . . . Petitioner . . . suggests that we should draw a distinction between "short-term" or "one-time" conditions (in which a state of mind requirement would apply) and "continuing" or "systemic" conditions (where official state of mind would be irrelevant). We perceive neither a logical nor a practical basis for that distinction. The source of the intent requirement is not the predilections of this Court, but the Eighth Amendment itself, which bans only cruel and unusual *punishment.* If the pain inflicted is not formally meted out *as punishment* by the statute or the sentencing judge, some mental element must be attributed to the inflicting officer before it can qualify.

---

unusual punishment have been violated. Generally, the tests are stated broadly and are thus open to interpretation. In its first case on the issue concerning prison conditions, the Court held that an inmate may bring a successful Section 1983 action against prison officials who deny him or her adequate medical care for a serious medical problem only if it can be shown that the officials acted with **deliberate indifference** to the inmate's needs. In *Estelle v. Gamble,* the Court stated that allegations of "inadvertent failure to provide adequate medical care," or of a "negligent . . . diagnos[is]" do not establish the requisite state of mind for a violation of the cruel and unusual punishment clause.[22]

In subsequent years, the Court construed the cruel and unusual punishment issue further. In June 1991, the Court decided *Wilson v. Seiter,* which involved a felon who was incarcerated at the Hocking Correctional Facility (HCF) in Nelsonville, Ohio. The inmate, Pearly L. Wilson, argued that his confinement constituted cruel and unusual punishment. He sought to distinguish *Estelle v. Gamble* on the grounds that the case involved a one-time act or violation. The majority rejected that distinction, stating that the mental element is implicit in the ban against cruel and unusual punishment. The excerpts from that case in Case Study 13.2 give more details.[23]

The Supreme Court sent the case back to the lower court because it could not determine the standard that court had applied, but for our purposes, the significance of the case is that the Court interpreted the Constitution to require that when inmates question prison conditions, they must show a negative state of mind of officials in order to win their cases. Specifically, they must prove that prison officials harbor *deliberate indifference.* Dissenters noted correctly that in many cases, this standard will be difficult, if not impossible, to prove.

Inhumane prison conditions are often the result of cumulative actions and inactions by numerous officials inside and outside a prison, sometimes over a long period of time. In those circumstances, it is far from clear whose intent should be examined, and the majority offers no real guidance on this issue. In truth, intent simply is not very meaningful when considering a challenge to an institution, such as a prison system.[24]

In June 1994, the Court applied a subjective rather than an objective standard to determining whether prison officials have the required state of mind to constitute deliberate indifference. *Farmer v. Brennan* involved an inmate who is biologically male but has some characteristics of a woman. He alleged that he was raped by another inmate after he was incarcerated in an all-male prison. He argued that placing a transsexual in an all-male population constituted deliberate indifference to his safety. Officials knew or should have known of the risks involved. The Court rejected that objective standard, stating that prison officials may be held liable for unsafe prison conditions only if they "know that inmates face a substantial risk of serious harm and disregard that risk by failing to take reasonable measures to abate it."[25]

Finally, the Court has held that it is not necessary for inmates to suffer significant injuries in order to prevail in a case alleging physical brutality in violation of the prohibition against cruel and unusual punishment. More attention is given to that issue later in the chapter's discussion of *Hudson v. McMillian*.[26] For now, we will examine the Court's position on current prison conditions.

Prison Conditions: Total View

Although the various constitutional rights of inmates are considered separately, it is important to understand that courts do not look at these rights in isolation. Generally, the concern is with overall incarceration conditions. For example, in two cases, the Supreme Court has held that **double celling,** or double bunking (i.e., more than one person per cell), of inmates is not unconstitutional. However, that does not mean that the Court would consider double celling constitutional under any circumstances.

The first case, *Bell v. Wolfish,* involved the housing of two inmates in the same cell in a modern jail facility. The Court noted that the inmates were not required to remain in their cells for long periods of time; thus, double celling might not be expected to have the negative effect that it could have under other circumstances when inmates do not have the freedom to move in and out of their cells. In 1981, in *Rhodes v. Chapman,* the Court considered double celling in an Ohio prison. Again, the Court was looking at a relatively new facility. The Southern Ohio Correctional Facility has several workshops, gymnasiums, school rooms, day rooms, two chapels, a hospital ward, a commissary, a barber shop, a library, a recreation field, a visitation area, and a garden. Cells are reasonably comfortable, with 63 square feet of space and bunk beds, a wall-mounted sink, a toilet, a cabinet, a shelf, a high nightstand, and a radio. Cells are ventilated and well heated; many have windows that can be opened. Noise has not been a serious problem, and, as in the *Bell v. Wolfish* case, most inmates are allowed considerable time outside their cells.[27]

In addition, it is necessary to distinguish *types* of facilities when analyzing whether certain prison conditions are unconstitutional. Most prisons are classified as maximum, medium, or minimum security. Conditions that might be justified for security in a maximum security prison may not be permitted in those designed for inmates who need only limited supervision. Likewise, conditions considered constitutional for convicted persons serving sentences in prison or jail may not be appropriate for pretrial detainees, who are in jail awaiting trial but have not been convicted.

This overview provided a background for an analysis of particular concerns in the area of inmates' rights. The following sections examine several amendments to the U.S. Constitution and their impact on inmates' rights.

One of the most important rights in the United States is the right to express ourselves—to communicate with other people. The First Amendment of the U.S. Constitution establishes, among other principles, that Congress cannot make any laws that prohibit the free exercise of religion, speech, or press. These rights are important to inmates as well. The difficult adjustment problems in prison may be eased by communication with family and friends. Injustices within prisons are eliminated primarily by courts; thus, the right of inmates to petition the courts is critical. Freedom of religion involves not only the right to think and believe, but also the right to engage in religious practices.

First Amendment Rights

Mail

Inmate correspondence has produced considerable litigation, partly because of the importance of contact with the outside world and partly because this right involves the rights of persons outside the prison. In the past, prison officials refused to mail or give letters to inmates, censored mail, deleted comments from outgoing and incoming letters, removed articles considered to be detrimental to the inmate, and decided who could correspond with particular inmates. Prison officials claimed that these actions were necessary to maintain prison security.

The Supreme Court considered prison censorship of personal mail in a case involving inmates who were not permitted to write letters in which they complained unduly or magnified grievances. They were forbidden to express any inflammatory views, whether political, racial, or religious, or to send letters that pertained to criminal activity. Letters that were lewd, obscene, defamatory, or contained foreign matter were forbidden. All incoming and outgoing mail was screened for violations of these regulations. When an official found a violation of these rules, the letter was returned to the inmate, who received a disciplinary report and punishment. In *Procunier v. Martinez*, the Court held that censorship of an inmate's mail is constitutional "if that is necessary to maintain security, order, rehabilitation. Even then, the censorship may be no greater than is necessary to protect those legitimate governmental interests."[28]

In 1989, in *Thornburgh v. Abbott*, the Court overruled *Martinez* to the extent that *Martinez* covered incoming mail. Regulations concerning incoming mail must be analyzed under the four criteria set forth in *Turner v. Safley*, discussed earlier, and are valid if they are "reasonably related to legitimate penological interests." The result is that the Court has approved more stringent rules for the regulation of incoming prison mail, which poses a greater threat to security than does outgoing mail. Spotlight 13.2 contains further information from *Abbott* and federal regulations concerning incoming publications that may be excluded from prison facilities.[29]

An example of the type of censorship that was not permitted by a federal court is found in *McNamara v. Moody*, in which prison officials refused to mail a letter written by an inmate to his girlfriend. The letter was returned to the inmate with a note indicating that:

> It was in poor taste and absolutely unacceptable for mailing from this institution.
> . . . The next time you write a letter such as the one attached, you may be sure that you will meet with the disciplinary team.[30]

The letter in question alleged that the censors lead such "blah" lives that they "must masturbate themselves while they read other people's mail." The letter alleged also that another inmate told the writer that the censor "has a cat and that he is suspected of having relations of some sort with his cat."

Spotlight 13.2

Federal Regulations Concerning Incoming Mail

In its 1989 decision, *Thornburgh v. Abbott*, the U.S. Supreme Court summarized the federal regulations concerning publications that an inmate might receive without prior administrative approval.[1] Some of these points are as follows:

- A publication may be rejected by prison officials "only if it is determined detrimental to the security, good order, or discipline of the institution or if it might facilitate criminal activity." Prison officials may not be reject a publication "solely because its content is religious, philosophical, political, social or sexual, or because its content is unpopular or repugnant."

- Publications may be rejected by prison officials if they meet any of the following criteria, which are specified by statute:

  1. It depicts or describes procedures for the construction or use of weapons, ammunitions, bombs, or incendiary devices.
  2. It depicts, encourages, or describes methods of escape from correctional facilities, or contains blueprints, drawings, or similar descriptions of Bureau of Prisons institutions.
  3. It depicts or describes procedures for the brewing of alcoholic beverages, or the manufacture of drugs.
  4. It is written in code.
  5. It depicts, describes, or encourages activities that may lead to the use of physical violence or group disruption.
  6. It encourages or instructs in the commission of criminal activity.
  7. It is sexually explicit material that by its nature or content poses a threat to the security, good order, or discipline of the institution, or facilitates criminal activity.[2]

- Prison officials may not establish an excluded list of publications but, rather, must examine each issue in every publication. To determine whether a publication is acceptable, the statute provides the following categories, which may be excluded:

  1. Homosexual (of the same sex as the institution population)
  2. Sado-masochistic
  3. Bestiality
  4. Involving children[3]

- Material in the first three categories may be admitted if officials determine it "not to pose a threat at the local institution." Ordinarily explicit heterosexual material will be admitted, and other material may be admitted if it has scholarly, literary, or general social value. Homosexual material that is not sexually explicit is admitted; material discussing the activities of gay-rights groups or gay religious groups, as well as literary publications with homosexual references or themes, is to be admitted.

- Prison officials may exclude materials only by following stated procedures, such as advising the inmate promptly in writing of the exclusion and the reasons. The inmate may appeal, and an independent review may be called for by the publisher. The Court notes that there is little doubt that this kind of censorship "would raise grave First Amendment concerns outside the prison context." But the Court recognizes also that exceptions to First Amendment rights may be made in prisons "with due regard for the 'inordinately' difficult undertaking that is modern prison administration."[3]

---

[1] *Thornburgh v. Abbott*, 490 U.S. 401 (1989).

[2] Code of Federal Regulations, Chapter 28, Section 540.70 (b) (1988).

[3] Code of Federal Regulations, Chapter 28, Section 540.71 (b) (7).

Prison officials argued that it was necessary to censor this mail for security reasons and that censorship was permissible because the words were obscene. The Court disagreed, holding that the words were not obscene ("Vulgar it is; obscene it is not") and that prison officials had not demonstrated that censorship was necessary for prison security and discipline. The Supreme Court refused to hear the case, thus allowing the lower court decision to stand.[31]

Likewise, disciplinary action against an inmate who wrote a letter to his brother, referring to various prison personnel as "punks" and "bitches," concluding with the comment, "I hope they all read this letter and get their kicks off of it," was a violation of that inmate's free speech rights.[32] Prison officials may not censor mail solely for the purpose of eliminating comments that may be unflattering to prison officials.[33]

In another case, the court held that a prison regulation requiring that all outgoing mail directed to the media and to the clergy be sent to the prison mailroom unsealed (in contrast to mail addressed to attorneys, which may not be inspected) does not violate an inmate's First Amendment rights. Such mail may be censored by prison officials only if it contains threats or escape plans.[34]

Limitations that prison officials may place on the right of inmates to communicate by mail with the outside world vary according to the type of mail. In federal prisons, mail falls into two categories: privileged (or special), and general. *General mail* is mail between an inmate and anyone not in the privileged category. General mail "is subject to being opened by prison officials, checked for contraband, read for plans to perform illegal acts, and then re-closed and delivered to the prisoner." *Privileged,* or *special mail* is mail between an inmate and attorneys or other persons connected with the courts or treatment of the inmate, legislative officials, and other public officials. Privileged mail "enjoys more protection than general mail in that it cannot be read by prison officials and can be opened to check for contraband only in the presence of the inmate to whom it is addressed."[35] States have similar regulations for prison mail.

Packages may be categorized as privileged or general mail. The Supreme Court has upheld the right of prison officials to prohibit the receipt of hardcover books by inmates unless they are mailed directly from publishers, book clubs, or bookstores. The Court considers that regulation to be a security measure. Correspondents might send *contraband* such as money and drugs, even weapons, into prison inside the hardback books. Officials may open packages to determine whether there is contraband, but prisons are given discretion in limiting, or in some cases prohibiting, receipt of packages because of the time required for these checks.[36]

The correspondence that causes the greatest concern for prison officials is correspondence between inmates in different prisons. In *Turner v. Safley,* the Supreme Court upheld a ban on such mail under the circumstances that existed in that case. The provisions in question permitted mail between "immediate family members who are inmates in other correctional institutions" and correspondence between inmates "concerning legal matters." Any other correspondence between inmates was permitted only if "the classification/treatment team of each inmate deems it in the best interest of the parties involved."[37]

Publishing Rights

The right of inmates to record and publish their thoughts should not be confused with the right to earn royalties on the sale of those publications. Many jurisdictions have "Son of Sam" statutes, which prohibit convicted persons from receiving profits from the sale of books written about their crimes. The name *Son of Sam* comes from the New York statute enacted because of public concern that Sam Berkowitz, who murdered six young people in New York in the late 1970s, would make millions from his writings about the killings.

The statute, which became the model for many of the subsequently enacted state statutes, provides that any proceeds from "the accused or convicted person's thoughts, feelings, opinions, or emotions regarding [the] crime" must be turned over to the Victim Compensation Board. The statute covers reenactment "by way of a movie, book, magazine, article, tape recording, phonograph, radio, or television presentation," and requires that the person contracting with the criminal must turn over proceeds to the Victim Compensation Board.[38] The New York statute contains provisions for victims to bring civil actions against their perpetrators and to recover from the victim's compensation fund.

The constitutionality of the New York statute was upheld by a New York court in 1979.[39] In 1987, the New York Crime Victim Compensation Board ruled that convicted murderer Jean Harris, author of *Stranger in Two Worlds*, must turn over her $45,000 advance for the book. If she did not have that money, the publisher was to pay the same amount to the board. Any profits above that advance were to be turned over to the family of the man whom Harris murdered. Harris planned to give the royalties, which were over $100,000, to charity, but the New York Court of Appeals upheld the statute. The court rejected arguments that the statute interferes with First Amendment rights. The inmate is free to exercise those rights, but he or she may not profit financially from the crime. This decision was vacated in early 1992 and sent back to the New York Court of Appeals for consideration in light of *Simon & Schuster, Inc., v. New York State Crime Victims Board.*[40]

In *Simon & Schuster, Inc.*, the book at issue was *Wiseguy: Life in a Mafia Family*, an account of the life of Henry Hill, a career criminal who became an informer. The lower federal court upheld the statute; the Supreme Court reversed, holding that the Son of Sam statute is inconsistent with the First Amendment right to free speech. In order to infringe on that right, the state must show "that its regulation is necessary to serve a compelling state interest and is narrowly drawn to achieve that end." Although the state has an interest in preventing crime, in preventing criminals from profiting from their crimes, and in compensating victims, the Court said the state could not show a compelling reason for targeting a criminal's assets from writing about the crime. Furthermore, the statute is too broad. For example, the Court noted that had it been in effect when Malcolm X wrote his autobiography, that work would have been included within the statute since it included comments of his crimes before he became a civil rights leader.[41]

New York enacted another Son of Sam statute in 1992. This statute permits state authorities to seize some assets of criminals and hold them for a period of seven years to cover any civil damages that victims might be awarded. The statute permits judges to award restitution to crime victims if they ask for it and if the award is in the interests of justice. The new statute may cover money that criminals received from talk shows as well as books, for it defines *profits of crime* as "any assets or income obtained through the use of unique knowledge obtained during the commission of . . . the crime." Presumably, the new statute avoids the defect of the previous one, which targeted speech.[42]

In May 1993, a Florida circuit judge ruled that Danny Rolling would not be permitted to profit financially from the crimes for which he was accused: the murders of five University of Florida students. Subsequently, Rolling pleaded guilty to those murders and was sentenced to death.[43]

Visitations

Professional treatment personnel, scholars, and courts recognize the importance of visits for inmates as well as for their families and friends. The National Conference of Commissioners on Uniform State Laws emphasizes that confinement without visitation:

> Brings alienation, and the longer the confinement, the greater the alienation. . . . Visitation has demonstrated positive effects on a confined person's ability to adjust to life while confined as well as his ability to adjust to life upon release.[44]

Prison visitation creates security problems and thus requires careful planning and supervision. Prison policies require that inmates submit lists of visitors for prior approval, and some persons on those lists may be denied visiting privileges for security or other reasons. Visits may be regulated by hours, days, frequency, and so on by prison officials as long as the regulations are reasonably related to legitimate prison goals. Prison officials may not be arbitrary and capricious in denying visitation privileges. For example, they may not deny an inmate visits with a person of another race solely because the two are of different races.[45] Nor may prison officials deny visitations to a gay or lesbian friend of an inmate solely because they are involved romantically. There is no reasonable connection between maintaining prison security and safety and denial of such visits.[46]

Contact visits may be denied to inmates who are dangerous to themselves or others or when the risk of smuggling contraband is high. Contact visits are to be distinguished from conjugal visits (discussed later), in which sexual relationships are permitted. In contact visits, inmates may be permitted to hug and embrace a family member or friend; in some institutions, that is the extent of contact permitted, and correctional officers monitor the visits. In other institutions, inmates may have limited contact with visitors throughout the visit. This may be important particularly when children are involved.

Inmates who are denied contact visits for security reasons may be permitted noncontact visits. For example, the inmate and his or her visitor may be separated by glass; they may talk over a phone or through a screened hole in the glass, but they may not touch each other. Another arrangement is to permit a dangerous inmate to be in the same room with the visitor, but restrain the inmate with handcuffs, body chains, or both.

Visits with Family and Friends

The Supreme Court has recognized the importance of permitting inmates to see their families and friends, suggesting that such visits might be "a factor contributing to the ultimate reintegration of the detainees into society." That statement, however, comes from a case involving pretrial detainees in detention in the largest jail in the country, the Los Angeles County Central Jail, which has a capacity of 5,000 inmates. In *Block v. Rutherford,* the Court upheld the total prohibition against visitations in that jail. The Court emphasized that security is a critical problem in a large population and that even small children may be used by family and friends to smuggle contraband into the jail.[47]

The position taken by the Supreme Court in *Block v. Rutherford* must be limited to the facts of the case. The Court emphasized that pretrial detainees, who are incarcerated because they have been denied bail or were unable to make bail, are likely to be charged with serious offenses. The Court also cited as additional reasons for denying visits the large size of the population, which would create tremendous administrative problems if visits were permitted, the danger of drugs being brought into the jail, and the short period of confinement. In other situations, the Court might not uphold a total prohibition on contact visits, and some lower courts have taken that position. Some prison officials maintain that prison contact visits reduce tensions and aid in inmates' rehabilitation.

Visitation is important for inmates' spouses, too. Studies of inmates' wives indicate that they suffer more than the obvious denial of companionship and sexual relations when their husbands are incarcerated. They are socially ostracized and rejected, despite their lack of involvement in the criminal activity that led to the incarceration. They face problems coping with their children, financial difficulties, problems of self-esteem, and so on.[48]

The importance of family has led some institutions to permit inmates to marry while they are incarcerated, and such marriages have been increasing in number. In Florida, hundreds of marriages have been conducted since 1985, when a federal court held that the state could not prohibit inmate marriages unless it could show a security risk or a threat to inmate rehabilitation. Prior to that decision, Florida permitted inmate marriages only if the inmate was near the end of his or her term or if marriage was necessary to legitimatize children.[49]

In 1989, a federal court in New York declared unconstitutional a policy forbidding inmates to marry unless they were ready for parole. The court said the prohibition was not reasonably related to the goal of punishment.[50]

Permitting inmate marriages does not necessarily mean that conjugal visits are permitted. *Conjugal visiting* refers to the system that administrators have employed in some jurisdictions to provide inmates with opportunities for sexual and other social contacts with their spouses in a relaxed, unsupervised, private area of the prison community. In some institutions, the visits may be extended to the complete nuclear family. Some involve a live-in weekend instead of a few hours on visiting day.

Conjugal visiting is common in many European prisons; rarely is it permitted in the United States. U.S. courts have refused to hold that inmates have a constitutional right to marry and engage in conjugal relations.[51] In *Turner v. Safley,* the Supreme Court held that states may place substantial restrictions on inmate marriages, but those restrictions must be "reasonably related to legitimate penological objectives," one of which is institutional security.[52]

It has been held that prison officials may deny an incarcerated inmate and his spouse the opportunity to attempt conception through artificial insemination. Numerous reasons are cited for denial of such requests. If proper procedures for artificial insemination are not followed, the procedures may be ineffective or result in the birth of a defective child. Proper procedures are expensive and would require additional prison facilities and personnel, or permitting the inmate to go to outside facilities, which creates a security risk. Providing the services for indigent inmates increases the costs. For these reasons, the Bureau of Prisons has adopted a policy prohibiting artificial insemination for inmates in federal prisons, and courts have upheld this policy.[53]

Visits with the Press

Another type of visit that is important to inmates is the right to visit with the press. In *Pell v. Procunier,* the Supreme Court upheld a California statute providing that "press and other media interviews with specific individual inmates will not be permitted." The Court said internal security required that some restrictions be made on face-to-face contacts with outsiders. The restriction on visits with the media must be viewed in perspective with alternatives. Inmates may communicate with the press through prison-approved visits and through the mail. The Court concluded that as long as reasonable and effective means of communications are available and there is no discrimination in the content of those communications, the prison must be given great latitude in regulating visits with the press.[54]

The Supreme Court has held that there is no right of access to government information or sources of information within the government's control, and the news media have no constitutional right of access to a county jail, over and above that of other persons, to interview inmates and make sound recordings, films, and photographs for publication and broadcasting by newspapers, radio, and television.[55]

Religious Worship

Some studies indicate that religion reduces discipline problems in prison.[56] Freedom of religion is a First Amendment right, and numerous court cases have arisen over this important right to freedom and what it means in a prison setting. The general rule was announced by the U.S. Supreme Court in 1972 in *Cruz v. Beto.* An inmate must be given "a reasonable opportunity of pursuing his faith comparable to the opportunity afforded fellow prisoners who adhere to conventional religious precepts." This does not mean that all religious sects or groups must have identical facilities or personnel. "But reasonable opportunities must be afforded to all prisoners to exercise the religious freedom guaranteed by the First and Fourteenth Amendments without fear of penalty."[57] The word "reasonable" is included in this statement since prison officials at times find themselves denying individuals "religious" practices that may pose a security risk to the institution. On the other hand, security is a reason for denying certain religious practices, such as the use of peyote by Native American inmates.[58]

An inmate may claim a right to practice religious beliefs only if the religion is a recognized one. Deciding whether a claimed religion is really a religion may be a problem, as Spotlight 13.3 indicates. A second issue is whether the inmate is a sincere believer in that religion. If the religion is found to be a recognized one and the inmate is a sincere believer, questions may arise over whether the inmate should be permitted to practice all aspects of the religious belief. It is clear that some observances may not be permitted for security reasons or because of the time and personnel required to secure the prison during those observances.[59]

Other issues may involve diet, grooming, and dress. Some inmates' requests for special food and diet compatible with their religious beliefs have been recognized. For example, some courts have upheld the request of Jewish inmates for kosher food, although some courts have refused. Generally, requests by Muslims to have a diet free of pork are upheld.[60] But a request from an inmate to be served a vegetarian diet because of his religious beliefs was denied. The court recognized the institutional concern with the inmate's health in justifying refusal of this request.[61]

In 1992, a court ruled against an inmate who claimed that cutting hair was against his religious beliefs and thus he should not be required to comply with the prison regulation concerning hair length. The court did not question the sincerity of the inmate but deferred to prison authorities concerning the rationale

Spotlight 13.3

Real or Imaginary Religions: The Prison Dilemma

One of the most litigated examples of inmate-claimed religions is that of the Church of the New Song (CONS), which was organized in the early 1970s by Harry William Theriault, a federal inmate. Theriault claimed himself the Bishop of Tellyus, obtained a mail-order divinity degree, and deemed his cell the Fountainhead Seminary. He converted other inmates to his Eclatarian Faith until prison authorities transferred him to solitary confinement. Previously, Theriault had been involved in litigation concerning his conviction and sentence, as well as prison conditions. He sued prison officials for deprivation of his constitutional right to the free exercise of religion. In spite of Theriault's admission that CONS was started as a game, the court said CONS was to be considered a bona fide religion under the First Amendment.[1]

Shortly after *Theriault v. Carlson* was decided, a sect within the church made a formal request to the Federal Bureau of Prisons to provide 700 Porterhouse steaks for the inmates to celebrate the sect's rituals. Theriault announced that he had no affiliation with that sect and that the request was not sanctioned.[2] The Court of Appeals remanded the case to the lower court to determine the validity of the alleged religion against the suspect background of Theriault and the dubious formation of the sect. On remand, the district court found that CONS was not a religion.[3]

Theriault appealed again and the Court of Appeals remanded the case because the district court had not indicated its basis for finding that CONS was not a religion.[4] On remand, the district court found that CONS was not a religion, but "a masquerade designed to obtain First Amendment protection for acts which otherwise would be unlawful and or reasonably disallowed by the various prison authorities but for the attempts which have been and are being made to classify them as 'religious' and, therefore, presumably protected by the First Amendment." The court noted that even if CONS were a religion (which it was held not to be), the prison could exercise reasonable controls over the practice of the religion. "To give a prisoner who is an admitted escape artist and who has been convicted of assault and battery on corrections officers the unrestricted freedom which he demands would make a mockery of the corrections system and would afford him privileges not available to other inmates, unless they joined his union."[5]

Theriault's appeal of this decision was dismissed because his petition contained vile and insulting references to the trial judge.[6] The issue of whether CONS is a religion is not settled. In Iowa, it was held to be a religion.[7] In Illinois, a court ruled that CONS was not a religion for First Amendment purposes.[8]

The question of what constitutes a religion arose in the case of the Metropolitan Community Church (MCC), frequently referred to as the homosexual or gay church, although membership does not exclude heterosexuals. The State of California denied requests by inmates to practice this religion in prison. The state contended that the MCC was not a bona fide religion. The court rejected that contention. The court ruled that in order to maintain the ban, the state would have to show that if the ban were removed, there would be a clear and present danger of a breach of prison security. At that point, California allowed the religion to be practiced within the prisons.[9]

---

[1] *Theriault v. Carlson,* 339 F. Supp. 375 (N.D. Ga. 1972), *vacated and remanded,* 495 F. 2d 390 (5th Cir. 1974), *cert. denied,* 419 U.S. 1003 (1974).

[2] Cited in comment, "The Religious Rights of the Incarcerated," *University of Pennsylvania Law Review* 125 (April, 1977): 818.

[3] *Theriault v. Silber,* 391 F. Supp. 578 (W.D. Tex. 1975).

[4] *Theriault v. Silber,* 547 F. 2d 1279 (5th Cir. 1977), *cert. denied,* 434 U.S. 943 (1977).

[5] *Theriault v. Silber,* 453 F. Supp. 254, 260, 262 (W.D. Tex. 1978).

[6] *Theriault v. Silber,* 569 F. 2d 301 (5th Cir. 1978).

[7] See *Remmers v. Brewer,* 361 F. Supp. 537 (S.D. Iowa 1973), *Aff'd. per Curiam,* 494 F. 2d 1277 (8th Cir. 1974), *cert. denied,* 419 U.S. 1012 (1974).

[8] *Hundley v. Sielaff,* 407 F. Supp. 543 (N.D. Ill. 1973).

[9] *Lipp v. Procunier,* 395 F. Supp. 871 (N.D. Cal. 1975).

Case Study 13.3

Jones v. North Carolina Prisoner's Union, Inc.

First Amendment associational rights, while perhaps more directly implicated by the regulatory prohibitions, likewise must give way to the reasonable considerations of penal management. . . . [N]umerous associational rights are necessarily curtailed by the realities of confinement. They may be curtailed whenever the institution's officials, in the exercise of their informed discretion, reasonably conclude that such associations, whether through group meetings or otherwise, possess the likelihood of disruption to prison order or stability, or otherwise interfere with the legitimate penological objectives of the prison environment.

for this rule. The court concluded that the "loss of absolute freedom of religious expression is but one sacrifice required by their incarceration."[62]

It has been held reasonable for prison authorities to refuse to permit an inmate to wear a rosary with an attached hard, plastic crucifix because the crucifix could be used to remove handcuffs.[63] On the other hand, in May 1994, a court granted preliminary permission to inmates who were adherents of the Santeria religion to wear multicolored beads. Prison officials argued that some inmates wear these beads as a sign of gang membership. The court said that might not be a reason to prohibit all inmates from wearing them for religious reasons. This case, however, followed the passage of the 1993 Religious Freedom Restoration Act, an act passed in 1993 for the purpose of reversing two Supreme Court decisions. The act requires that freedom of religion may not be restricted except under circumstances that constitute a "compelling state interest" and is accomplished by the "least restrictive means" available. Prison officials lobbied unsuccessfully for exemptions, arguing that the act would have devastating results in prisons.[64]

Freedom of Assembly and Self-Government

The First Amendment guarantees the right of persons to assemble freely. Inmates have argued that this freedom, along with the right to engage in self-government to some extent, applies also to them. In 1977, in *Jones v. North Carolina Prisoner's Union, Inc.,* the Supreme Court upheld the right of prison officials in North Carolina to restrict the activities of prison unions, a decision described by two dissenting justices as a "giant step backward" in inmates' rights. In *Jones,* the Court contemplated the right of inmates to associate with each other and the restrictions that officials could place on this right, as the brief excerpt in Case Study 13.3 indicates.[65]

Access to Courts

The right of access to courts, recognized by the Supreme Court in *Ex Parte Hull* in 1941, is an inmate's most important right.[66] Without access to courts, most other rights have limited meaning. In 1969, in *Johnson v. Avery,* the Supreme Court invalidated a Tennessee prison regulation that forbade inmates to assist one another in preparing legal cases. Because many institutions do not provide legal services, the effect of that regulation was to deny some inmates access to courts. *Johnson* recognized the right of an inmate to the services of a jailhouse lawyer, but the Court restricted the use of such services to inmates in institutions that

Case Study 13.4

Bounds v. Smith

[This] fundamental constitutional right of access to the courts requires prison authorities to assist inmates in the preparation and filing of meaningful legal papers by providing prisoners with adequate law libraries or adequate assistance from persons trained in the law. . . .

Among the alternatives are the training of inmates as paralegal assistants to work under lawyers'
supervision, the use of paraprofessionals and law students, either as volunteers or in formal clinical programs, the organization of volunteer attorneys through bar associations and other groups, the hiring of lawyers on a part-time consultant basis, and the use of full-time staff attorneys, working in either new prison legal assistance organizations or as part of public defender or legal services offices.

provided no reasonable alternative.[67] Some jailhouse lawyers are highly recognized for their legal services while they are inmates.[68] The individuals have a fairly good understanding of case law. They use their skills to assist some of their peers in their effort to petition the courts for a review of their cases.

In 1977, in *Bounds v. Smith* (see Case Study 13.4), the Court presented some guidelines concerning the meaning of the right of access to courts.[69] The meaning of *Bounds* has been litigated. It has been held that the case does not require that the assistance of attorneys be made available to inmates; the requirement of adequate access to courts may be met through providing adequate law libraries.[70] On the other hand, not permitting inmates (such as those on death row or in administrative segregation) to go to the law library and browse may be unconstitutional, depending on the facts. Some courts have upheld these restrictions because of the threat to security posed by death-row inmates, but some recent cases have held to the contrary. In 1992, a federal court in Arizona held that prison officials denied inmates access to courts by restricting their access to the prison law library and by restricting inmates' opportunities to engage in confidential phone calls to their attorneys. The court stated:

> The vast majority of adult prisoners incarcerated by [the Arizona Department of Corrections] have no adequate means to research the law, crystalize their issues, present their papers in a meaningful fashion, and get them filed in court.[71]

The court noted that some inmates are not permitted to go to the library, and that policy denies them an opportunity to browse, a privilege that is necessary for those who do not know exactly which materials they need. For those who do not speak or read English, a law library is not adequate access to courts.

In upholding a policy of permitting death-row inmates access to the law library only through a paging system in which requested books are delivered to them in their cells, a federal court in Pennsylvania emphasized that court decisions "like the decisions of the prison administrators, must not be made in a vacuum, but rather must give due consideration to the depraved nature of the crimes committed and the 'character of the inmates.'"[72]

Security might be a sufficient reason for denying an inmate the opportunity to go to the library, but in that case, some courts hold that legal assistance must be provided. Further, indigent inmates must be provided sufficient papers, pens, and other materials to make it possible for them to do research, and law libraries must be staffed with persons trained in legal research.[73] This does not mean that those persons must be attorneys or even trained paralegals.[74]

One court stated that it is sufficient that they be "intelligent lay people who can write coherent English and who have had some modicum of exposure to legal research and to the rudiments of prisoner-rights law." In addition, there must be sufficient numbers of persons to assist the inmate population.[75] Harassment of inmate paralegals by prison officials may deny other inmates adequate access to courts.[76] Adequate access to courts extends to pretrial jail detainees who are proceeding *pro se* (on their own, without attorneys).[77]

The right of inmates to access to courts does not include the right to appointed counsel for all appeals. An indigent defendant is entitled "as a matter of right to counsel for an initial appeal from the judgment and sentence of the trial court," but is not entitled to appointed counsel for all subsequent appeals.[78]

In general, inmates do not have a right to appointed counsel for civil cases. One court has held, however, that female inmates may have greater rights than male inmates. Thus, it was held unconstitutional for Michigan to cut back on its policies to provide legal assistance to female inmates in civil parental rights cases. This is because parenthood is part of the "liberty" guaranteed by the Fourteenth Amendment.[79] Female inmates may need more legal assistance than do male inmates (and thus require the assistance of paralegals or attorneys) because "female prisoners lack their male counterparts' history of 'self-help' in the law, . . . [and] equal protection considerations may require that library facilities be supplemented by assistance from a lawyer."[80] It will be interesting to see if this trend continues as women become more involved in the workforce.

In addition to the right to access to legal materials, inmates have the right to reasonable and confidential communication with their retained attorneys. Prisons must provide reasonable visitation policies and adequate facilities for inmate visits with attorneys. Inmates must be permitted to communicate by mail with their attorneys. The Supreme Court allows prison officials to open letters from attorneys to inmates and to search for contraband as long as it is done in the presence of the inmates to whom the letters are addressed. This action is not censorship because the mail is not read. Prisons may require attorneys to indicate on the outside of the envelope that the mail is from a legal office.[81]

Inmates who retain attorneys for their legal actions against prison officials may be entitled to attorney fees upon winning their cases. In 1989, a federal judge ordered Michigan state correctional officials to pay $1.48 million in attorney fees to compensate inmates' attorneys for their time and legal services. The compensation included an award for the "stress, frustration and outrage" the inmates' attorneys suffered from the misconduct of state attorneys. In the case at issue, the judge ruled that inmates were denied adequate access to courts, endured excessive restrictions on their legal mail, were deprived of adequate warm clothing and adequate access to toilets, and that officials failed to deter correctional staff from subjecting African American inmates to racial slurs.[82] The legal fees are thought to be one of the largest awards in a prison lawsuit.[83]

One final point on adequate access to courts is that this right may be, and is, used to file frivolous suits. A recent article noted a few examples. One inmate filed a suit claiming he was the victim of cruel and unusual punishment because he was served melted ice cream. Another alleged that he was served creamy peanut butter after ordering chunky, while another inmate who had an ulcer claimed he should be provided with lamb, veal, and oysters. His physician said these foods were permitted, but not required, for his health. Since the 1960s, when only a few hundred inmate suits were filed each year, the number grew to

Case Study 13.5

Hudson v. Palmer

[T]he Fourth Amendment proscription against unreasonable searches does not apply within the confines of the prison cell. The recognition of privacy rights for prisoners in their individual cells simply cannot be reconciled with the concept of incarceration and the needs and objectives of penal institutions.

Prisons, by definition, are places of involuntary confinement of persons who have a demonstrated proclivity for antisocial criminal, and often violent, conduct. . . .

Within this volatile "community," prison administrators are to take all necessary steps to ensure the safety of not only the prison staffs and administrative personnel, but visitors. They are under an obligation to take reasonable measures to guarantee the safety of the inmates themselves. They must be ever alert to attempts to introduce drugs and other contraband into the premises. . . .

Virtually the only place inmates can conceal weapons, drugs, and other contraband is in their cells. Unfettered access to these cells by prison officials, thus, is imperative if drugs and contraband are to be ferreted out and sanitary surroundings are to be maintained.

33,000 in 1993. Those lawsuits constituted up to 15 percent of the total number of civil lawsuits filed in federal courts that year.[84] This is probably because restrictions on the ability of inmates to file lawsuits have been lifted since the 1960s. As discussed earlier, attempts are currently underway to reintroduce restrictions to limit the number of inmate lawsuits. This is permissible to the extent that it eliminates frivolous lawsuits *only*. It is not permissible if it denies inmates adequate access to courts for legitimate claims. Of course, the problem is to distinguish between these categories.

Fourth Amendment Rights

Among other things, the Fourth Amendment prohibits unreasonable searches and seizures. The key word is *unreasonable*. In the prison setting, the need for security has highest priority; that need enables prison officials to conduct searches and seizures that are not permissible in other settings. In 1984, in *Hudson v. Palmer* (see Case Study 13.5), the Supreme Court considered the application of the Fourth Amendment to prison cell searches. With an emphasis on the difficult problems of maintaining security in a prison setting, the Court reviewed the recent history of violence in prisons and in that context issued its opinion.[85]

Hudson was decided by a 5–4 vote by the Court. Justice John Paul Stevens, who wrote an opinion in which he concurred in part and dissented in part, took the unusual step of reading his opinion from the bench when the decision was announced:

> By telling prisoners that no aspect of their individuality, from a photo of a child to a letter from a wife, is entitled to constitutional protection, the Court breaks with the ethical tradition that I had thought was enshrined forever in our jurisprudence.

Hudson v. Palmer was brought by an inmate who alleged that the officer who searched his cell did so for malice, not for security, and that the officer destroyed his personal property. Justice Stevens agreed with the Court that random searches are necessary and permissible, but he disagreed with the Court's conclusion that no matter how malicious, destructive, or arbitrary a cell search and seizure may be, it cannot constitute an unreasonable invasion of any privacy or possessory interest that society is prepared to recognize as reasonable.

According to Justice Stevens, the small amount of possessions and limited privacy that an inmate might have in a cell are little compared to what the rest of society has, but "that trivial residuum may mark the difference between slavery and humanity." In *Block v. Rutherford,* the Supreme Court upheld routine searches of cells while inmates were absent.[86]

Searches of the person are more intrusive, but even here there are degrees of intrusiveness. In general, searches by means of mechanical devices may be conducted at any time without prior authorization of a supervisor. A casual search of a person or frisk of an inmate may be conducted at any time, and is routine before and after the inmate has contact visits with family and friends.

The most intrusive search is the body search, which may involve a strip search or a manual search of body cavities. The Supreme Court has upheld body cavity searches after inmates have had contact visits.[87] The U.S. Court of Appeals for the Second Circuit has upheld random visual inspections of inmates' body cavities even without suspicion of contraband. In a 1992 decision, the court said this is permitted because of the high percentage of inmates who engage in substance abuse and violent behavior.[88]

Permitting strip searches of inmates because of the practice of secreting contraband inside the body is illustrated by the excerpt from *State v. Palmer* in Case Study 13.6. *Palmer* illustrates some of the issues associated with strip searches: the manner and place in which they occur and who conducts the search. [89]

Although it may be argued that pretrial detainees have a greater expectation of privacy than offenders who have been convicted and incarcerated in prisons, courts have upheld some types of body searches, such as visual body cavity searches.[90]

Strip searches have been held unconstitutional when conducted on a person who visits an inmate, unless the prison official has reasonable cause to think that visitor is attempting to smuggle contraband into the jail or prison. In other words, strip searches of visitors are permitted only when it is reasonable to think that is necessary for security reasons.[91] Thus, it is unreasonable to search a visitor who is leaving the prison, as that visitor is no longer in a position to introduce contraband into the prison.[92] Some courts have held that it is unconstitutional to have a policy of strip searching all persons brought to jail, even those charged with minor offenses.[93]

One final point with regard to personal searches is important. Male and female inmates have questioned searches by or in the presence of correctional officers of the opposite gender. Generally pat-down searches have been upheld as meeting the requirements of *Turner v. Safley.*[94] Searches are necessary to satisfy the security need of prisons, and opposite-gender searches (along with permitting opposite-gender officers to supervise showers and other inmate activities) may be necessary to satisfy another legitimate institutional goal, that of equal opportunity employment.[95]

Not all judges and justices agree with permitting opposite-gender pat-down searches. In a 1990 case upholding these searches, one dissenting judge said:

> To treat men and women as equals does not require that courts ignore that differences exist. Even prisoners are entitled to a modicum of privacy and are entitled not to be embarrassed by needlessly requiring that they expose their nakedness and private parts to guards of the opposite sex. My colleagues have stripped the prisoners of their limited privacy rights. . . .[96]

Case Study 13.6

State v. Palmer

All 12 inmates, including appellant, in appellant's "pod" of Cell Block Six were to undergo body cavity searches. The intelligence officer testified that he authorized an initial digital rectal search and, if that search revealed the presence of an object, the inmate would be X-rayed. Finally, if the inmate did not voluntarily give up or excrete the object, it would be removed. An initial digital rectal search was performed on appellant by a correctional medical assistant. Appellant was then escorted to a medical examining room where a medical doctor performed a second digital search. During the search, the doctor felt the presence of an object and ordered an X-ray of appellant's pelvic area. The X-ray revealed the presence of a foreign object believed to be a shotgun shell.

Following the X-ray, appellant was transported to the central unit hospital's emergency room. A second doctor, trained in sigmoidoscopy examinations, first performed a rectal examination which consisted of the insertion of a small scope to determine the nature of the foreign object. Appellant refused to submit to that examination and, eventually, was forced to lay on the table by corrections officers. Appellant finally agreed to position himself on the table so that the item could be removed, and the doctor removed the shotgun shell which had been wrapped in tissue paper in a condom. During the procedure, appellant testified that he suffered severe pain and discomfort and, following the removal he suffered some bleeding.

Searches of other inmates revealed balloons filled with gunpowder and a detonation cord, and subse-quent searches led to the discovery of blasting caps and a homemade rip gun capable of shooting a shotgun shell. Other inmates had consented to voluntarily pass or remove the contraband they possessed. One other inmate, who did not immediately excrete his contraband, was placed in an isolation cell and eventually passed a balloon filled with gunpowder.

[The appellate court discusses the dispute between the appellant and the prison officials over the method in which these searches occurred; the appellate court sees no reason to disturb the trial court's findings that the procedures were appropriate under the circumstances.]

Many factors must be considered in determining whether a search is reasonable. They include the crime allegedly being committed, society's interest in punishing the act, and the reliability of the means employed to conduct the search. They also include the strength of law enforcement suspicions that evidence of crime will be revealed, the importance of the evidence sought, and the possibility that the evidence may be recovered by less intrusive means. . . . We acknowledge that the search and removal probably resulted in discomfort, pain and humiliation, however, the removal resulted from the method by which appellant chose to hide the contraband and by appellant's refusal to voluntarily pass it. . . .

The immediate methods employed in this case were reasonable. . . . In view of all the facts and circumstances surrounding this case, we do not find that the search and seizure violated appellant's Fourth Amendment right.

Eighth Amendment Rights

Physical Abuse

Among other things, the Eighth Amendment prohibits cruel and unusual punishment. This phrase has been interpreted to include various activities within prisons. For example, it is not permissible for inmates to attack other inmates physically. Corporal punishment of inmates may constitute cruel and unusual punishment. Correctional officers and administrators may use reasonable force to maintain security, but if they go too far, they may be liable to inmates who bring civil suits against them, claiming that their Eighth Amendment rights have been violated.

In February 1992, the Supreme Court considered physical abuse of inmates by correctional officers. In *Hudson v. McMillian,* the Court held that inmates may bring actions for cruel and unusual punishment against prison officials who use physical force that may result in injuries, even if the injuries are not significant. This case involved an inmate who got into an argument with a correctional officer. Other officers intervened, and the inmate was placed in restraints and walked from his cell to a lockdown area. During this excursion, the officers kicked and punched the inmate, who suffered minor bruises, loosened teeth, and a cracked dental plate. The inmate brought a civil suit against the officers and won a modest damage award, which was overturned on appeal to a federal circuit court. The U.S. Supreme Court reversed, holding that the inmate was entitled to damages even though he did not suffer significant injuries.

Although all of the justices did not agree on the reasons, seven justices joined the affirmative in this case, which extends inmates' rights. Clarence Thomas was the most recently appointed justice at that time. His dissenting opinion, in which Justice Scalia joined, may provide significant insight into Justice Thomas's impact on the future of the Court. Thomas argued that not only must an inmate show a serious injury in order to bring a successful suit for injuries against a prison official, but he also attacked the Court's modern interpretations of the Eighth Amendment's cruel and unusual punishment clause. The result is that in only a short time on the bench, Justice Thomas aroused considerable debate about his judicial positions, far more so than did Justice David Souter, who was appointed the previous year.[97]

In December 1993, the Eighth Circuit held that the use of a stun gun on an inmate who refused to sweep his cell when ordered to do so constituted the kind of "torment without marks" that the Supreme Court prohibited in *Hudson v. McMillian.* According to the court, prison officials do not have the legal right to use force any time an inmate disobeys an order.[98]

Courts have held that the cruel and unusual punishment clause of the Eighth Amendment extends to general prison conditions. We noted earlier that when assessing general prison conditions, courts look to the totality of conditions within prisons to determine whether the conditions are so bad that they constitute cruel and unusual punishment. Those conditions may include overcrowding, unsanitary conditions, methods of discipline, food that is not prepared properly or nutritiously or that contains foreign matter, and about any other condition that threatens inmates' welfare. One of the primary areas of lawsuits concerns medical care.

Medical Care

Prison officials have broad discretion in determining the medical care that inmates should receive. It is difficult, if not impossible, for courts to make such determinations. The Supreme Court has articulated a standard for care, stating in 1976 in *Estelle v. Gamble,* that "deliberate indifference to serious medical needs of prisoners constitutes the kind of cruel and unusual punishment that is prohibited by the Eighth Amendment."[99] A decade later, the Court stated that to be actionable, delay in providing medical care for inmates must be prompted by "obduracy and wantonness, not inadvertence or error in good faith."[100]

In 1982, in *Ruiz v. Estelle,* a lower federal court looked at the Texas prison system (TDC) and concluded that the Eighth Amendment was being violated. The court found a "continuous pattern of harmful, inadequate medical treatment" that led to "anguish and inexpedient medical treatment to inmates on a large scale."[101]

In *Ruiz,* the court ordered substantial changes, including more qualified medical staff, elimination of inmate labor in medical and pharmacological functions, improvement of physical facilities, establishment of diagnostic and sick-call procedures and work classification procedures, and a complete overhaul of the record-keeping system. Improvements were made in the Texas system, leading to the end of court monitoring in December 1992.[102]

Spotlight 13.4

HIV in U.S. Prisons and Jails

A 1993 report of the Bureau of Justice Statistics, reporting on 1991 data, underscored the extent of the problems with HIV and AIDS in U.S. prisons and jails. Inmates are at a higher risk than the general population for contracting the deadly virus because of their increased use of cocaine or crack, with one out of four inmates rejecting illegal drugs into their bodies at some time in their lives. Among the conclusions of the analysis are the following:

- In 1991, 2.2 percent of all federal and state prison inmates were infected with the HIV virus.

- State prisons reported 2.3 percent of inmates were HIV positive, and federal prisons reported 1 percent.

- Of HIV-positive inmates in state or federal prisons, 9.6 percent had confirmed AIDS.

- All prison jurisdictions tested at least some inmates for HIV.

- In 1991, 28 percent of all deaths in state prisons were attributed to AIDS.

- In 1991, about 51 percent of state prison inmates reported having been tested for HIV and knew the results.

- In 1991, among those prison inmates tested, an estimated 3.3 percent of women, 3.7 percent of Hispanics, and 3.7 percent of those between age thirty-five and forty-four tested positive for HIV.

Source: Bureau of Justice Statistics. U.S. Department of Justice. *HIV in U.S. Prisons and Jails.* (Washington, DC: September, 1993), p. 1.

It is important to distinguish cases in which inmates argue that they are subjected to cruel and unusual punishment because of inadequate medical care as opposed to other conditions, such as prison physical conditions. We have noted that with regard to medical care, since *Estelle v. Gamble* (decided in 1976), the Court has required that to prevail in such cases, inmates must prove that officials' deprivation of medical services indicates a *deliberate indifference* to inmates. This stricter test has not been applied to prison physical conditions. We noted earlier in this chapter, however, that in 1991, the Court imposed the deliberate indifference standard to other prison cases, thus making it much more difficult for inmates to prevail in cases involving prison conditions.[103]

AIDS: A Special Prison Medical Problem

AIDS (acquired immune deficiency syndrome) has become a household word in the United States, as educational efforts to alert people to the deadly and rapidly spreading disease have had some success. Thousands of people have died of AIDS and, to date, there is no known cure. There is evidence that AIDS is spread primarily through sexual contact and intravenous drug use. Jails and prisons face acute problems concerning the spread of AIDS, as Spotlight 13.4 indicates. In addition, the prevalence of AIDS raises numerous legal issues in prisons.

One of those issues concerns whether prison officials may isolate or segregate persons with the HIV virus or AIDS. In 1991, the Eleventh Circuit upheld a segregation policy in the Alabama prisons. The court noted that this policy is a reasonable means of limiting behavior that might cause rapid spread of the disease. The lawsuit was brought by 150 inmates with HIV or AIDS who sought to have the policy eliminated. However, the court held that the lower court should reassess the plaintiffs' argument that by being segregated they were denied equal access to educational and recreational programs as well as legal assistance to which they had access before they were segregated.[104]

The following year, the Fifth Circuit upheld a Mississippi State Penitentiary policy of identifying and segregating HIV-positive inmates.[105] On the other hand, a federal district court in New York ruled that a policy of identifying and segregating an HIV-positive inmate violated her privacy and due process rights. Louise Nolley, who was confined for three months at the Erie County Holding Center, was incarcerated in a cell block reserved for mentally ill inmates and those with contagious diseases. Special red identifying marks were placed on her files, her transportation documents, and her clothing bag. The court held that the red sticker served no purpose other than to publicize Nolley's condition to prison officials as well as inmates serving in custodial positions and constituted an overreaction to AIDS hysteria; that Nolley did not constitute a threat to the general population; and that she was in greater danger by being placed in a cell block with persons who have contagious diseases.[106]

A report released in 1994 indicates that only Alabama and Mississippi segregate all inmates known to be HIV-positive. The trend in U.S. prisons and jails is away from blanket segregation of these inmates. Rather, they are considered on a case-by-case basis.[107] In addition, some prison systems are looking more closely into general conditions under which HIV-positive inmates are confined. California inmates protested their conditions and won some concessions, such as enhanced programs, improved medical care, and training of correctional officers to handle the problems of HIV-positive inmates.[108] Some other restrictions on HIV-positive inmates may be upheld, however. In 1993, the Ninth Circuit upheld a policy of prohibiting contact visits between such inmates and their attorneys.[109]

One final point concerning AIDS in prisons is the issue of contact visits between inmates and their families. In 1987, New York's highest court upheld prison officials' decision to prohibit conjugal visits between an inmate infected with AIDS and his wife. The court held that this refusal was not an unreasonable interference with the rights of the inmate or of his spouse.[110]

Right to a Smoke-Free Environment: A New Challenge

One last Eighth Amendment area deserves mention. For some years, our society has been faced with medical evidence of the harmful effects of smoking, including secondhand smoke. Many states have enacted legislation providing smoke-free environments or restricted smoking areas within establishments such as restaurants and public buildings. Administrative officials within some jails and prisons have instituted smoking restrictions or bans. In some facilities that do not have restrictions on smoking, inmates have filed suits arguing that the lack of a smoke-free environment exposes them to health risks and constitutes cruel and unusual punishment. These demands pose a serious dilemma, for as one court noted, "Nowhere is the practice of smoking a more imbedded institution than in the nation's prisons and jails, where the proportion of smokers to nonsmokers is many times higher than that of society in general." That court, however, refused to rule in favor of the inmate's demand for a smoke-free environment, suggesting that it was unworkable. The U.S. Supreme Court refused to review the case.[111]

Prior to 1993, lower federal courts issued conflicting rulings on the issue of whether the failure to provide inmates with a smoke-free environment constituted cruel and unusual punishment, and the U.S. Supreme Court had refused to hear and decide some of these cases.[112] In 1993, however, the Court agreed to hear a case, *Helling v. McKinney,* from the Ninth Circuit. In this case, the Court recognized the right of a Nevada inmate to offer proof that celling him with another inmate who smoked five packs of cigarettes a day subjected him to short-term as well as long-term health hazards. At the time the Supreme Court heard the case, however, the inmate had been moved to another institution and was not celled with the five-pack-a-day smoker. On remand, the inmate would have to prove that he was subjected to unreasonably high levels of environmental tobacco smoke (ETS), an objective factor.

Fourteenth Amendment Rights

Among other things, the Fourteenth Amendment prohibits the denial of life, liberty, or property without due process or equal protection, which are basic concepts of U.S. criminal justice systems. These concepts arise in prison settings for various reasons.

The due process clause may be invoked in inmate discipline cases. Such claims involve decisions regarding *good-time credits* (reducing the prison sentence based on number of days the confined offender behaved well), deprivation of freedom and privileges within the prison environment, segregated housing or solitary confinement, and transfers for disciplinary reasons. The focus in due process claims is on the procedures by which these decisions are made.

Inmates' due process claims must pass a two-part test. First, the claim must involve a liberty or property interest within the Fourteenth Amendment. If it does, the test is to determine what process is due in that situation. If there is no liberty or property right, decisions may be made without giving reasons to inmates. Further, the Court has held that inmates' freedom does not fall within the meaning of liberty. That right is extinguished when they are convicted. Thus, an inmate sentenced to ten years in prison has no liberty interest in getting out sooner. States may create liberty interests by statute; if they do, due process must be provided when that liberty is denied.

Olim v. Wakinekona illustrates the due process issue regarding transfer. Wakinekona was serving several sentences, including a life sentence without possibility of parole, in the Hawaii State Prison. When problems erupted in the maximum security control unit to which Wakinekona had been assigned after he was classified as a maximum security risk, a committee held hearings to determine who caused the disturbance. Testimony was taken from other inmates, and the discipline committee concluded that Wakinekona and another inmate were the troublemakers.

Wakinekona was notified of a hearing to determine whether he should be reclassified within the prison and whether he should be transferred to another prison. That hearing was held by the same committee that found him to be the troublemaker. Wakinekona attended the hearing with his retained counsel. He was told that despite his progress in vocational training in that prison, and his desire to continue that training, he was a security risk and a threat to the staff. Since Hawaii had no other maximum security facilities, he was transferred 4,000 miles away to Folsom State Prison in California.

Wakinekona sued, alleging that his right to due process was denied because the same committee that labeled him a troublemaker decided on the transfer. He claimed he was entitled to an unbiased tribunal in the latter decision. The Supreme Court held that Wakinekona did not have a liberty interest in remaining in Hawaii and therefore was not entitled to an unbiased tribunal. This translates to the notion that Wakinekona would not have been freed if he had remained in Hawaii. In other words, the possibility of being freed would not have been affected by his transfer. Consequently, the Court emphasized that often it is necessary to transfer inmates from one prison to another, even from one state to another, and that they have no liberty interest against such transfers.[113]

Even if the inmate can show that there is a liberty interest, the due process requirements are limited. In *Hewitt v. Helms,* inmate Helms, serving a term in a state correctional institution in Pennsylvania, sued prison officials on the claim that he was placed in administrative segregation without due process. Helms had been given a misconduct report for his alleged part in a riot in which correctional officers were injured. The Court agreed that he had a liberty interest in remaining in the general population. That interest derived from the state statutes and therefore does not necessarily apply in other cases. But, said the Court, that liberty interest does not entitle the inmate to more than a nonadversary and informal hearing.[114]

The Court's holding in *Helms* illustrates why it is so important to read the facts of cases and the reasoning of judges and justices carefully. The Supreme Court had decided *Wolff v. McDonnell,* a case involving reducing the good-time credits of an inmate (mentioned earlier in this chapter). In *Wolff,* the Court required that inmates who faced disciplinary charges for misconduct must be given twenty-four hours advance written notice of the charges against them; a right to call witnesses and present documentary evidence in defense, unless doing so would jeopardize institutional safety or correctional goals; the aid of a staff member or inmate in presenting a defense, provided the inmate is illiterate or the issue complex; an impartial tribunal; and a written statement of reasons relied on by the tribunal. *Wolff* did not require all elements of due process. The Court did not require that inmates be provided with an attorney at disciplinary hearings, and it limited the right to call and cross-examine witnesses. Prison officials may reduce the number of witnesses without giving reasons.[115]

In *Helms,* the Court emphasized that its holding in *Wolff* involved procedures that affected the length of time the inmate would be incarcerated. *Wolff* involved good-time credits, which cut the prison time served. Prison officials had revoked those credits. The Court said that is different from changing the status of an inmate within a prison or transferring an inmate to another prison. Subsequently, the Court held that when states provide for good-time credits, revocation of those credits may occur only when sufficient evidence has been presented for revocation.[116] In addition, the Court has held that due process requires that when prison officials refuse to call witnesses requested by an inmate at a disciplinary hearing, the officials must give reasons for their refusal, although they do not have to give written reasons.[117]

Another requirement of the Fourteenth Amendment is that all persons are guaranteed equal protection of the law. Equal protection claims in prisons are brought primarily by female inmates who allege that they do not have the same access as male inmates have to medical care, vocational training, and educational opportunities. An earlier study disclosed that, in most cases, this allegation was correct even in those instances in which female and male inmates occupied the same general facilities. In addition, it is argued that female inmates have additional needs, such as maternity care. Women have unique problems that may not be met within jail and prison facilities.[118]

On the other hand, women are more likely to have private rooms, which in some institutions are more like dormitory rooms than cells. Women may have greater freedom of movement within the prison. Male inmates may allege that these differences violate their equal protection rights. Prison officials may counter with the argument that, generally, female inmates do not engage in the serious violence that is characteristic of many maximum security prisons for men.

The critical issue, then, is to determine at what point female, as compared to male, inmates (or vice versa) are denied equal protection in prison. As a class, are women being discriminated against? The Supreme Court has not ruled on this issue; thus, the cases in the lower courts must be analyzed carefully. It is important to remember that the issue here is not whether a particular service such as educational programs *must* be provided, but, rather, whether if it is provided for one gender it must be provided for the other as well.[119]

One of the recent cases (*Klinger v. Nebraska Department of Correctional Services*) to analyze the equal protection claims of female inmates held that programs for female and male inmates must be "substantially equivalent." Equal protection requires "parity of treatment." There is no justification for paying women less per hour than men are paid. Nor is there justification for providing female inmates inferior medical services and dental care, less access to the law library, and fewer educational opportunities. Moreover, prison officials are liable in damages for these differences because they knew of the differences, refused to do anything to alleviate them, and thus exhibited deliberate indifference to the rights of female inmates.[120]

Prison Programs and Legal Rights

The rights discussed thus far are guaranteed by the Constitution, but what about activities and programs that are not required by that document? If inmates do not have a constitutional right to an education, to vocational training, and to work opportunities, should those activities be provided?

There is evidence that education and work opportunities are therapeutic for inmates.[121] Courts have not ruled that inmates have a right to any educational opportunities they may choose, and some courts have ruled that inmates do not have a right to a free college education.[122] In the past, the lack of educational or work opportunities, combined with a lack of other opportunities, has been cited by courts as evidence that the overall prison system does not meet minimum constitutional requirements. Recall, however, our earlier discussions in this chapter, indicating that in 1991, the Court ruled that to prevail on allegations of unconstitutional conditions within the prison, inmates must show deliberate indifference on the part of prison officials.

Inmates may be paid for their work, but compensation is not mandatory. A 1990 federal court noted that compelling an inmate to work without pay is not unconstitutional. The Thirteenth Amendment specifically allows involuntary servitude as punishment after conviction of a crime, and this court held that "compensating prisoners for work is not a constitutional requirement but, rather, 'is by the grace of the state.'"[123]

Analysis of Prison Reform

Despite changes in prison conditions, many jails and prisons remain under federal court orders, and this situation will continue until specified changes are made. Of particular concern are the problems of jail and prison overcrowding and inmate violence. These problems are related to all of the other issues discussed in this chapter.

Overcrowding

Overcrowding is the main problem faced by present-day prisons and jails. Part of jail overcrowding results from holding those sentenced to prison until space is

Case Study 13.7

Ruiz v. Estelle

The overcrowding at TDC exercises a malignant effect on all aspects of inmate life. Personal living space allotted to inmates is severely restricted. Inmates are in the constant presence of others. Although some degree of regimentation and loss of privacy is a normal aspect of life in any prison, the high population density at TDC leaves prisoners with virtually no privacy at any time of the day or night. Crowded two or three to a cell or in closely packed dormitories, inmates sleep with the knowledge that they may be molested or assaulted by their fellows at any time. Their incremental exposure to disease and infection from other inmates in such narrow confine-

ment cannot be avoided. They must urinate and defecate, unscreened, in the presence of others. Inmates in cells must live and sleep inches away from toilets; many in dormitories face the same situation. There is little respite from these conditions, for the salient fact of existence in TDC prisons is that inmates have wholly inadequate opportunities to escape the overcrowding in their living quarters.

Even when they are away from the housing areas, inmates are confronted with the inescapable reality that overcrowding is omnipresent within the prison confines. . . .

available in state and federal prisons. State and federal prison populations rose 7.4 percent in 1993, reaching a new record high that was nearly three times the 1980 level: a total of 948,881 inmates. It was estimated that between 18 and 29 percent of the nation's facilities were overcrowded at the end of 1993. These figures represent a 12 percent increase in the number of federal inmates.[124] One of the main reasons for the increase in prison inmates in recent years is the increase in persons convicted of drug offenses.[125] As of February 1994, thirty-nine states plus the District of Columbia, the Virgin Islands, and Puerto Rico were under federal court orders to reduce prison populations or to remedy other unconstitutional conditions.[126]

What effect does overcrowding have on jail and prison inmates? Research on the effects of overcrowding has been conducted for some years, but only recently has attention been given to the serious effects it might have on inmates.[127] Federal courts have accepted the position that overcrowding has negative effects on inmates. The excerpt in Case Study 13.7 from the 1980 federal court case involving the Texas prison system (TDC) is an example. In *Ruiz v. Estelle*, nearly every aspect of the TDC operation was found to be unconstitutional, and the prison was placed under court order to develop plans for bringing the system into compliance with constitutional standards. Living conditions in Texas prisons have improved in recent years, and as mentioned earlier, the system has been removed from monitoring, although overcrowding remains a daily concern. As the case citation indicates, *Ruiz* has a long history.[128]

In the fall of 1990, a federal court ruled that prison overcrowding was so severe that it constituted cruel and unusual punishment at the Pennsylvania State Correctional Institution at Pittsburgh. Inmates were double-celled in cells built for one person, resulting in such closeness that both could not stand at the same time—one had to lie on his bed. Inmates were confined to their cells for sixteen to twenty-two hours a day, and when they were out, they faced violence from other inmates, resulting in rapes and other assaults. The prison needed plumbing repairs. In addition to inmates, it housed mice, lice, birds, and bedbugs. The state was told bluntly to clean up its prison.[129]

Many, if not most, jail and prison problems are related to overcrowding.[130] Perhaps the most serious consequence is violence, a challenge correctional administrators will continue to face in the years to come.

WiseGuide Wrap-Up   Inmates must retain reasonable opportunities to exercise basic human rights while they are incarcerated. According to the U.S. Supreme Court:

> The continuing guarantee of these substantial rights to prison inmates is testimony to a belief that the way a society treats those who have transgressed against it is evidence of the essential character of that society.[131]

If that is the case, what must we think of ourselves for permitting a prison system in which three inmates in a California prison for the mentally ill died because of the extreme heat in their cells? The deaths in July 1991 occurred just one week after inmates at that institution filed a lawsuit protesting prison conditions as being medieval.

The preceding quote came from a 1984 Supreme Court decision. As noted earlier in this chapter, in 1991, the Court ruled that in order to prevail in lawsuits concerning prison conditions, inmates must prove that prison officials are indifferent to their plight. This new approach makes it more difficult for inmates to prevail. Surely one could argue that permitting inmates to die shows indifference. But could one have proved that before the inmates' deaths?

The Supreme Court has made it clear that some rights are forfeited by inmates and that security needs may permit restriction of rights normally recognized in prison. This chapter surveyed the historical and current approaches to the legal rights of inmates, beginning with a look at the traditional hands-off doctrine, in which federal courts refused to become involved in the daily administration and maintenance of prisons. As a result of recognized abuse of prisoners and the civil rights movement that brought the nation's attention to the problems of minorities in society and the conditions under which inmates lived, courts began to abandon the hands-off policy. Courts still defer to prison officials, but they no longer tolerate violations of basic rights.

This chapter examined the procedures for filing lawsuits, followed by an overview of the First, Fourth, Eighth, and Fourteenth Amendments of the Constitution. We discussed the First Amendment rights of inmates, including the importance of mail and other communication. We examined visitation, religious worship, freedom of assembly and self-government, and access to courts—all rights within the First Amendment. The chapter discussed the Fourth Amendment right to be free from unreasonable searches and seizures, the Eighth Amendment right to be free from cruel and unusual punishment, and the Fourteenth Amendment rights to due process and equal protection. All of these rights may be restricted if prison officials show it is necessary to maintain a legitimate prison goal such as security and safety.

Many of the problems of incarceration are related to overcrowding. There are two basic ways to solve this problem. We can build more facilities, a prospect discussed in an earlier chapter. Costs are overwhelming, however. Perhaps even more important, if we build them, we fill them, and the problem of a lack of prison space remains. The second solution is to reduce prison populations. This has been done in some states by enacting statutes that permit governors to declare an emergency situation when notified that the prison population has reached 95 percent (or some other figure) of legal capacity. Problems occur, however, when those released inmates commit new crimes.

This chapter focused on the rights of inmates, but these rights must be viewed in the context of society's needs. How can prisons achieve a balance between inmates' rights and the needs of safety? One problem with the recognition of inmates' rights is that there is not always public support for the approach; nor is there public support for spending more money on facilities. Inmates who file frivolous lawsuits are finding strong reactions not only from prison officials and the public, but also from judges and Supreme Court justices who are devising ways to reduce frivolous appeals.

The courts, the public, inmates, and prison officials all may be expected to continue the struggle of finding a reasonable balance that will permit society to be protected and to exercise its right to punish those who offend, while providing a system of punishment that does not demean and degrade inmates.

Notes

1. *Ruffin v. Commonwealth,* 62 Va. 790, 796 (1871).
2. *Wolff v. McDonnell,* 418 U.S. 539 (1974).
3. For a discussion on the law of prisoners' rights, see John W. Palmer, *Constitutional Rights of Prisoners,* 4th ed. (Cincinnati, OH: Anderson, 1991).
4. *Siegel v. Ragen,* 180 F.2d 785, 788 (7th Cir. 1950), cert. denied, 339 U.S. 990 (1950), reh'g denied, 340 U.S. 847 (1950).
5. *Bell v. Wolfish,* 441 U.S. 520 (1979).
6. *Time* (February 9, 1968), p. 14.
7. Murton, Thomas O. *The Dilemma of Prison Reform.* (New York: Holt, Rinehart and Winston, 1976).
8. *Holt v. Sarver,* 309 F. Supp. 362 (E.D. Ark. 1970). This case has a long history of remands and reversals leading to the Supreme Court case *Hutto v. Finey,* 437 U.S. 678 (1978), reh'g denied, 439 U.S. 1122 (1979).
9. *Graham v. Richardson,* 313 F. Supp. 34 (D. Ariz. 1970), aff'd., 403 U.S. 365, 375 (1971).
10. See *O'Lone v. Estate of Shabazz,* 482 U.S. 342 (1987), on remand, 829 F. 2d 32 (3rd Cir. 1987), and on remand, 829 F. 2d 31 (3rd Cir. 1998), superceded by statute as stated in *Allah v. Menei,* 844 F. Supp. 1056 (E.D. pa. 1994).
11. *Turner v. Safley,* 482 U.S. 78 (1987), superceded by statute as stated in *Campos v. Coughlin,* 1994 U.S. Dist LEXIS 5721 (S.D.N.Y. 3 May 1994).
12. *Turner v. Safley.*
13. *Turner v. Safley.*
14. *Joint Anti-Fascist Refugee Committee v. McGrath,* 341 U.S. 123, 162-163 (1951), Justice Frankfurter, concurring.
15. *Lowrane v. Achtyl* 20 F. 3d 529, 537 (2nd Cir. 1994).
16. *Liberta v. Kelly,* 839 F2d 77, 93 (2nd Cir. 1988), cert. denied, 488 U.S. 832 (1988), citations omitted.
17. *McCleskey v. Zant,* 499 U.S. 467 (1991), reh'g. denied, 501 U.S. 1224 (1991), and stay denied sub. nom., 112 S. Ct. 37 (1991), cert. denied sub. nom., 112 S. Ct. 38 (1991).
18. "A Window on the Court," *The New York Times,* (May 6, 1992), p.1, referring to the Court's decision in *Keeney v. Tamayo-Reyes,* 112 S. Ct. 1715 (May 1992). The federal statute at issue is codified in the U.S. Code, Title 28, Section 2254 (1994).
19. *O'Neal v. McAninch,* 513 U.S. 432 (1995).
20. U.S. Code, Title 42, Section 1983 (1994).
21. For an extensive analysis of 1983 actions, see H. E. Barrineau III, *Civil Liability in Criminal Justice,* (Cincinnati, OH: Anderson, 1987). For a discussion of the possibilities for suing prison officials in their personal capacities for violation of Section 1983 rights, see David L. Abney and Lynne W. Abney, "Corrections Law: The Fate of Prisoner Damages Actions after *Will v. Michigan Department of State Police," Criminal Law Bulletin* 26 (March-April, 1990): 167–171. For a contrary opinion, see Robert Bartels, "Corrections Law: Why Will Won't Destroy Section 1983 Damages Actions," *Criminal Law*

Bulletin 27 (January-February, 1991): 59–66. The case in question is *Will v. Michigan Department of State Police,* 491 U.S. 58 (1989).
22. *Estelle v. Gamble,* 429 U.S. 97, 106 (1976), reh'g. denied, 429 U.S. 1066 (1977), and on remand, 554 F. 2d 653 (5th Cir. 1977), reh'g. denied, 59 F. 2d 1217 (5th Cir. 1977), cert. denied, 434 U.S. 974 (1977), citations omitted.
23. *Wilson v. Seiter,* 501 U.S. 294 (1991), footnotes and citations omitted, remanded, 940 F. 2d. 664 (6th Cir. 1991).
24. *Wilson v. Seiter,* 501 U.S. 294 (1991), Justice White, dissenting, remanded, 940 F.2d. 664 (6th Cir. 1991).
25. *Farmer v. Brennan,* 1994 U.S. LEXIS 4274 (1994).
26. *Hudson v. McMillian,* 112 S. Ct. 995 (1992), on remand. 962 F. 2d. 522 (5th Cir. 1992).
27. *Bell v. Wolfish,* 441 U.S. 520, 545 (1979); *Rhodes v. Chapman,* 452 U.S. 337 (1981).
28. *Procunier v. Martinez,* 416 U.S. 396, 413 (1974), overruled in part by *Thornburgh v. Abbott,* 490 U.S. 401 (1989), superceded by statute as stated in *Lawson v. Dugger,* 844 F. Supp. 1538 (S.D. Fla. 1994).
29. *Thornburgh v. Abbott,* 490 U.S. 401 (1989), superceded by statute as stated in *Lawson v. Dugger,* 844 F. Supp. 1538 (S.D. Fla. 1994).
30. *McNamara v. Moody,* 606 F. 2d. 621 (5th Cir. 1979), cert. denied, 447 U.S. 929 (1980).
31. *McNamara v. Moody.*
32. *Bressman v. Farrier,* 825 F. Supp. 231 (N.D. Iowa, 1993).
33. *Travis v. Norris,* 805 F. 2d. 806, 808 (8th Cir. 1986).
34. *Smith v. Delo,* 995 F. ed 827 (1993).
35. *United States v. Stotts,* 925 F. 2d. 83, 85 (4th Cir. 1991), later proceeding sub. nom., 1991 U.S. Dist. LEXIS 15643 (E.D.N.C. 1991).
36. *Bell v. Wolfish,* 441 U.S. 520 (1979).
37. *Turner v. Safley,* 482 U.S. 78 (1987), superceded by statute as stated in *Campos v. Coughlin,* 1994 U.S. Dist. LEXIS 5721 (S.D.N.Y. 3 May 1994).
38. N.Y. CLS Exec., Section 632-a (1994).
39. *In re Berkowitz,* 430 N.Y.S. 2d. 904 (N.Y. Sup. Ct. 1979).
40. *Children of Bedford, Inc. v. Petromelis,* 573 N.E. 2d. 541 (N.Y. 1991), vacated, 112 S. Ct. 859 (1992), and different results reached on reh'g., 79 N.Y. 2d 972 (N.Y. 1992).
41. *Simon and Schuster, Inc. v. Members of the New York State Crime Victims Board,* 724 F. Supp. 170 (S.D.N.Y. 1989), aff'd. sub. nom., 916 F. 2d 777 (2nd Cir. 1990), reversed, 112 S. Ct. 501 (1991).
42. New York CLS Exec. 632-a (1994).
43. "Rolling and Fiancee Can't Profit from Story," *Tallahassee Democrat* (May 19, 1993), p. 2c. The case is *Rolling v. State,* 619 So. 2d. 20 (Fla. Dist. Ct. App. 5th Dist. 1993), corrected, 18 Fla. L. Weekly D 1294 (Fla. Dist. Ct. App. 5th Dist. 1993).
44. National Conference of Commissioners on Uniform State Laws (NCCUSL), Model Sentencing and Corrections Act, Section 40115. Comment (1979) (citations omitted).

45. *Martin v. Wainwright,* 525 F. 2d. 983 (5th Cir. 1976).

46. *Doe v. Sparks,* 733 F. Supp. 227 (W.D. Pa. 1990).

47. *Block v. Rutherford,* 468 U.S. 576 (1984).

48. See Laura T. Fishman, *Women at the Wall: A Study of Prisoners' Wives Doing Time on the Outside.* (New York: State University of New York Press, 1990); Fishman, "Prisoners and Their Wives: Marital and Domestic Effects of Telephone Contacts and Home Visits," *International Journal of Offender Therapy and Comparative Criminology* 32 (April, 1988): 55–65.

49. "Prisoner Marriages Setting Records," *Tallahassee Democrat,* (December 11, 1989), p. 5.

50. *Langone v. Coughlin,* 712 F. Supp. 1061 (N.D.N.Y. 1989).

51. See *McCray v. Sullivan,* 509 F. 2d 1332 (5th Cir. 1975), remanded, 399 F. Supp. 271 (S.D. Ala. 1975), cert. denied, 423 U.S. 859 (1975).

52. *Turner v. Safley,* 482 U.S. 78 (1987), superceded by statute as stated in *Campos v. Coughlin,* 1994, U.S. Dist. LEXIS 5721 (S.D.N.Y. 3 May 1994).

53. See *Goodwin v. Turner,* 908 F. 2d. 1395 (8th Cir. 1990), reh'g. denied in banc, 1990 U.S. App. LEXIS 17169 (8th Cir. 1990).

54. *Pell v. Procunier,* 417 U.S. 817 (1974).

55. *Houchins v. KQED, Inc.,* 438 U.S. 1 (1978).

56. See, for example, a report by the National Council on Crime and Delinquency, "Does Involvement in Religion Help Prisoners Adjust to Prison?" It is available from the Council, 685 Market Street, Suite 620, San Francisco, CA, 94105.

57. *Cruz v. Beto,* 405 U.S. 319, 322, text and n. 2 (1972), appeal after remand, *Cruz v. Estelle,* 497 F. 2d. 496 (5th Cir. 1974).

58. See *Employment Division of Oregon v. Smith,* 494 U.S. 872 (1990), reh'g. denied, 496 U.S. 913 (1990), remanded, 799 p. 2d. 148 (Ore. 1991).

59. See, for example, *O'Lone v. Estate of Shabazz,* 482 U.S. 342 (1987), and on remand, sub. nom., 829 F. 32 (3rd Cir. 1987), and on remand, sub. nom., 839 F.2d. 32 (3rd Cir. 1987), superceded by statute as stated in *Allah v. Menei,* 844 F. Supp. 1056 (E.D. pa. 1994).

60. See David L. Abney, "Our Daily Bread—Prisoners' Rights to a Religious Diet," *Case and Comment* 90 (March-April, 1985): 28–38.

61. *LaFevers v. Saffle,* 936 F. 2d. 1117 (10th Cir. 1991).

62. *Scott v. Mississippi Department of Corrections,* 961 F. 2d 77 (5th Cir. 1992).

63. *Mark v. Nix,* 983 F. 2d. 138 (8th Cir. 1993), reh'g. denied, 1993 U.S. LEXIS 2409 (8th Cir. 15 February, 1993).

64. See "Religious Freedom Act Worries AGs," *American Bar Association* 80 (February, 1994): 20. The Act is codified at U.S. Code, Title 42, Sections 200bb et seq. (1994).

65. *Jones v. North Carolina Prisoner's Union, Inc.,* 433 U.S. 119, 132 (1977).

66. *Ex Parte Hull,* 312 U.S. 546 (1941), reh'g. denied, 312 U.S. 716 (1941).

67. *Johnson v. Avery,* 393 U.S. 483 (1969). For a discussion of jailhouse lawyers, see Dragan Milovanovic, "Jailhouse Lawyers and Jailhouse Lawyering," *International Journal of the Sociology of Law* 16 (November, 1988): 455–475.

68. See, for example, "His Own Case Was Futile, So He Now Works for Others," *The Miami Herald,* (November 19, 1989), p. 4B.

69. *Bounds v. Smith,* 430 U.S. 817, 821, 828, 831 (1977), citations omitted.

70. See *Blake v. Berman,* 877 F. 2d 145 (1st Cir. 1989).

71. *Casey v. Lewis,* 834 F. Supp. 1553 (D. Ariz. 1992), later proceedings, 834 F. Supp. 1553 (D. Ariz. 1993), 834 F. Supp. 1569 (1993), 834 F. Supp. 1009 (D. Ariz. 1993).

72. *Peterkin v. Jeffes,* 661 F. Supp. 895 (E.D. Pa. 1987), aff'd. in part and vacated in part, 855 F. 2d. 1021 (3rd Cir. 1988), on remand, 1989 U.S. Dist. LEXIS 13828 (E.D. Pa. 1989), later proceedings, 953 F. 2d 1380 (3rd Cir. 1992).

73. See *Casey v. Lewis,* 834 F. Supp. 1553 (D. Ariz. 1992); later proceedings, 834 F. Supp. 1477 (D. Ariz. 1993); 834 F. Supp. 1569 (D. Ariz. 1993); 837 F. Supp. 1009 (D. Ariz. 1993).

74. See *Knop v. Johnson,* 977 F. 2d 996 (6th Cir. 1992), cert. denied sub. nom., 113 S. Ct. 1415 (1993), and cost/fees proceeding sub. nom., 1994 U.S. Dist. LEXIS 867 (W.D. Mich. 7 Jan. 1994), reversing a lower court holding that prison officials must provide either attorneys or paralegals for inmates.

75. *Knop v. Johnson,* 977 F. 2d 966 (6th Cir. 1992), cert. denied sub. nom., 113 S. Ct. 1415 (1993).

76. *Prisoners' Legal Association v. Roberson,* 822 F. Supp. 185 (D.N.J. 1993).

77. *Kaiser v. Sacramento County,* 780 F. Supp. 1309 (E.D. Cal. 1991).

78. *Murray v. Giarratano,* 492 U.S. 1 (1989). See also *Douglas v. California,* 372 U.S. 353 (1963), reh'g. denied, 373 U.S. 905 (1963); and *Griffin v. Illinois,* 351 U.S. 12 (1956), reh'g. denied, 351 U.S. 958 (1956).

79. *Glover v. Johnson,* 1994 U.S. Dist. LEXIS 5999 (E.D. Mich. 1994). The Supreme Court case concerning the right of parenthood is *Meyer v. Nebraska,* 262 U.S. 390 (1923).

80. *Knop v. Johnson,* 977 F. 2d. 996 (6th Cir. 1992), cert. denied sub. nom., 113 S. Ct. 1415 (1993).

81. *Wolff v. McDonnell,* 418 U.S. 539 (1974).

82. *Knop v. Johnson,* 685 F. Supp. 636 (W.D. Mich. 1988), cert. denied sub. com., 713 S. Ct. 1415 (1993).

83. "Judge Awards $1.48 Million to Lawyers in Michigan Prison Case," *Criminal Justice Newsletter* 20, (April 17, 1989): 6.

84. "Flood of Prisoner Rights Suits Brings Effort to Limit Filings," *New York Times,* (March 21, 1994), p. 1.

85. *Hudson v. Palmer,* 468 U.S. 517 (1984), citation omitted, remanded, *Palmer v. Hudson,* 744 F. 2d. 22 (4th Cir. 1984).

86. *Block v. Rutherford,* 468 U.S. 576 (1984).

87. *Bell v. Wolfish,* 441 U.S. 520 (1979).

88. See *Covino v. Patrissi,* 967 F. 2d. 73 (2nd. Cir. 1992).

89. *State v. Palmer,* 751 P. 2d. 975, 976, 977 (Ariz, App. 1987), footnotes and citations omitted.

90. See, for example, *Covino v. Patrissi,* 967 F. 2d. 73 (2nd Cir. 1992).

91. See *Hunter v. Auger,* 672 F. 2d. 668 (8th Cir. 1982); and *Marriot v. Smith,* 931 F. 2d. 517, reh'g en banc denied, 1991 U.S. App. LEXIS 13199 (8th Cir. 1991).

92. See *Marriott v. Smith,* 931 F. 2d. 517 (8th Cir. 1991), reh'g. en banc denied, 1991 U.S. App. LEXIS 13199 (8th Cir. 1991).

93. *Giles v. Ackerman,* 746 F. 2d. 614 (9th Cir. 1984), cert. denied, 471 U.S. 1053 (1985).

94. *Turner v. Safley,* 482 U.S. 78 (1987).

95. See *Tim v. Gunter,* 917 F. 2d. 1093 (8th Cir. 1990). Cert. denied, 501 U.S. 1209 (1991) (permissible for female officers to conduct pat-down search on male inmates).

96. *Timm v. Gunter,* 917 F. 2d. 1093 (8th Cir. 1990), cert. denied, 501 U.S. 1209 (1991), Judge Bright dissenting.

97. For a discussion of the case, see the following: Doretha M. Van Slyke, Note. "*Hudson v. McMillian,* and Prisoners' Rights: The Court Giveth and the Court Taketh Away," *American University Law Review* 42 (1993):1727–1760; Dale E. Butler, Comment. "Cruel and Unusual Punishment Takes One Step Forward, Two Steps Back," *Denver University Law Review* 70 (1993): 393–412; and Donald H. Wallace, "The Eighth Amendment and Prison Deprivations: Historical Revisions," *Criminal Law Bulletin* 30 (January-February, 1994): 5–29.

98. *Hickey v. Reeder,* 12 F. 3d. 754 (8th Cir. 1993), reh'g. denied, 1994 U.S. App. LEXIS 1614 (8th Cir. 1 Feb. 1994).

99. *Estelle v. Gamble,* 429 U.S. 97 (1976), reh'g. denied, 429 U.S. 1066 (1977), remanded, 554 F 2d. 653 (5th Cir. 1977), cert. denied, 434 U.S. 974 (1977).

100. *Whitley v. Albers,* 475 U.S. 312, 313 (1986), appeal after remand, 788 F. 2d. 650 (9th Cir. 1986). See also *Ruark v. Drury,* 21 F. 3d 213 (8th Cir. 1994).

101. *Ruiz v. Estelle,* 679 F. 2d. 1115 (5th Cir. 1982), amended in part, vacated in part, reh'g. denied in part, 688 F. 2d 266 (5th Cir. 1982), cert. denied, 460 U.S. 1042 (1983), appeal after remand sub. nom.,

724 F. 2d. 1149 (5th Cir. 1984), later proceedings sub. nom., 661 F. Supp. 112 (S. D. Tex. 1986); 981 F. 2d. 1256 (5th Cir. 1992).

102. "Settlement Ends Federal Control of Texas Prisons," *New York Times,* (December 13, 1992), p. 17. For an analysis of the Texas prison system, see Steve J. Martin and Sheldon Ekland-Olson, *Texas Prisons: The Walls Came Tumbling Down.* (Austin: Texas Monthly Press, 1987).

103. *Estelle v. Gamble,* 429 U.S. 97 (1976), reh'g. denied, 429 U.S. 1066 (1977), remanded, 554 F. 2d 653 (5th Cir. 1977). The 1991 case is *Wilson v. Seiter,* 501 U.S. 294 (1991), remanded, 940 F. 2d. 664 (6th Cir. 1991).

104. "Court Backs Policy to Separate Inmates with the AIDS virus," *The New York Times,* (September 20, 1991), p. 4. See *Harris v. Thigpen,* 941 F. 2d. 1495 (11th Cir. 1991).

105. *Moore v. Mabus,* 976 F. 2d 268 (5th Cir. 1992).

106. *Nolley v. County* of Erie, 776 F. Supp. 715 (W.D.N.Y. 1991), supplemental opinion, 802 F. Supp. 898 (W.D.N.Y. 1992), set aside, on reconsideration, remanded, 798 F. Supp. 123 (W.D.N.Y. 1992).

107. "Prisons and Jails Integrating More HIV-Positive Inmates," *Criminal Justice Newsletter,* 25 (March 1, 1994): 6.

108. For a discussion see "California Inmates Win Better Prison AIDS Care," *The New York Times,* (January 25, 1993), p. 7.

109. *Casey v. Lewis,* 834 F. Supp. 1553 (D.Ariz. 1992), later proceedings, 834 F. Supp. 1477 (D. Ariz. 1993), 834 F. Supp. 1569 (D. Ariz. 1993), 837 F. Supp. 1009 (D. Ariz. 1993). For a discussion of female inmates and AIDS, see David K Marcus and Roger Bibace, "A Developmental Analysis of Female Prisoners' Conceptions of AIDS," *Criminal Justice and Behavior* 20 (September, 1993): 249–253.

110. *Doe v. Coughlin,* 523 N.Y.S. 2d. 782 (N.Y.Ct. App. 1987), reargument denied, 70 N.Y. 2d. 1002 (1988), cert. denied, 488 U.S. 879 (1988).

111. *Doughty v. Board of County Commissioners for the County of Weld,* 731 F. Supp. 423 (D. Colo., 1989).

112. See, for example, *McKinney v. Anderson,* 959 F. 2d. 853 (9th Cir. 1992), on remand of 924 F. 2d. 1500 (9th Cir. 1991), aff'd., remanded, 113 S. Ct. 2475 (1993), on remand, remanded, 5 F. 3d. 365 (9th Cir. 1993), holding that under some circumstances smoke within a prison may constitute cruel and unusual punishment.

113. *Olim v. Wakinekona,* 461 U.S. 238 (1983), remanded, 716 F. 2d. 1279 (9th Cir. 1983).

114. *Hewitt v. Helms,* 459 U.S. 460 (1983), remanded, 712 F. 2d. 48 (3rd Cir. 1983).

115. *Wolff v. McDonnell,* 418 U.S. 539 (1974).

116. *Superintendent, Massachusetts Correctional Institution v. Hill,* 472 U.S. 445 (1985).

117. *Ponte v. Real,* 471 U.S. 491 (1985), remanded sub. nom., 482 N.E. 2d, 1188 (Mass. 1985).

118. *Jails in America: An Overview of Issues.* (Laurel, MD: American Correctional Association in Cooperation with the National Coalition for Jail Reform, 1985), p. 24.

119. For a general discussion, see Charlotte A. Nesbitt, "Female Offenders: A Changing Population, *Corrections Today* 48 (February, 1986): 76–80.

120. *Klinger v. Nebraska Dept. of Correctional Services,* 824 F. Supp. 1374 (D. Neb. 1993).

121 See Hans Toch, "Regenerating Prisoners Through Education," *Federal Probation* 51 (September, 1987): 61–66.

122. See *Hernandez v. Johnston,* 833 F. 2d. 1316 (9th Cir. 1987).

123. *Murray v. Mississippi Department of Corrections,* 911 F. 2d. 1167 (5th Cir. 1990), cert. denied, 111 S. Ct. 760 (1991).

124. Bureau of Justice Statistics. *Prisoners in 1993.* (Washington, DC: U.S. Department of Justice, 1994), p. 1.

125. See "Drug Crimes Push Record Prison Population," *The New York Times,* (May 10, 1993), p. 16.

126 *Status Report: The Courts and the Prisons.* (Washington, DC: National Prison Project, 1994), as cited in "Status Report on Prison Lawsuits," *Criminal Justice Newsletter* 25 (February 15, 1994): 8.

127. For more information on the effects of jail and prison overcrowding, see Michael S. Vaughn, "Listening to the Experts: A National Study of Correctional Administrators' Responses to Prison Overcrowding," *Criminal Justice Review* 18 (Spring, 1993): 12–25.

128. *Ruiz v. Estelle,* 503 F. Supp. 1265 (S.D. Tex. 1980), aff'd. in part, and vacated in part, modified in part, appeal dismissed in part, 679 F. 2d 1115 (5th Cir. 1982), amended in part, vacated in part, 688 F. 2d. 266 (5th Cir. 1982), cert. denied, 460 U.S. 1042 (1983), appeal after remand, sub. nom, 724 F 2d 1149 (5th Cir. 1984), later proceedings sub. nom., 661 F. Supp. 112 (S.D. Tex. 1986); 981 F. 2d 1256 (5th Cir. 1992).

129. *Tillery v. Owens,* 719 F. Supp. 1256 (W.D. Pa. 1989), aff'd., 907 F. 2d. 418 (3rd Cir. 1990), cert. denied sub. nom., 112 S.Ct. 343 (1991), and aff'd. w/o opinion, 993 F. 2d. 879 (3rd Cir. 1993).

130. For more detailed analyses of jail and prison overcrowding and their effects, see Paul B. Paulus, *Prison Crowding: A Psychological Perspective.* (New York: Springer-Verlag, 1988).

131. *Hudson v. Palmer,* 468 U.S. 517, 523, 525, (1984), on remand, 744 F. 2d. 22 (4th Cir. 1984).

Special Issues

Corrections: Y2K and Beyond

The school massacre in Littleton, Colorado, in the spring of 1999 was one of several criminal acts involving juveniles that have taken center stage in public attention. As this book is being finalized, news stories raise perplexing questions about the nature of this particular violent act. Stories focusing on the two killers and their backgrounds are not hard to find in light of a social need to explain the unexplainable. The question that you, the student of corrections, should ask is "What are we to do with offenders—juveniles and adults alike—who commit violent criminal acts? Hopefully, by now, this book has provided enough insight to help you formulate several responses to this question.

In earlier chapters, we examined the various options available to members of society who are concerned with the handling of criminal offenders. As was clear from the first few chapters of this book, punishment has been administered in such unique ways that it seems sometimes as if we have exhausted all of our options for new ideas. In fact, I wonder if some of those who call themselves "innovators" of correctional ideas ever take the time to study the history of punishment. If they do, they would quickly learn that most of what they regard as "new ideas" have been used before, and have resulted in high recidivism and incarceration rates.

This final chapter explores the decline of an emphasis on the rehabilitative ideal, noting the return to a punishment philosophy of retribution. It also explores various perspectives on the future of corrections, including the aging of the inmate population. We also examine the existing correctional trends and their impact on the future of corrections.

Key Terms

AVIAN (Advanced Vehicle Notification System)
privatization

Decline of the Rehabilitative Ideal

In 1959, law professor Francis A. Allen coined the term "rehabilitative ideal."[1] This "ideal" was characterized by the juvenile court, probation, parole, and individualized sentencing and treatment. The rehabilitative ideal was based on the premise that human behavior is the result of antecedent causes that may become known by objective analysis, thus permitting the scientific control of human behavior. The assumption was that the offender could and should be treated, not punished.

As we have learned, the rehabilitative ideal has come under strong attack in recent years. In 1977, Allen admitted that the "case against the rehabilitative ideal has achieved spectacular success. Rarely, has there been so precipitous and complete a reversal of professional opinion. . . . The concept of deserved punishment is to be refurbished and pressed into service."[2] The result has been a nationwide attack on the indeterminate sentence and parole and a decrease in the support of a treatment/rehabilitation rationale for imprisonment.

The main reason for the decline of faith in the rehabilitative ideal is that many perceive that the treatment approach has not been successful. Several years ago, David L. Bazelon, Chief Judge of the United States Court of Appeals in Washington, D.C., concluded that the basic problem with rehabilitation as a justification for punishment was that it "should never have been sold on the promise that it would reduce crime."[3] Nevertheless, it was promised that treatment would be effective in reducing the rates of recidivism when offenders are released from prison. As crime rates continued to soar, the public became disillusioned with the rehabilitative approach.

The basic attack on the effectiveness of treatment came in 1974 when Robert Martinson published his article entitled, "What Works?—Questions and Answers About Prison Reform,"[4] in which he reported the results of his survey of the literature on corrections programs published between 1945 and 1967. Martinson concluded that treatment has been ineffective in reducing rates of recidivism.

Many criticized Martinson's work. It was alleged that he really had very little to do with the original report on the effectiveness of treatment. The original report was criticized because only treatment studies prior to 1967 were selected for analysis. He was criticized for his failure to include all types of treatment programs and for ignoring the effects of some treatment programs on some individuals. He did not focus on the "differential value" and the "degree of effectiveness" of the method. It has been argued that the conclusions in his article were inconsistent with the information reported in his book. Ted Palmer attacked Martinson for asking "What works?" instead of "Which methods work best for *which* types of offenders, and under *what* conditions or in what types of settings?"[5]

It was further argued that Martinson ignored the possibility that the characteristics of the researcher are important in analyzing the results of the research. Further, Martinson's study failed to consider the possibility that treatment might be effective immediately, but may "fade" after the inmate is released from the correctional facility. Martinson did not design his study to permit quantitative and objective analysis of the partial effects of treatment programs. Finally, it was alleged that treatment in correctional institutions has been about as effective as have efforts to combat other social problems.

Was Martinson correct? It really seems to have made little difference whether he was correct in his initial assessment of the failure of treatment methods. He said what many people wanted to hear. He gained considerable exposure among professionals as well as the lay public, and his work is among the most frequently cited "evidence" that treatment has not been effective, and that we should return to a philosophy of retribution as a justification for punishment.

The Return to Retribution

For centuries, philosophers have debated justifications for punishment. We have traced the movement from an emphasis on retribution and deterrence to the embodiment of the rehabilitative ideal and, most recently, back to a form of retribution. What is the nature and meaning of this movement?

Historically, the concept of retribution usually meant revenge, often manifested in the doctrine of "an eye for an eye and a tooth for a tooth." Under the doctrine of revenge, an offender should be treated by society in the same way that the offender treated his or her victim. Thus, the hands of a thief would be removed and the eye of the spy gouged. The extreme form of the doctrine was manifested in the use of capital punishment in the cases of those who murdered.

More recently, the doctrine of retribution has come back into favor, but this time the emphasis is on "just deserts," which does not necessarily mean an "eye for an eye and a tooth for a tooth," although in some cases that would be considered appropriate. "Just deserts" means that the offender receives the punishment he or she deserves, and no more. According to the proponents of this model, deterrence of others, protection of society, or rehabilitation of the offender may result from punishment, but they should not be the *reason* for punishment.

The Justice Model

One of the persons most cited as responsible for the popularity of the Justice Model is David Fogel, who expressed his views in his book ". . . *We are the Living Proof . . .": The Justice Model for Corrections.*[6] Fogel argued that punishment is necessary for implementation of the criminal law, a law based on the theory that people act as a result of their own free will. His approach is similar to that of the classical writers, who took the position that criminal behavior is rational and is based on hedonism. People choose to behave in a certain way because they gain pleasure from that behavior. However, if the pain (that is, punishment) to be inflicted as a result of that behavior is greater than the pleasure to be gained from the act, people will refrain from the illegal act.

According to Fogel, offenders act on the basis of free will, and they should be held responsible for their acts. They (the offenders) become the focal point of the criminal justice system. Fogel emphasized that all of the agencies of the criminal justice system should be carried out in "a milieu of justice." That means that justice for the offender does not stop with the due process accorded at trial; it continues throughout all of the stages of the system. Justice for offenders means that once they are incarcerated, the state will not attempt to force them to change, to reform, to be rehabilitated.

The Aging Prison Population

There is a current trend to demonize (i.e., label as evil) all offenders who are found guilty for any drug-related offense. These individuals are presently facing punitive and long prison sentences—some of these sentences were enacted during the Reagan administration in the 1980s. Inevitably, these longer sentences have precipitated the rising trend of the prison population. As baby boomers approach their retirement age, prisons find themselves with the complex problem of having to deal with older inmates who were either incarcerated at an older age or were sentenced to prison for life when they were young.

Most of these individuals occupy trustworthy jobs in prisons. They are viewed as inmates who pose very little risk of escaping. In fact, some correctional staff members have sympathy for them. The fact that most of the elderly offenders have been in prison for long terms prompts them to be dependent on the correctional system. If released, this dependency is usually not met in a world where independence is not only valued, but becomes a method of survival.

Specifically, the "Three Strikes and You're Out" law has been instrumental in the incarceration of inmates who, after committing a third, similar violent crime, are sentenced to life without parole. As other states adopt this law, more and more inmates are expected to die from natural causes behind prison bars. Thus, the citizenry should expect to pay not only for more prisons, but also for the "special" needs of older inmates. These include, among many other items, long-term medical treatment, special housing, and appropriate facilities to accommodate wheelchairs and walkers. In addition to the "obvious" needs of inmates, it is expected that older inmates will require special diets, prescription drugs, eyeglasses, and so on. Also, staff will need special training to accommodate the special needs of some older inmates.

Another concern is the older inmate's vulnerability to younger inmates. Since prison represents Darwin's survival of the fittest, it can only be expected that older inmates will often be victimized by the younger, more agile inmates. If a particular facility was to separate the older and younger inmates (what may appear as a plausible solution to the problem mentioned earlier), the citizens in that particular jurisdiction should be ready to pay higher taxes in order to build these special units.

Lessons Learned from the Past

The National Institute of Corrections (NIC) sponsored a national conference in 1996 to discuss what works and what doesn't in planning for the future of corrections.[7] The NIC asserted that programs specially designed for the specific needs of offenders were "effective." Some of these programs range from boot camps for young street offenders to dormitories for illiterate substance abusers. These programs are designed for sex offenders, high school dropouts, the mentally ill and retarded, and the elderly. Conference attendees recommended that these programs continue to be part of the correctional system.

Also, community corrections was regarded as successful in that it allows the state to effectively impose local sanctions on nonviolent offenders. The argument was made that although many new laws call for longer, more definite sentences for recidivists, some also contain a "presumption for local punishment." Thus, the laws leave it up to the states to administer punishment, especially for nonviolent offenders. This trend allows states to have more control and should continue as a part of the correctional system.

One of the last points made by those who attended the NIC conference was that technology has been and will continue to be part of corrections.[8] Technology works by allowing everyone to work harder and smarter. For instance, many states are now implementing telemedicine—a program that allows inmates to participate in medical conferences with doctors electronically instead of being transported to a medical facility for a consultation. This technology, although expensive to implement, is reported as being highly effective in reducing the costs associated with the transportation and supervision of inmates during medical consultations outside the prison facility. NIC conference attendees also concluded that computers and databases are highly effective in the proper management and operation of prison facilities around the United States. Unquestionably, technology will continue to serve the custodial and operational needs of American corrections.

As we have seen throughout this text, prison populations were relatively stable in the 1960s. Since that time, however, we have witnessed an unprecedented increase in incarceration rates in the United States. Although I have attempted to explain the reasons for this increase, we must ask "What does this trend mean for the future of corrections?"

To answer this question, we must first keep in mind that there is no shortage of images of what the future holds for the correctional system in the United States. Furthermore, there is no universal consensus on predictions about the future of American corrections. For instance, criminologist James Fox recently predicted that the rising violence of juveniles is the leading edge of a "blood bath" that is bound to take place in the future. This view was disputed by Professor James Austin, executive director of the National Council on Crime and Delinquency. For some, increases in violent crime demand even more extensive incarceration sentences. However, for others, incarceration fails to deter crime, and furthers the plight of already disadvantaged minorities.

Ben Crouch has recently examined some aspects of society and corrections that, in his opinion, point toward what things might be like in ten or fifteen years for the correctional system.[9] Specifically, Crouch contended that the existing social, demographic, economic, and political conditions in the United States account for a great proportion of the correctional status quo. These factors also enable a further understanding of what the future holds for this complex system.

Crouch begins his assessment by stating that demographic shifts in the United States have influenced crime and imprisonment rates. Specifically, he points out that as the baby boomers entered their late teens (in the late 1960s), crime increased rapidly.[10] However, it was not until the mid-1970s that a higher crime rate affected the incarceration rate. One reason for this delay is the fact that criminal justice systems in the 1960s may have been hesitant to incarcerate young offenders, who were instead given probation. Crouch explains that it did not take long for the system to run out of patience. As a result, offenders were incarcerated more frequently.

Economic and occupational structure shifts also led to the increase of crime and incarceration rates. Many argue that as America moved from a unionized, manufacturing economy to a more competitive and less unionized economy, the urban poor and minorities were severely affected.[11] Of all the minorities, African Americans are reportedly one of the most affected groups—although Hispanics are becoming more affected as their population grows.

It is clear, then, that all of these changes created an environment suitable for violence, drug addiction, and other vices. The growing incarceration rate and the increase in juvenile violence have led many to predict a future full of chaos and disparity. These predictions have also reached the shores of American corrections. In fact, Crouch and others have ventured into the task of predicting the future of corrections.

According to Crouch, the shifts mentioned earlier provide information about the future of American corrections. Crouch argues that the economy will increasingly demand skills and attitudes that large, poor, and urban populations have a very small opportunity to acquire. Thus, members of these populations are unable to compete in the conventional economy. Out of their inability, Crouch argues, they will likely turn to crime and, at times, even high-profile acts or collective violence. This will continue to prompt public demand for tougher sanctions.[12]

Today's Trends and Their Impact on the Future of Corrections

Although some disagree, Crouch sustains that crime rates will fall over the next few decades because there will be a decrease in the number of young people and an increase in the number of older persons. This may lower the incarceration rate. However, Crouch warns that this may not occur if prison officials find it easy to fill the newly built prisons and if the existing conservative agenda continues its influence over the legislative and political processes. If these two trends continue, prisons in the twenty-first century will likely be large enterprises that house high numbers of unskilled, poor, powerless, and angry minorities.[13] In other words, as many critical criminologists contend, prisons will continue their legacy of serving as houses for the oppressed. We will now explore some of the specific predicaments that prisons are likely to face at the turn of the century.

Hispanics

According to the U.S. Census Bureau, Hispanics will make up 18.9 percent of the total U.S. population by the year 2030.[14] Although today's correctional system is already over-represented by Hispanics, it can only be speculated that this trend will continue. Aside from the fact that this growth will further deteriorate the current overcrowded conditions in prison, it can be argued that it will present more serious challenges to prison administrators.

Most of these problems will occur because today's prison system is ill-equipped to handle the cultural differences that surround the Hispanic inmate. Aside from the language barrier, other differences exist in the areas of religion, politics, and regard for law and authority. The lack of planning by correctional administrators and policy-makers alike can and probably will result in a major predicament to the correctional system of the twenty-first century.

Technology

Although most U.S. households enjoy the benefit of a personal computer, most correctional facilities lack the resources and political support to make computers available to inmates. Thus, as "Pentium Fours" are being developed and released to the general public, prison inmates continue to be isolated from the benefit of using computers. This further limits their marketability in the job market (which expresses the need for computer-literate individuals) upon release.

Despite the limited availability of computers to the inmate population, it is important to note that correctional staff is increasingly relying upon the use of computers in the everyday operation of correctional facilities. As correctional web sites are being developed and placed on the Web, it can only be speculated that computers will continue to play an important role in the operation of correctional facilities.

Aside from computers, prison administrators are currently benefitting from several technological advances. California is one of the states currently using the latest technology. Prison administrators in California, upon hearing rumors of a potential inmate out-break via an underground tunnel, sought the help of Special Technologies Laboratories (STL). The STL team, using a "ground penetrating radar" (GPR), was able to locate the underground tunnel and therefore prevent the escape.[15]

Another technological advance involves the use of the Advanced Vehicle Notification System (**AVIAN**), which detects the heartbeat of a person who may be hidden inside a vehicle. This is particularly useful to correctional staff in their daily inspections of service vehicles leaving the correctional institution.[16] It is speculated that corrections, much like society at large, will increase its dependency on technology in the year 2000 and beyond.

Privatization

A recent phenomenon—the **privatization** of correctional facilities—has taken place. This phenomenon serves as evidence that the private sector has responded to the growing need of warehousing offenders. As the prison population continues to grow, it can be speculated that the need for the creation of these private facilities will be even greater. Despite this, it is worth noting that the birth of privately owned correctional facilities has been the subject of much controversy. Some of this concern is founded on incidents of inmate abuse, coupled with substandard accreditation requirements. Although some feel pessimistic about the future of private prisons, others argue that they will improve their record by virtue of their vulnerability to public opinion. Regardless, privatization will continue to make a significant impact on the correctional system.

WiseGuide Wrap-Up In the final analysis, the public asks, "What went wrong?" That is a very difficult, perhaps impossible, question to answer, but some suggestions might be offered:

1. We usually move too quickly into a suggested remedy or solution for a problem in corrections. We move without carefully analyzing what might be the result. Solutions are demanded and stop-gap measures are taken. We fail to evaluate, to experiment, to measure. This, coupled with a public that constantly demands a fast response to what they perceive is a "growing crime problem," sets the stage for failure.

2. We promise too much. Without knowing what the effect of a proposed solution will be, we suggest—at times even argue strongly—that it is the "answer" to the crime problem, or at least that it will have a significant effect on crime. Samuel Walker, a nationally recognized criminologist, has concluded that a "decline in faith in the idea of rehabilitation . . . rehabilitation has become an unpopular goal. . . . The war on crime, like the Johnsonian War on Poverty, promised too much, and the backlash resulting from the failure has been costly. . . ."[17]

    Perhaps we should recognize that a significant reduction in the crime rate may be an unrealistic goal for our reform proposals. Surely we must recognize that by changing only one area of the criminal justice system, we will not necessarily have a significant, positive effect on all other areas. For example, it is reasonable to assume that the public believes the return to a philosophy of retribution, of just deserts, will reduce crime. After all, they are told that if criminals get "what they deserve," others will be deterred from crime. If convicted offenders are incarcerated for long enough periods of time, they will be deterred from committing crimes upon release. But the more likely effect is that a return to the retribution philosophy will exacerbate the problems in corrections. It will increase the numbers of inmates, leading to greater problems of overcrowding in our already inadequate prison facilities. This new "get-tough" approach may lead to a lessening of any attempts at rehabilitation, even on a voluntary basis. The programs and the personnel will not be available for the increasing numbers of inmates and the public will be unwilling to appropriate the necessary funds for expansion of treatment programs.

3. We should not abandon all efforts at treatment even if we adopt the "just deserts" approach. It is one thing to argue against forced treatment and quite

another to eliminate opportunities for inmates to participate in treatment programs voluntarily. Likewise, we should not confuse treatment with humanitarianism. Our efforts to make prisons more humane have led some to believe that we have been involved in the "treatment" of inmates. We should recognize the distinction that Don Gibbons has emphasized between treatment and humanitarianism: "Humanitarian reform designates those changes that have been introduced into corrections in recent decades which serve to lessen the harshness or severity of punishment."[18] In essence, the humanitarian movement with regard to prisons is based on the early philosophy that deprivation of liberty is the punishment. It would be excessive punishment, and therefore inhumane, to force the person deprived of liberty to live in filth, to live among rats, in damp, cold, dark cells, to eat poorly prepared food constituting an unbalanced diet, and to suffer corporal punishment. Gibbons pointed out that actions such as an increase in the number of visits may decrease tensions in prison and may have positive effects on the inmates who receive the visitors. They might also, however, have negative effects. The point is that the visits are not "treatment" and should not be considered therapeutic in character. Increased visits, classification, education, and vocational training might be referred to as *adjuncts* to treatment. Other adjuncts are religious activities, recreational participation, and prerelease planning. These programs are not aimed at particular therapy problems of inmates and therefore are not treatment per se.

Treatment, said Gibbons, consists of "explicit tactics or procedures deliberately undertaken to change those conditions thought to be responsible for the violator's misbehavior."[19] We should continue providing the opportunities by which those inmates who wish to change their behavior might be able to do so. As Chief Justice Warren E. Burger of the United States Supreme Court said, "We take on a burden when we put a man behind walls, and that burden is to give him a chance to change. If we deny him that, we deny his status as a human being, and to deny that is to diminish our own humanity and plant the seeds of future anguish for ourselves."[20]

4. We should recognize and be prepared to deal with economic and political problems that are inevitable if change is to take place. We should realize that in our attempts to locate places for community-based corrections, we will run into community opposition. Therefore we should educate citizens on the need for such facilities. The public will also resist the costs of reform; they must be convinced that the cost is greater if needed reforms do not occur.

5. We should emphasize the need for research and evaluation of all attempted programs and reforms. Improvements in research methodology as well as in the development of theories must receive a high priority in corrections. Specifically, we must ensure that the evaluators of correctional programs are independent from those providing the funding or overseeing the institutions. Furthermore, research in the area of corrections should include discussions on the history of correctional programs in order to provide a better sense of initiatives that work or don't work.

6. We should emphasize diversion *from* the criminal justice system, especially in the case of juveniles. Unfortunately, since the term *diversion* was first popularized by the President's Crime Commission in the late 1960s, it has been used in too many cases to "widen the net" and draw in juveniles who never should have been involved in official processing. In regard to the process of diversion, we need to decriminalize, or reduce the number of

offenses covered by criminal law. Some juvenile offenders with alcohol and drug dependency problems, should not be swept into the criminal justice system unless they have violated other laws.

7. We should emphasize the need for the law and social sciences to work together in the area of corrections. Although corrections is a component of the criminal justice system, changes may have repercussions in the other components of the system of justice.

Although we do not have all of the answers to the problems in corrections, it is clear that some action must be taken. Any action that results in significant rehabilitation of those who serve time in our institutions will, of necessity, involve significant changes in the structure of society. No program behind prison walls can be successful if the inmate returns to a society determined to reject those who have been convicted of crime and have served time in correctional institutions. Most inmates do eventually return to society; if they and society do not adequately prepare for that return, we can expect recidivism to continue to be a major problem in the twenty-first century.

Notes

1. This term is credited to Francis A. Allen in "Criminal Justice, Legal Values and the Rehabilitative Ideal," *Journal of Criminal Law, Criminology, and Police Science* 50 (September-October, 1959), 226–232.

2. Allen, Francis A. "Central Problems of American Criminal Justice," *Michigan Law Review* 75 (April-May, 1977), 813–822. Quotation is on p. 821. For a further discussion of rehabilitation, see Harry E. Allen and Clifford E. Simonsen, *Corrections in America*, 8th ed. (Englewood Cliffs, NJ: Prentice-Hall, 1998).

3. Bazelon, David L. "Street Crime and Correctional Potholes," *Federal Probation* 41 (March, 1977), 3.

4. Martinson, Robert. "What Works?—Questions and Answers about Prison Reform," *The Public Interest* No. 35 (Spring, 1974), 22–54. For a more recent assessment on programs that "work," see Reginald A. Wilkinson, "What Works? (Correctional Practice)" *Corrections Today*, (August, 1996), vol. 58, no. 5, 6(2).

5. Palmer, Ted. "Martinson Revisited," chapter 2 in Robert Martinson, Ted Palmer, and Stuart Adams, *Rehabilitation, Recidivism, and Research*. (Hackensack, NJ: National Council on Crime and Delinquency, 1976), pp. 41–152.

6. Fogel, David. ". . . *We Are the Living Proof* . . .": *The Justice Model for Corrections*. (Cincinnati, OH: W. H. Anderson, 1975). For a further discussion of the Justice Model, see Sue Titus-Reid, *Criminal Justice*, 5th ed. (Madison, WI: Coursewise Publishing, 1999).

7. Wilkinson, "What Works?" 6(2).

8. Wilkinson, "What Works?" 6(2).

9. Crouch, Ben M. "Looking Back to See the Future of Corrections" *Prison Journal*, (December, 1996), vol. 76, no. 4, 468(7).

10. Crouch, "Looking Back," 468(7).

11. Crouch, "Looking Back," 468(7).

12. Crouch, "Looking Back," 468(7).

13. Crouch, "Looking Back," 468(7).

14. For the latest census figures, go to http://www.Census.gov/

15. deGroot, Gabrielle. "Hot New Technologies," *Corrections Today*, (July, 1997), vol. 59, no. 4, 60–61, and "Ionscan Drug Detection Devices Will be Installed in New California Prison," *Corrections Digest*, (Feb. 17, 1995), vol. 26, no. 7, 7.

16. deGroot, "Hot New Technologies," 60–61.

17. Walker, Samuel. "Reexamining the President's Crime Commission: The Challenge of Crime in a Free Society after Ten Years," *Crime and Delinquency* 24 (January, 1978), 1, 12. For a discussion on rehabilitative programs offered in today's correctional system, see Jeanne B. Stinchcomb and Vernon B. Fox, *Introduction to Corrections*, 5th ed. (Englewood Cliffs, NJ: Prentice-Hall, 1999).

18. Gibbons, Don. *Changing the Law Breaker: The Treatment of Delinquents and Criminals*. (Englewood Cliffs, NJ: Prentice-Hall, 1965), pp. 130–131.

19. Gibbons, *Changing the Law Breaker*, p. 130.

20. Burger, Warren E. "No Man Is an Island," *American Bar Association Journal* 56 (April, 1970), 328.

Glossary

A

Auburn, or congregate, system: Prison system that espoused congregate work during the day with an enforced rule of silence; also demanded that the prisoners be housed in isolation at night.

AVIAN: Advanced Vehicle Notification System. Detects the heartbeat of an individual who may be hidden inside a car.

B

bail: A system of posting bond in order to secure a defendant's presence at trial while allowing the accused to be released until such time.

battered woman syndrome: An act of aggression on the part of a woman who has been physically abused by a man with whom she had a close relationship.

behavior modification: Method based on learning theory; applied to change behavior by rewarding appropriate behaviors and removing reinforcements for negative actions.

beyond a reasonable doubt: Legal standard utilized in criminal trials for the purpose of establishing the guilt of the defendant.

boot camps: A correctional program modeled after military boot camps and aimed at reforming first-time juvenile offenders.

C

Cherry Hill: Institution known as the Eastern Penitentiary; was the first attempt to establish solitary confinement for offenders at all times; work was provided for offenders in their individual cells.

chivalry hypothesis: Early view on female criminality; held that police were less likely to arrest women, and juries were less likely to convict women, due to a general attitude of protectiveness toward this gender.

classical school of criminology: A school of thought that held that the punishment should fit the crime.

classical theorist: Writers and philosophers who promoted the principles set forth by the classical school of criminology.

classification clinic: Location where an individual was classified according to security and rehabilitative programs. This concept failed because it was independent from the institution that incarcerated the offender.

community-based corrections: An approach to punishment that emphasizes reintegration of the offender into the community through the use of local facilities.

conditions of confinement: Circumstances that surround the incarceration experience of the offender.

conjugal visits: Visitation program that allows inmates to engage in sexual and social contact with their respective partners in a specified area of the prison facility.

continuing custody theory: Theory that holds that the parolee remains in the custody of the granting authority. The subject is under the same rules and regulations that governed the daily conduct of the offender before release from prison.

contract system: System under which the state maintained inmates but sold their labor to a contractor, who, in turn, supervised them while providing the necessary work equipment.

contract theory: Theory that holds that the parolee agrees to assume the conditions of release when parole is offered. If those conditions are violated, the contract has been broken, and parole may be revoked.

corrections: The component of the criminal justice system concerned with the investigation, confinement, supervision, and treatment of offenders.

criminal law: The norms and statutes that, if violated, subject the accused individual to governmental prosecution.

criminologist: Professionals who engage in the scientific study of crime, criminals, and criminal behavior.

cruel and unusual punishment: Punishment prohibited by the Eighth Amendment of the U.S. Constitution. The interpretation of what constitutes cruel and unusual punishment is left to the courts' discretion.

cultural consistency: Theory that suggests that methods and severity of punishment will be consistent with other developments within the culture at a given time.

D

deinstitutionalization: The process of institutional incarceration with community-based correctional facilities and programs.

deliberate indifference: Criteria used when considering the failure of a prison official to address the needs of an inmate properly.

deprivation model: A prisonization theory based on the concept that the inmate subculture stems from prisoners' adaptation to the physical and psychological losses created by incarceration.

determinate sentence: Type of sentence that mandates fixed periods of incarceration minus any good-time credits offenders may earn.

determinism: Doctrine that states that a person's decisions and actions are decided by inherited or environmental factors that act on a person's character.

deterrence: A justification frequently used for punishing individuals. It is based on the concept that the punishment will prevent or discourage an individual from engaging in criminal behavior.

diagnostic (or reception) center: Correctional units in which professional staff determines which treatment program and correctional facility are appropriate for the individual offender.

direct supervision: Prisonization theory based on the notion that an environment will be provided in which normative, civilized behavior of inmates housed in podular units is expected. In addition, each living area is designed to enhance the observation of and communication between inmates and staff members.

double celling: The practice of housing two (or more) offenders in a room that was originally designed for one.

double jeopardy: Prosecuting an individual twice for the same offense; prohibited by the Fifth Amendment of the U.S. Constitution.

due process: A fundamental idea under the U.S. Constitution that an individual should not be deprived of life, liberty, or property without reasonable and lawful procedures.

due process theory: Theory based on the concept that parole is an important phase in the process of rehabilitation.

E

early release: See *parole.*

Elmira Reformatory: The first true reformatory, built in 1876. It advocated the rehabilitation and reformation of offenders.

F

FBI Crime Index offenses: Classification of offenses found in the Uniform Crime Report. These include homicide, arson, forcible rape, robbery, aggravated assault, burglary, larceny/theft, and auto theft.

Federal Bureau of Prisons: Institution created in 1929 by the House Special Committee on Federal Penal and Reformatory Institutions.

felicific calculus: Theory that holds that people are rational creatures who will consciously choose pleasure and avoid pain; authored by Jeremy Bentham.

free will: A punitive philosophy that demands severe punishment for people who choose to commit criminal acts.

furlough: An authorized temporary leave from prison during which the offender may engage in certain types of behavior (i.e., attend a funeral, visit family members, seek employment).

G

gangs: A group of individuals who create an allegiance toward a common goal. In prison, these gangs often engage in unlawful or criminal behavior.

general deterrence: A punitive philosophy based on the belief that punishment in a specific case will inhibit others from committing the same offense.

group psychotherapy: A type of psychotherapy aimed at an individual within a group setting.

H

habeas corpus: A written court order requiring that the accused be present before the court in order to determine the legality of custody and confinement.

halfway house: A prerelease center that helps the offender engage in an adequate transition from prison to community life. Also, a facility that addresses particular problems experienced by some inmates (i.e., alcohol and drug abuse)

hands-off doctrine: A policy used by federal courts to justify a nonintervention approach in the administration of correctional facilities.

hedonism: Pleasure-pain principle; people choose those actions that give pleasure and avoid those that give pain.

HIV: Human immunodeficiency virus; virus that causes AIDS.

I

importation model: A theory of prisonization based on the concept that the inmate subculture is not created from internal prison experiences but rather on external patterns of behavior that inmates bring to prison.

incapacitation: A punitive theory based on the concept that an individual offender is incarcerated to prevent the commission of any other crimes.

incarceration: Imprisonment in an institution. Jails usually house individuals sentenced to less than one year, while state and federal prisons house those sentenced to custody for more than one year.

indeterminate sanctions: Penalties considered to be not as harsh as prison but more stringent than probation. These include, but are not limited to, fines, parole, house monitoring, halfway houses, day treatment centers, boot camps, and intensive supervision probation (ISP).

indeterminate sentence: A sentence whose length is not determined by legislators or the courts, but by professionals at an institution who determine when an offender is ready to return to society.

individual deterrence: A philosophy of punishment based on the idea that the threat of punishment may prevent a specific individual from engaging in criminal activity.

individual psychotherapy: A form of psychotherapy aimed at addressing the specific needs of an individual. The success of this type of therapy in a controlled environment such as prison is highly questionable.

inquisitory system: System in which the accused is presumed to be guilty and must prove his or her innocence.

integrated classification system: Inmate classification system in which a classification committee, usually chaired by the warden or superintendent of the institution, was formed. The decisions of this committee were binding on the administration, and any changes in the treatment program of the inmate had to be approved by the committee.

interaction space: Architectural concept used as a foundation to build the new generation jails. This concept offers architectural designs aimed at controlling inmate interaction in the prison environment.

intermediate sanctions: A series of punishments that are more restrictive than probation and less severe than incarceration.

intermittent incarceration: Type of incarceration that allows the offender who was sentenced to probation to spend weekends or nights in a local jail. The idea is that the offender is part of the community while still being supervised in a controlled correctional facility.

J

jail: A locally administered confinement facility used to detain individuals awaiting trial or serving a sentence of less than one year.

jail confinement: One of the three types of sentences that, in 1994, comprised most of the sentences that were imposed in federal and state courts for felony convictions. This type of confinement usually involves less that one year in a jail facility.

juries: In a criminal case, a number of individuals summoned to court and sworn to hear a trial, determine certain facts, and issue a verdict of guilty or not guilty. In some jurisdictions, juries determine the offender's sentence.

just deserts: A principle based on the concept that an individual who commits a crime deserves to suffer for it.

justice model: A philosophy based on the notion that justice is achieved when offenders receive punishments based on what is deserved for their offenses as specified in the law; the crime determines the punishment.

L

LEAA: Law Enforcement Assistance Administration. This grew out of the President's Crime Commission between 1965 and 1967. Although it was created to provide resources and coordination to state and local law enforcement agencies, it was short-lived; it was terminated in the late 1970s.

lease system: System whereby the prison labor force was placed in the hands of a lessee for a previously agreed-upon fee.

M

mandatory sentence: A sentence determined by statutes that requires that a specific penalty is imposed for certain convicted offenders.

Manhattan bail project: An experiment in the reform of bail that introduced the concept of release on own recognizance.

maximum security prisons: Correctional institutions that hold inmates requiring the highest degree of custody and control.

medium security prisons: Correctional institutions in which inmates are allowed to engage in recreational activities.

minimum security prisons: Correctional institutions in which inmates are allowed extensive freedoms under limited correctional supervision.

modification of sentence: The adjustment of an offender's sentence based on a number of factors, including the individual's good behavior in prison.

N

neoclassical theorist: Individual who holds that situations or circumstances that make it impossible to exercise free will are reasons to exempt the accused from being convicted.

O

obedience model: Model that emphasizes habits, respect for authority, and training in conformity.

P

panopticon: Prison plan developed by Bentham.

parens patriae: The historical doctrine of the states' power to serve as the ultimate parent of the child.

parole: The continued custody and supervision, at the state and federal levels, of a released offender in the community.

penitentiary: A state or federal prison that confines offenders convicted of serious crimes and sentenced for terms longer than one year.

Pennsylvania System: Prison system based on solitary confinement whereby inmates were isolated at all times.

personal space: One of three architectural designs used to build the new generation jails. The design of the new generation jail is based on the philosophy that an environment will be provided in which normative, civilized behavior of inmates housed in podular units is expected. It is believed that personal space should be encouraged to attain the previously mentioned goals.

piece-price system: System in which a contractor pays a fixed price for each finished piece of work done by inmates.

podular design: One of three architectural designs used to build the new generation jails. It proposes living areas designed to enhance the observation of and communication (i.e., interaction) between inmates and staff members.

positive school of criminology: A school of thought that emphasizes the individual scientific treatment of the criminal.

positivist: Theorists who believe in the positive school of thought and who hold that the punishment should fit the criminal and not the crime.

prerelease centers: Centers where individuals would be housed as a last step before being released from correctional supervision. These have been suggested to help alleviate the problem of overcrowding.

principle of least eligibility: Idea that inmates should be the least eligible of all citizens to receive any social benefits beyond those required by the law.

prison confinement: One of the three types of sentences that, in 1994, comprised most of the sentences that were imposed in federal and state courts for felony convictions. Prison confinement usually entails a sentence of one year or more in prison.

prison overcrowding: Condition facing prisons today. This condition has been due mostly to the creation of longer and more punitive sentences.

privatization: Trend in the correctional field in which the private sector is becoming increasingly involved in the operation of correctional institutions.

probation: A type of sentence in which the offender is subjected to conditioned supervision in the community.

probation officer: An official employed by a probation agency who is mostly responsible for preparing presentence investigation reports, supervising offenders on probation, and helping to incorporate offenders back into society as lawful citizens.

progressives: A group of individuals who espoused social reforms, including individualized treatment of criminals to achieve their rehabilitation. They believed that treating criminals as individuals, each with a different set of needs and problems, would achieve rehabilitation and prepare criminals for mainstream society.

PSI: Presentence Investigation Report. This report is filed by probation or parole officers. It provides background information about the offender for the purpose of influencing the sentence imposed by the judge or parole board.

R

reality therapy: Therapy that operates on the principle that the past is significant in an individual's behavior only to the extent that he or she so permits; the focus is therefore on the present.

reception center: See *diagnostic center.*

reception program: First element of a classification program; new inmates should be segregated for purposes of medical tests and for orientation.

recidivist: An individual found guilty of violating the law repeatedly.

reeducation model: Model that places emphasis on changing inmates through training. It is characterized by close inmate-staff relations, emphasis on changes in attitudes and social behaviors, the acquisition of skills, and the development of personal resources.

reformation: A way in which the "prevention of crime" can be analyzed using Herbert Packer's conceptualization of behavioral prevention. In corrections, this term often refers to the idea that offenders can be changed or transformed into law-abiding citizens.

rehabilitation: The theory for reformation of offenders based on the concept that human behavior is the direct result of predetermined causes that may be found by objective analysis.

reintegration: A punitive philosophy that emphasizes the return of the offender to the community with restored educational, employment, and family ties.

restitution: The compensation to victims for the physical, financial, and emotional loss suffered as a result of a criminal incident. This compensation can be monetary or in the form of service to the community.

retribution: A theory of punishment based on the premise that an offender should be punished for the crimes committed because he or she deserves it.

revenge: A doctrine based on the concept that an individual who violates the law is punished in a way that replicates the victim's suffering.

S

scientific method: When applied to corrections, a positivist theory that holds that social scientists should decide the punishment and treatment of offenders (rather than allowing judges or juries to decide).

segregation: One of the forms of social control used by various correctional institutions; based on the expulsion or separation of an individual from the group.

sentencing disparity: The variations that take place when defendants convicted of the same crime receive sentences of different types or lengths.

shock incarceration: The process of incarcerating an individual for a brief period of time and then releasing him or her on probation.

social contract: Doctrine that held that an individual was bound to society only by his or her consent and therefore society was responsible for the individual, and the individual was responsible for society.

social-structural theory: A theory that relates the methods and severity of punishment to the organization and traits of the social structure; includes the division of labor in a society at a given time.

social therapies: Also known as environmental therapies. Social therapies promote the idea that the client is not to be rehabilitated in isolation from the environment. The two major social therapies are group therapy and milieu management.

solitary confinement: A type of confinement whereby inmates are isolated at all times; originated in the Walnut Street Jail in Philadelphia, Pennsylvania, in the late 1700s.

split sentence: A type of sentence whereby a judge renders a sentence involving incarceration for a specific period of time followed closely by a probationary period for a fixed period of time.

state account system: A system that brought the entire prison labor system under the control of the state.

state use system: A system whereby inmates were allowed to sell their goods to state-run institutions.

status offender: A juvenile who commits an offense that would not be considered a crime if it had been committed by an adult.

supermax prisons: Often referred to as "maxi-max." These institutions are built to house the most violent and aggressive individuals in the correctional system.

T

three-strikes and you're out law: A crime prevention tactic based on the notion that offenders who commit and are convicted of the same three serious violent offenses will be sentenced to life in prison without parole. The goal is to incarcerate repeat offenders while reducing the crime rate.

transactional analysis: Theory based on the belief that each person has three persons within—a parent, an adult, and a child. Games, psychodrama, and script analysis help the individual to understand how these three persons control his or her behavior. The goal is to understand and develop spontaneity and a capacity for intimacy.

treatment model: Model that promotes the idea that offenders should be treated and consequently released back to the community.

U

utilitarianism: A theory that makes the happiness of the individual or society the criterion of the morally good and right.

W

warden: The chief administrator of a correctional facility.

Case Index

Name Index

General Index